THE
COLLEGE
PRESS
NIV
COMMENTARY

PROVERBS, ECCLESIASTES, & SONG OF SONGS

THE
COLLEGE
PRESS
NIV
COMMENTARY

PROVERBS, ECCLESIASTES,
& SONG OF SONGS

DAVE BLAND

Old Testament Series Co-Editors:

Terry Briley, Ph.D.   Paul Kissling, Ph.D.
Lipscomb University   Great Lakes Christian College

 COLLEGE PRESS
PUBLISHING COMPANY
Joplin, Missouri

Library of Congress Cataloging-in-Publication Data

Bland, Dave.
    Proverbs, Ecclesiastes, Song of Songs/ by Dave Bland.
        p.   cm. — (The College Press NIV commentary. Old
    Testament series)
    Includes bibliographical references.
    ISBN 0-89900-889-5
    1. Bible. O.T. Proverbs—Commentaries.   2. Bible. O.T.
Ecclesiastes—Commentaries.   3. Bible. O.T. Song of Solomon—
Commentaries.   I. Title. II. Series.
BV1465.53 .B53 2002
223'.077—dc21
                                                          2002035091

A WORD
FROM THE PUBLISHER

Years ago a movement was begun with the dream of uniting all Christians on the basis of a common purpose (world evangelism) under a common authority (the Word of God). The College Press NIV Commentary Series is a serious effort to join the scholarship of two branches of this unity movement so as to speak with one voice concerning the Word of God. Our desire is to provide a resource for your study of the Old Testament that will benefit you whether you are preparing a Bible School lesson, a sermon, a college course, or your own personal devotions. Today as we survey the wreckage of a broken world, we must turn again to the Lord and his Word, unite under his banner and communicate the life-giving message to those who are in desperate need. This is our purpose.

ABBREVIATIONS

BDB . . . . .*Brown, Driver, and Briggs* (Hebrew and English Lexicon of the Old Testament)

CBQ . . . . .*Catholic Biblical Quarterly*

IDB . . . . . .*Interpreter's Dictionary of the Bible*

JBL . . . . . .*Journal of Biblical Literature*

JETS . . . .*Journal of the Evangelical Theological Society*

JSOT . . . .*Journal for the Study of the Old Testament*

LXX . . . . .*Septuagint, Greek Old Testament*

NASB . . . .*New American Standard Bible*

NIV . . . . .*New International Version*

NRSV . . . .*New Revised Standard Version*

MT . . . . . .*Masoretic Text*

NIB . . . . . .*New Interpreter's Bible*

RSV . . . . .*Revised Standard Version*

TDOT . . . .*Theological Dictionary of the Old Testament*

VT . . . . . .*Vetus Testamentum*

ZAW . . . . .*Zeitschrift für die Alttestamentliche Wissenschaft*

Simplified Guide to Hebrew Writing

Heb. letter	Translit.	Pronunciation guide
א	’	Has no sound of its own; like smooth breathing mark in Greek
ב	b	Pronounced like English B *or* V
ג	g	Pronounced like English G
ד	d	Pronounced like English D
ה	h	Pronounced like English H, silent at the end of words in the combination āh
ו	w	As a consonant, pronounced like English V or German W
ו	û	Represents a vowel sound, pronounced like English long OO
ו	ô	Represents a vowel sound, pronounced like English long O
ז	z	Pronounced like English Z
ח	ḥ	Pronounced like German and Scottish CH and Greek χ (chi)
ט	ṭ	Pronounced like English T
י	y	Pronounced like English Y
כ/ך	k	Pronounced like English K
ל	l	Pronounced like English L
מ/ם	m	Pronounced like English M
נ/ן	n	Pronounced like English N
ס	s	Pronounced like English S
ע	‘	Stop in breath deep in throat before pronouncing the vowel
פ/ף	p/ph	Pronounced like English P *or* F
צ/ץ	ṣ	Pronounced like English TS/TZ
ק	q	Pronounced very much like כ (k)
ר	r	Pronounced like English R
שׂ	ś	Pronounced like English S, much the same as ס
שׁ	š	Pronounced like English SH
ת	t/th	Pronounced like English T *or* TH

Note that different forms of some letters appear at the end of the word (written right to left), as in כָּפַף (kāphaph, "bend") and מֶלֶךְ (melek, "king").

Vowels in Hebrew (except where the ו is used to represent a vowel sound), are represented by "vowel points" added to the consonant. For example: הַ (ha, "the"). The letter *yod* (י, y) also becomes a *part of* certain vowel sounds, as in the conjunction כִּי (kî, "that"). Originally, Hebrew was written as "unpointed" text, with just the consonants. For convenience, the different vowel points are shown below on the letter Aleph (א).

אָ	ā	Pronounced not like long A in English, but like the broad A or AH sound
אַ	a	The Hebrew short A sound, but more closely resembles the broad A (pronounced for a shorter period of time) than the English short A
אֶ	e	Pronounced like English short E

א	ē	Pronounced like English long A, or Greek η (eta)
א	i	Pronounced like English short I
א	î	The same vowel point is sometimes pronounced like אִ (see below)
אָ	o	This vowel point sometimes represents the short O sound
אֹ	ō	Pronounced like English long O
אֻ	u	The vowel point ֻ sometimes represents a shorter U sound and
אֻ	ū	is sometimes pronounced like the וּ (û, see above)
אֵ	ê	Pronounced much the same as א
אֵ	ê	Pronounced much the same as א
אִי	î	Pronounced like long I in many languages, or English long E
א	ə	An unstressed vowel sound, like the first E in the word "severe"
אֳ, אֲ, אֱ	ŏ, ă, ĕ	Shortened, unstressed forms of the vowels אָ, אַ, and אֶ, pronounced very similarly to א

ACKNOWLEDGMENTS

I am indebted to several individuals who offered helpful feedback on various portions of the commentary. I want to thank Steve McKenzie for the comments he made on the introductions to each of the three books included in this commentary. Mark Hamilton was especially helpful in offering valuable advice on the Song of Songs, as well as portions of the book of Proverbs. Glenn Pemberton gave insightful critique on the first nine chapters of Proverbs. My graduate assistant, Jonathan Woodall, helped me in the editing process.

I especially want to thank Mark Sneed for a thorough reading of the manuscript from beginning to end that gave me much food for thought and held me accountable for a number of conclusions I came to that needed more thought. Some of my conclusions still need more thought. I also want to thank Marcella Trevathan who pored over the manuscript in detail, identifying grammatical and stylistic problems. Her work produced a more readable volume.

**With gratitude
I dedicate this volume
to my parents
who by their lives
first introduced me to wisdom
and by their lives
taught me that
"a good name is better than great wealth."**

INTRODUCTION

How one gains wisdom is the subject of the books of Wisdom Literature (Proverbs and Ecclesiastes). Wisdom is a quality that one must pursue diligently (Prov 2:1-5). Ironically, those who earnestly seek it will never acquire it by themselves. It is a gift from God (Prov 2:6).

Seeking this gift of wisdom does not guarantee fame, fortune, or financial success, even though such things may come to the wise. Rather wisdom offers individuals the ability to negotiate the difficulties of life in a way that enables them to live responsibly before God and others. Wisdom is primarily relational. Thus, in order to find wisdom, individuals must not seek it primarily in solitude or private meditation, but in community with God and with other human beings. This commentary is an exercise in seeking the wisdom that God gives by exploring the Wisdom Literature of Scripture.

This commentary focuses on two wisdom books, Proverbs and Ecclesiastes, and one nonwisdom book, the Song of Songs. The Song of Songs differs significantly from Proverbs and Ecclesiastes. It is sometimes associated with the wisdom corpus because of its affiliation with Solomon (S of S 1:1; cf. Prov 1:1; Eccl 1:1). Outside that relationship, little else about the Song in both its form and content can be identified as wisdom material. As a love poem, it is a genre unto itself.

Nevertheless, because of its proximity in our English Bibles to Proverbs and Ecclesiastes it is fitting to include the Song of Songs in this commentary. The introductory comments that follow, however, will deal primarily with Proverbs, Ecclesiastes, and Wisdom Literature material. Introductory materials related to the Song of Songs are presented later at the beginning of the commentary to that book.

CHARACTERISTICS OF WISDOM LITERATURE

By scholarly consensus, the wisdom books of the Bible include Proverbs, Ecclesiastes, and Job. In addition, two apocryphal books stand within the wisdom tradition, Sirach (also known as Ben Sira or Ecclesiasticus) and Wisdom of Solomon. Both are included in the Catholic canon of Scripture but not in the Protestant canon.

Some of the Psalms are classified as wisdom, including Psalms 1, 34, 37, 49, and 73. Characteristics of Wisdom Literature permeate a number of other parts of the Old Testament, including the Joseph story in Genesis 37–50. In the New Testament, wisdom-type material includes certain teaching sections of the Gospel of Matthew (e.g., Matthew 5–7) and James.

A distinction sometimes is made between two types of Wisdom Literature. On the one hand, there is "lower wisdom" or experiential wisdom. The book of Proverbs represents this type. Generally speaking, lower wisdom is practical and written with the day-to-day affairs of life in mind. Its perspective is that through observing the world one can make sense out of it and live more fully. This material is generally quite optimistic.

On the other hand, "higher wisdom" or theoretical wisdom tends to be skeptical and asks more "impractical" questions that have to do with "why." This perspective is concerned with issues such as, "Why is there evil in the world?" and "What is the nature of death?" With higher wisdom, the sages address crisis situations. Job and Ecclesiastes represent this type of wisdom inquiry.

The Old Testament does not contain a distinct Wisdom Literature section. The three sections of the Old Testament according to the Jews were the Law, Prophets, and Writings. Proverbs, Ecclesiastes, and Job are in the third section, but because they have a number of characteristics in common with one another, it is natural to cluster them under the subheading of Wisdom Literature.

I began by saying that scholarly consensus creates the genre of Wisdom Literature. However, there are legitimate grounds for that consensus. These three books (Proverbs, Ecclesiastes, and Job) have a number of characteristics in common with one another. Generally speaking, there are two ways to identify wisdom material. One is by content. The other is by form.[1]

The content of Wisdom Literature sets it apart from other literature in the Old Testament in several ways. First, within this genre, there is very little interest in the major traditions of Israel's history. The exodus, wilderness wanderings, the conquest, and the allotment of the land play no major role in the agenda of Wisdom Literature. In addition, seldom do miracles or supernatural interventions make an appearance. Little is mentioned of the Levitical sacrifices and worship practices. Seldom does this literature appeal to the commands revealed by God in the Torah. Usually the word "command" in wisdom material is associated with the parents' words and not with the Law of Moses. The teachings of wisdom are not presented as a "Thus says the LORD" as they are in the prophets. Rarely is there a reference to the tradition of Israel's covenant with Yahweh or the institution of the monarchy. Few of the books make reference to the great personalities in Israel's rich tradition such as Abraham, Moses, and David.

Second, all three wisdom books share a hearty didactic tone. The books are concerned with passing on the knowledge of an older generation to a younger generation (Prov 4:1-4; Job 8:8-9; 12:7-12; Eccl 12:1,12). The imperative mood dominates in Proverbs 1–9, as a father instructs his son regarding the perils of life.

Third, a common vocabulary unites these books into a corpus. The word "wisdom" (חָכְמָה, ḥokmāh) permeates the material. The word is used 161 times in the Old Testament with the highest concentration found in Proverbs, Job, and Ecclesiastes. In the book of Proverbs "wisdom" appears 42 times, in Job 18 times, and in Ecclesiastes 28 times. The books are concerned with wisdom, how one gains it, its practical meaning for life, and what its relationship is to the LORD of the universe (for further details, see "What Is Wisdom?" on page 28).

Wisdom material also contains a rich and diverse vocabulary for the fool. The sages used at least half a dozen synonyms to describe the fool.[2] Fox places these words on "a continuum from ingrained

---

[1]James Crenshaw, *Old Testament Wisdom: An Introduction*, revised and enlarged (Louisville, KY: Westminster John Knox Press, 1998), p. 8.

[2]Crenshaw lists eight words, *Old Testament Wisdom*, p. 68. Michael V. Fox lists seven terms in his article, "Words for Folly," *Zeitschrift für Althebraistik* 10 (1997): 1-12.

moral defect and unchangeability to relative innocence and improvability."[3] The most hardened of the lot is the "fool" (אֱוִיל, *'ĕwîl*).[4] This fool is morally dense and has excised from himself any moral conscience. He is morally debased. The NIV consistently translates the term with the English word "fool" (Prov 1:7; 10: 8,10,14; 11:29; 12:15,16; 15:5; 17:28; 18:2; 20:3; 24:7; 27:3,22; 29:9).

Next on the continuum is the "scoffer" (לֵץ, *lēṣ*).[5] The NIV usually translates this word "mocker" (Prov 9:7,8,12; 13:1; 14:6; 15:12; 19:25; 20:1; 21:11,24; 22:10; 24:9). The mocker is the one who is "wise in his own eyes" and therefore is not open to correction or rebuke. He manifests arrogance (cf. 21:24).

Following the mocker in degree of hardened character is the כְּסִיל (*kᵊsîl*).[6] The NIV also translates this word "fool" (Prov 10:18,23; 13:16; 14:16; 15:2,14; 17:10,12,16; 19:1,10; 23:9; 28:26; 29:11; 29:20). The NIV does not distinguish between the *kᵊsîl* and the *'ĕwîl*. On some occasions in the Hebrew text, the two terms are used interchangeably (13:16). Generally speaking, the *kᵊsîl* is the fool who is mentally lazy when it comes to making decisions. His laziness renders him incompetent in speech (15:2,14; 19:1; 26:6,7,9; 29:20). The *kᵊsîl* lacks vision and focus (17:24).

Another term, unique to Proverbs, used to describe the fool is the one which the NIV translates "lacks judgment" (חֲסַר־לֵב, *ḥăsar-lēb*; lit., "needy of heart," or better, "lacking a mind"; Prov 6:32; 7:7; 9:4,16; 10:13; 10:21; 11:12; 12:11; 15:21; 17:18; 24:30). Such a person does not use his mental faculties. Fox says that the English counterpart to the phrase would be "empty-headed."[7]

Finally there is the gullible person or what the NIV translates as the one who is "simple" (פֶּתִי, *pethî*; Prov 1:4,22,32; 7:7; 8:5; 9:4,6,16; 14:15,18; 19:25; 21:11; 22:3; 27:12).[8] This is the inexperienced person whose naïveté makes him or her vulnerable. These individuals could be easily influenced for either good or ill depending on to

---

[3] Fox, "Words for Folly," 6. See also Fox, *Proverbs 1–9*, The Anchor Bible 18a (New York: Doubleday, 2000), pp. 38-39.

[4] This word for fool is used nineteen times in Proverbs and twice in Job.

[5] לֵץ is used eighteen times in Proverbs.

[6] This term for fool is used forty-nine times in Proverbs, more than any other term. It is used eighteen times in Ecclesiastes and twice in Job.

[7] Fox, *Proverbs 1–9*, pp. 39-40.

[8] פֶּתִי is used fifteen times in Proverbs.

whom they listen. So the Hebrew term is not pejorative per se. Both Woman Wisdom and Woman Folly call to the simple (9:6,16).

Two other less frequent terms are also used to describe the fool. One is "stupid" or brutish (בַּעַר, ba'ar; Prov 12:1; 30:2; Ps 73:22). This person rejects the reproof of the sage and thus does not develop good judgment (Prov 12:1). The other is "senseless" (נָבָל, nābāl; 17:7,21; 30:22,32). These seven terms used to describe the fool are found throughout Proverbs and the wisdom material. All the terms, except for the "simple" (pethî) indicate some kind of moral breach.[9] Vocabulary for wisdom and folly is concentrated in the Wisdom Literature and serves to set it apart as common material.

Besides the content that sets it apart, Wisdom Literature also displays a distinct form. It is not that the literary forms appear exclusively in these three books, but these forms are more commonly identified with Wisdom Literature and are typically thought to be the literary tools the sages use to convey insight and instruction.

The first and most fundamental form is the proverb. The Hebrew word for proverb (מָשָׁל, māšāl) comes from the verb "to rule" or "to compare." If the former is the meaning, then the proverb may connote mastery over the use of words or over life. If the latter is the meaning, which is what I favor, then the word suggests some kind of comparison. As a literary tool, the proverb uses analogy to compare phenomena in the natural world with phenomena in the human world.

The sentence saying (i.e., the proverb) is a multipurpose rhetorical unit that remains the bread and butter of the sages' instructional tools. One definition of the saying describes it as "a short sentence based on a long experience." More technically, a proverb is "a concise statement of an apparent truth which has currency among the people."[10] Proverbs describe a reality of life that is true in a specific context. Proverbs are the children of experience. The sentence saying finds its home primarily in Proverbs 10–29.

A second genre found in wisdom material is the instruction saying or wisdom poem, which is located primarily in Proverbs chapters 1-9, 22-24, and 30-31. These poems usually use the imperative

---

[9]Fox, Proverbs 1-9, p. 39.

[10]Quoted by Wolfgang Mieder in Proverbs Are Never Out of Season: Popular Wisdom in the Modern Age (New York: Oxford University Press, 1993), p. 14.

mood to express their thought and typically begin with the formulaic phrase, "listen, my son."

A third wisdom genre is autobiography. This sometimes takes the form of a journal. The sages offer their hearers the learning drawn from long and varied experience. Ecclesiastes or Qoheleth uses this form of presentation, especially in 1:12–2:26. Some parts of Proverbs also use this form (4:3-9; 7:6-27; 24:30-34).

Fourth, the sages also use riddles. Although no pure riddle is found in Wisdom Literature, the introduction to the book of Proverbs claims that a riddle was one of the tools found in the sage's repertoire (1:6).[11] A riddle-like format is found in many of the "comparison" proverbs in chapters 25–27. In these proverbs, the first line gives an analogy (e.g., "apples of gold in a setting of silver," 25:11a) followed in the second line by the referent (e.g., "a word fitly spoken," 25:11b). The reader is briefly left in the dark about the proverb's subject until the second line. The numerical proverbs found in Proverbs 30:15-33 also contain a riddle-like quality.

Speaking in broad terms then, the two primary ways of identifying Wisdom Literature are by its content and form. The sages instruct youth in the way of wisdom and moral development through the use of distinct rhetorical forms. As James Crenshaw concludes, "When a marriage between form and content exists, there is wisdom literature."[12]

AUTHORSHIP

The book of Proverbs is a collection of collections. Various sections of the book are assigned to various individuals or groups, so the authorship of Proverbs is multiple. The headings in Proverbs 1:1 and 10:1 assign these collections to Solomon. There are, however, other headings scattered through the book.

Scribes in Hezekiah's court, mentioned in 25:1, are said to have copied and transmitted proverbs from a Solomonic collection that circulated among the population of the day. Two foreign authors or

---

[11]For a possible explanation, see comments on 1:6 later in this commentary.
[12]Crenshaw, *Old Testament Wisdom,* p. 11.

collectors are mentioned in 30:1 (Agur) and 31:1 (King Lemuel's mother). An anonymous group of sages is referred to in 24:23.

In addition, 22:17 reveals the beginning of a collection from another anonymous group, the "sayings of the wise." This collection has long been associated with wisdom material from an Egyptian source. There is almost unanimous agreement that the collection of proverbs in 22:17–23:11 in some way is influenced by the work of the Egyptian sage known as Amenemope (ca. 1100 B.C.).[13] This section does not slavishly depend on his writing, but does demonstrate a level of creative appropriation. Through an interpretive process, the Israelite sages filtered this material through their understanding of Yahweh and incorporated it into the wisdom corpus of Proverbs.

An examination of the book of Proverbs, then, reveals multiple authorship and origin. Ultimately the sages understand these collections as God's word to humans (cf., Prov 30:5-6). Proverbs is a part of the canon of sacred Scripture.

THE SOCIAL BACKGROUND OF WISDOM LITERATURE

Scholars have wrestled over several important issues that relate to understanding Wisdom Literature. One issue deals with how Wisdom fits into the overall context of Old Testament theology. Another theological concern relates to Wisdom's interest in order and how rigid or flexible is this order that the sages teach. Some proverbs seem to convey a black and white outlook on life (26:27), while others are more flexible (16:1). The issue that receives the most attention among scholars is the social context of Wisdom Literature.

The social background of wisdom includes several important issues. For one, what is the socioeconomic culture of the wisdom corpus? That is, from what economic class does wisdom derive? Does it primarily come from the upper class or from the peasant farmer? Certainly the perspective on wealth and poverty in the book of Proverbs is influenced by the socioeconomic status of the sages

---

[13]Roland Murphy, *Proverbs*, Word Biblical Commentary, vol. 22 (Nashville: Thomas Nelson, 1998), p. 291.

and whether they are members of the elite or whether they come from the rank and file of the common people. Differences of opinion exist among scholars regarding the economic status reflected in the book of Proverbs.

Some scholars argue that the book derives from the elite of Israelite culture.[14] These scholars maintain that Proverbs is a product of the upper-class strata of Israelite society. One argument made in favor of this view is the international scope of wisdom (22:17–24:22; 30:1-8; 31:1-9). Only the wealthy could travel to other areas of the world such as Egypt and Mesopotamia. Another argument in favor of the wealthy is the urban context that is often portrayed in Proverbs (namely, chs. 1–9 and 31). For the most part the wealthy people lived in towns and cities while the poor lived in the rural areas and countryside (although some of the rural landowners were quite wealthy). Further, the final editing of the corpus is ascribed to royal authors (Solomon, 1:1; 10:1; Hezekiah, 25:1; Lemuel, 31:1). An upper-class lifestyle is portrayed in speaking about eating meat (17:1; 15:17) and drinking wine (23:29-35). The moral admonitions betray an upper class milieu. Frequent reproof against laziness (6:6-9; 24:30-34; 26:13-16) and the admonitions to practice moderation with food and drink and in seeking riches reveals upper-class values.

In addition, the three basic types of women described in Proverbs are rich, emancipated women. There is the temptress of chapters 5, 6, and 7 who lives a life of ease, using her wealth to entrap unsuspecting young men (7:15-20). The quarrelsome woman, described in the sentence literature (10–29), lives in a spacious house and drives her husband to live in the corner rooftop (21:9; 25:24). Finally, the woman of noble character manages a household and engages in foreign trade (31:10-31). All three types of women are from the wealthy class. It is argued that this univocal perspective unites the Wisdom Literature.

Other scholars argue in favor of an oral folk-wisdom culture.[15] The proverbs are the voice of the common people in Israel. This

---

[14]See Robert Gordis's classic article in support of the upper-class status, "The Social Background of Wisdom Literature," *The Jewish Theological Seminary of America* 18 (1944): 77-118. Gordis set the tone in contemporary scholarship for accepting the idea of a single, uniform, upper-class background for the book of Proverbs.

[15]For one example of this perspective see Carole R. Fontaine, *Traditional*

stream of scholarship believes the sayings in Wisdom Literature were not textually transmitted from the outset. When one looks at the historical texts in the Old Testament, what one discovers is that proverbs were already in circulation among the people, and these proverbs were handed down orally from generation to generation (e.g., 1 Sam 10:12; 19:24). Ultimately, they were edited and gathered into collections of sayings.

Another argument proposed in favor of the folk context is that agrarian sayings dominate the book of Proverbs. The aphorisms depict life in rural villages with subsistent living conditions. Furthermore, when one compares biblical proverbs to contemporary preliterate cultures (such as certain African cultures), one discovers surprising similarities. Such anthropological studies offer strong confirmation that wisdom is the property of the common people.[16]

In between these two positions lies the perspective that advocates a variety of social settings. Contrary to Robert Gordis's thesis, there is no uniform social class reflected in the book of Proverbs.[17] Rather a variety of class levels is projected. Certain sections of the book image different socioeconomic levels. For example, chapters 1–9 portray a more urban and well-to-do class of people.[18] We see the images of the temptress who enjoys a comfortable lifestyle. She has all the luxuries that life affords (7:16-18). She is married to a wealthy businessman (7:19-20). In addition, there is the advice that the father gives to the son in 1:8-19 to stay away from the ill-gotten

---

Sayings in the Old Testament: A Contextual Study (Sheffield: Almond Press, 1982). Claus Westermann maintains "that the genus of proverbs had its heyday in preliteracy cultures" (p. 4). See Westermann, *Roots of Wisdom: The Oldest Proverbs of Israel and Other Peoples* (Louisville, KY: Westminster John Knox Press, 1995).

[16]See Friedemann W. Golka, *The Leopard's Spots: Biblical and African Wisdom in Proverbs* (Edinburgh: T & T Clark, 1993).

[17]See footnote 14 above.

[18]R.N. Whybray, *Wealth and Poverty in the Book of Proverbs* (Sheffield: JSOT Press 1990). Whybray also includes chapters 22:16–24:22 as depicting an urban upper-class setting. However, Harold Washington makes some pretty persuasive arguments against such a setting for this unit of material. In comparing this section of Proverbs to the Instruction of Amenemope, he concludes that both materials come from village folk wisdom and not from the elite upper class. See Harold C. Washington, *Wealth and Poverty in the Instruction of Amenemope and the Hebrew Proverbs* (Atlanta: Scholars Press, 1994).

wealth accumulated by gangs. One of the reasons the gang was so attractive was that the group promised equal distribution of wealth to all members (1:14). Woman Wisdom, first introduced to the reader in chapter 1, dwells in a secure urban setting. She is one who is active in the marketplace and gates of the city (1:20-33).

In these chapters, there are few references to agricultural life (one reference to agriculture is in 3:9-10). The gang members of chapter 1 are interested foremost in making quick, easy money. The temptress is concerned primarily with flaunting the wealth that she has. She lavishes it on herself. Woman Folly uses her wealth to lure the fool to her table (9:13-18). These characters use money to destroy.

In chapters 1–9, there are yet images of the constructive employment of wealth. Woman Wisdom builds a seven-pillared house and invites all who diligently seek wisdom to come to her extravagant banquet at which bread, wine, and meat are served (9:1-6). Even though this is metaphorical language, it is rooted in realistic experiences. The paradigmatic statement in 3:9-10 affirms that the one who faithfully serves the LORD receives material blessings, at least an abundance of the necessities of life.

So even among the urban rich, the attitude toward wealth varies. There are those who are concerned primarily with "get-rich-quick" schemes. They are concerned with getting to the top and flaunting their wealth, using it to gain power. However, there are the rich who, having been blessed by God, use their wealth as a means of serving others. Overall, to the urban rich, wealth is a positive value. Striving to increase what one has is not necessarily bad, but there are striking contrasts in the way in which the wealthy gain and use their money.

Another class of the wealthy is reflected in the royal proverbs. Ideally the king as God's representative on earth ensures that righteousness, justice, and fairness prevail (16:10-15). He makes sure that wealth is not used to exploit others, that it is properly distributed to those in need. He guards against unjust means of people gaining wealth through false balances or other faulty business practices (16:11). The king maintains the rights of the poor and the oppressed (31:1-9). Wealth is his to dispense appropriately. The king and the urban elite, these are also among the wealthy in the book of Proverbs.

They are, however, the minority group. It appears that the small subsistence farmer represents the dominant social class in the book of Proverbs. This farmer is the one who has just enough to support himself and his family. He lives on the edge of ruin, always existing from hand to mouth. Whybray identifies two strata of farmers in the text of Proverbs. On the one hand, there is the prosperous farmer who has achieved a level of wealth by hard work.[19] The description of the capable woman in 31:10-31 is of a family that seems to have acquired financial security, but wealth is not their ambition in life.[20] It is serendipitous to their goals. In the process of being diligent in work, the offshoot is that they prosper. In the process of caring for the family, reaching out to the poor, offering counsel, and instructing others, God blesses them materially. Here is an image of the realization of the blessing pronounced in 3:9-10: "Honor the LORD with your substance and with the firstfruits of all your produce; then your barns will be filled with plenty, and your vats will be bursting with wine." This is the prosperous farmer.

On the other hand, the image portrayed in the sentence literature of Proverbs, primarily chapters 10:1–22:16 and chapters 25–29, is that of the small subsistence farmer.[21] This person is the hard-working individual, the ordinary one in Israelite society. Several characteristics portrayed in the sentence literature seem to indicate the small-farmer status. First, many of the proverbs reflect the precarious nature of life. One's economic status can change quickly depending on the conditions of the weather.[22] A drought, blight, or plague could easily wipe out the livelihood of such a family.[23] Illness, injury, or death could also put a family in jeopardy (26:27; 28:10; 15:25). The sentence literature contains a plethora of language about falling (11:5,14,28), terror (10:24), misfortune, danger, or trouble (11:27; 13:21; 16:4; 17:13; 22:3). A level of anxiety about potential disasters always looms on the horizon. Such a perspective fits more

---

[19]Whybray, *Wealth*, p. 111.

[20]What a contrast to the gang in 1:8-19 that is totally obsessed with getting more and more!

[21]Whybray, *Wealth*, pp. 11-74.

[22]Whybray says that in 10:1–22:16 and 25–29 a total of 103 verses refer to the uncertainty of their existence (ibid., p. 24).

[23]See Whybray for a list of references to disaster in Proverbs (ibid., pp. 24-25).

the ordinary life of an Israelite than it does of someone from royal or upper-class strata. In 10:1–22:16, the speakers are preoccupied with the ever-present danger of falling into poverty.

Second, the work ethic that is advocated in chapters 10–29 is one that calls for continual diligence. Such an ethic better describes the average hardworking farmer than it does the wealthy (16:26; 20:13). Whybray claims that the emphasis in the sentence literature is "on the necessity for hard work and the reward which the hardworking person will gain."[24] The wisdom poem in 27:23-27 is a more typical picture of the social setting in which the sentence literature finds its home. There is a need for continuous hard work if the farmer is to make a living. He is not wealthy by any means. Rather he has just enough to feed and clothe his family, with a little extra to buy a field (vv. 26-27). He must continually care for his flocks and herds because wealth is fleeting (v. 24).

Third, there are four proverbs in the literature that speak of the poor and rich as having equal status before God (14:31; 17:5; 22:2; 29:13). According to these proverbs, Yahweh is the creator of both the rich and the poor. Proverbs 22:2 observes, "The rich and the poor have this in common: the LORD is the maker of them all." That is, both rich and poor have equal standing in the eyes of God. Thus each must regard the other with mutual respect. The rich should not despise the poor. Nor should the poor envy the rich. While these proverbs do not rule out being written by the upper class, some would argue that it seems more likely that these statements are made by someone who is at least not among the wealthy.

The book of Proverbs does not represent just one economic class of individuals. Because wisdom permeates all of life, it is not the sole possession of a particular group; thus it should not come as a surprise that a variety of social strata are represented.[25] Neither do the distinct sections of the book (e.g., chapters 1–9; 10:1–22:16; 31) within themselves represent a uniform perspective as Whybray claims. Instead, within the various sections are a variety of perspectives. For example, within Proverbs 10–22 several social perspectives are sug-

[24]Ibid., p. 38. Although, the poem on observing the work ethic of the ant is found among the urban upper-class material in chapters 1–9.
[25]Whybray says that the only class of society not represented in the book of Proverbs is the indigent poor (ibid., p. 113).

gested. A cluster of royal proverbs appears in 16:10-15. Chapters 28–29 imply a court setting. In the context of chapters 10–29, which some believe reflect primarily the life of a peasant farmer, sayings addressed to wealthy landowners exist. Proverbs 15:17 and 17:1 envision a familial context in which meat serves as the main course. Proverbs 11:26 does not describe the common folk but a wealthy grain distributor: "People curse the man who hoards grain, but blessing crowns him who is willing to sell" (מַשְׁבִּיר, mašbîr). The "one who sells grain" (mašbîr) is not the subsistence farmer but the individual who has wealth and power. Joseph (Gen 42:6), Sihon (Deut 2:28), and the greedy men in Amos (8:5) are all described as wealthy grain distributors (מַשְׁבִּירִים, mašbîrîm).

Ultimately court officials (25:1) assembled the final composition of the wisdom corpus. These wealthy officials possessed the wisdom to incorporate material from a variety of social classes and economic strata.[26] For example, in the book of Proverbs, chapters 1–9 reflect more of a wealthy, urban mentality. The sentence literature of chapters 10–29, to some degree, incorporates the thought of folk wisdom. Chapter 31:1-9 portrays the royal class. Finally, 31:10-31 projects the image of a prosperous farmer. This makes Proverbs's view on wealth and poverty quite complex but also realistic for those who are receiving moral training in righteousness, justice, and fairness (Prov 1:3).

SCHOOLS IN ISRAEL

The controversy over the social status of Wisdom Literature is closely related to a second major debate that occupies scholarly interest. That is the question of education. Were there schools in ancient Israel? In brief, there are three major arguments for the existence of schools.

---

[26]Mark Sneed points out the parallels between Amenemope and Proverbs. Using a sociological methodology, he argues for an upper-class milieu and that the upper and lower classes in Israel shared a common set of values. Sneed, "The Class Culture of Proverbs: Eliminating Stereotypes," *Scandinavian Journal of the Old Testament*, 10, no. 2 (1996): 296-308. One of the conclusions that Sneed comes to is that care must be taken in stereotyping the different classes: "Surely we cannot stereotype every member of the upper class as incapable of even one unselfish thought. And the lower class surely has no monopoly on altruism and goodwill" (303).

The first is based on comparison between Israel and other ancient Near Eastern cultures. The evidence is conclusive that schools existed in Egypt and Mesopotamia. During the Davidic and Solomonic monarchies, the Israelite nation expanded and was influenced by these international powers. Some scholars maintain that it is reasonable to assume that Israel imitated these nations in their bureaucratic structures and in particular in implementing their educational system. Nili Shupak has compared the words unique to Wisdom Literature to the vocabulary used in schools found in Egyptian Instruction. She discovers strong connections between the two types of material.[27] Nevertheless, such comparison is a weak argument, especially when the Old Testament is "notoriously reticent" on the subject of schools.[28] Biblical authors never mention schools.[29] Bernard Lang appeals to the image of Woman Wisdom in the city gate rebuking the young men assembled to learn who were not listening (Proverbs 1:20-33), as evidence for the existence of schools.[30] However, it is difficult to offer a *conclusive* argument for schools in Israel based on a text that is poetic.

In addition, comparing Israel to Egyptian and Mesopotamian civilizations is like comparing apples to oranges. These civilizations were more complex and advanced than Israelite culture.[31] One cannot simply assume that Israel imitated the bureaucratic structures of Egyptian and Mesopotamian cultures. Therefore, it is not a foregone conclusion that Israel developed a public education system like her ancient Near Eastern neighbors.

In fact, to compare Israel with Egypt and Mesopotamia works against proponents for schools. The wisdom instructions from these countries may have been used in schools, but they do not present

---

[27]Nili Shupak, "The 'Sitz Im Leben' of the Book of Proverbs in the Light of a Comparison of Biblical and Egyptian Wisdom Literature," *Revue Biblique* 94 (1987): 98-119.

[28]See Stuart Weeks, *Early Israelite Wisdom* (Oxford: Clarendon Press, 1994), p. 132.

[29]There are, however, the possible allusions to schools in Isaiah 28:9-13 and 50:4 and Proverbs 22:17-21.

[30]See Bernard Lang, *Wisdom and the Book of Proverbs: A Hebrew Goddess Redefined* (New York: The Pilgrim Press, 1986), pp. 29-33.

[31]James Crenshaw, *Education in Ancient Israel: Across the Deadening Silence* (New York: Doubleday, 1998), p. 108.

themselves as being composed first and foremost for them. The authors of these books do not seem to be schoolteachers. As Fox observes, "The books are ascribed to men from a variety of professions, from king and vizier to ordinary scribes. Some ascriptions are probably fictitious, but some certainly are not. . . ."[32] He continues:

> The ostensive, and often true, authors are men from various walks of life who are speaking to their actual sons. Ptahhotep addresses his "staff of old age," who is his biological son. Amenemope writes his book for his youngest son only, out of all his children, a narrowing of audience that would have no fictional function and does not belong to the generic formulae. . . . Anii is a scribe of the palace and his son Khonshotep is himself a scribe. Various maxims in the Wisdom Instructions speak of passing this wisdom on to one's own children, never to one's pupils.[33]

Egyptian sages present themselves as paternal sages. The father-to-son setting is common in this material, and this setting is maintained, as well, in Proverbs.[34]

Second, the high literary quality of much of the Old Testament is difficult to explain without the existence of schools.[35] André Lemaire claims that in the context of schools, biblical material was written as literary resources for students to use in the classroom.[36] But a sapiential community within the larger Israelite community that collected and edited the material in its final form could explain the biblical literature.[37] Schools do not have to exist to produce literature of this caliber.

With the work of André Lemaire[38] and Bernard Lang,[39] a new

---

[32]Michael V. Fox, "The Social Location of the Book of Proverbs," in *Texts, Temples and Traditions: A Tribute to Menahem Haran*, ed. by Michael V. Fox et al. (Winona Lake, IN: Eisenbrauns, 1996), p. 230.

[33]Ibid.

[34]Fox, *Proverbs 1–9*, pp. 8-9.

[35]Gerhard von Rad, *Wisdom in Israel* (Nashville: Abingdon, 1972), p. 17.

[36]André Lemaire, *Les écoles et la formation de la Bible dans l'ancien Israël*, OBO 39, Fribourg: Editions Universitaires (Göttingen: Vandenhoeck & Ruprecht, 1981).

[37]Crenshaw, *Education,* p. 111.

[38]Lemaire, *Les écoles et la formation de la Bible dans l'ancien Israël.*

[39]Lang, *Wisdom and the Book of Proverbs: A Hebrew Goddess Redefined.*

kind of evidence was brought forth for the existence of schools in Israel. This was the introduction of archaeological studies. Fragmentary inscriptions found and dated around the twelfth century B.C. seem to be the school exercises of young students. Lemaire's conclusion is that schools existed in major Israelite centers such as Shiloh, Gilgal, Shechem, Bethel, etc., in premonarchical times. Graham Davies also argues fervently in favor of schools from the epigraphic evidence.[40]

Both James Crenshaw and Stuart Weeks maintain that no definitive answer for the existence of schools can be known from the current evidence.[41] In his most recent landmark work, Crenshaw concedes that the evidence is just not there to make a decisive statement regarding when schools in Israel came into existence. That there were schools in ancient Israel seems clear from Palestinian inscriptions. Before the eighth century, however, no definitive date can be set. Neither do we have clear information on how the schools operated or how the learning process took place.[42] An interpretive approach to Wisdom Literature that assumes a school context is tentative at best. The primary literary context of Proverbs is the family. Father and mother instruct the son. At the same time, some instruction poems imply a teacher/student relationship (e.g., 1:20-33).

WHAT IS WISDOM?

The Hebrew word for "wisdom" (חָכְמָה, ḥokmāh; feminine noun) carries a number of meanings in the Old Testament. It can refer to the "skill" (חֲכַם־לֵב, ḥăkam-lēb; literally "wise of heart") of a "craftsman" (ḥokmāh, "wisdom"; Exod 31:6; cf. 31:3). In Psalm 107:23-27, the term refers to sailors handling a ship in rough waters. In that Psalm sailors, in the midst of a storm, are described as being "at their wits end" (literally, "their wisdom was swallowed up," v. 27).

---

[40]See G.I. Davies, "Were There Schools in Ancient Israel?" *Wisdom in Ancient Israel: Essays in Honour of J.A. Emerton,* ed. by John Day, Robert Gordon and H.G.M. Williamson (Cambridge: Cambridge University Press, 1995), pp. 199-211.

[41]See Crenshaw in "Education in Israel," *JBL,* 104, no. 4 (1985): 601-615; Stuart Weeks, *Early Israelite Wisdom.*

[42]James L. Crenshaw, *Education in Ancient Israel.*

Wisdom can also refer to good judgment in running the affairs of state (e.g., Joseph in Gen 41:33; David in 2 Sam 14:20; Solomon in 1 Kgs 3:9,12,28). Sometimes wisdom means understanding (Job 12:2-3; 26:3; 38:36). Wisdom is accessible not only to the royal class but also to the ordinary person. Fox maintains that the Hebrew term for wisdom refers to "a high degree of knowledge and skill in any domain."[43] He argues that the closest English equivalent to *ḥokmah* is "expertise."[44]

In the Wisdom Literature of Proverbs and Ecclesiastes the term wisdom refers to developing the expertise to negotiate the complexities of life. Wisdom occupies itself with discovering God's order in life and then learning to fit into that order successfully, all the while keeping in mind the boundaries and limits of humanity.

Wisdom is earnestly sought by humans, like a miner searching for silver (Prov 2:4). The wisdom that humans seek is the understanding of the world in which they live, but wisdom is also a quality given by Yahweh (Prov 2:6). Yahweh activates the wisdom that humans possess. In activating that wisdom, Yahweh gives protection from evil men (Prov 2:12) and evil women (2:16).

The ultimate goal of attaining wisdom is the formation of moral character.[45] Wisdom's thicker, richer meaning, according to Fox, has to do with an ethical quality, a quality of character.[46] He states, "Proverbs consistently applies the word *ḥokmah* to wisdom as manifest in the skill and knowledge of right living" in the ethical and pragmatic senses.[47] Near the end of his work, Fox states wisdom's objective succinctly, "And fostering moral character, it is no overstatement to say, is at all times the greatest goal of education."[48] The content of this moral education is found throughout Proverbs 10–29, but it is most tightly condensed in Job 31 where Job lists a litany of vices of which he claims innocence. In listing the vices, Job reveals wisdom's code of ethics. These are the qualities the sages teach to those in transition from youth to adulthood.

---

[43]Fox, *Proverbs 1–9*, p. 32.

[44]Ibid.

[45]William Brown, *Character in Crisis: A Fresh Approach to the Wisdom Literature of the Old Testament* (Grand Rapids: Eerdmans, 1996), p. viii.

[46]Fox, *Proverbs 1–9*, p. 29.

[47]Ibid., p. 33.

[48]Ibid., p. 348.

CHARACTERISTICS OF THE WISE

Another angle from which to approach the question "What is wisdom?" is to identify the qualities of the person who is wise (i.e., qualities that are manifested in the life of a wise person). Such a person demonstrates certain actions and attitudes.

As one studies the material in Proverbs and Ecclesiastes, certain qualities rise to the surface that set the wise apart from others. The degree to which one possesses these characteristics is the degree to which that person lives by wisdom. The following list is not exhaustive by any means, but it identifies some of the more prominent features of those who display wisdom.

First, the wise are those who know what is appropriate. They understand what the occasion calls for them to say and do. They know the right word to say (Prov 15:23; 25:11). Knowing what to say and when to say it is an act of wisdom. The writer of Ecclesiastes was a wordsmith who weighed and studied and arranged proverbs (Eccl 12:9-10). The sage knows that there is a proper time for everything (Eccl 3:1-8). The wise learn to live with that timing.

Second, those who are wise value the importance of interaction with others. Wisdom is not gained primarily in solitude but in the midst of human activity (Prov 1:20-33). The wise person is the one who is open to the give and take of relationships (27:5,6,17,19). The capable woman in Proverbs 31:10-31 has invested herself in the lives of others. In contrast, the fool is the one who believes he does not need anyone else. He feels he has it all together and so he is "wise in his own eyes" (Prov 3:7; 26:5). Wisdom is primarily relational.

Third, the wise person develops understanding and discernment (Prov 1:2,4-6). Such a person understands that the decisions of life are often complex and require the utmost thought. Seldom does life provide "pat answers" (e.g., Prov 26:4,5). The sage is not afraid to challenge and question conventional beliefs (think of Job and Ecclesiastes). In contrast, the fool does not use his mental faculties (Prov 17:16) because he "lacks judgment" (10:13, 21).

Fourth, the one who pays careful attention to the routine affairs of life displays wisdom. Wisdom Literature contains little material about the mighty acts of God or the miracles or the major events in Israel's history. Rather it attends to the mundane matters of the ordinary person: relationships, desires, eating, drinking, planning, anger, compassion, work, sleep, etc. The wise observe these and learn from them. The wise then reflect on these experiences. "The Teacher" in Ecclesiastes does this. He looks back on his experiences and shares what he has observed and learned (note how frequently the writer says "I saw"; 1:14; 2:13,24; 3:10,16,22, etc.). The sage learns from nature, from the least to the most powerful of God's creation (Prov 30:24-31).

Fifth, the one who demonstrates wisdom is the one who gleans from the best culture has to offer. The wise person takes every available opportunity to learn, even from secular and foreign cultures (cf., the foreigners from Massa, Prov 30:1; 31:1). The sages incorporate wisdom material from Egyptian culture into their thought patterns (Prov 22:17–24:22). However, the wise practice discretion in doing this by filtering the thoughts of other worldviews through the Yahwistic lens of their belief system. The wise person lives in the world but is not of the world.

Sixth, the sage is one who takes a balanced view of life. He or she is neither lazy nor a workaholic, neither an underachiever nor an overachiever. The wise person keeps life and its challenges in perspective. Such a person seeks to discover the order of the universe and then fit into the ebb and flow of that order. The French call this *savoir faire*. The wise know when to work and when to play, when to speak and when to listen, when to sleep and when to wake, when to advance and when to retreat. They are in tune with the rhythm of life that God established.

Finally, and most fundamentally, the truly wise person takes a God-centered focus on life. The one who wishes to gain wisdom begins by being in relationship with Yahweh and trusting him (Prov 3:5-8). Underlying all of the sayings in the book of Proverbs, including the most "secular" ones, is a fundamental belief in the God who created the universe. The fear of the LORD is the beginning as well as the culmination of wisdom (Prov 9:10; see also 1:7; Job 28:28; Eccl 12:13).[49]

---

[49]See commentary on 1:7.

BOOK OF PROVERBS

This commentary will first look at wisdom as it is described in the book of Proverbs. Proverbs introduces the student to the world of wisdom and to the way the wise think and act. The book is concerned with negotiating the day-to-day affairs of life in a way that reflects the fear of the LORD in one's character. Proverbs is a textbook on practical theology. As Derek Kidner puts it, Proverbs is Scripture's effort to put godliness in working clothes.[50]

---

[50]Derek Kidner, *The Proverbs*, Tyndale Old Testament Commentaries (Downers Grove, IL: Tyndale, 1964), p. 35.

PROVERBS

OUTLINE

BIBLIOGRAPHY

Aitken, Kenneth T. *Proverbs.* The Daily Study Bible Series. Philadelphia: Westminster Press, 1986.

Alter, Robert. *The Art of Biblical Poetry.* N.p.: Basic Books, 1985.

Atkinson, David. *The Message of Proverbs.* Downers Grove, IL: InterVarsity Press, 1996.

Barker, Kenneth L. "Proverbs 23:7—'To Think' or 'To Serve Food'?" *The Journal of the Ancient Near Eastern Society* 19 (1989): 3-8.

Bland, Dave. "Formation of Character in the Book of Proverbs." *Restoration Quarterly* 40, no. 4 (1998): 221-237.

_____ . *Rhetorical Perspective on the Sentence Sayings of the Book of Proverbs.* Dissertation, University of Washington, 1994.

Bonhoeffer, Dietrich. *Letters and Papers from Prison.* New York: Macmillan, 1972.

Boström, G. *Proverbiastudien. Die Weisheit und das fremde Weib in Spr. 1–9.* LUÅ N.F. Avd. I, Bd 30, Nr. 3. Lund, 1935.

Botterweck, G. Johannes. "יָסַר." *Theological Dictionary of the Old Testament.* Ed. by G. Johannes Botterweck and Helmer Ringgren. Trans. by David E. Green. Grand Rapids: Eerdmans, 1990.

Brown , William P. *Character in Crisis: A Fresh Approach to the Wisdom Literature of the Old Testament.* Grand Rapids: Eerdmans, 1996.

_____ . *The Ethos of the Cosmos: The Genesis of Moral Imagination in the Bible.* Grand Rapids: Eerdmans, 1999.

Bryce, Glendon E. "Another Wisdom-'Book' in Proverbs." *Journal of Biblical Literature* (1972): 145-157.

_____ . "'Better'—Proverbs: An Historical and Structural Study." *The Society of Biblical Literature Book of Seminar Papers.* Ed. by L.C. McGaughy, Missoula, MT: SBL, 1972.

Bullinger, E.W. *Figures of Speech Used in the Bible.* Grand Rapids: Baker, 1968.

Camp, Claudia. *Wisdom and the Feminine in the Book of Proverbs.* Decatur, GA: Almond Press, 1985.

Clements, Ronald E. "The Concept of Abomination in the Book of Proverbs." In *Texts, Temples and Traditions: A Tribute to Menahem Haran.* Ed. by Michael V. Fox, Victor Avigdor Hurowitz, Avi Hurvitz, Michael L. Klein, Baruch J. Schwartz, and Nili Shupak. Winona Lake, IN: Eisenbrauns, 1996.

—————. "The Good Neighbour in the Book of Proverbs." In *Of Prophets' Visions and the Wisdom of Sages.* Ed. by Heather A. McKay and David J. A. Clines. Sheffield: JSOT Press, 1993.

—————. *Wisdom in Theology.* Grand Rapids: Eerdmans, 1992.

Clifford, Richard J. *Proverbs.* The Old Testament Library. Louisville: Westminster John Knox, 1999.

—————. *The Wisdom Literature.* Interpreting Biblical Texts. Nashville: Abingdon Press, 1998.

Crenshaw, James L. "Clanging Symbols." In *Justice and the Holy.* Ed. by D.A. Knight and P.J. Paris. Philadelphia: Fortress Press, 1989.

—————. *Education in Ancient Israel: Across the Deadening Silence.* New York: Doubleday, 1998.

—————. "Education in Israel." *Journal of Biblical Literature* 104, no. 4 (1985): 601-615.

—————. *Old Testament Wisdom: An Introduction.* Louisville: Westminster John Knox Press, 1998, revised and enlarged.

—————. *Urgent Advice and Probing Questions: Collected Writings on Old Testament Wisdom.* Macon, GA: Mercer University Press, 1995.

—————. "Wisdom and Authority: Sapiential Rhetoric and Its Warrants." *Congress Volume: Vienna, 1980.* Ed. by John A. Emerton. Leiden: Brill, 1981.

Davies, G.I. "Were There Schools in Ancient Israel?" *Wisdom in Ancient Israel: Essays in Honour of J.A. Emerton.* Ed. by John Day, Robert Gordon, and H.G.M. Williamson. Cambridge: Cambridge University Press, 1995.

Davis, Ellen F. *Proverbs, Ecclesiastes, and the Song of Songs*. Westminster Bible Companion. Louisville: Westminster John Knox Press, 2000.

Day, John, Robert P. Gordon, and H.G.M. Williamson, eds. *Wisdom in Ancient Israel: Essays in Honour of J.A. Emerton*. Cambridge: Cambridge University Press, 1995.

Eaton, John. *The Contemplative Face of Old Testament Wisdom in the Context of World Religions*. Philadelphia: Trinity Press, 1989.

Emerton, J.A. *The Interpretation of Proverbs 21:28*. Zeitschrift für die Alttestamentliche Wissenschaft Supplement 100 (1988).

Estes, Daniel J. *Hear, My Son: Teaching & Learning in Proverbs 1–9*. Grand Rapids: Eerdmans, 1997.

Fabry, H.-J. "חָקַק." *Theological Dictionary of the Old Testament*, vol 5. Ed. by G. Johannes Botterweck and Helmer Ringgren. Trans. by David E. Green. Grand Rapids: Eerdmans, 1986.

Follis, E. *Directions in Biblical Hebrew Poetry*. Journal for the Study of the Old Testament Supplement 40 (1987).

Fontaine, Carole R. *Traditional Sayings in the Old Testament: A Contextual Study*. Sheffield: Almond Press, 1982.

Fox, Michael V. "'AMON AGAIN." *Journal of Biblical Literature* 115 (1996): 699-702.

_____ . "Ideas of Wisdom in Proverbs 1–9." *Journal of Biblical Literature* 116 (1997): 613-633.

_____ . "The Pedagogy of Proverbs 2." *Journal of Biblical Literature* 113, no. 2 (1994): 233-243.

_____ . *Proverbs 1–9*. Vol. 18a, Anchor Bible. New York: Doubleday, 2000.

_____ . "The Social Location of the Book of Proverbs." In *Texts, Temples and Traditions: A Tribute to Menahem Haran*. Ed. by Michael V. Fox et al. Winona Lake, IN: Eisenbrauns, 1996.

_____ . "Words for Folly." *Zeitschrift für Althebraistik* 10 (1997): 1-12.

_____ . "Words for Wisdom." *Zeitschrift für Althebraistik* 6 (1993): 149-165.

Garrett, Duane. *Proverbs, Ecclesiastes, Song of Songs.* New American Commentary. Nashville: Broadman Press, 1993.

Goldingay, John. "The Arrangement of Sayings in Proverbs 10–15." *Journal for the Study of the Old Testament* 61 (March 1994): 75-83.

Golka, Friedemann W. *The Leopard's Spots: Biblical and African Wisdom in Proverbs.* Edinburgh: T & T Clark, 1993.

Gordis, Robert. "The Social Background of Wisdom Literature." *The Jewish Theological Seminary of America* 18 (1944): 77-118.

Gutstein, Naphtali. "Proverbs 31:10-31: The Woman of Valor as Allegory." *The Jewish Bible Quarterly* 27 (1999): 36-39.

Hildebrandt, Ted. "Motivation and Antithetic Parallelism in Proverbs 10–15." *Journal of the Evangelical Theological Society* 35 (December, 1992): 433-444.

_____. "Proverbial Pairs: Compositional Units in Proverbs 10–29." *Journal of Biblical Literature* 107 (1988): 207-224.

_____. "Proverbs 22:6a: Train Up a Child?" *Grace Theological Journal* 9, no. 1 (1988): 3-19.

Huwiler, Elizabeth Faith. "Control of Reality in Israelite Wisdom." Dissertation, Duke University, 1988.

Kersovec, J. *Antithetic Structure in Biblical Hebrew Poetry.* Leiden: Brill, 1984.

Kidner, Derek. *Proverbs.* Tyndale Old Testament Commentary. Downers Grove, IL: Tyndale, 1964.

Lang, Bernard. *Wisdom and the Book of Proverbs: A Hebrew Goddess Redefined.* New York: The Pilgrim Press, 1986.

Lemaire, André. *Les écoles et la formation de la Bible dans l'ancien Israël.* OBO 39. Fribourg: Editions Universitaires. Göttingen: Vandenhoeck & Ruprecht, 1981.

Lyons, Ellen Louise. "A Note on Proverbs 31:10-31." In *The Listening Heart: Essays in Wisdom and the Psalms in Honor of Roland E. Murphy.* Ed. by Kenneth G. Hoglund et al. Sheffield: JSOT Press, 1987.

Malchow, Bruce V. "A Manual for Future Monarchs." *Catholic Biblical Quarterly* 47 (April, 1985): 238-245.

McCreesh, Thomas P. "Wisdom as Wife: Proverbs 31:10-31." *Revue Biblique* 92 (1985): 25-46.

McKane, William. *Proverbs: A New Approach*. Philadelphia: The Westminster Press, 1970.

Mieder, Wolfgang. *Proverbs Are Never Out of Season: Popular Wisdom in the Modern Age*. New York: Oxford University Press, 1993.

Murphy, Roland E. "The Personification of Wisdom." In *Wisdom in Ancient Israel: Essays in Honour of J.A. Emerton*. Ed. by John Day, Robert Gordon and H.G.M. Williamson. Cambridge: Cambridge University Press, 1995.

_____. *Proverbs*. Word Biblical Commentary. Nashville: Thomas Nelson, 1998.

_____. *The Tree of Life: An Exploration of Biblical Wisdom Literature*. 2nd ed. Grand Rapids: Eerdmans, 1996.

Newsom, Carol A. "Woman and the Discourse of Patriarchal Wisdom: A Study of Proverbs 1–9." In *Gender and Difference in Ancient Israel*. Ed. by Peggy L. Day. Minneapolis: Fortress, 1989.

O'Connor, Kathleen M. "Wisdom Literature and Experience of the Divine." In *Biblical Theology: Problems and Perspectives*. Ed. by Steven J. Kraftchick, Charles D. Myers Jr., and Ben C. Ollenburger. Nashville: Abingdon, 1995.

Pemberton, Glenn D. "The Rhetoric of the Father: A Rhetorical Analysis of the Father/Son Lectures of Proverbs 1–9." Ph.D. diss., University of Denver/Iliff School of Theology, 1999.

Perdue, Leo G. *Proverbs*. Interpretation. Louisville: John Knox Press, 2000.

_____. *Wisdom & Creation: The Theology of Wisdom Literature*. Nashville: Abingdon, 1994.

Peterson, Eugene. *The Message: Proverbs*. Colorado Springs: Navpress, n.d.

Rad, Gerhard von. *Wisdom in Israel*. Nashville: Abingdon, 1972.

Roth, Wolfgang M.W. "The Numerical Sequence X/X+1 in the Old Testament." *Vetus Testamentum* 12 (1962): 300-311.

Scherer, Andreas. "Is the Selfish Man Wise? Considerations of Context in Proverbs 10:1–22:16 with Special Regard to Surety, Bribery and Friendship." *Journal for the Study of the Old Testament* 76 (December 1997): 59-70.

Scott, R.B.Y. *Proverbs, Ecclesiastes: Introduction, Translation, and Notes.* Anchor Bible. Garden City, NY: Doubleday, 1965.

Seebass, H. "נֶפֶשׁ." *Theological Dictionary of the Old Testament*, vol 9. Ed. by G. Johannes Botterweck and Helmer Ringgren. Trans. by David E. Green. Grand Rapids: Eerdmans, 1986.

Shupak, Nili. "The 'Sitz Im Leben' of the Book of Proverbs in the Light of a Comparison of Biblical and Egyptian Wisdom Literature." *Revue Biblique* 94 (1987): 98-119.

Sneed, Mark. "The Class Culture of Proverbs: Eliminating Stereotypes." *Scandinavian Journal of the Old Testament* 10, no. 2 (1996): 296-308.

Snell, Daniel C. "The Most Obscure Verse in Proverbs: Proverbs XXVI 10." *Vetus Testamentum* 41 (1991): 350-356.

_____. "The Wheel in Proverbs XX 26." *Vetus Testamentum* 39 (1989): 503-505.

Van Leeuwen, Raymond C. *Context and Meaning in Proverbs 25–27.* Atlanta: Scholars Press, 1988.

_____. "Liminality and Worldview in Proverbs 1–9." *Semeia* 50 (1990): 111-144.

_____. "Proverbs." In *The New Interpreter's Bible*, vol. 5. 1997.

_____. "Proverbs xxv 27 Once Again." *Vetus Testamentum* 36 (1986): 105-114.

_____. "Proverbs 30:21-23 and the Biblical World Upside Down." *Journal of Biblical Literature* 105 (1986): 599-610.

_____. "Wealth and Poverty: System and Contradiction in Proverbs." *Hebrew Studies* 33 (1992).

Washington, Harold C. *Wealth and Poverty in the Instruction of Amenemope and the Hebrew Proverbs.* Atlanta: Scholars Press, 1994.

Weeks, Stuart. *Early Israelite Wisdom.* Oxford: Clarendon Press, 1994.

Westermann, Claus. *Roots of Wisdom: The Oldest Proverbs of Israel and Other Peoples*. Louisville, KY: Westminster John Knox Press, 1995.

Whybray, R.N. *Proverbs*. The New Century Bible Commentary. Grand Rapids: Eerdmans, 1994.

_____. *The Book of Proverbs*. Cambridge: University Press, 1972.

_____. *The Book of Proverbs: A Survey of Modern Study*. New York: E.J. Brill, 1995.

_____. *The Composition of the Book of Proverbs*. Sheffield: JSOT Press, 1994.

_____. *Wealth and Poverty in the Book of Proverbs*. Sheffield: JSOT Press, 1990.

PROVERBS 1–9

OVERVIEW

As mentioned in the introduction, the material in chapters 1–9 is primarily of two kinds. One kind is lectures taught by a father to his son. The second kind is speeches made by personified wisdom. With the first, parents instruct their son in the importance of pursuing wisdom and understanding. With the second, wisdom praises herself for her value to youth. The speeches are interludes that reflect on the value of wisdom.

The first nine chapters contain ten instruction poems (lectures to the son) and five interlude poems on Woman Wisdom. The lectures are as follows: 1:8-19; 2:1-22; 3:1-12; 3:21-35; 4:1-9; 4:10-19; 4:20-27; 5:1-23; 6:20-35; 7:1-27. All ten begin with some form of the parental admonition, "My son, listen to my instruction. . . ." Where each of the instructions conclude is harder to locate. Generally speaking, these instruction poems contain three parts. First, the sage makes an appeal for his son to listen to his words. Second, the sage offers advice to the son to embrace wisdom and avoid folly. Third, the sage uses motivational appeals to persuade the son of the benefits of obedience to his words and the consequences of disobedience.

Glenn Pemberton, however, warns against assuming that all ten lectures are alike. He shows how these lectures contain distinct rhetorical functions, and therefore classifies them into three different categories, based on the terms used in the introductory formula.[1] In one category of instruction, the father is concerned solely with gaining the undivided attention of the youth (1:8-19; 2:1-22; 4:1-9; 4:10-19). The father gives no instruction; he only seeks to persuade

---

[1] Glenn D. Pemberton, "The Rhetoric of the Father: A Rhetorical Analysis of the Father/Son Lectures in Proverbs 1–9," dissertation at Iliff School of Theology and University of Denver, 1999, pp. 84-87.

the son to listen to his advice. In a second category of instruction, the father reminds the son of the content of moral instruction and exhorts the son to obey (3:1-12; 3:21-35; 4:20-27). The concern is with retention. In the third category, the father warns the son about illicit sexual behavior (5:1-23; 6:20-35; 7:1-27). In these, the father elaborates on a single theme of moral instruction, sexual misconduct. The ten instructions address three different problems, each using different rhetorical strategies in the process.

Five other interlude poems are strategically placed within the instruction literature. They include three poems in which Woman Wisdom speaks: 1:20-33; 8:1-36; 9:1-6. Among other things, the poems of Wisdom emphasize that the instruction of the parents is more than just reflection on human experience; it has divine approval. Behind the voice of Wisdom is the authoritative voice of Yahweh himself. Two other interlude poems reflecting on wisdom include 3:13-20 and 6:1-19.

The first two chapters of Proverbs introduce the main players in chapters 1-9. Chapter 1:8-19 introduces the father and mother, the son, and the deceptive men. Chapter 1:20-33 introduces Woman Wisdom. Chapter two introduces the quest for wisdom and places side by side the two enemies that Wisdom will battle: the deceptive men (always in the plural; 2:12-15; also 1:8-19; 4:10-19), and the deceptive woman or the adulteress (always in the singular; 2:16-19; also 5:1-23; 6:20-35; 7:6-27; 9:13-18). The adulteress is literally the "strange" or "foreign" woman (the woman other than one's wife; the "other woman"). No attempt should be made to stereotype women as sex objects based on the deceptive woman passages anymore than men should be stereotyped as violent based on the deceptive men passages. In Proverbs, women are also positively portrayed as Wisdom personified (9:1-12) and as one possessing noble character (31:10-31).

In chapters 1-9, the father exposes the youth basically to three temptations he will face. These temptations claim to offer life but ultimately lead to destruction. The first is the temptation to acquire money (1:8-19). The second is peer pressure (1:8-19; 2:12-15; 4:10-19). The third temptation dominates the first nine chapters and is the temptation to illicit sex (chapters 5, 6, 7). The opposite of life in chapters 1-9 is illegal financial gain, conformity to the wrong group, and illicit sex.[2] These temptations come from "external" sources, the evil men and the evil woman. But there are also "internal" threats that the youth faces. These threats come from his own character, which include such things as indolence (6:9-11) and poor judgment (6:1-5).

These instructions from the father come primarily in the form of imperatives (admonitions and commands) followed by a motive clause and then frequently followed by a description of the consequences. Chapters 1–9 serve as the narrative introduction to the sentence literature that follows in chapters 10–29. They are, along with 31:10-31, intended as an editorial framework for the whole book of Proverbs.

PERSONIFICATION OF WISDOM

"Wisdom" is used in a variety of ways in Proverbs 1–9. Sometimes the word is equated with abstract terms like knowledge, understanding, or discretion (1:2; 2:1-2; 3:13; 4:4-5). At other times "wisdom" is described as a precious object that humans seek out (2:4; 3:14-15). In other passages "wisdom" is associated with Yahweh (1:7; 2:5; 9:10). Chapters 1–9 also use descriptions that unambiguously use feminine terms to represent Wisdom as a person. In the Old Testament, wisdom is generally a quality that is ascribed to either God or humans. Only in the first nine chapters of Proverbs are human and divine qualities given to Wisdom.

The personification of Wisdom is most fully developed in three texts: 1:20-33; 8:1-36; 9:1-12. Two of these (1:20-33 and 8:1-36) are speeches by Wisdom. The third (9:1-6) is a description of the invitation that Wisdom offers to the "simple." The precise nature of this personification has baffled many scholars. Interpreters offer a number of different views on how to understand Woman Wisdom. I will briefly mention three.

The first view is that Wisdom is a *hypostasis* of Yahweh. That is, Woman Wisdom is an attribute of God. She is a divine extension of God that assumes an independent character. Just as love or anger or

---

[2]See Daniel J. Estes, *Hear, My Son: Teaching & Learning in Proverbs 1–9* (Grand Rapids: Eerdmans, 1997), p. 57.

compassion are qualities of God, so is wisdom. The sages in Proverbs give this quality of God an autonomous identity. The problem with this view is that Woman Wisdom is depicted as subordinate to Yahweh, especially in 1:20-33 and 8:22-31. To interpret Wisdom as an extension of deity violates the essence of Old Testament belief in Yahweh as one God. In Proverbs, Wisdom is not a rival to the LORD. In 8:22-31, Wisdom was in the beginning with God as God created the world. The passage (namely, v. 30) does not mean, however, that Wisdom was *hypostasis*. Rather than wisdom being an attribute of God, wisdom is an attribute of the world. It is the personifying principle of order in creation.

Second, Kathleen M. O'Connor argues that Woman Wisdom is fully and equally God and not simply an aspect (*hypostasis*) of God.[3] Wisdom stands as a symbol for the God of Israel. O'Connor briefly examines several of the wisdom poems to demonstrate how, in each instance, Woman Wisdom is identified with God. The reason for identifying Wisdom with God in these poems is to "alter the imagination of the readers by persuading them that their God is Wise-God and that they do not need to abandon Israel's God to live with Wisdom for she and God are one. She is God among humans."[4] But when it comes to treating 8:22-33 and the claim that God created Wisdom, O'Connor is not convincing in her argument that Wisdom and God are one.

A third position is that Woman Wisdom is purely a literary device. The author creates a verbal portrait of wisdom by using the figure of personification. Thus Woman Wisdom piques the curiosity of the youth (male) and makes the arduous educational process more attractive. I believe it is best to interpret Woman Wisdom as a personification (a literary device) that expresses a way in which God communicates with humans.

In the final analysis, what can be said about this personified figure of Wisdom? First, Wisdom originates with Yahweh. In an amazing poem in 8:22-31, Wisdom extols herself. Her birth is from God.

---

[3]Kathleen M. O'Connor, "Wisdom Literature and Experience of the Divine," in *Biblical Theology: Problems and Perspectives*, ed. by Steven J. Kraftchick, Charles D. Myers, Jr., and Ben C. Ollenburger (Nashville: Abingdon, 1995), p. 189.

[4]Ibid., p. 195.

She is present before and during creation. She does not compete with God. Second, Wisdom delights in being with humans (8:31).[5] She has a particular mission to them. Wisdom wants and needs human attention. She loves to interact with them (8:4,30-36). Wisdom is not a static body of information. She is like a living organism that needs interactive stimulus to achieve actualization. She promises blessings and prosperity to those who follow her (3:13-18; 8:1-5; 9:1-6). Third, Wisdom is a gift from God (2:6). At the same time, she is associated with discipline and hard work (4:10-27).[6]

PURPOSE OF THE INSTRUCTION LITERATURE

Two issues surface as the reader tries to understand the relationship between the instruction poems (chapters 1–9) and the sentence literature (chapters 10–29). For one, when proverbs, like those found in chapters 10–29, are assigned to a collection, they lose their "performance" context. Proverbs fulfill their function in specific oral contexts. Taken out of that context, they lie dormant. For another, in Israel when proverbs lose their performance context, they also lose their covenant context. That is, they appear detached from any theological basis and appear only to reflect common sense. The loss of a covenant context gives the appearance that a sacred and secular dichotomy exists in the book of Proverbs.

Claudia Camp's solution to these problems is to "recontextualize" proverbs. She proposes that this is accomplished by framing the sentence literature (chapters 10:1–22:16 and 25:1–29:33) in a narrative within the wisdom poems (chapters 1–9 and 31). Wisdom personified as feminine offers a narrative framework for the collection of proverbs. The feminine image enables the book of Proverbs to be a unified whole and function as part of a canon of

---

[5]See Roland Murphy, "The Personification of Wisdom," in *Wisdom in Ancient Israel: Essays in Honour of J.A. Emerton*, ed. by John Day, Robert P. Gordon, and H.G.M. Williamson (Cambridge: Cambridge University Press, 1995), p. 231.

[6]For a more detailed profile of Woman Wisdom see Roland Murphy's chapter "Lady Wisdom," in *The Tree of Life: An Exploration of Biblical Wisdom Literature* (Grand Rapids: Eerdmans, 1996), pp. 145-146.

religious literature.[7] Nevertheless, Camp does not specify how the beginning and ending interpret the whole.

I would like to push the issue further and suggest that the purpose of this material (chapters 1-9) is to equip youth making the transition into adulthood to live within wisdom's boundaries.[8] Two levels exist in the instruction given in the series of poems, both operating simultaneously. On one level, the wisdom poems address specific moral issues that the youth will face head on: the influence of evil companions, the power of greed and money, marriage, and sexual temptations. The lion's share of the instructional warnings goes to sexual temptations, which occupies chapters 5-7.

Yet a second level underlies or, better, overarches these moral issues. It has to do with what the youth will ultimately pursue. The wisdom poems serve as powerful metaphors of two lifestyles: wisdom and life on the one hand, folly and death on the other. These contrasting metaphors depict the moral boundaries or limits in which humans are to operate. To venture outside the boundaries is folly and death. To stay within the bounds is wisdom and life.

The temptations to which the wisdom poems expose the youth demonstrate the powerful attraction of the instant gratification of human desires. But they also demonstrate the even more powerful attraction of a fulfilling life for those willing to delay gratification and live within the limits of wisdom's order.

The wisdom poems of chapters 1-9 serve as a context for understanding the sentence literature in chapters 10-29. The opening chapters use broad strokes to describe the boundaries of wisdom. To keep within wisdom's boundaries is to follow the way of righteousness, justice, and fairness (1:3; 2:9; 8:8-9,15-16,20). It is to live in the fear of the LORD (1:7; 9:10). Folly is the way of evil men and women (2:12-19). The sentence literature, then, specifies what it means to choose one of these two ways and to stay within the parameters of wisdom.

The wisdom poems provide the emotional incentive for the young man to dedicate himself to the pursuit of wisdom by pre-

---

[7]Claudia V. Camp, *Wisdom and the Feminine in the Book of Proverbs* (Decatur, GA: Almond Press, 1985), p. 182.

[8]This is the position of Raymond C. Van Leeuwen in an article entitled "Liminality and Worldview in Proverbs 1-9," *Semeia* 50 (1990): 111-144.

senting Wisdom as a woman offering a sumptuous banquet (chs. 8–9) and granting happiness, a long life, and riches (3:5-12; 3:13-18). The opening poems also depict the total ruin of one who chooses the path of folly (1:17-19; 5:7-14; 7:21-23). The final poem (31:10-31) describes what life looks like when trained in wisdom. The poem is wisdom incarnated. It provides incentive for living the disciplined life called for by wisdom.

In addition, Wisdom's close association with Yahweh (e.g., 8:22-31) validates her instruction. Wisdom has deep theological roots. Thus Woman Wisdom highlights the theological dimension of the book of Proverbs (especially chapters 10–29), which sometimes has been accused of being too secular for the biblical neighborhood.

The wisdom poems set the tone for the reader to receive the specific instruction of the sentence literature in chapters 10–29. Thus the sentence literature fleshes out the exhortations of the wisdom poems. As Fox aptly describes it, the first nine chapters serve as "a hermeneutical preamble to the rest of the book."[9]

I. INTRODUCTION (1:1-7)

[1]**The proverbs of Solomon son of David, king of Israel:**
[2]**for attaining wisdom and discipline;**
> **for understanding words of insight;**

[3]**for acquiring a disciplined and prudent life,**
> **doing what is right and just and fair;**

[4]**for giving prudence to the simple,**
> **knowledge and discretion to the young—**

[5]**let the wise listen and add to their learning,**
> **and let the discerning get guidance—**

[6]**for understanding proverbs and parables,**
> **the sayings and riddles of the wise.**

[7]**The fear of the LORD[a] is the beginning of knowledge,**
> **but fools despise wisdom and discipline.**

[a]**7 The Hebrew words rendered** *fool* **in Proverbs, and often elsewhere in the Old Testament, denote one who is morally deficient.**

---

[9]Fox, *Proverbs 1–9*, p. 46.

1:1-2 The opening wisdom poem serves as an introduction to the whole collection of proverbs. It identifies four key elements in understanding the book: the author, the purpose, the rhetorical tools, and the audience. The author is identified as **Solomon**. According to 1 Kings 4:29-34 Solomon collected, encouraged the collection of, and wrote proverbs. To what degree, however, he is the author of proverbs in the book of Proverbs remains uncertain. This is because the book of Proverbs is a collection of collections. Numerous individuals are mentioned as authors and collectors of proverbs. Solomon is mentioned here and in 10:1. Anonymous collectors are mentioned in 22:17 and 24:23. Two foreign authors are referred to in 30:1 (Agur) and 31:1 (Lemuel's mother).

The poem summarizes the overarching purpose of the book. Stockpiling synonyms for wisdom emphasizes this purpose: **understanding**, prudence, discipline, and knowledge. Verses 2-6 (except v. 5) begin with the Hebrew preposition "to" (translated **for** in the NIV) plus the infinitive construct indicating purpose. These verses set the tone for the book by identifying the course objectives for moral training. The objectives stated here at the beginning are once again affirmed in chapter 9:7-10: to give instruction and teach righteousness to the wise. This goal comes to reality in the final poem of the book (31:10-31).

1:3 The goal of moral instruction is to learn to do what is **right, just and fair**. These three values are the core virtues of wisdom. They are all concerned with one's relationship and responsibility to the community. To do **what is right** or practice righteousness is to demonstrate loyalty to the community. Justice and fairness are closely related terms referring to making responsible, judicial decisions that reflect one's speech and actions (cf. 2:9). The Hebrew word for "fair" comes from the root word which means "straight" or "right" (יָשָׁר, yāšar). The word is often associated with honesty in speech and judgment. When listeners acquire these three virtues, they attain wisdom.

1:5-6 The **wise** are also exhorted to **listen and add to their learning**. For the wise to add to their learning connotes the capacity to increase their ability to understand and share their expertise on life. The word for "learning" (לֶקַח, leqaḥ), as Fox notes, "usually (and perhaps always) connotes eloquence and persuasiveness" (cf. 16:23).[10]

---

[10]Ibid., p. 62.

Verse 6 introduces the rhetorical tools of the sages. It is connected with the previous verse in that the sages study these rhetorical forms in order to gain further insight into life. The primary educational tool used by the sages is the **proverbs** (מָשָׁל, *māšāl*; see "Overview" under III. Sentence Literature of the First Solomonic Collection [10:1–22:16]). A proverb is a short sentence consisting of two parallel lines (located primarily in chapters 10–29). It serves to impart the moral instruction to youth.

The term the NIV translates **parables** (מְלִיצָה, *mᵉlîṣāh*) is an uncommon word in the Old Testament (appearing elsewhere only in Hab 2:6). The rhetorical form probably refers to a type of satire or enigmatic poem of the kind found in Proverb 6:6-19. The verse also mentions education in understanding **riddles** (חִידֹת, *ḥîdôth*). However, it is difficult to discover this literary form in the book of Proverbs. The "comparative" proverbs clustered in chapters 25–27 contain riddle-like qualities with the first line using some type of analogy and the second line specifying the reference. But those are not true riddles.

Fox proposes that this reference to riddles in the prologue alerts the wise to the fact that there is more to these collections of proverbs than meets the eye.[11] It prepares the wise to engage in careful study. In other words, what follows in this book are proverbs that are collected not simply for the sake of listening to and heeding, but for examining and learning interpretive skills. All three terms, "proverbs," "parables," and "riddles," in this context are closely related. **The wise** mentioned here appears to refer to a special class of individuals who collected and preserved wisdom (cf. 22:17 and 24:23).

1:7 The fear of the LORD is one of the most repeated phrases in Proverbs (cf. 1:29; 2:5; 9:10; 10:27; 14:26,27; 15:16,33; 16:6; 19:23; 22:4; 23:17). This is the *leitmotif* of proverbial wisdom. The phrase carries with it the qualities of humility (15:33; 22:4), wisdom (1:7), practicing steadfast love and faithfulness (16:6), and a concern for a relationship with God (2:5; 9:10). In the book of Proverbs, fear of the LORD is related to faith in God that seeks understanding.[12] This phrase is the book's motto forming parentheses around the first nine

---

[11]Ibid., pp. 66-67.

[12]See Leo G. Perdue, *Wisdom & Creation: The Theology of Wisdom Literature* (Nashville: Abingdon, 1994), p. 79.

chapters, coming here at the beginning as well as the conclusion of the unit (9:10). It also frames the whole book (1:7 and 31:31).

In what way is the fear of the LORD **the beginning of knowledge?** The best way is to understand "beginning" in the temporal sense. The prerequisite to gaining wisdom is the fear of the LORD (cf. 9:10 and 15:33). As Fox concludes, "The motto says that the **fear** of God is the starting point of the educational process. . . ."[13] In order to be wise, one must first seek godliness. From this starting point, the wise grow in practicing what is right, just, and fair (v. 3). The fear of the LORD, however, is not just the beginning point for gaining wisdom; it is its essence (Job 28:28).

Fear of God involves a relationship with him but also apprehension in the presence of an awesome power. Contrary to attempts to tone down the idea of fear, it does include an element of trepidation. Proverbs 24:21 speaks of fear in the presence of the LORD and the king. One fears those powers that can inflict harm (24:21-22). This serves as a powerful motivational force for seeking wisdom.

In the book of Proverbs, the fear of the LORD does not primarily refer to the reverent worship of Yahweh. The subject of worship is seldom addressed in the book. Rather it refers to the total life commitment of a person to God. The way in which the book of Deuteronomy defines the fear of the LORD can also be applied to Proverbs:

> And now, O Israel, what does the LORD your God ask of you but to fear the LORD your God, to walk in all his ways, to love him, to serve the LORD your God with all your heart and with all your soul, and to observe the LORD's commands and decrees that I am giving you today for your own good? (10:12-13).

This text defines the fear of God as the dedication of one's whole life to the devotion of the LORD. It is not simply the display of awe and reverence in public worship. Instead, it is the demonstration of daily response to God's will in one's decisions and actions.

The prologue of 1:1-7 introduces three characters: the youth, the wise, and the fool. The terms **simple** (פֶּתִי, *pethî*; used fifteen times) and **young**[14] are synonymous and refer to those who are inexperi-

---

[13]Fox, *Proverbs 1-9*, p. 68.

[14]In the book of Proverbs, youth (נַעַר, *na'ar*) does not refer to an infant or an elementary age child but to the teen or the young adult.

enced in the ways of living (v. 4). To refer to someone as "simple" can either have positive or negative connotations. Sometimes this term is used synonymously with fool (e.g., 1:32; 8:5); sometimes the term is used to refer to those who are inexperienced, that is, open to instruction and moldable (e.g., 8:5; 21:11).

The young, however, are not the exclusive audience of Proverbs. The instructions given in this book are also for the wise (v. 5), those who are older and more mature in their life experiences. The noun "wise" is used synonymously with the person who is referred to throughout Proverbs as "the discerning" or "understanding one" (נָבוֹן, nābôn; 16:21; 19:25). The wise can also increase in their understanding of life. According to Proverbs 9:9, when instruction is given to the wise, they increase in learning. Wisdom is not something attained once and for all. The pursuit of wisdom is a lifetime enterprise. Young and old, male and female alike, must seek it out.[15]

In addition to the young and the wise, a third character is introduced in verse 7 and that is the fool. At least a half dozen different words are used to describe **fools** in Proverbs and in Wisdom Literature.[16] The term used here is one that describes the person who is hardened in his ways (אֱוִיל, 'ĕwîl; used 19 times). This is what the simpleminded become who do not listen to instruction. The simpleminded person described in verse 4 is the one who is naïve and gullible; he is the impressionable youth. The gullibility of the simple, if not properly instructed, can lead to a morally calloused fool (see 9:16; 14:18).

This opening instruction sets forth the task of the sage, identifies the ones to whom instruction is directed, and establishes the purpose of the book. The recipients are those who possess receptive

---

[15]It is true that in the instruction material of chapters 1–9, the admonitions are addressed to the son. Nonetheless, daughters may also apply the material to themselves. Richard Clifford suggests that even though Proverbs is addressed to young men, all ages can easily apply the "transitional time" of decision making to themselves: "she addresses all of us at a critical moment in our lives, when we are, so to speak, in the process of building our lives, founding a household, seeking a relationship. The book takes a particular moment in a youth's coming of age and uses it as an analogy." See Richard Clifford, *The Wisdom Literature*, in Interpreting Biblical Texts (Nashville: Abingdon Press, 1998), p. 56.

[16]See discussion of the words for "fool" in the Introduction under "Characteristics of Wisdom Literature" pp. 15ff.

minds and who are open to learning (the simple, the youth, and the wise). They are open to receiving **wisdom**, and understanding, and **knowledge**. The sages instruct them in knowledge. But this is not simply information that they are passing on. The instruction goes beyond the mere transfer of a body of knowledge to the goal of forming moral character that reflects obedience to God.

II. INSTRUCTION LITERATURE (1:8–9:18)

This is the first of ten instruction poems in chapters 1–9. The instruction begins with the formulaic admonition from a father and mother to a son. A debate arises over whether "father" and "mother" actually refer to a parent and child relationship or whether it refers to a teacher and student relationship. The fact that both parents are frequently referred to as fulfilling this teaching role strongly points to the recognition that it was the pupil's natural parents that were involved. The father's reminiscence of his father's teachings in 4:3 further depicts parental, not school, education. So whether or not Proverbs was composed for use in schools, its *literary* context is the instruction of the (actual) father to his (actual) son. "Father" means father, just as the parallel "mother" (1:8; 4:3; 6:20) must mean the actual mother, not a "schoolmarm." A home, not a school is the *literary* milieu of Proverbs.[17] At the same time, the book of Proverbs had broader application than just to the education in the home (see Schools in Israel in Introduction).

Proverbs does not usually talk about such extreme cases that involve felony crimes, as envisioned in this first instruction poem. Proverbs usually addresses ethical choices related to common everyday decisions such as controlling anger, restraining the tongue, learning patience, developing integrity, and practicing generosity. So in speaking of those involved in pillaging and killing, the first lecture to the son comes as a shock! The admonition is basically, "Do not choose to involve yourself with felons and their criminal activity."

---

[17]Michael V. Fox maintains that, "There is no justification for the common assumption that the speaker is a schoolteacher." See Fox, "Ideas of Wisdom in Proverbs 1–9," *JBL* 116 (1997): 620. See further comments he makes about this in footnotes 10 and 11.

Fox proposes that the unusual scenario causes the youth to ask the question, "Is life really *that* dangerous?"[18] The implication is, yes, it is. The choices that youth make in the daily decisions of life can lead to self-destruction.[19]

A. FIRST INSTRUCTION: WARNING AGAINST GANGS
(1:8-19)

[8]**Listen, my son, to your father's instruction**
    and do not forsake your mother's teaching.
[9]**They will be a garland to grace your head**
    and a chain to adorn your neck.
[10]**My son, if sinners entice you,**
    do not give in to them.
[11]**If they say, "Come along with us;**
    let's lie in wait for someone's blood,
    let's waylay some harmless soul;
[12]**let's swallow them alive, like the grave,**[a]
    and whole, like those who go down to the pit;
[13]**we will get all sorts of valuable things**
    and fill our houses with plunder;
[14]**throw in your lot with us,**
    and we will share a common purse"—
[15]**my son, do not go along with them,**
    do not set foot on their paths;
[16]**for their feet rush into sin,**
    they are swift to shed blood.
[17]**How useless to spread a net**
    in full view of all the birds!
[18]**These men lie in wait for their own blood;**
    they waylay only themselves!

---

[18]Fox, *Proverbs 1-9* , p. 93.

[19]Carol A. Newsom also assumes that the gang is a metaphor for something else; a metarhetoric is at work in this opening instruction. See Newsom, "Woman and the Discourse of Patriarchal Wisdom: A Study of Proverbs 1-9," in *Gender and Difference in Ancient Israel*, ed. by Peggy L. Day (Minneapolis: Fortress, 1989).

[19]**Such is the end of all who go after ill-gotten gain;**
   it takes away the lives of those who get it.

[a]*12 Hebrew Sheol*

1:8-9 The best translation is **son** rather than "child" (NRSV).
"Child" carries the connotation of dependence and inability to make
decisions, someone who is preteen in age. One could translate the
term "disciple" for the sake of using inclusive language. However,
"son" best clarifies the status of the original recipient. By discernment, later audiences, both male and female, can appropriate the
instructions to themselves.

The admonition is for the son to follow the **father's** and **mother's**
instruction.[20] Their instruction is to adorn the youth like fine jewelry,
a garland to grace your head. This is probably some kind of plaited
wreath that was placed on the head to signify a position of honor.

The actual instruction begins with verse 10. The instruction
addresses the temptation of a young man to associate with criminals,
gangs, and felons. All of the instruction literature address concrete
issues. The admonition is for the son to stay away from these kinds
of corrupt companions. Underlying this admonition one picks up
tension that may have existed between parent and adolescent as the
parent seeks to urge the youth along the wise path. At the same time
the youth, moving into the adult world, wants to explore the great
adventures that await him.

1:11-14 These verses contain a description of the gang lifestyle.
The sage creates a hypothetical situation in which a youth is enticed
to join a gang. The father's imitation of the dialogue of the gang
recreates a "virtual reality" of the temptation. This is the gang's

---

[20]Does this mean that daughters were not a part of instruction? No. The
women in Proverbs are mature in wisdom and morally educated. Woman
Wisdom is involved in instruction (chapters 1–9). King Lemuel's mother
instructs him (31:1-9). The capable woman of Proverbs 31 is a teacher (31:26).
These are educated women. In addition E. Follis observes, "Sons commonly
are thought to represent the adventuresome spirit of a society, constantly
pressing beyond established boundaries, at the outmost part, the circumfer-
ence, of the community. Daughters, on the other hand, have been associated
with stability, with the building up of society, with nurturing the community
at its heart and center." See Follis, *Directions in Biblical Hebrew Poetry*, JSOT
Supp. 40 (1987), p. 178. In other words, sons were tempted to stray more than
were daughters, thus more in need of instruction and reproof.

speech, which involves an appealing egalitarian ethos. The greatest temptation from the gang comes not from their actions but from their enticing words. They claim to offer adventure (v. 11), easy money (v. 13), and camaraderie (v. 14). What they do, they do for the fun of it (v. 11).

1:15-17 The parents exhort the son to stay away from the gang for two reasons. For one, their actions are evil (v. 16). For another, their vision is shortsighted (vv. 17-19). They only desire instant gratification. However, the primary basis upon which the father appeals to the son is not on rational arguments but on the basis of the father's credibility with the son. The father describes the enticement of the gang's lifestyle and responds by saying, **my son do not go along with them** (v. 15). It is an appeal to the relationship the father has with the son.

Verse 17 contains a proverb difficult to interpret. Who do the **birds** represent? If the birds represent the son, then the proverb is an observation on the importance of remembering the lesson the parent has taught when the gang of criminals entices the son to join. Now that the son is aware of the trap, he can avoid it. Any snare that the wicked set fails because of the instruction the son has received. In other words, "forewarned is forearmed."

Or the lesson may apply to the gang members which then sets up a *contrast* between the gang and the bird. Birds can see a net spread before them and avoid it, but sinners are blind to the consequences of their own actions (v. 18). Thus a contrast is set up between the actions of a bird and those of sinners. Birds have more sense than do some people.[21]

The interpretation I believe to be most natural to the context is the second: the gang members have less sense than a bird that is clever enough to stay out of a fowler's trap. Verse 18 implies a contrast between the actions of the birds and the behavior of the hoodlums. These thugs are so enslaved by their appetite that they throw caution to the wind. Those who plan violence walk resolutely to their own death (cf. 7:22-23).

---

[21]Fox understands the proverb to carry a double meaning. Initially it applies to the youth who through instruction now has the sense to stay away from a trap. But after reading the whole scenario, it also applies to the robbers who have less sense than a bird (*Proverbs 1–9*, p. 89).

It is not uncommon in the instruction poems for the sage to use a maxim like the one in verse 17 to clinch his argument (see also vv. 27-28 in 6:20-35; v. 17 in 9:13-18; vv. 10-11 in 6:6-11). The sages use proverbs in the course of these wisdom poems to persuade the young regarding the seriousness of the matter before them.[22]

1:18-19 In this instruction poem, the parent appeals to his son to heed his words, offers practical advice for avoiding temptation, and finally lays out the motivation for not engaging in the lifestyle of the gang. In the end, though, the parent leaves it to the youth to decide for himself. Only the son can choose.

The first instruction poem contains no specific moral instruction. The father's sole purpose is to gain the undivided attention of the youth.[23] The daily decisions that youth face are "life and death" matters. Rejecting the wisdom and moral standards of the community is as dangerous as joining a murderous gang.

It is no accident that what follows on the heels of parental instruction in this poem is the instruction of Wisdom. To affirm the authority of the parents' advice, Woman Wisdom speaks in the next poem, inviting youth to take a seat in her school. When Woman Wisdom speaks, she confirms the authority of the parent.

B. FIRST SPEECH BY PERSONIFIED WISDOM (1:20-33)

[20]**Wisdom calls aloud in the street,**
   she raises her voice in the public squares;
[21]**at the head of the noisy streets[a] she cries out,**
   in the gateways of the city she makes her speech:
[22]**"How long will you simple ones[b] love your simple ways?**
   How long will mockers delight in mockery
   and fools hate knowledge?
[23]**If you had responded to my rebuke,**
   I would have poured out my heart to you
   and made my thoughts known to you.

---

[22]James L. Crenshaw, "Wisdom and Authority: Sapiential Rhetoric and Its Warrants," *Congress Volume: Vienna, 1980,* ed. by John A. Emerton (Leiden: Brill, 1981), pp. 10-29.

[23]See Pemberton, "Rhetoric," pp. 87-109.

²⁴**But since you rejected me when I called**
        and no one gave heed when I stretched out my hand,
²⁵**since you ignored all my advice**
        and would not accept my rebuke,
²⁶**I in turn will laugh at your disaster;**
        I will mock when calamity overtakes you—
²⁷**when calamity overtakes you like a storm,**
        when disaster sweeps over you like a whirlwind,
        when distress and trouble overwhelm you.
²⁸**"Then they will call to me but I will not answer;**
        they will look for me but will not find me.
²⁹**Since they hated knowledge**
        and did not choose to fear the LORD,
³⁰**since they would not accept my advice**
        and spurned my rebuke,
³¹**they will eat the fruit of their ways**
        and be filled with the fruit of their schemes.
³²**For the waywardness of the simple will kill them,**
        and the complacency of fools will destroy them;
³³**but whoever listens to me will live in safety**
        and be at ease, without fear of harm."

ᵃ*21 Hebrew; Septuagint / on the tops of the walls*   ᵇ*22* **The Hebrew word rendered** *simple* **in Proverbs generally denotes one without moral direction and inclined to evil.**

Verses 20-21 introduce Woman Wisdom and her omnipresence in the city. Verses 22-33 contain Wisdom's speech. The harshest warning given to the youth in chapters 1–9 is found in this poem. Wisdom proclaims her condemnation of the simple and the fool with a prophetic voice (vv. 24 and 28). The term "rebuke" or "reproof" is used no less than three times in verses 20-33 (vv. 23,25,30). This speech by Woman Wisdom is parallel to her speeches in chapters 8 and 9.

It is quite doubtful that any youths in the audience to whom Wisdom speaks would identify themselves as mockers and fools (v. 22). More than likely, Wisdom uses a rhetorical ploy to get the attention of her audience.[24] She turns from speaking to the youth

---

[24]In rhetoric this is often referred to as an "apostrophe," the turning away from the real audience to address an imaginary one (E.W. Bullinger, *Figures of Speech Used in the Bible* [Grand Rapids: Baker, 1968], p. 901).

and begins to address an imaginary audience of hardened fools with the intention that the youth present will overhear the warning and take heed (note the shift from the second person to the third in vv. 27-28). In this first speech, Woman Wisdom focuses on attitude rather than action. Her concern is that listeners develop a responsive and open heart toward wisdom.

1:20-21 Wisdom confronts learners in the **city** gates and **noisy streets.** Being present in such public places demonstrates the relevance of what she has to offer. Though Wisdom is not a prophet, she uses a prophetic tone to alert the listeners to their vulnerability. What they are facing is a life and death matter, but these students appear indifferent. So Wisdom issues a wakeup call to help her hearers realize the seriousness of what they are up against; it is a word of judgment. However, in the end she extends hope to those who respond (v. 33). The poem appears to suppose some type of public school setting in which Wisdom teaches. Wisdom assumes the role of a teacher instructing in the context of a public school.

1:22-23 Verse 22 appeals to three types of people. First, the **simple** (פֶּתִי, *pethî*) love simple ways. They are easily swayed, gullible. As yet they have not developed strong moral foundations for life. **Mockers** represent the second type. Mockers (לֵצִים, *lēṣîm*; cf. Ps 1:1) are arrogant individuals who think they know it all. Proverbs 9:7-8 describes mockers as unteachable. The mocker assumes his own superiority. Finally, the **fool** (כְּסִיל, *kᵊsîl*) has made folly a habit, a way of life.

In contrast, the wise person develops a teachable spirit. The basis of teachability is the **fear** of **the LORD** (v. 29). Wisdom begins by submitting to Yahweh. Then the wise accepts the **advice** and **rebuke** of parents and elders (v. 30). The teachable person learns from tradition. He or she learns from the accumulated insights of others. This means a couple of things. First, a wise person is committed to lifelong learning (9:9). Second, as Daniel Estes says, "learning from the past provides a solid foundation for personal choices in the present."[25] If the fool had **responded** (lit., "turned to") to wisdom's rebuke, he would have received the **heart** (or "desire"; רוּחַ, *rûaḥ*) of wisdom (v. 23).

1:24-27 The first denunciation of the simple is addressed directly to them in the second person (**you**; v. 24). There will come a time when Wisdom will simply let the foolish suffer the consequences of

---

[25]Estes, *Hear, My Son*, p. 48.

their own behavior. She will not intervene to rescue but will only watch in scornful observation. To **laugh** is an expression of one's superiority and of confidence in one's situation in life (Ps 2:4). For example, the woman of noble character laughs at the time to come (31:25).

1:28-31 The second denunciation switches to the third person (**they**; v. 28). The irony is that those who earlier ignored Wisdom are now calling out to her. Wisdom does not respond. The tables are turned. Verse 28 indicates that timing is crucial. There is a point of no return, when one cannot reverse the decisions made. Wisdom repeatedly emphasizes the importance of timing.

Verses 29-30 state the reason fools reject Wisdom's voice. They **hated knowledge** and the **fear** of the **LORD**. If fools refuse wisdom, they also refuse the fear of Yahweh (v. 29). Though Wisdom has authority and is assigned traits that are traits of Yahweh, she is not a goddess. As William McKane concludes, "Wisdom is located in the market-place, not in the Godhead."[26]

Wisdom takes to the street to invite all who would listen to come to her classroom. Wisdom does not take a passive role; she is in the thick of the action in the public square. In this context Wisdom is not contemplative; one does not find her in solitude but in the hustle and bustle of life, in the public arena. This is ironic given that women were excluded from public life in the gate (cf. Prov 31:23, where the woman's husband is in the city gates). Normally, a woman seen in the street was looking for men, going for water, or working (1 Sam 9:11-14). In this instance Woman Wisdom, who is a distinguished and reputable woman, is roaming the streets looking for those open to instruction.

In 1:20-33, Wisdom assumes the role of a teacher. She is concerned with a class of students who lack motivation. She has lost patience with her inattentive students (1:24-27). She pulls out all stops to convince them of the seriousness of the subject matter. Her instruction deals with matters of life and death. In other ancient Near Eastern cultures, education was primarily career oriented. In Israel, the sages were more than transmitters of basic skills (e.g., reading, writing, and learning a trade). They were communicators of wisdom and ethical instruction.

---

[26]William McKane, *Proverbs: A New Approach* (Philiadelphia: Westminster Press, 1970), p. 277.

C. SECOND INSTRUCTION: THE SEARCH FOR WISDOM (2:1-22)

The instruction poem in chapter 2 is an amazing literary composition. In Hebrew, it is one long complex sentence made up of twenty-two lines, the number of letters in the alphabet. The poem is in the form of an acrostic. Each of the first three strophes (vv. 1-4,5-8,9-11) begins with the first letter of the Hebrew alphabet, *aleph* (א , except for v. 1). The strophes in the second half of the poem (vv. 12-15,16-19,20-22) all begin with *lamed* (ל), the middle letter of the alphabet. This wisdom poem is programmatic for the following chapters (3–7). In chapter 2 the reader is introduced to the "wicked men," who are again described in chapter 4. The reader is also introduced to the strange woman or the adulteress, who gets the lion's share of attention in chapters 5–7. The sole purpose of the instruction poem is to persuade the son to listen to the sage and not give up on the pursuit of wisdom.[27]

¹My son, if you accept my words
 and store up my commands within you,
²turning your ear to wisdom
 and applying your heart to understanding,
³and if you call out for insight
 and cry aloud for understanding,
⁴and if you look for it as for silver
 and search for it as for hidden treasure,
⁵then you will understand the fear of the LORD
 and find the knowledge of God.
⁶For the LORD gives wisdom,
 and from his mouth come knowledge and understanding.
⁷He holds victory in store for the upright,
 he is a shield to those whose walk is blameless,
⁸for he guards the course of the just
 and protects the way of his faithful ones.
⁹Then you will understand what is right and just
 and fair—every good path.
¹⁰For wisdom will enter your heart,
 and knowledge will be pleasant to your soul.

---

[27]Pemberton, "Rhetoric," pp. 130-132.

[11]Discretion will protect you,
>and understanding will guard you.
[12]Wisdom will save you from the ways of wicked men,
>from men whose words are perverse,
[13]who leave the straight paths
>to walk in dark ways,
[14]who delight in doing wrong
>and rejoice in the perverseness of evil,
[15]whose paths are crooked
>and who are devious in their ways.
[16]It will save you also from the adulteress,
>from the wayward wife with her seductive words,
[17]who has left the partner of her youth
>and ignored the covenant she made before God.
[18]For her house leads down to death[a]
>and her paths to the spirits of the dead.
[19]None who go to her return
>or attain the paths of life.
[20]Thus you will walk in the ways of good men
>and keep to the paths of the righteous.
[21]For the upright will live in the land,
>and the blameless will remain in it;
[22]but the wicked will be cut off from the land,
>and the unfaithful will be torn from it.

[a]*17* Or *covenant of her God*

Verses 1-11 serve as a lengthy introduction to the instruction given in verses 12-22. The purpose of the introduction is to offer encouragement to the youth. As youths begin to seek wisdom, they will find the pursuit wearisome. Wisdom is a quality that humans do not necessarily have a natural inclination to possess. They must acquire a taste for it. If youths can work through the initial struggles and maintain openness and patience, they will find it. This kind of encouragement demonstrates that pedagogy in ancient Israel was not harsh and insensitive.

2:1-4 Learning begins with the parent instructing the youth. The parent takes the initiative in imparting wisdom, but the youth shoulders the major responsibility for acquiring it. In the previous poem, Wisdom cries out in the streets and public squares but the fool does not respond. In this instruction poem, the receptive youth cries aloud for wisdom. The youth is required to exert much effort in gaining wisdom. He is to **cry aloud for understanding, look for it as for silver, search for it as for hidden treasure**. Gaining wisdom is compared to miners digging for precious metal. It involves diligence, commitment. To gain wisdom is not simply to gain insight into life. Wisdom is also an attitude; it is the desire to pursue what is right.

2:5-8 This strophe and the next (vv. 9-11) describe the consequences for one who diligently seeks wisdom. Verses 5-8 describe the relationship between Yahweh and the youth. Paradoxically, Yahweh gives (נָתַן, *nāthan*) wisdom to those who have cried out for it. Along with it, he provides protection from evil. The first result of seeking wisdom is that those who seek it will have a right relationship with Yahweh.

2:9-11 The second result of seeking wisdom affects one's relationship with humans. Verse 9 summarizes the tripartite ethic of human relationships: **right, just,** and **fair** (see 1:3; see also 8:20). When persons acquire a mature ethic, they not only know how to behave responsibly, they delight in doing so (v.10). The wicked, on the other hand, delight in evil (v. 14). Wisdom equips youth to fear God and live appropriately in community.

2:12-15 The positive relationship in community described above is now contrasted with potential negative relations with wicked men and women. When others try to lead youth astray, youth have the ability to resist such temptations because of wisdom. Verses 12-15 describe the ways of wicked men. They are known primarily by their **perverse** speech and **crooked** actions. The parent introduced the son to these men earlier in 1:8-19.

2:16-19 Both this and the previous unit are introduced by the same Hebrew phrase, "to deliver from . . ." (לְהַצִּילְךָ מִ, *l°haṣîlkā mi*). Here the son is delivered **from the adulteress** (lit., "strange" or "foreign" woman; מֵאִשָּׁה זָרָה, *mē'iššāh zārāh*). She is "strange" because she is the wife of another man (v. 17). Nothing in the instruction poems indicates that she is a "foreigner" in the sense of a non-Israelite or in terms of religious practices. The counterpart to this woman is "the wife of your youth" described in 5:15-20.

Like her male counterpart, what identifies the adulteress is her speech. Unlike the "perverse" speech of the male tempter, the speech of the temptress is smooth. She knows how to entice the simpleton. She makes what she has to offer irresistible to the naïve person. She has not remained faithful to the husband of her youth (v. 17). In leaving **the partner of her youth** this woman has **ignored the covenant she made before God**. That is, she has ignored her marriage vows made in the presence of God as witness. To follow this woman in her lifestyle is to follow the way of death.

2:20-22 The concluding paragraph serves as a reminder to the son. When guided by wisdom, his life will be productive. But, be assured, the life of the wicked will be cut off.

This poem sheds some light on the goals and the process of moral education in Israel. Fundamental to the goal of education is instilling in the heart of the student an intense desire to learn. Wisdom involves more than understanding; it includes an attitude. That is the image portrayed in 2:1-4. A heavy responsibility is placed on the individual. He must engage in a painstaking search for wisdom. The primary focus of this instruction is on the formation of godly character. This concern for character focuses on internal qualities, which in turn manifest themselves in the way in which the learner activates righteousness, justice, and fairness in the community. As Estes has aptly described, the goal of Wisdom "is not concerned primarily with the acquisition and development of professional skills; it is concerned with the development of that moral maturity with which professional skills may be competently utilized."[28] Estes continues, "The goal of education is not just to transmit a body of facts, but it is to develop in the learner the kind of character that will continually impel him to keep learning and growing."[29] The goals for education in Proverbs 1–9 "focus for the most part on the cultivation of the learner as a mature godly person, rather than upon the transmission of a discrete body of knowledge."[30]

The process of education in Israel has not always been clearly understood. Contrary to the popular stereotype of pedagogy in Israel, instruction was not a barbarous affair.[31] The admonition in 2:1-22 offers encouragement and reassurance. In the sentence liter-

---

[28]Estes, *Hear, My Son*, p. 69.
[29]Ibid., pp. 69-70.
[30]Ibid., p. 85.
[31]See Michael V. Fox, "The Pedagogy of Proverbs 2," *JBL* 113, no. 2 (1994): 233-243.

ature of chapters 10–29, reference is made to the use of the rod (e.g., 13:24; 29:15). But as one examines Proverbs 1–9, corporal punishment is not among the tools used to educate youth. Though Woman Wisdom reproves, she never uses the rod. The description of the education process in chapter 2 is a collaborative effort among parents, youth, and Yahweh.[32] Yahweh and Wisdom offer reproof; parents give instruction. None resort to the rod.

D. THIRD INSTRUCTION: BEHAVIOR TOWARD GOD (3:1-12)

This passage is the third of ten instruction poems in Proverbs 1–9. True to form, the poem begins with the formulaic admonition, "My son, do not forget my teaching." What follows are exhortations designed to encourage the learner to grow in "trust in the LORD" (v. 5) and establish a good reputation "in the sight of God and man" (v. 4).

This poem only uses the word "wisdom" once, and that with a negative connotation (v. 7). The poem is not directly about wisdom but about stimulating in the listener faith and trust. Notice the vocabulary used in this poem: "Trust," "lean not," "acknowledge," "fear," "honor," "do not despise," "do not resent." All of these refer to one's attitude toward God. Reliance on God is the prerequisite for attaining wisdom.

Chapter 3:1-12 holds together in the following way. Verses 1-4 exhort youth to incorporate parental instruction into their lives. Verses 5-8 describe proper humility before Yahweh. Verses 9-10 issue an imperative to submit wealth to Yahweh. And finally, verses 11-12 exhort the learner to accept the LORD's discipline. The instruction contains six commands paired with corresponding reasons or motive clauses.[33] The parent does not demand obedience based solely upon his authority but upon legitimate reasons offered.

¹My son, do not forget my teaching,
> **but keep my commands in your heart,**
²for they will prolong your life many years
> **and bring you prosperity.**

---

[32]Ibid., 243.
[33]Estes, *Hear, My Son,* p. 112.

³Let love and faithfulness never leave you;
  bind them around your neck,
  write them on the tablet of your heart.
⁴Then you will win favor and a good name
  in the sight of God and man.
⁵Trust in the LORD with all your heart
  and lean not on your own understanding;
⁶in all your ways acknowledge him,
  and he will make your paths straight.ᵃ
⁷Do not be wise in your own eyes;
  fear the LORD and shun evil.
⁸This will bring health to your body
  and nourishment to your bones.
⁹Honor the LORD with your wealth,
  with the firstfruits of all your crops;
¹⁰then your barns will be filled to overflowing,
  and your vats will brim over with new wine.
¹¹My son, do not despise the LORD's discipline
  and do not resent his rebuke,
¹²because the LORD disciplines those he loves,
  as a fatherᵇ the son he delights in.

ᵃ6 Or *will direct your paths*   ᵇ*12 Hebrew; Septuagint / and he punishes*

3:1-4 The opening verses call on the youth to absorb parental instruction into the very core of his being. He must adorn himself with the **teaching** (תּוֹרָה, *tôrāh*; v. 1) of his parents. The image refers to the task of memorization, a standard way of learning in antiquity (v. 3b). Yet to **write** these instructions **on the tablet of your heart** means something more than just memorizing them. It also means that one's character is shaped by them (cf., Jer 31:33). Youth must also clothe themselves in **love and faithfulness** (v. 3), which are here used synonymously to refer to trust in God (v. 5).

Such adornment results in **favor** with **God and man** (v. 4). It is interesting to note that verse 4 contains one of the few references in Proverbs to the divinity as God (אֱלֹהִים, *'ĕlōhîm*, cf. 2:5; 2:17; 3:4; 25:2; 30:9). Normally the covenant name Yahweh (יהוה) is used to refer to the Creator of the universe.

3:5-8 These verses contain key words and phrases in sapiential thought. First of all, the phrase **trust in the LORD** (16:20; 22:17-19;

28:25; 29:25), and its close associate **fear the LORD**, is the fundamental definition of wisdom in Proverbs. Trust usually implies some
threat or evil looming on the horizon.[34] To trust in the LORD **with all
your heart** refers to the total surrender of self. The admonition is
the theological foundation upon which all the proverbs rest.

When the sage calls on the reader to **acknowledge him** (v. 6), he
speaks on the level of attitude; the disciple desires to do God's will.
When the disciple learns to trust completely in Yahweh, then the
promise is that **he will make straight your paths**. This does not mean
that Yahweh promises a life free from difficulties. Rather it means
that one's life has clear direction and purpose. Abraham set off on a
journey not knowing where he was going, only that God would lead
him. In other words, God promised to make his paths straight.

The next imperative in the instruction is **Do not be wise in your
own eyes** (v. 7). This is a stock phrase in wisdom's dictionary used
some nine times in Proverbs.[35] The sage often portrays the fool as
someone who is "wise in his own eyes" (cf. 26:5,12,16). Those who
are wise in their own eyes are those ruled by conceit, who depend
on their own intellectual finesse to make it in the world (cf. Jer 9:23-
24). Here the phrase is antithetic to "fear the LORD." To be wise in
one's own eyes is a demonstration of pride. To fear the LORD
demonstrates humility.

For those who do fear the LORD, the rewards are significant. It
will result in **health to your body and nourishment to your bones**
(v. 8). "Nourishment" (שִׁקּוּי, *šiqqûy*) can literally be translated "medicine." A healthy life flows out of one's relationship to the Creator.
Such trust brings healing to the flesh and medicine for the body.
This reference to the body is to the physical body and to physical
health, yet it includes more than that. It incorporates the whole of a
person's being.

The wisdom of Proverbs does not divide individuals or life into
parts. There is no dichotomy between mind and body, physical and
spiritual, or sacred and secular. Such a dichotomy is artificial. From
the perspective of Proverbs, the physical, mental, emotional, moral,
and spiritual are parts of the whole. When one is affected, the others

---

[34]Fox, *Proverbs 1-9*, p. 148.
[35]This phrase, with slight variation, is used repeatedly in Proverbs to
describe human pride (3:7; 12:15; 16:2; 21:2; 26:5,12,16; 28:11; 30:12).

are affected as well. Proverbial wisdom is about health, health that incorporates the whole person.

3:9-10 These verses call for those who are truly wise to surrender their **wealth** to Yahweh. The image of **firstfruits** recalls texts like Deuteronomy 26:2 and 10 where the people offer back to God the firstfruits of their labor, not in order to get rich but to acknowledge that all they have is a gift from God. The offering of the firstfruits was an act of worship, not a means of gaining more wealth. In verse 10, the image of prosperity described as **barns** and **vats filled to overflowing** does not refer to the luxuries of life but to the necessities. Barns and vats represent "bread" and "wine," the staples of life.

The promise of prosperity for those who submit to Yahweh is not automatic. In Proverbs, wealth is the most relative of all values. Its worth depends on the character of the user. Thus verses 9-10 are intentionally contrasted with what follows in verses 11-12.

3:11-12 Here the sage anticipates an objection: if a prosperous life is not realized, then consider it, ironically, as a sign of divine favor. The LORD disciplines those who are the object of divine love. Often in Proverbs, **discipline** (מוּסָר, *mûsār*) points to a God-centered way of life. Discipline gives assurance of sonship.

Righteousness and prosperity in verses 9-10 stand in juxtaposition with righteousness and poverty in verses 11-12.[36] Wisdom does not always promise material prosperity. Neither the rich nor the poor are to put their trust in wealth but in the LORD (v. 5).[37] It is not uncommon in Proverbs for the sage intentionally to place contrasting images side by side (see 26:4-5).

This instruction poem juxtaposes nicely with the following interlude. Chapter 3:1-12 admonishes one to seek faith in God and not to rely on one's own wisdom or understanding. The following verses (vv. 13-20) extol Wisdom and promise a blessing to those who pursue her.

---

[36]Raymond Van Leeuwen, "Proverbs," in *NIB* (Nashville: Abingdon, 1997), pp. 48-51.

[37]For insightful biblical commentary on the discipline of the LORD in Proverbs 3:11-12, see Deuteronomy 8:3-5 and Hebrews 12:5-11.

E. THE PRAISE OF WISDOM (3:13-20)

This unit is the second of the five wisdom poems found in chapters 1–9. It is a hymn personifying Wisdom and praising her for her value. Wisdom is portrayed as a woman. The hymn in verses 13-18 begins and concludes with an inclusio, "blessed" (אַשְׁרֵי, 'ašrê). The hymn foreshadows the praise of the woman of noble character in 31:10-31.

¹³Blessed is the man who finds wisdom,
        the man who gains understanding,
¹⁴for she is more profitable than silver
        and yields better returns than gold.
¹⁵She is more precious than rubies;
        nothing you desire can compare with her.
¹⁶Long life is in her right hand;
        in her left hand are riches and honor.
¹⁷Her ways are pleasant ways,
        and all her paths are peace.
¹⁸She is a tree of life to those who embrace her;
        those who lay hold of her will be blessed.
¹⁹By wisdom the LORD laid the earth's foundations,
        by understanding he set the heavens in place;
²⁰by his knowledge the deeps were divided,
        and the clouds let drop the dew.

3:13-15 Verse 13 echoes the language of proverbs that describe a young man finding a faithful wife (18:22; 31:10). Finding **wisdom** is like finding a devoted spouse. Wisdom is also compared to wealth (vv. 14-15). That wisdom is superior to material gain, as the reader will see throughout the book of Proverbs, qualifies the relationship between wisdom and prosperity. Verse 14 contains the first "better than" saying in the book of Proverbs.[38] Wisdom offers a **better** return on investment **than** either **silver** or **gold**. Wisdom, unlike riches, is enhanced by use, not diminished.

3:16-18 To a youth, the path of wisdom may not initially be **pleasant** and peaceful (see 2:1-4). Yet for those who allow wisdom to instruct them, it will lead to **peace** (v. 17). The **tree of life** is an image

---

[38]See commentary on 15:16-17 for an explanation of the "better than" proverbs.

that conveys health and fulfillment (v. 18). Wisdom as tree of life not only brings health, but later in Proverbs one finds "tree of life" associated with other characteristics as well. They include the fruit of righteousness (11:30), hope (13:12), and words of integrity (15:4).

3:19-20 Why is Wisdom able to offer rich blessings and a fulfilling life? Because Wisdom is one of the resources God himself uses. These verses assert that God used Wisdom to create the world. In the context of this poem and of the parental advice that follows, the cosmological image of Wisdom emphasizes the idea "that whoever abandons wisdom runs against the very structure by which the world was made."[39] Notice here that Wisdom is subordinate to Yahweh. Wisdom is not the source of life. Wisdom is not a goddess. Only Yahweh is God.

F. FOURTH INSTRUCTION: BEHAVIOR TOWARD NEIGHBORS (3:21-35)

This unit contains the fourth lecture to the son. It is the counterpart to 3:1-12. Whereas verses 1-12 instruct the disciple regarding his relationship with Yahweh, verses 21-35 instruct the disciple regarding his relationship to the community. Like the previous lecture, this one contains a series of prohibitions. These verses specify what the three wisdom virtues of righteousness, justice, and fairness look like in one's relationship with others (1:3; 2:9). Richard Clifford describes the logic of the lecture in the following way. Verses 27-28 issue the mandate regarding the responsibility toward a neighbor with whom one has an obligation. Verses 29-30 describe the conduct toward a neighbor with whom one lives on good terms. Finally, verses 31-32 describe the conduct that must be exhibited toward neighbors who are wicked and prosperous.[40]

The instructions in this unit are organized around commands given, followed by reasons for complying with the commands. The teacher does not demand obedience based on his or her authority alone, but on reasoning. Here both the teacher and the learner play a crucial role. There is a synergistic element at work.

---

[39]Duane A. Garrett, *Proverbs, Ecclesiastes, Song of Songs,* The New American Commentary (Nashville: Broadman Press, 1993), p. 83.

[40]Richard Clifford, *Proverbs*, The Old Testament Library (Louisville: Westminster/John Knox Press, 1999), p. 57.

²¹**My son, preserve sound judgment and discernment,**
    do not let them out of your sight;
²²**they will be life for you,**
    an ornament to grace your neck.
²³**Then you will go on your way in safety,**
    and your foot will not stumble;
²⁴**when you lie down, you will not be afraid;**
    when you lie down, your sleep will be sweet.
²⁵**Have no fear of sudden disaster**
    or of the ruin that overtakes the wicked,
²⁶**for the LORD will be your confidence**
    and will keep your foot from being snared.
²⁷**Do not withhold good from those who deserve it,**
    when it is in your power to act.
²⁸**Do not say to your neighbor,**
    "Come back later; I'll give it tomorrow"—
    when you now have it with you.
²⁹**Do not plot harm against your neighbor,**
    who lives trustfully near you.
³⁰**Do not accuse a man for no reason—**
    when he has done you no harm.
³¹**Do not envy a violent man**
    or choose any of his ways,
³²**for the LORD detests a perverse man**
    but takes the upright into his confidence.
³³**The LORD's curse is on the house of the wicked,**
    but he blesses the home of the righteous.
³⁴**He mocks proud mockers**
    but gives grace to the humble.
³⁵**The wise inherit honor,**
    but fools he holds up to shame.

3:21-26 Verses 21 and 22 introduce the instruction material and are quite similar to other introductions (1:8-9; 3:1-3; 6:20-21; etc.). Verse 21 is also quite similar to 4:20-21. When the youth adheres to the instruction, he will be protected from life's mishaps. He will not stub his toe (v. 23). He will feel secure in **sleep** (v. 24). In contrast, the wicked who think they are secure will run into all kinds of pitfalls.

3:27-28 The unit (vv. 27-32) consists of five admonitions identified by the use of the negative **do not** (אַל, *'al*) at the beginning of verses 27-31. **Do not withhold good from those who deserve it** is a difficult phrase to interpret in Hebrew (v. 27), but "good" possibly refers to material wealth. Those who deserve good may be workers who have earned their pay, or it could refer to those who have loaned money and deserve to be paid back. The second colon (or line) of verse 27 uses an idiom that the NIV translates by the phrase **when it is in your power to act** (לְאֵל יָדֶיךָ, *l³'ēl yādêkā*), a phrase that more literally means "by the power of your hand." Since the context of the whole instruction is about that which is right, just, and fair, the passage is more about practicing fairness to one's neighbor than it is about doing good to the poor.

Verse 28 reaffirms the thought of verse 27. The act of fairness is directed toward one's **neighbor** (רֵעַ, *rēaʿ*), not the poor. In this context, "neighbor" does not refer to an intimate friend but to one who resides in one's sphere of influence.

3:29-30 This proverbial pair describes those who **plot** evil against innocent victims (cf. 1:11). These people have no concern for the solidarity of the community. The situation reminds one of Jezebel's conspiracy against Naboth in 1 Kings 21.

3:31-32 The prohibition against **envy**ing the **violent man** has affinities with the wealth of the violent men in 1:8-19 (see also 14:30). The wise were quite aware that wicked people can prosper. The consequences of their lifestyle are destructive. The violent man loses favor with Yahweh. In fact, the violent man is **detest**ed (תּוֹעֲבַת, *thôʿăbath*) by **the LORD** (v. 32). The term for "detest" is one of the strongest words used to describe God's displeasure. Sometimes the word is translated "abomination" and is used repeatedly in Proverbs (e.g., 6:16; 11:1; 15:8; 16:5; 17:15; 20:10; 28:9). Since the sage cannot punish individuals for their motives or intentions, he resorts to reproof, calling such improper motives detestable to the LORD. In contrast, **upright** motives lead to good behavior. See 11:1 for further treatment of the phrase "the LORD detests."

3:33-35 The final verses of the instruction offer God's verdict on the righteous and the evil. The LORD detests or invokes a **curse** on the **house** of the evil, but the righteous **inherit honor**. The **righteous** (צַדִּיקִים, *ṣaddîqîm*), **humble** (עֲנִיִּים, *ʿănîyîm*), and **wise** (חֲכָמִים,

ḥăkāmîm) are all closely related to each other as are the **wicked** (רָשָׁע, *rāšāʿ*), **mockers** (לֵצִים, *lēṣîm*), and **fools** (כְּסִילִים, *kᵉsîlîm*). Verse 34 is quoted in James 4:6 and 1 Peter 5:5.

G. FIFTH INSTRUCTION: A FATHER'S EXAMPLE (4:1-9)

Fairly common agreement exists among scholars that chapter 4 contains three instruction poems: verses 1-9, 10-19, and 20-27. Chapter 4, then, contains lectures five, six, and seven of the ten found in chapters 1–9. Chapter 4:1-9 includes a quote from the speaker's father (vv. 4b-9). Quotations are also found in 1:11-14 and 7:14-20.

[1]**Listen, my sons, to a father's instruction;**
        pay attention and gain understanding.
[2]**I give you sound learning,**
        so do not forsake my teaching.
[3]**When I was a boy in my father's house,**
        still tender, and an only child of my mother,
[4]**he taught me and said,**
        "Lay hold of my words with all your heart;
        keep my commands and you will live.
[5]**Get wisdom, get understanding;**
        do not forget my words or swerve from them.
[6]**Do not forsake wisdom, and she will protect you;**
        love her, and she will watch over you.
[7]**Wisdom is supreme; therefore get wisdom.**
        Though it cost all you have,[a] get understanding.
[8]**Esteem her, and she will exalt you;**
        embrace her, and she will honor you.
[9]**She will set a garland of grace on your head**
        and present you with a crown of splendor."

[a]7 Or *Whatever else you get*

4:1-2 The fifth lecture opens using a similar formulaic expression that the others employ: **Listen, my sons, to a father's instruction**. The term for "instruction" is the Hebrew word מוּסָר (*mûsar*), which is elsewhere translated "discipline." This is discipline in the broadest sense — meaning preparation for living a successful life. Verse 2 concludes with a parallel admonition, **do not forsake my teaching**. Here the word for teaching is *torah* (תּוֹרָה, *tôrāh*), which means "law" or "instruction." The sons are to heed the parents' *torah*. In Proverbs, the primary place where moral instruction takes place is in the home.

4:3-4a The implication of the phrase **still tender, and an only child of my mother** is that education began early (v. 3). Israelite families believed that parents could not begin too early in instilling fundamental principles for successful living (e.g., Deut 6:1-9).

4:4b-9 The speaker quotes his father, the grandfather of the sons. The admonition is to **get wisdom**. The relationship between the student and wisdom is pictured as that between husband and wife (v. 6). Contrary to stereotypical attitudes, it is the wife who is the protector (v. 6).

Verse 7 sounds repetitive: **get wisdom . . . get understanding**. But the sequence might refer first to gathering in and collecting wisdom by rote or observation. After that one will learn to appreciate and understand wisdom.[41] The pupil must first acquire a taste for wisdom. The reward for acquiring wisdom is that **she will exalt you** and will **present you with a crown of splendor** (vv. 8-9). In other words, the possessor will receive public recognition.

H. SIXTH INSTRUCTION:
WARNING AGAINST EVIL COMPANIONS (4:10-19)

The sixth lecture depicts the two ways of living life, either in the way of the righteous or in the way of the wicked. This is the third description in chapters 1-9 of the evil men. The earlier descriptions were found in 1:8-19 and 2:12-15.

[10]**Listen, my son, accept what I say,**
   and the years of your life will be many.
[11]**I guide you in the way of wisdom**
   and lead you along straight paths.
[12]**When you walk, your steps will not be hampered;**
   when you run, you will not stumble.
[13]**Hold on to instruction, do not let it go;**
   guard it well, for it is your life.

---

[41]Fox, *Proverbs 1-9*, p. 175.

¹⁴**Do not set foot on the path of the wicked**
    or walk in the way of evil men.
¹⁵**Avoid it, do not travel on it;**
    turn from it and go on your way.
¹⁶**For they cannot sleep till they do evil;**
    they are robbed of slumber till they make someone fall.
¹⁷**They eat the bread of wickedness**
    and drink the wine of violence.
¹⁸**The path of the righteous is like the first gleam of dawn,**
    shining ever brighter till the full light of day.
¹⁹**But the way of the wicked is like deep darkness;**
    they do not know what makes them stumble.

4:10-11 Guide is the verb from which the word *torah* is derived (cf. 4:4). These are the directives to accept in order to succeed on the journey of life. To be led **along straight paths** means to have a focus on the proper goals of life. The straight paths may not only refer to clarity in direction, it may also refer to straight in the sense of honesty and fairness (cf. "paths" in Ps 1:1; Jer 6:16).

4:12-13 Verse 12 uses the images of **walk**ing and **run**ning as metaphors for the struggles of life. The ethical life (i.e., the life of honesty and fairness) will keep one safe. Verse 13 exhorts the youth to **hold on to instruction** (lit., discipline; מוּסָר, *mûsār*). Here discipline is synonymous with wisdom. Often wisdom comes with discipline, discomfort, and suffering.

4:14-15 Who are the **wicked** and the **evil** in verse 14? A specific group of scoundrels who are out to take advantage of the weak and innocent? It is better to look at the wicked with the righteous in Proverbs 1–9 (as well as life and death) as two archetypal paths of life. The implication in verses 14 and 15 is that the paths of the wicked frequently intersect with the paths of the righteous. The youth may inadvertently come across **the path of the wicked** (cf. the adulteress in 7:11-12).

4:16-17 The wicked lie awake at night fantasizing about **do**ing **evil** (v. 16). Micah describes the wicked in his day and time as doing the same thing (Micah 2:1). Like a wild animal that cannot rest until it kills again once it has tasted blood, the wicked cannot rest until they have inflicted further injury on a person. They thrive on corruption itself. They **eat** and **drink wickedness** (v. 17). Feeding on perversion alone satisfies their emotional and physical desires.

4:18-19 The aphorisms in the final two verses epitomize the message of the poem. The **righteous** experience increasing joy; as they move along life's path, the way becomes **brighter** and clearer (v. 18). Fox believes the image in verse 18 "suggests the education and moral growth of a youngster."[42] In contrast to the righteous whose way shines brightly, **the way of the wicked is like deep darkness**. Light and dark are not only metaphors for joy and misery, but also represent qualities of moral insight and ignorance. In this instruction poem, the sage works to create an appetite for wisdom and instruction in the heart of the student. If one develops a taste for wisdom, then the proper behavior will follow.

I. SEVENTH INSTRUCTION: THE HEALTHY BODY (4:20-27)

This is the seventh lecture in chapters 1–9. Notice how the parent/teacher stacks references to various parts of the body, no less than seven organs: ear (v. 20), eye (vv. 21,25), heart (v. 23), mouth (v. 24), lips (v. 24), eyelids (v. 25), and feet (vv. 26-27). The disciple is to exert every ounce of "body" strength to the task of staying on the right path. When each part of the body is properly functioning, the whole body is morally healthy. In addition, when every part of a person's body is under control, he or she incarnates the principles of wisdom. Such is the case of the woman of strong character in 31:10-31.

²⁰**My son, pay attention to what I say;**
  listen closely to my words.
²¹**Do not let them out of your sight,**
  keep them within your heart;
²²**for they are life to those who find them**
  and health to a man's whole body.
²³**Above all else, guard your heart,**
  for it is the wellspring of life.
²⁴**Put away perversity from your mouth;**
  keep corrupt talk far from your lips.
²⁵**Let your eyes look straight ahead,**
  fix your gaze directly before you.

---

[42]Ibid., p. 182.

²⁶**Make level^a paths for your feet**
      and take only ways that are firm.
²⁷**Do not swerve to the right or the left;**
      keep your foot from evil.

^a*26 Or* Consider the

4:20-24 In contrast to the previous instruction in 4:10-19, which spoke of two paths to choose from, this instruction admonishes the youth to walk a single path. Keep focused straight ahead. Do not turn to the right or to the left where temptation always lurks.

The instruction of the parent will bring wellness: **for they are life to those who find them, and health to a man's whole body** (v. 22). The health mentioned here (מַרְפֵּא, *marpē'*) includes mental, moral, and physical well-being. The son is called upon to give his undivided attention to his father's instruction.

The instruction begins first by affirming that wholeness comes about through keeping the instructions learned from the wise in one's **heart** (i.e., mind). The prudent person will listen and heed moral teaching. The wise person will **guard** his or her **heart** (i.e., mind) with all vigilance; **for it is the wellspring of life** (v. 23). Second, the sage exhorts the student with the following piece of advice: be careful about **your mouth**, that is, the way you speak (v. 24). **Keep corrupt talk far from your lips** (v. 24) is a rebuke of duplicity of speech. We might say, "Do not talk out of both sides of your mouth." The sages have much to say about the power of words. In Proverbs, the mouth and the heart (i.e., the mind) are the most important organs. One's speech reflects the inner character.

4:25 Let your eyes look straight ahead is an idiom for staying on course. The disciple must have a focus, purpose, and direction. Side glances and the winking of the eye indicate deception (cf., 6:13; 10:10; 16:30).

4:26-27 Make sure the **feet . . . do not swerve to the right or the left**. This phrase exhorts the student to practice discipline and to ensure that such discipline is a part of the daily walk. Once a student chooses a path early in life (v. 26), then he must stay the course throughout the journey (v. 27).

In addition to the description of a healthy person, this text demonstrates a fundamental belief about the nature of humans. The sages hold to a belief in the tremendous freedom individuals have to act. The organs represent the ability of the individual to act responsibly. Individuals have the power to see, speak, think, listen, and walk. As such, they have the ability to set the course for their own lives. That is why the sages have such contempt for the sluggard who chooses to live an inactive lifestyle (6:6-11).

J. EIGHTH INSTRUCTION: WARNINGS AGAINST THE ADULTERESS (5:1-23)

The eighth lecture, as were the previous ones, is addressed to the son. In 2:16-19, readers were introduced to the "adulteress" or the "strange woman" (זָרָה, zārāh). In chapter 5, readers now get a fully developed picture of her.

Is the adulteress a literal woman (another man's wife), or is she a metaphorical image representing religious infidelity and the way of folly? Fox argues that she is a character in her own right and not just a personification of folly. She "is the negative counterpart to the human wife, not of personified Lady Wisdom."[43] Van Leeuwen maintains that, in the context of chapters 1–9, she serves in both capacities.[44] On the one hand, the son is warned about the seductive power of the temptress and the deadly consequences of giving in to his sexual desires. On the other hand, the temptress serves as a symbol of those who yield to a life of folly.

Because of the detailed description of the adulteress and her activities, it seems most natural to understand her as the embodiment of an actual human. Woman Wisdom already has her counterpart in Woman Folly. In like manner, the counterpart of the adulteress is the son's wife in 5:15-19. Given the literary context of Proverbs, the reader should imagine the father addressing an adolescent who is either married or on the verge of marriage.

---

[43]Ibid., p. 262.

[44]Van Leeuwen argues, "If the short poems are isolated, they serve as warnings against marital infidelity. But in the larger context of Proverbs 1–9, they serve as powerful metaphors to reinforce the primary message of the collection. *In this world there are two contrary loves: for Wisdom, Good, and Life or for Folly, Pseudo-good, and Death.*" See Van Leeuwen, "Liminality," p. 130. A little later he concludes, "Thus the passage into a wholesome and healthy adulthood, which entailed for the Israelite male a faithful marriage, has its deeper source in a love for Wisdom" (p. 131).

[1]My son, pay attention to my wisdom,
        listen well to my words of insight,
[2]that you may maintain discretion
        and your lips may preserve knowledge.
[3]For the lips of an adulteress drip honey,
        and her speech is smoother than oil;
[4]but in the end she is bitter as gall,
        sharp as a double-edged sword.
[5]Her feet go down to death;
        her steps lead straight to the grave.[a]
[6]She gives no thought to the way of life;
        her paths are crooked, but she knows it not.
[7]Now then, my sons, listen to me;
        do not turn aside from what I say.
[8]Keep to a path far from her,
        do not go near the door of her house,
[9]lest you give your best strength to others
        and your years to one who is cruel,
[10]lest strangers feast on your wealth
        and your toil enrich another man's house.
[11]At the end of your life you will groan,
        when your flesh and body are spent.
[12]You will say, "How I hated discipline!
        How my heart spurned correction!
[13]I would not obey my teachers
        or listen to my instructors.
[14]I have come to the brink of utter ruin
        in the midst of the whole assembly."
[15]Drink water from your own cistern,
        running water from your own well.
[16]Should your springs overflow in the streets,
        your streams of water in the public squares?
[17]Let them be yours alone,
        never to be shared with strangers.
[18]May your fountain be blessed,
        and may you rejoice in the wife of your youth.
[19]A loving doe, a graceful deer—
        may her breasts satisfy you always,
        may you ever be captivated by her love.

²⁰**Why be captivated, my son, by an adulteress?**
   Why embrace the bosom of another man's wife?
²¹**For a man's ways are in full view of the LORD,**
   and he examines all his paths.
²²**The evil deeds of a wicked man ensnare him;**
   the cords of his sin hold him fast.
²³**He will die for lack of discipline,**
   led astray by his own great folly.

^a5 Hebrew *Sheol*

5:1-6 The instruction begins with the typical formula, **My son, pay attention to my wisdom . . . my words of insight** (v. 1). The purpose of the instruction is so the son will maintain **discretion** (מְזִמּוֹת, *mizmôth*; v. 2). "Discretion" is another term used in the word family of "wisdom." Its root meaning relates to hidden or private thoughts.[45] Sometimes it is used in a negative sense to speak of harmful schemes (12:2; 14:17; 24:8). Sometimes, as in this verse, it is used to describe legitimate human planning (cf., 2:11; 8:12). The thoughtful planning of youth serves as a defense against the **adulteress**.

The instruction consists of a stern warning to stay clear of the temptress. The main weapon the adulteress uses is not her physical appearance but her **speech** (v. 3). It is smooth and enticing. In the end, however, it is like **gall** (lit., "wormwood;" לַעֲנָה, *la'ănāh*).[46] The speech of the adulteress destroys. The wayward woman has deliberately chosen the path she follows. Yet she does not understand the ultimate consequences of where she is going or what she is doing (vv. 5-6). Such is also the end of the gangsters in chapter 1:8-19 (especially, vv. 18-19).

5:7-14 These verses describe the consequences of the fatal attraction for the youth who does not listen to his teachers. Fox suggests the four nouns in verses 9-10 belong together in two pairs. The first pair, **strength** and **years**, refers to the loss of sexual vigor because it is spent on another man's wife. The second pair, **wealth** and **toil**,

---

[45]Michael V. Fox, "Words for Wisdom," *Zeitschrift für Althebraistik* 6 (1993): 159.
   [46]Wormwood is an aromatic plant, quite bitter to the taste. At one time the plant was used to protect clothing and furniture from insects.

refers to the loss of the young man's earnings to compensate the adulteress's husband (cf., 6:35).[47]

In verse 11, the phrase **at the end** does not necessarily mean the end of his own life but the end of the affair. The phrase, **when your flesh and body are spent**, may possibly refer to a sexually transmitted disease.[48]

In verses 12-14, the teacher puts dialogue in the mouth of the youth, imagining the youth lamenting his failure to listen to his instructors. The youth laments the public shame he experiences and the loss of his reputation in the eyes of others (v. 14). Shame was a powerful deterrent against antisocial behavior such as adultery. **Teachers** and **instructors** (v. 13) are broad designations for those who pass on wisdom and moral instruction. They are not terms that necessarily refer to schoolteachers.

The one who yields to sexual temptation stands to lose everything: sexual vitality (v. 9), wealth (v. 10), physical health (v. 11), and honor (v. 14). Though readers can understand the general thrust of the terms describing the consequences of sexual misconduct in these verses, they are intentionally left vague in order to capture the imagination of the youth. The consequences of adultery are also described in other wisdom texts (cf., Job 31:9-12; Sirach 26:19-21).

5:15-19 When the temptress is first introduced in chapter 2, Yahweh and Wisdom provide protection to the youth from her seductive powers (2:8-19). Here a new character is introduced. The **wife** is also a source of protection from the adulteress. The best way for the husband to resist sexual temptation is to have a loving relationship with his wife.

Water is a metaphor for sexual intercourse (v. 15). This is implied in 9:17, where Woman Folly says to those who lack discretion, "Stolen water is sweet; food eaten in secret is delicious!" In the Song of Songs, the young man refers to his beloved as "a garden fountain, a well of flowing water streaming down from Lebanon" (S of S 4:15). With the exception of the Song of Songs, this is the only text in Scripture that celebrates marital sex.

Verse 16 has given translators problems since antiquity. The Masoretic text literally reads, "Let your springs flow into the streets,

---

[47]Fox, *Proverbs 1-9*, pp. 194-195.
[48]Van Leeuwen, "Proverbs," p. 68; Fox, *Proverbs 1-9*, p. 197.

streams of water into the squares." That is just opposite the advice given in verse 15. The issue is whether the verse should be rendered as a statement or a question. No interrogative particle in the Hebrew text indicates that the verse should be translated as a question, but doing so fits the exclusive language of verses 15 and 17. The sentence then becomes a rhetorical question that expects a "no" answer. The man must not go to other **springs** to find sexual fulfillment.

The blessing referred to in verse 18a is the blessing of offspring and not sexual pleasure (cf. Deut 28:4; Ps 128:3-4). Verse 18b expresses the thrust of the passage: **may you rejoice in the wife of your youth** (cf. 2:17). The phrase clarifies what the metaphors of water refer to in the previous verses. It refers to experiencing sexual fulfillment with one's wife.

5:20-23 Two other reasons for marital fidelity are added. For one, God sees everything (v. 21a). For another, the youth will eventually find himself trapped by his own sin and folly (vv. 22-23). His **lack of discipline** will enslave him to his own sin and to others (v. 23). The lack of discipline is the youth's inability to control his behavior.

Five images of water sources are used to symbolize intercourse in the marital relationship: "cistern," "well," "springs," "streams," and "fountain." In an arid country where every drop of water was precious, to spill water recklessly out onto the street was a tragedy.

As liquid, water is difficult to contain. It flows where it wills. When water spills over its boundaries, it turns into floodwaters that destroy. But when confined within a cistern or a well or a riverbank, it brings life and refreshment. The metaphor of water is well suited to describe sexual intercourse within marriage. Within the confines of marriage, sexual intercourse helps sustain the bonds of love between two people. Fox observes that in a culture where marriages were arranged by parents, the father may be convincing a son who is less than enthusiastic about his new wife that she "is as sexy as any woman out there."[49]

---

[49]Fox, *Proverbs 1–9*, p. 208.

K. FOUR PIECES OF PRACTICAL ADMONITION (6:1-19)

1. Admonition against Pledging Security for a Neighbor (6:1-5)

With the initial words "my son," this paragraph begins like an instruction saying, but it is different. It does not have the usual appeal to listen to the words of the father. Chapter 6:1-19 is an interlude between the eighth and ninth instruction speeches. This interlude consists of four distinct paragraphs, 1-5, 6-11, 12-15, and 16-19, that contain practical advice to the son.

¹**My son, if you have put up security for your neighbor,**
    if you have struck hands in pledge for another,
²**if you have been trapped by what you said,**
    ensnared by the words of your mouth,
³**then do this, my son, to free yourself,**
    since you have fallen into your neighbor's hands:
Go and humble yourself;
    press your plea with your neighbor!
⁴**Allow no sleep to your eyes,**
    no slumber to your eyelids.
⁵**Free yourself, like a gazelle from the hand of the hunter,**
    like a bird from the snare of the fowler.

6:1-5 These verses sternly warn against standing surety or **putting up security for your neighbor** or **another** (i.e., a stranger, זָר, *zār*). The father offers a hypothetical situation (as he does on other occasions; e.g., 1:10-19; 7:6-27) to the **son**. As such, it acts as a preventative warning about becoming entangled in financial commitments.

Making a **pledge** on behalf of another refers to the practice of intervening in a business relationship to provide financial backing to a person indebted to another. The one who goes surety pledges to pay the debt if the debtor is unable to fulfill his or her financial responsibility.[50] In this case, the transaction involves three parties, two of whom are explicitly mentioned in the text: the son and the

---

[50]In Genesis 44:32, Judah gives himself as surety to Joseph for the sake of Benjamin.

neighbor.[51] One man (the son) gives a pledge on behalf of a neighbor in order that the neighbor can borrow from a third party, a creditor. Obviously the creditor loaning the money prefers a commitment from a person he knows will keep his word over that of one he does not know. The problem arises when the neighbor reneges on the payment. This leaves the one who pledged with the responsibility to pay back the loan to the creditor.

The motives for going surety are unclear. One reason might be that the one going surety for a neighbor may expect the neighbor to pay a fee for his risk, thinking that this is a quick way to make a little money. Another motive might be purely altruistic. Whatever the reason, the sage urges the son not to offer his possessions as collateral for another person's debt. The sage does this by setting up a scenario describing the trap that awaits the patron.

The pledge involves an outward sign of someone who has **struck hands** with the neighbor or "stranger" (*zār*; v. 1), not unlike shaking hands after we have made an agreement with someone. Such a pledge to another should never be made. It puts the person at the mercy of the creditor and the neighbor (vv. 1 and 3). Other warnings against making pledges are given in the sentence literature: 11:15; 17:18; 20:16; 22:26-27; 27:13.

This passage does not express insensitivity to the poor or the oppressed. One was to give, not lend money to the poor. Many proverbs speak of one's responsibility to the underprivileged (for further comment see 17:17-18). The advice serves as a strict "warning not to become involved in the complicated credit arrangements of commerce. . . ."[52] It may be that it reflects the harsh economic conditions of the day. Making a pledge on behalf of someone else now puts two families in financial jeopardy, the one who made the pledge and the one who was in debt. If such a pledge is made, one should do everything in his or her power to get out from under it,

---

[51]Some commentators see all three parties mentioned in the passage. One man (the son) gives a pledge to another (the stranger) on behalf of a neighbor in order that the neighbor can borrow from "the stranger" (v. 1). See R.N. Whybray, *Proverbs*, The New Century Bible Commentary (Grand Rapids: Eerdmans, 1994), pp. 94-95. However, the neighbor and the stranger mentioned in verse one appear to be synonyms.

[52]McKane, *Proverbs*, p. 322.

even to the point of losing face (v. 3). Making such a pledge is an act of folly. It spreads the disaster rather than contains it.[53] The sage mandates that one use money wisely.

2. Admonition against Laziness (6:6-11)

[6]**Go to the ant, you sluggard;**
    consider its ways and be wise!
[7]**It has no commander,**
    no overseer or ruler,
[8]**yet it stores its provisions in summer**
    and gathers its food at harvest.
[9]**How long will you lie there, you sluggard?**
    When will you get up from your sleep?
[10]**A little sleep, a little slumber,**
    a little folding of the hands to rest—
[11]**and poverty**[a] **will come on you like a bandit**
    and scarcity like an armed man.

[a]*11 Or like a vagrant / and scarcity like a beggar*

6:6-11 This is the first of three poems in Proverbs devoted to the **sluggard** or "lazybones" as the NRSV translates the term (עָצֵל, *'āṣēl*, cf., 24:30-34; 26:13-16). There are other miscellaneous proverbs on laziness scattered throughout the collection (e.g., 10:4,26; 15:19; 19:24; 20:4; 21:25; 22:13). The Hebrew term **ant** is both feminine and singular (נְמָלָה, *nᵉmālāh*). As singular, the emphasis is on the individual responsibility the ant takes.

The ant, which has **no overseer or ruler**, is self-motivated (v. 7). She acts autonomously, without the need for supervision or direction from others. She manifests self-discipline, an important quality in sapiential wisdom. She fulfills her responsibilities because she sees the larger picture of life (v. 8). The point is, if the little does this, then how much more should humans take the initiative to fulfill responsibilities?

---

[53]See Ronald E. Clements "The Good Neighbour in the Book of Proverbs," in *Of Prophets' Visions and the Wisdom of Sages*, ed. by Heather A. McKay and David J.A. Clines (Sheffield: JSOT Press, 1993), pp. 221-222.

One of the ways in which wisdom is acquired is through observation. Observation as an avenue of instruction is highlighted here in the lesson of the ant. The sages believed that one could gain much insight by simply observing the created world (Job 12:7; Isa 1:3; Jer 8:7). One could learn about order, discipline, dependence, trust, and care.

3. Admonition against the Scoundrel (6:12-15)

¹²**A scoundrel and villain,**
> **who goes about with a corrupt mouth,**
¹³ > **who winks with his eye,**
> **signals with his feet**
> **and motions with his fingers,**
¹⁴**who plots evil with deceit in his heart—**
> **he always stirs up dissension.**
¹⁵**Therefore disaster will overtake him in an instant;**
> **he will suddenly be destroyed—without remedy.**

6:12-15 The **scoundrel** (lit., "man of Belial;" אָדָם בְּלִיַּעַל, *'ādām bᵉlîyaʿal*) is described in detail in this text. He is put in the company of some pretty notorious characters in 16:27-30 (16:27 uses the same term, *'ādām bᵉlîyaʿal*). As a scoundrel, he works to undermine the solidarity of the community for the sake of his own benefit. He is one who continually **stirs up dissension** (v. 14). The scoundrel possesses no moral conscience (cf., Judg 19:22; 1 Kgs 21:10-11).

It is difficult to know the meaning of the nonverbal symbols in verse 13. The use of body language, as described in Proverbs, usually implies efforts at deception. The winking of the eye, the shuffling of feet, the pointing of the finger — these are designed to cover evil schemes (cf. 10:10; 16:30). This indirect communication indicates one who attempts to manipulate. In contrast, direct communication, such as reproof, indicates one who has the best interest of the other in mind (27:5-6).

4. Admonition Listing Things Detestable to the Lord (6:16-19)

¹⁶**There are six things the LORD hates,**
> **seven that are detestable to him:**

¹⁷   **haughty eyes,**
                a lying tongue,
                hands that shed innocent blood,
¹⁸   **a heart that devises wicked schemes,**
                feet that are quick to rush into evil,
¹⁹   **a false witness who pours out lies**
                and a man who stirs up dissension among brothers.

6:16-19 While verses 12-15 characterize the portrait of the evil man, this unit portrays evil activity which God despises. This is the only numerical proverb to appear outside of chapter 30 in the book. The numerical sequence **six things . . . seven** is a Hebrew idiom frequently used in the Old Testament.[54] Here the numbers six and seven are used rhetorically to develop the parallelism between the two lines as well as to develop a climax.

One could describe this list as Israel's seven deadly sins.[55] What these seven evils have in common is that they are **detestable** ("abomination"; תּוֹעֲבַת, tō'ăbath) to Yahweh. Evil motives are condemned just as much as destructive actions. These sins not only break covenant with Yahweh, but they also disrupt the life of the community. Each of the sins is associated with a body part, proceeding from top to bottom, so the sage gives an image of an unhealthy body using five organs: **eyes, tongue, hands, heart, feet**. Verses 17b and 18b echo the description of the evil men in 1:16. Persons who learn to subdue their bodies, live by wisdom (see 4:20-27).

The list culminates with **a man who stirs up dissension among brothers** (cf. v. 14). The NRSV reads "one who sows discord in a family." Evil always destroys the solidarity of the family and the community. **Brothers** refers to those who live in community with others as well as to one's family. Proverbs alludes to the family on numerous occasions (see Overview of 10:1–22:16).

---

[54]See Wolfgang M.W. Roth, "The Numerical Sequence x/x+1 in the Old Testament," *VT* 12 (1962): 300-311.

[55]Garrett, *Proverbs, Ecclesiastes, Song of Songs*, p. 97.

L. NINTH INSTRUCTION:
WARNINGS AGAINST THE ADULTERESS (6:20-35)

This is the ninth of ten lectures in the opening chapters of Proverbs. Chapter 6:1-19 addressed the gamut of sins that result in the destruction of the family and the community. Now verses 20-35 focus on what the sages view as the quintessential sin in chapters 1–9: adultery. Adultery is representative of how sin destroys human relationships. It also symbolizes living outside the boundaries of wisdom. Because of the enticing and destructive consequences of adolescent lust, the sage uses powerful rhetorical images and even scare tactics to discourage youth from acting out their sexual drives in adultery (vv. 31-35).

[20]My son, keep your father's commands
     and do not forsake your mother's teaching.
[21]Bind them upon your heart forever;
     fasten them around your neck.
[22]When you walk, they will guide you;
     when you sleep, they will watch over you;
     when you awake, they will speak to you.
[23]For these commands are a lamp,
     this teaching is a light,
  and the corrections of discipline
     are the way to life,
[24]keeping you from the immoral woman,
     from the smooth tongue of the wayward wife.
[25]Do not lust in your heart after her beauty
     or let her captivate you with her eyes,
[26]for the prostitute reduces you to a loaf of bread,
     and the adulteress preys upon your very life.
[27]Can a man scoop fire into his lap
     without his clothes being burned?
[28]Can a man walk on hot coals
     without his feet being scorched?
[29]So is he who sleeps with another man's wife;
     no one who touches her will go unpunished.
[30]Men do not despise a thief if he steals
     to satisfy his hunger when he is starving.

³¹**Yet if he is caught, he must pay sevenfold,**
      though it costs him all the wealth of his house.
³²**But a man who commits adultery lacks judgment;**
      whoever does so destroys himself.
³³**Blows and disgrace are his lot,**
      and his shame will never be wiped away;
³⁴**for jealousy arouses a husband's fury,**
      and he will show no mercy when he takes revenge.
³⁵**He will not accept any compensation;**
      he will refuse the bribe, however great it is.

6:20-22 These opening verses echo the language of Deuteronomy 6:6-8. The instructions of the parents are analogous to the teachings of Moses. The parental voice is grounded in divine instruction. Verse 21 uses images similar to those in 1:8 and 3:3,22. The image depicts the clothing of oneself in the *torah* (**teaching** or "instruction") of the parents (v. 20).

6:23-25 The phrase in verse 24 **from the immoral woman** is literally "from the evil woman" (רָע אֵשֶׁת מֵ, *mē'ēšeth rā'*). It is possible to translate the word "evil" (רַע, *ra'*) as "neighbor" (רֵע, *rēa'*). If so, the phrase would then be rendered "from the wife of a neighbor." Two reasons exist for translating the word as "neighbor." First, the parallel in the second line of verse 24 is **wayward wife** or adulteress. Second, verses 26 and 29 offer a variant to "wife of another." Verses 24 and 25 echo the command "Do not covet your neighbor's wife." The woman described is a married woman (cf. v. 29).

6:26 This is a problematic verse to translate from Hebrew,[56] but most commentators agree that the verse makes a contrast between the consequences of being with a **prostitute** and of being with an **adulteress**. The fee of the prostitute is a loaf of bread. The fee of the adulteress is the loss of life. The verse does not promote prostitution. It simply states that the consequences of engaging in sexual intercourse with a prostitute are paltry when compared to being involved with a married woman. The unfaithful married woman is a deadly stalker who hunts lives.

6:27-29 These rhetorical questions highlight the absurdity of the

---

[56]The MT literally reads, "for on behalf of a woman, a harlot, unto a loaf of bread. . . ."

man who engages in adultery. The questions assume an "absolutely not" answer. The one who plays with fire will be burned. No one can escape the consequences of such actions (v. 29).

6:30-32 Adultery is compared with theft. The unit develops a "how much more" argument. A **thief** may steal because he is desperate, that is, hungry. The community understands why he stole. He is not despised. But the thief still has to face the consequences. It was a crime committed out of necessity not foolishness. However, if this is true, how much more will the one who commits **adultery** receive punishment! There remains absolutely no compassion for the adulterer who steals his neighbor's wife, not because of a need but because of lust. Such a person is a fool; the community despises him. Ultimately, he **destroys himself**.

6:33-35 The consequences of adultery are specified. The consequences are practical and not theological in nature. The adulterer will face the fury of a jealous husband. Nothing the perpetrator can do will appease his wrath. The kind of punishment pictured in these verses seems to be physical punishment and shame. The main point of this lecture is that, though one commits the adulterous act in secret, it will most certainly be found out and the adulterer will not escape the consequences.

M. TENTH INSTRUCTION:
WARNINGS AGAINST THE ADULTERESS (7:1-27)

This is the tenth and final lecture found in chapters 1–9 and is the last of four lectures that describe the adulteress (2:16-22; 5:1-23; 6:20-35; 7:1-27). Verses 6-23 serve as an example story.[57] The father may be engaging in an act of role playing with the son. Because of the details of the story, it appears to be based on a personal experience of the father.[58] Maybe the father, in the not too distant past, found himself in such a moral quandary.

---

[57]See Proverbs 24:30-34 as another example story.

[58]He reveals the dialogue between the son and adulteress, which he could not have overheard from his window. He describes the bedroom, the aroma, and the type of linen.

1. Remember Parental Instuction (7:1-5)

¹My son, keep my words
    and store up my commands within you.
²Keep my commands and you will live;
    guard my teachings as the apple of your eye.
³Bind them on your fingers;
    write them on the tablet of your heart.
⁴Say to wisdom, "You are my sister,"
    and call understanding your kinsman;
⁵they will keep you from the adulteress,
    from the wayward wife with her seductive words.

7:1-5 The **son** is to keep parental instructions ever before him.
He must commit them to memory (v. 3; see 3:3). Verses 4 and 5 are
parallel to 5:15-20. The narrative poem sets up a contrast between
two women. When the son falls in love with the right woman (here
Wisdom), he receives protection from the evil woman (the **adulteress**). The son is to establish an intimate relationship with Wisdom in
order to protect him from the temptress. Notice once again that the
temptress is known for her smooth talk (2:16; 5:3; 6:24).

2. Actions of the Adulteress (7:6-23)

⁶At the window of my house
    I looked out through the lattice.
⁷I saw among the simple,
    I noticed among the young men,
    a youth who lacked judgment.
⁸He was going down the street near her corner,
    walking along in the direction of her house
⁹at twilight, as the day was fading,
    as the dark of night set in.
¹⁰Then out came a woman to meet him,
    dressed like a prostitute and with crafty intent.
¹¹(She is loud and defiant,
    her feet never stay at home;
¹²now in the street, now in the squares,
    at every corner she lurks.)

¹³She took hold of him and kissed him
    and with a brazen face she said:
¹⁴"I have fellowship offeringsᵃ at home;
    today I fulfilled my vows.
¹⁵So I came out to meet you;
    I looked for you and have found you!
¹⁶I have covered my bed
    with colored linens from Egypt.
¹⁷I have perfumed my bed
    with myrrh, aloes and cinnamon.
¹⁸Come, let's drink deep of love till morning;
    let's enjoy ourselves with love!
¹⁹My husband is not at home;
    he has gone on a long journey.
²⁰He took his purse filled with money
    and will not be home till full moon."
²¹With persuasive words she led him astray;
    she seduced him with her smooth talk.
²²All at once he followed her
    like an ox going to the slaughter,
like a deerᵇ stepping into a nooseᶜ
²³   till an arrow pierces his liver,
like a bird darting into a snare,
    little knowing it will cost him his life.

ᵃ*14* Traditionally *peace* offerings   ᵇ*22* Syriac (see also Septuagint);
Hebrew *fool*   ᶜ*22* The meaning of the Hebrew for this line is uncertain.

7:6-23 The adulteress is active, busy, restless, and above all aggressive. The woman uses all five senses to seduce the lad. In contrast, the youth is passive and silent.

In her dialogue, the adulteress refers to fulfilling her **vows** of a "peace offering" (זִבְחֵי שְׁלָמִים, *zibḥê š°lāmîm*, v. 14). Such a reference to **fellowship offerings** is obscure. Does she need money (a prostitute's salary) for the sake of fulfilling her vows (it seems unlikely since her husband is wealthy, vv. 19-20)? Is the woman a foreigner (stranger; see 2:16) who lures the youth to participate in a sexual fertility rite?[59] However, her foreignness is not related to her ethnic

---

[59]See G. Boström, *Proverbiastudien. Die Weisheit und das fremde Weib in Spr. 1–9*, LUÅ N. F. Avd. I, Bd 30, Nr 3, (Lund, 1935), pp. 104ff.

status; she is another man's wife. Is the woman trying to further entice the youth to a sexual encounter with a good dinner? Or is she letting the youth know that she has made herself right with God (2:17)? That is, now her conscience is clear to engage in sexual activity. The youth can feel relieved that she has taken care of the religious obligations. The reader cannot know for certain to what fellowship offerings and vows refer. Either of the last two interpretations seems more feasible (see Lev. 7:11-18).

The temptress is clearly a woman of wealth who now flaunts certain items of luxury to entice the youth. The items mentioned in verses 16 and 17 are all imported goods. These spices are also associated with lovemaking and possess an aphrodisiac quality (cf. S of S 4:6; Ps 45:8). The woman describes these spices to seduce the young man.

In addition, the youth and the adulteress have plenty of time to enjoy sexual pleasures because, as she claims, **my husband . . . has gone on a long journey** (v. 19). The adulteress's strategy is to argue that there is no chance for the two of them to get caught in their illicit affair and experience the wrath of her husband (cf. 6:34-35).

The adulteress uses her speech as the primary weapon to entice the young man (v. 21; cf. 2:16; 5:3; 6:24).[60] She knows how to use **words** persuasively to get her way. The sages knew the **persuasive** power of words for both good and evil.

Verses 22 and 23 describe the defenselessness of the youth. At this point in the encounter, the youth is completely helpless. He is a senseless animal; he is like an **ox going to the slaughter**. He responds only on instinct and reaps the deadly consequences.

3. Warning to Avoid the Adulteress (7:24-27)

[24]**Now then, my sons, listen to me;**
      pay attention to what I say.
[25]**Do not let your heart turn to her ways**
      or stray into her paths.
[26]**Many are the victims she has brought down;**
      her slain are a mighty throng.

---

[60]Murphy says, "The power of the word to persuade, even to seduce, is highlighted as much as sexual indulgence itself." See *Tree of Life,* p. 18.

²⁷Her house is a highway to the grave,^a
    leading down to the chambers of death.

^a*27* **Hebrew** *Sheol*

7:24-27 The father now turns and offers advice not only to his
son but others as well (**sons**, v. 24, even though the singular appears
again in v. 25). He pleads for the youth not to be lured into the trap.
Many have been the **victims** of the adulteress. To follow in her steps
leads the youth to an early **grave**.[61] This instruction calls on youth to
be constantly alert to temptation. The adulteress is ever present,
lurking at every corner (vv. 11-12). No man can avoid her. For youth
to resist her requires constant vigilance.

N. SECOND SPEECH BY PERSONIFIED WISDOM (8:1-36)

Chapter 8 contains the second speech by Wisdom. The first was
1:20-33. Once again Wisdom is personified. The third and final personification of Wisdom is found in 9:1-12. Wisdom's speech in chapter 8 serves to complement her first speech in 1:20-33. There wisdom spoke harshly to her students. Here she offers affirmation.

1. Wisdom Seeks an Audience (8: 1-11)

¹Does not wisdom call out?
    Does not understanding raise her voice?
²On the heights along the way,
    where the paths meet, she takes her stand;
³beside the gates leading into the city,
    at the entrances, she cries aloud:
⁴"To you, O men, I call out;
    I raise my voice to all mankind.
⁵You who are simple, gain prudence;
    you who are foolish, gain understanding.

---

[61]The reference to Sheol in verse 27 is not a reference to hell as understood in the New Testament. Here, as well as throughout the Old Testament, Sheol is the place of the dead.

[6]Listen, for I have worthy things to say;
    I open my lips to speak what is right.
[7]My mouth speaks what is true,
    for my lips detest wickedness.
[8]All the words of my mouth are just;
    none of them is crooked or perverse.
[9]To the discerning all of them are right;
    they are faultless to those who have knowledge.
[10]Choose my instruction instead of silver,
    knowledge rather than choice gold,
[11]for wisdom is more precious than rubies,
    and nothing you desire can compare with her.

8:1-11 Wisdom is a prophetlike person who **calls** for the undivided attention of the youth. In order to do that, Woman Wisdom takes to the streets. In verses 1-3, Woman Wisdom does not stand in one place to deliver her message. She speaks from the high points within the city (**the heights**) and stands **where the paths meet**, that is, at the crossroads where several streets in the city intersect. Outside the city, she proclaims her message **beside the gates** and **at the entrances** (cf. 2 Sam 15:2). Her call is not just to the **simple** (v. 5) but also **to all mankind** (v. 4). Inside and outside the city walls she announces her invitation to all who would hear. She speaks her message where the daily distractions of business are the fiercest.

And what is that message? Verses 6-7 declare that she speaks what is **right** and **true**. To speak what is true (אֱמֶת, *'ĕmeth*) is to speak that which is reliable. She calls on the learners to choose her **instruction** rather than material riches (vv. 10-11).

2. The Blessings of Wisdom (8:12-21)

[12]"I, wisdom, dwell together with prudence;
    I possess knowledge and discretion.
[13]To fear the LORD is to hate evil;
    I hate pride and arrogance,
    evil behavior and perverse speech.
[14]Counsel and sound judgment are mine;
    I have understanding and power.

¹⁵**By me kings reign**
> **and rulers make laws that are just;**
¹⁶**by me princes govern,**
> **and all nobles who rule on earth.**^a
¹⁷**I love those who love me,**
> **and those who seek me find me.**
¹⁸**With me are riches and honor,**
> **enduring wealth and prosperity.**
¹⁹**My fruit is better than fine gold;**
> **what I yield surpasses choice silver.**
²⁰**I walk in the way of righteousness,**
> **along the paths of justice,**
²¹**bestowing wealth on those who love me**
> **and making their treasuries full.**

^a*16* **Many Hebrew manuscripts and Septuagint; most Hebrew manu-**
scripts *and nobles—all righteous rulers*

8:12-21 What Wisdom offers is **prudence, knowledge, discretion**
(v. 12), **counsel, sound judgment, understanding, and power**
(v. 14). Wisdom makes herself available not just to the covenant people of Israel but also to everyone, especially **rulers** of other nations
(v. 15). Those who display political virtues (vv. 15-16) and rule in
righteousness (v. 20) demonstrate wisdom. Wisdom is that quality
which brings order to a society. The qualities that Wisdom offers
demonstrate that Wisdom's authority does not reside in an office
but rather in persuasive power.

3. Wisdom Comes from God (8:22-31)

²²**"The L**ORD **brought me forth**^a **as the first of his works,**^b
> **before his deeds of old;**
²³**I was appointed**^c **from eternity,**
> **from the beginning, before the world began.**
²⁴**When there were no oceans, I was given birth,**
> **when there were no springs abounding with water;**
²⁵**before the mountains were settled in place,**
> **before the hills, I was given birth,**
²⁶**before he made the earth or its fields**
> **or any of the dust of the world.**

²⁷I was there when he set the heavens in place,
    when he marked out the horizon on the face of the deep,
²⁸when he established the clouds above
    and fixed securely the fountains of the deep,
²⁹when he gave the sea its boundary
    so the waters would not overstep his command,
  and when he marked out the foundations of the earth.
³⁰   Then I was the craftsman at his side.
  I was filled with delight day after day,
    rejoicing always in his presence,
³¹rejoicing in his whole world
    and delighting in mankind.

ᵃ22 Or *The LORD possessed me*   ᵇ22 Or *way*, or *dominion*   ᶜ23 Or *fashioned*

8:22-31 The reason that Wisdom should be pursued and trusted is that she comes from God. She was the **first** of God's creation (vv. 22-23; cf. 3:19-20). And she was with God as he created the rest of the world (vv. 27-31). Wisdom was **brought forth** (קָנָה, *qānāh*) by God (v. 22). The lexical definition of the Hebrew word means "to acquire" (cf. 17:16), but there is evidence for also translating *qānāh* "to create" (cf. Deut 32:6).[62] Here it is fitting to understand the word as conveying the idea of bringing into existence (thus the NIV **brought me forth**).

In verses 24 and 25, Wisdom claims that she **was given birth**. The emphasis in verses 22-26 is that Wisdom was first on the scene; before the rest of the world was created, God created Wisdom. Early Christians used verse 22 to argue that Wisdom was found in Jesus (cf. John 1:1-2; Col 1:15-16). Verses 27-31 affirm that Wisdom was with the LORD as he created the cosmos. Wisdom **was filled with delight** in being in God's presence as the world was brought into existence (v. 30).

Much debate surrounds verse 30 and the meaning of the word *amon* (אָמוֹן, *'āmôn*). At least three possible interpretations exist. One school of thought, which the NIV follows, translates the word as **craftsman** or "artisan." Wisdom somehow aids the LORD in the creation of the world (cf. 3:19; 9:1). Fox rejects the possibility of "craftsman"

---

[62]Clifford, *Proverbs*, p. 96.

because the images in verse 30b indicate that Wisdom was not crafting but playing. Wisdom is an *instrument* and not an *agent* in the process of creation (3:19).[63] A second possibility is to translate the word as "trustworthy" or "constant." The English word "amen" derives from the Hebrew word אָמֵן (*'āmēn*), but this translation does not shed much light on what Wisdom is doing. Third, the word can be translated "ward" or "nursling." In his commentary, Fox concludes that while Yahweh was creating the world, Wisdom grew up with and was nurtured by him.[64] The basic idea is that God nurtured and cared for Wisdom during the act of creation.

In what does Wisdom rejoice and **delight day after day** (v. 30)? It seems likely that she delights in exploring, discovering, and learning. She delights in watching God create the world. She delights in the human race (v. 31).

4. Wisdom Is the Way of Life (8:32-36)

[32]"Now then, my sons, listen to me;
   blessed are those who keep my ways.
[33]Listen to my instruction and be wise;
   do not ignore it.
[34]Blessed is the man who listens to me,
   watching daily at my doors,
   waiting at my doorway.
[35]For whoever finds me finds life
   and receives favor from the LORD.
[36]But whoever fails to find me harms himself;
   all who hate me love death."

8:32-36 The intention of the poem in chapter 8 is to persuade youth to **listen** to Wisdom and follow her. If world leaders rule by wisdom (vv. 15-16), if wisdom was the first item God created (v. 22), if she was in intimate relationship with God through the whole process of creation (v. 30), then she is someone most worthy to seek.

---

[63]Michael V. Fox, " 'AMON AGAIN," *JBL* 115 (1996): 699-702.
[64]Fox, *Proverbs 1–9*, p. 285. Later Fox claims, "wisdom was not an active agent in creation. . . . Wisdom played while God worked. God alone (as in Gen. 1 and Job 38) imposes order on chaos" (pp. 354-355).

Wisdom's father is God; he raised and trained her (v. 30). So her instruction is trustworthy. **Whoever finds me finds life and receives favor from the LORD** (v. 35).

Wisdom is described not simply as an intellectual component but as an attitude, a desire. Wisdom's function is to generate a passion for doing good and for building a wall of protection from temptation.

O. THIRD SPEECH BY PERSONIFIED WISDOM (9:1-12)

Chapter 9 is composed of three different units. Verses 1-6 contain the invitation that Woman Wisdom offers to those who are simple and lack experience. Verses 7-12 are a distinct unit that echoes the introduction in 1:1-7 and serves as an inclusion to chapters 1–9. Finally, in verses 13-18 Woman Folly offers her invitation, which stands counter to Woman Wisdom's call in the first six verses. In terms of length, the voices of both Wisdom and Folly get an equal share of six verses (vv. 1-6 and vv. 13-18). The two invitations of Woman Wisdom and Woman Folly point forward to the sentence literature in chapters 10–15 which set forth a more detailed description of the boundaries between the way of the righteous and the way of the wicked.

1. Invitation Issued by Wisdom (9:1-6)

[1]**Wisdom has built her house;**
     she has hewn out its seven pillars.
[2]**She has prepared her meat and mixed her wine;**
     she has also set her table.
[3]**She has sent out her maids, and she calls**
     from the highest point of the city.
[4]**"Let all who are simple come in here!"**
     she says to those who lack judgment.
[5]**"Come, eat my food**
     and drink the wine I have mixed.
[6]**Leave your simple ways and you will live;**
     walk in the way of understanding.

9:1-6 Wisdom has built her house (v. 1). This house represents the ordered life that Wisdom constructs. The house is described in its completeness in 31:10-31. It is a home or a world where individuals grow and learn and serve and love. It is a world where individuals work together in harmony and live in a community in which everyone contributes to the well-being of the whole. Much speculation surrounds the image of the **seven pillars** mentioned at the end of verse 1. Does this refer to the seven liberal arts, the seven days of creation, the seven churches in Revelation? None of these are valid suggestions. "Seven" rather is a metonymy for the majestic house Wisdom has built. It indicates that which is complete or appropriate.

Wisdom prepares a banquet to celebrate the completion of the house (v. 2). The celebration serves as a kind of "house warming" but one that is continual, not a onetime activity. Wisdom sends out **maids** to the most prominent parts of the city to announce the banquet (v. 3). Her invitation is extended to the gullible and immature (v. 4). The invitation is to change, that is, to leave simplicity behind. The imperative implies that those who are **simple** (פֶּתִי, *pethî*) choose that lifestyle for themselves (cf. 1:22). This banquet is an invitation to learning. Wisdom is training toward life and the development of moral character.

2. Educating the Wise and the Foolish (9:7-12)

[7]"Whoever corrects a mocker invites insult;
    whoever rebukes a wicked man incurs abuse.
[8]Do not rebuke a mocker or he will hate you;
    rebuke a wise man and he will love you.
[9]Instruct a wise man and he will be wiser still;
    teach a righteous man and he will add to his learning.
[10]"The fear of the LORD is the beginning of wisdom,
    and knowledge of the Holy One is understanding.
[11]For through me your days will be many,
    and years will be added to your life.
[12]If you are wise, your wisdom will reward you;
    if you are a mocker, you alone will suffer."

9:7-12 These verses do not appear to relate to the two banquet scenes that precede and follow it. However, this text forms a nice inclusion with the introduction in 1:1-7 to round out chapters 1–9. Verse 7 has an affinity with 1:7b and the fool who is not open to learning. Verse 9 echoes 1:5 with the focus on instructing the wise who are open to learning. Verse 10 recalls 1:7 and the **fear of the Lord** as the foundation of wisdom. So this unit rounds out the thought of chapters 1–9. It appears to address the ones who instruct others, describing who can and who cannot learn.

In Proverbs the sages do not believe that everyone can be taught moral instruction (cf. 27:22; 29:1). The **mocker** (לֵץ, *lēṣ*) and the **wicked** (רָשָׁע, *rāšā'*) cannot learn. Anyone who tries to teach them will only bring harm to themselves (v. 7). The simple can learn (9:4,6; 1:4; 19:25), but only if such a one is willing to give up simplicity and be open to instruction (9:6). The **wise** and the **righteous** can also continue to grow in **wisdom** and **understanding** (v. 9; cf. 1:5). The bottom line is that wisdom grows only in the context of a relationship with God (v. 10; cf. 1:7). True education begins with the affirmation of God's active work in the daily affairs of life.

P. INVITATION ISSUED BY FOLLY (9:13-18)

¹³**The woman Folly is loud;**
 she is undisciplined and without knowledge.
¹⁴**She sits at the door of her house,**
 on a seat at the highest point of the city,
¹⁵**calling out to those who pass by,**
 who go straight on their way.
¹⁶**"Let all who are simple come in here!"**
 she says to those who lack judgment.
¹⁷**"Stolen water is sweet;**
 food eaten in secret is delicious!"
¹⁸**But little do they know that the dead are there,**
 that her guests are in the depths of the grave.ᵃ

ᵃ*18* Hebrew *Sheol*

9:13-18 These six verses stand as the counterpart to verses 1-6. Like Woman Wisdom, Woman **Folly** finds the most prominent place in **the city** to issue her invitation (v. 14; cf. v. 3). She issues the same invitation as Woman Wisdom, **"Let all who are simple come in here!"** (v. 16; cf. v. 4). Whereas Woman Wisdom calls on individuals to leave simplicity, Woman Folly invites them to capitalize on it and develop this "quality."

Woman Folly is loud (הָמָה, *hāmāh*; v. 13). She is boisterous and restless. She is easily distracted, her attention span short. Unlike Woman Wisdom who is clear about her purpose and actively pursues it, Woman Folly is inactive. She does not build a house; she does not prepare a meal because the food she offers is stolen (v. 17). **She only sits at the door of her house** (v. 14). Hers is a dysfunctional world.

In order to entice the simple, Folly quotes a proverb that sums up what she has to offer, **"Stolen water is sweet; food eaten in secret is delicious!"** (v. 17). What she offers is the titillating opportunity to defy the norms of the community and cross over boundaries to challenge authority. She offers a risk and an adventure not dissimilar to what the gang offered the youth in 1:8-19 (especially vv. 11-14). There is something exhilarating about the feeling that one can get away with an activity that is "off limits" or outside the boundaries. It gives one a sense of power, a false sense of freedom.

"Stolen water" can refer to adultery. In 5:15-17, water is used as a metaphor for the sexuality of the wife (cf. also with S of S 4:13-15), but the metaphor here is broader than a reference to sexuality. It has to do with a whole lifestyle characterized by greed and deception. Yet this lifestyle, in stark contrast to Wisdom, ends in death (v. 18).

The two women depicted in chapter 9 represent the two choices set before youth: life and death. If one chooses the banquet of Wisdom, then one follows the path of learning and growing and moral development. It is a nutritious meal that leads to a healthy life. If one chooses Folly's banquet then one has chosen a feast that by all appearances looks good. However, it is a meal loaded with sweets and containing little nutrition. In fact, the meal is toxic. In the chapters that follow, a more detailed description is given of the two banquets. The sentence literature in chapters 10:1–22:16 lays out the specifics of what is found on the table of each host.

PROVERBS 10:1–22:16

OVERVIEW

Beginning with chapter 10, the literary form of Proverbs changes. Chapters 1–9 contained longer units of material known as instruction or wisdom poems. With chapter 10, the form changes to a collection of single verse proverbs that in many ways are self-contained, autonomous sayings.[1] However, how these proverbs are arranged is the subject of debate. Are these sayings randomly collected? Is reading through this material like reading a dictionary, with no connection between what precedes and what follows an individual saying? Or is there an intentional strategy in the way in which these proverbs are arranged? Are they clustered together in larger rhetorical units?

My response is that there is an element of truth to both of the above perspectives. By definition, the proverbs in this collection are self-contained. Each proverb must be interpreted in light of the two-line parallelism of its structure. (Hebrew parallelism, based on thought rhyme rather than word rhyme, means that one can use the second line to help interpret the first.) The proverb maintains its independence. At the same time, there are clearly proverbs that have been intentionally clustered together in artful arrangement. For example, the proverbs in 16:10-15 all deal with the theme of the monarchy. The letter "b" (ב in Hebrew) begins each of the proverbs in chapter 11:9-12. Chapter 26:13-16 provides a humorous picture of the lazy person. The word טוֹב (tôb, "good" or "better") and לֵב (lēb, "heart") serve as catchwords that tie 15:13-17 together as a unit.

---

[1]Chapters 10:1–22:16 and chapters 25–29 contain the bulk of the sentence literature in Proverbs. The two collections contain a total of 512 aphorisms. Three hundred seventy-five proverbs are found in the first collection. One hundred thirty-seven proverbs are clustered in the second collection of sentence literature.

It is not that all the proverbs in the sentence literature are arranged in artful, rhetorical clusters. However, there are units of sayings that do clearly hold together. The careful interpreter will be on the lookout for such clustering. The individual proverb may have a literary context. At the same time, a responsible interpreter will not force individual proverbs into unreasonable rhetorical units. Fox succinctly summarizes the relationship:

> The proverbs sometimes have ties to their contexts and can form thematic clusters, but the basic interpretive units are usually the individual sayings. They require a special approach to exegesis, one appropriate to the atomistic character of the collections and sensitive to the proverb's autonomy, which enables it to function in a limitless variety of life situations.[2]

On a broader scale, the proverbs in chapters 10:1–22:16 appear to be clustered according to the type of parallelism used. Antithetic parallelism dominates the proverbs in chapters 10–15. That is, the second line in these proverbs contrasts the first and usually is introduced by the conjunction "but." Synonymous parallelism is more common among the proverbs of chapters 15–22. Frequently the second line begins with the conjunction "and" or "so."

Beyond this rhetorical clustering, there appears to be a type of theological development. Proverbs 10–15 are dominated with sayings contrasting righteousness with wickedness (especially chapters 10–11).[3] These proverbs emphasize the traditional act-consequence or character-consequence scenario, which affirms the belief that those who practice righteousness reap blessings from God. In contrast, those who practice wickedness receive like consequences. Proverbs in these chapters express the fundamentals, the ABCs, of wisdom.[4] In essence, it is like a parent saying to a youth, "Let's start with the basics of wisdom before you are introduced to the complexities of life." Or like a coach who says to his team struggling in the playoffs, "Let's get back to the basics." Before one gets to the exceptions, one must learn the fundamental rules first.

---

[2]Fox, *Proverbs 1–9*, p. 44.

[3]See for example, John Goldingay, "The Arrangement of Sayings in Proverbs 10–15," *JSOT* 61 (March, 1994): 75-83.

[4]Van Leeuwen, "Proverbs," p. 107.

When the reader comes to chapters 16:1–22:16 the theological perspective becomes more complex. Within these chapters reside a number of sayings referred to as "limit proverbs" like the following: "In his heart a man plans his course, but the LORD determines his steps" (16:9). Along with the limit proverbs, the majority of "better than" sayings appear in this section: "Better a dry crust with peace and quiet than a house full of feasting, with strife" (17:1). Both the limit proverbs and the better-than sayings question the strict act-consequence scenario. Issues of life become more intricate. Certain issues, like wealth, are relative in value. The result of a righteous life is not always predictable. The two major blocks of material in 10–15 and 16–22 maintain subtle distinctions between each other in both form and content.

In addition, an image that runs like a scarlet thread all through this first Solomonic collection is that of the "family" or "household." According to one commentator, these chapters "contain over fifty references to the father, mother, son, house, wife, and servant; only chapter 16 is without a reference."[5] Such a theme builds on the image of the first nine chapters and is in keeping with the whole context of Proverbs. The basic responsibility assigned to any who read this book is "the task of building a 'house' in the sense of a personal and communal life."[6] The domestic saying in chapter 24:3-4 serves as a paradigmatic summary of the sentence literature: "By wisdom a house is built, and through understanding it is established; through knowledge its rooms are filled with rare and beautiful treasures."

In this commentary, I deal with the sentence literature in small units. I do this for pragmatic reasons. Space does not permit me to comment on every proverb, so I comment on them in groups. The way I group them is sometimes arbitrary but sometimes, as I mentioned earlier, the proverbs may be intentionally clustered together. Where the clustering appears intentional, I will make note of that in the comments.

One obviously cannot read through Proverbs 10–22 (as well as 25–29) like a novel. The material contains no overarching plot that unfolds or characters that develop. Reading through chapters 10–22 in one sitting is like taking a crosscountry road trip with some eccentric

---

[5]Clifford, *Proverbs*, p. 109.
[6]Ibid., p. 108.

relative who doles out an overdose of advice. The reader cannot quickly skim over these proverbs. Their literary nature demands that the reader carefully mull them over in the mind.

Even though no overarching plot exists in these chapters, each proverb does contain an implied narrative. One definition of a proverb describes it as "a short sentence based on a long experience." The key to reading a proverb is to unpack the "long experience" that lies behind the short sentence. The reader should ask, "What were the experiences that went into the making of this aphorism?" Another narrative quality exists within the two parallel lines of the proverb. The second line of the proverb contains either an analogy or comparison or contrast or expansion of the first line. As a result, there is micromovement from the first line to the second in terms of advancing the thought or increasing the emotional intensity. The reader must probe to discover the relationship between the two lines. In discovering the relationship, one also gains new insight into the meaning of the proverb.

On one level, a proverb's meaning appears obvious. That is part of its power. One can immediately acknowledge its truth. This surface meaning sometimes seems pedestrian, even mundane. On another level, the power of the proverb lies in the fact that its metaphorical and poetic nature enables it to have more than one meaning. The proverb possesses a riddle-like quality that requires the reader to dwell on it and probe it more deeply (see 1:6). There is more to the proverb than meets the eye. Thus, one must wrestle for a while with even the most mundane proverb, not turning it loose until it reveals its deeper meaning.

III. SENTENCE LITERATURE OF THE FIRST SOLOMONIC COLLECTION (10:1–22:16)

A. TRADITIONAL WISDOM IN ANTITHETIC PROVERBS (10:1–15:30)

Chapters 10–15 are dominated by sayings contrasting the righteous with the wicked. In 10:1–11:31 the root word "righteous" (צַדִּיק, ṣaddîq) appears nineteen times, the root word "wicked" (רָשָׁע, rāšāʿ) is used eighteen times.[7] Altogether in chapters 10–15, the terms "righteous" and "wicked" each appear thirty-nine times in these six chapters.[8] Such a concentration of sayings at the beginning of the sentence literature sets the ethical context for what follows. What is at stake is the choosing of the right path.

Antithetic parallelism dominates the proverbial structure in these chapters. Ninety percent of the proverbs in chapters 10–15 display this kind of parallelism. Some scholars view this structure as pedantic, requiring little mental energy to understand.[9] Ted Hildebrandt shows why the sages preferred the antithetic structure.[10] Such structure enabled the motivational potency of the sentences to be doubled. That is, the antithetic structure enabled the sage to give *two* reasons for engaging in appropriate behavior, one positive and one negative. Hildebrandt concludes that ". . . the sage's use of antithetic structure is extremely potent motivationally."[11] The very first proverb (10:1b) in this section sets the motivational tone for the rest.

[10:1]**The proverbs of Solomon:**

A wise son brings joy to his father,
> **but a foolish son grief to his mother.**
[2]Ill-gotten treasures are of no value,
> **but righteousness delivers from death.**
[3]The LORD does not let the righteous go hungry
> **but he thwarts the craving of the wicked.**
[4]Lazy hands make a man poor,
> **but diligent hands bring wealth.**
[5]He who gathers crops in summer is a wise son,
> **but he who sleeps during harvest is a disgraceful son.**

10:1 Verse 1a serves as a heading to the proverbs that are collected in chapters 10 through 22. The reference to the **wise son** and **foolish son** in 1b stands as a programmatic statement for the rest of the sentence literature, which is concerned with building a home on

[7]Goldingay, "Arrangement," pp. 75-76.

[8]Murphy, *Proverbs*, p. 267.

[9]J. Kersovec, *Antithetic Structure in Biblical Hebrew Poetry* (Leiden: Brill, 1984), p. 17.

[10]Ted Hildebrandt, "Motivation and Antithetic Parallelism in Proverbs 10–15," *JETS* 35 (December, 1992): 433-444.

[11]Ibid., 439.

proper moral foundations. The statement echoes the formulaic exhortation in 1:8, which began the instruction poems: "Listen, my son, to your father's instruction and do not forsake your mother's teaching."

10:2-5 These proverbs focus on the subject of wealth. They are relatively strict character-consequence scenarios: one's character will generate certain consequences. Evil behavior produces evil consequences. The righteous one prospers. Yet these proverbs do not state absolutes. For example, the proverb of verse 4 does not state an absolute truth about poverty. As is confirmed elsewhere, poverty sometimes results from injustice (13:23). One proverb cannot say it all.

The sages in the book of Proverbs do not simply make secular observations and admonitions about life but root those observations in a firm belief in the one creator God of the universe, Yahweh. Verse 3 reveals this underlying theology as it affirms the work of **the LORD** in caring for the **righteous** and punishing the **wicked**. This is the first of what is known as the "Yahweh proverbs" in the sentence literature of the first Solomonic collection.[12]

These initial proverbs set the tone for the rest of the proverbs in chapters 10–15. What is noteworthy are the incentives for proper conduct. Scholarship has typically emphasized the *extrinsic* act-consequence sequence. In other words, the sages emphasize that certain actions lead directly to certain consequences. For example, 11:15 is a typical example of this kind: "He who puts up security for another will surely suffer, but whoever refuses to strike hands in pledge is safe." The act performed involves putting up a pledge or a loan for someone else. The consequence, which is stated in the second half of the proverb, leads to suffering.

Far more common than the *extrinsic* act-consequence, however, is the *intrinsic* character-consequence sequence. According to Hildebrandt, about 70 proverbs in chapters 10–15 are based on the act-consequence formula and about 152 proverbs are character-consequence based.[13] For example, 10:1 states, "A wise son brings joy to his father, but a foolish son grief to his mother." The positive character, that is the "wise son," produces the consequence of joy in the

---

[12]Eleven Yahweh proverbs appear in chapters 10–14. However the bulk, forty-four, are clustered in 15:1–22:16.

[13]Hildebrandt, "Motivation," p. 437.

eyes of his parents. In contrast, the negative character, the "foolish son," produces grief. The sage uses a twofold approach to motivating the son. Chapter 10 verse 5 follows the same sequence (cf. also 2b,3a). The emphasis on character over behavior displayed in the opening proverbs sets the tone for the motivational basis used by the sage in chapters 10–15.

Chapter 10:6-32, frequently uses and refers to the organs of speech, nineteen references in all. These include the mouth (פֶּה, peh),[14] lips (שָׂפָה, śāphāh),[15] tongue (לָשׁוֹן, lāšôn),[16] and heart or mind (לֵב, lēb). Verses 13-21 contain an especially heavy concentration: lips (used four times), heart/mind (three times), mouth (once), and tongue (once).

[6]Blessings crown the head of the righteous,
    but violence overwhelms the mouth of the wicked.[a]
[7]The memory of the righteous will be a blessing,
    but the name of the wicked will rot.
[8]The wise in heart accept commands,
    but a chattering fool comes to ruin.
[9]The man of integrity walks securely,
    but he who takes crooked paths will be found out.
[10]He who winks maliciously causes grief,
    and a chattering fool comes to ruin.
[11]The mouth of the righteous is a fountain of life,
    but violence overwhelms the mouth of the wicked.
[12]Hatred stirs up dissension,
    but love covers over all wrongs.

[a]6 Or *but the mouth of the wicked conceals violence*; also in verse 11

10:6-7 Notice that the second line in verse 6 is repeated in the second line in verse 11. The book of Proverbs contains a number of "overlapping sayings," where one line is interchanged with another proverb in another part of the collection. The two lines of the proverb equip it to undergo a type of literary fission (cf. 10:8b and 14b). The sages used proverbs with flexibility, changing and adding lines in dif-

---

[14]Used forty-one times in Proverbs.
[15]Used forty-eight times in Proverbs.
[16]Used nineteen times in Proverbs.

ferent situations. Verse 7 confirms that the name of the **righteous** is immortalized, but the name of the **wicked** is soon forgotten.

10:8-9 The proverb in verse 9 depicts human life as a journey. In fact, the book of Proverbs is about youth on a journey into adulthood and the choices that lie before them. The righteous person, that is the person of strong character, finds security in life. Yet God also sees the way of the unprincipled person. God knows the heart (cf. 16:2).

10:10-11 He who winks maliciously causes grief refers to nonverbal communication that is deceptive, insincere, and indirect (cf. 6:13). This is the language of the evil woman in chapters 5–7. For the sage, language that is honest and direct is the most healthy: "Better is open rebuke than hidden love" (27:5). However, a rebuke must be offered wisely (25:12) and must never belittle another (cf. 11:12).

10:12 The sages have much to say about **dissension** or strife. Both men (26:21) and women (27:15) are guilty of this offense. In contrast, the truly wise person seeks not to inflame but to bring about reconciliation. The phrase **love covers over all wrongs** has two possible meanings. One can interpret the phrase to refer to overlooking the faults of another. Proverbs 12:16 affirms this possible meaning (cf. 19:11). However, one can also interpret the phrase to mean forgiving the sins of another. Proverbs 17:9 offers support for this interpretation (cf. NRSV translation; see also 16:6). It is difficult to know which of the two is meant. Fundamentally, the saying contains an indirect admonition to love one's enemies (cf. 25:21-22). This one-line statement, "love covers over all wrongs," is quoted as a reference to God's forgiveness in the last line of the book of James (5:20). It is also quoted in 1 Peter 4:8 in referring to Christians' responsibility to forgive one another.

In this section of proverbs, two clusters revolve around the subject of speech, verses 13-14 and verses 18-21.

[13]**Wisdom is found on the lips of the discerning,**
    but a rod is for the back of him who lacks judgment.
[14]**Wise men store up knowledge,**
    but the mouth of a fool invites ruin.
[15]**The wealth of the rich is their fortified city,**
    but poverty is the ruin of the poor.

¹⁶**The wages of the righteous bring them life,**
    but the income of the wicked brings them punishment.
¹⁷**He who heeds discipline shows the way to life,**
    but whoever ignores correction leads others astray.
¹⁸**He who conceals his hatred has lying lips,**
    and whoever spreads slander is a fool.
¹⁹**When words are many, sin is not absent,**
    but he who holds his tongue is wise.
²⁰**The tongue of the righteous is choice silver,**
    but the heart of the wicked is of little value.
²¹**The lips of the righteous nourish many,**
    but fools die for lack of judgment.

10:13-14 The phrase **lacks judgment** (חֲסַר־לֵב, *ḥăsar-lēb*; v. 13) is used in Proverbs to refer to the fool who does not think before he speaks.[17] He is "empty-headed." The **wise** are those who learn from the past, from experience, and store up or treasure that **knowledge** for the right occasion and person (v. 14). In contrast, the **fool** has no such control. He simply blurts out to anyone who listens whatever happens to be on his mind at the time. The result is imminent destruction.

10:15-17 Verses 15 and 16 are a proverb pair. This pair contrasts the **righteous** and the **wicked**, **wealth** and **poverty**, as many of the proverbs do in chapters 10 and 11. The first line of each proverb sets forth the value of wealth and hard work in the hand of the righteous. It is not uncommon in Proverbs for wealth to include more than just material prosperity.

10:18-19 The thought of verse 19 is tied closely to verses 13 and 14. Here one important sign of wisdom is the ability to control speech. The one who incessantly talks is the one who inevitably gets into trouble. A contemporary proverb expresses it well, "Least said, soonest mended."[18] Because such individuals are so busy talking, they are not sensitive to the situation or the individuals involved.

10:20 This verse uses the image of precious metal to describe the speech of the **righteous** person. The wise use of speech is a work of art. **Choice silver** is silver that has been purified by the furnace.

---

[17]The phrase appears eleven times only in Proverbs (6:32; 7:7; 9:4,16; 10:13,21; 11:12; 12:11; 15:21; 17:18; 24:30).

[18]An old saying from World War II serves as a fitting counterpart to the extensive damage done by thoughtless speech, "Loose lips sink ships."

Thus it is not just raw material, but it has been handled and tested and readied for use as some kind of ornament or jewelry. The organs of speech of the righteous (in this case, the **tongue**) are of the highest quality. The organs of speech of the **wicked** (in this case the **heart** or mind) are of **little value**.

10:21 Verse 21 describes the speech of the **righteous**, or principled, person as that which provides nourishment to others. The word "to **nourish**" is literally in Hebrew "to shepherd" (רָעָה, *rā'āh*). Such healthy instruction provides the nutrition necessary for the development of godly character.

In several of the proverbs in verses 13-21, the use of speech is pictured as a work of art and as such its proper use entails restraint. Such restraint means the ability to remain silent when necessary, speaking only after one understands the situation. Restraint also means the ability to hear and accept wise criticism. The sage is one who accepts "discipline" (verse 17). Discipline is a central part of listening and is necessary in order to appropriate constructive criticism. The results of disciplined speech include nurture, wisdom, and life. The absence of such discipline leads to destruction, sin, hatred, lying, leading others astray, and ultimately death.

> [22]The blessing of the LORD brings wealth,
>> and he adds no trouble to it.
> [23]A fool finds pleasure in evil conduct,
>> but a man of understanding delights in wisdom.
> [24]What the wicked dreads will overtake him;
>> what the righteous desire will be granted.
> [25]When the storm has swept by, the wicked are gone,
>> but the righteous stand firm forever.
> [26]As vinegar to the teeth and smoke to the eyes,
>> so is a sluggard to those who send him.
> [27]The fear of the LORD adds length to life,
>> but the years of the wicked are cut short.
> [28]The prospect of the righteous is joy,
>> but the hopes of the wicked come to nothing.
> [29]The way of the LORD is a refuge for the righteous,
>> but it is the ruin of those who do evil.
> [30]The righteous will never be uprooted,
>> but the wicked will not remain in the land.

³¹**The mouth of the righteous brings forth wisdom,**
   but a perverse tongue will be cut out.
³²**The lips of the righteous know what is fitting,**
   but the mouth of the wicked only what is perverse.

10:22-25 These proverbs continue to emphasize the fundamentals of wisdom. Those who are **righteous** experience security and the blessings of the Lord. The **wicked** experience punishment and destruction. Jesus' parable of the wise and foolish builders in Matthew 7:24-27 expands on verse 25.

10:26 Just as vinegar and smoke irritate the human body, so a lazy person irritates human relationships. The phrase refers to one who has been entrusted with a specific responsibility. The term **sluggard** (עָצֵל, *'āṣēl*) appears fourteen times in the book of Proverbs and only once in the rest of the Old Testament (Eccl 10:18). The sages were concerned about the destructive results of indolence.

10:27 This is the first appearance in the Solomonic collection (10:1–22:16) of the phrase **the fear of the LORD.** One who fears the LORD lives a longer life. The same promise is made in regard to heeding parental instruction in chapters 1–9 (cf. also Eph 6:3).

10:28-32 In these verses, a contrast between the **righteous** and the **wicked** continues to develop. **The way of the LORD** reflects one of the two ways set before youth in chapters 1–9. Clear choices must be made. Youth must live within wisdom's boundaries.

Throughout chapter 10, the proverbs describe a world in which there are choices between two ways of life, the way of the righteous or the way of the wicked. What one chooses has a profound impact on the rest of life. These proverbs emphasize that the choice one makes has far reaching consequences. There is an intrinsic order to the way in which the universe runs. Actions have consequences. For the wicked, there is poetic justice; the punishment fits the crime. In contrast, the lives of the righteous stand secure. This is the "elementary" teaching of wisdom. More of this fundamental instruction will be forthcoming in the next few chapters.

What must be kept in mind is that the sages who wrote the book of Proverbs did not employ the elementary teachings mechanically. The character-consequence scenario was not always predictable. Thus when readers come to chapters 16–22, they are introduced to the more complex realities of the world, a more advanced wisdom.

Then readers come to discover that there are limits to what humans can do and expect and understand about Yahweh's world. For the time being, understanding the fundamentals of wisdom, that is, the way of the righteous and the way of the wicked, are the focus of attention. There are clear boundaries of right and wrong.

[11:1]**The LORD abhors dishonest scales,**
> **but accurate weights are his delight.**
[2]**When pride comes, then comes disgrace,**
> **but with humility comes wisdom.**
[3]**The integrity of the upright guides them,**
> **but the unfaithful are destroyed by their duplicity.**
[4]**Wealth is worthless in the day of wrath,**
> **but righteousness delivers from death.**
[5]**The righteousness of the blameless makes a straight way for them,**
> **but the wicked are brought down by their own wickedness.**
[6]**The righteousness of the upright delivers them,**
> **but the unfaithful are trapped by evil desires.**
[7]**When a wicked man dies, his hope perishes;**
> **all he expected from his power comes to nothing.**
[8]**The righteous man is rescued from trouble,**
> **and it comes on the wicked instead.**

11:1 The word for **abhors** (תּוֹעֵבָה, *tô'ēbāh*, "abomination") is used twenty-one times in Proverbs. This verse is the first time it appears in the sentence literature. The phrase "abomination of the Lord" is used twelve times. In contrast to Deuteronomy and Ezekiel, where the word frequently appears in reference to objectionable non-Israelite worship activities and aberrant sexual behavior, the word in Proverbs is imposed as a sanction against inappropriate moral and social behavior.

When the sages could not appeal to specific punishment that would naturally follow irresponsible actions, to speak of something as "an abomination to the LORD" was powerful reproof for engaging in wrong activity.[19] The use of dishonest scales was next to impossible

---

[19]See Ronald E. Clements, "The Concept of Abomination in the Book of Proverbs," in *Texts, Temples and Traditions: A Tribute to Menahem Haran*, ed. by Michael V. Fox et al. (Winona Lake, IN: Eisenbrauns, 1996), pp. 211-225.

to detect (see 20:10 and 20:23). There were ways of cheating the customer that technically did not violate the law.[20] So the sages employed the sharpest reproof available. Such dishonest activity is "an abomination to the LORD." The combination **abhor** (*tôʿēbāh*) and **delight** (רָצוֹן, *rāṣôn*) occurs only four times in the Old Testament. All four are in chapters 10–15 (11:1,20; 12:22; 15:8).

11:2 The Hebrew text contains a rhyme of assonance in the first line. When **pride** (זָדוֹן, *zārôn*) comes, then comes **disgrace** (קָלוֹן, *qālôn*). R.B.Y. Scott tries to capture the assonance when he translates the first line as follows: "To show disdain is to show you're vain."[21] In Proverbs, pride is the fundamental sin of the fool. **Humility** is the fundamental virtue of the wise.

11:3 These proverbs speak of the results of living a **righteous** life. According to verse 3, the internal character of the **upright** governs their life (cf. 6:22-23). Character is viewed not as a single act, but as a habit.

11:4 The proverb in verse 4 contrasts **wealth** with **righteousness**. In Proverbs, wealth is a relative value. Even here in chapters 10–15, where the lessons of life are more clear-cut and "righteous people prosper," wealth is not always an indication of God's blessing. The **day of wrath** does not refer to the cosmic end of time but to the demise of an individual who does not use wealth responsibly. The day of wrath may refer to financial ruin or a life-threatening disaster (see Job 21:30). Proverbs's focus is on individual responsibility, not on the end times.

Wealth does not protect one from disaster. Only righteousness ultimately sees one through the difficulties (v. 4). Deliverance from **death** does not mean immortality beyond death but deliverance from the deathlike experiences of this life. The second line in verse 4, **but righteousness delivers from death**, duplicates the second line of 10:2, and is an example of an "overlapping" proverb. The sages employed proverbs with flexibility, feeling free to change a line when necessary to fit their instructional purpose (see 10:6 for an explanation of "overlapping" proverb).

---

[20]Ibid., p. 221.

[21]R.B.Y. Scott, *Proverbs, Ecclesiastes: Introduction, Translation, and Notes,* Anchor Bible (Garden City, NY: Doubleday, 1965), p. 85.

11:5-6 These two verses are quite similar in meaning. Again, these two proverbs highlight the value of one's character, **righteousness**, as that which enables a person to negotiate the difficult terrain of life. For the meaning of the phrase **makes a straight way**, see 3:6.

11:7 This proverb captures the essence of what happens to the wicked in verses 1-6. Whybray interprets the proverb, "When someone wicked dies, all his hopes perish, and any expectations of affluence ends" [sic].[22] Eugene Peterson captures the succinctness and wit of the proverb with this paraphrase, "When the wicked die, that's it—the story's over, end of hope."[23]

11:8 Verse 8 implies that the **righteous** are not immune from **trouble**, but God delivers them. The proverb encapsulates the narrative of Daniel in the lion's den (Dan 6:23-24). In contrast, the **wicked** fall into the pit that they have dug for themselves (26:27).

[9]**With his mouth the godless destroys his neighbor,**
         but through knowledge the righteous escape.
[10]**When the righteous prosper, the city rejoices;**
         when the wicked perish, there are shouts of joy.
[11]**Through the blessing of the upright a city is exalted,**
         but by the mouth of the wicked it is destroyed.
[12]**A man who lacks judgment derides his neighbor,**
         but a man of understanding holds his tongue.
[13]**A gossip betrays a confidence,**
         but a trustworthy man keeps a secret.
[14]**For lack of guidance a nation falls,**
         but many advisers make victory sure.
[15]**He who puts up security for another will surely suffer,**
         but whoever refuses to strike hands in pledge is safe.
[16]**A kindhearted woman gains respect,**
         but ruthless men gain only wealth.

11:9-15 These proverbs all deal with how an individual's life influences the larger community. The verses describe the individual's relationship to the **neighbor** (vv. 9,12), the **city** (vv. 10-11), and

---

[22]Whybray, *Proverbs*, p. 179.
[23]Eugene Peterson, *The Message: Proverbs* (Colorado Springs: Navpress, nd), p. 37.

the **nation** (v. 14). The proverbs in verses 9-12 all begin with the Hebrew letter "בּ" (in English "b"; a preposition meaning "in," "by," "with," etc.).

By the words they use, the **godless** (v. 9, literally, the "profane" or the "irreligious") can destroy a neighbor (or "friend," same word in Hebrew).[24] A whole community is affected by the actions of an individual or a smaller group. The godless show their ignorance of God by the way they treat their neighbor.

Verses 10 and 11 describe the effect of one's character on a **city**. A city's moral and social health is grounded in the character of individual citizens. A proverb found later in 14:34 also affirms this effect, "Righteousness exalts a nation, but sin is a disgrace to any people." A city **rejoices** over both the prosperity of the **righteous** and the demise of the **wicked** (v. 10).

One important quality of a person's character that contributes to the moral climate of a community is the use of speech. Verses 12 and 13 offer a comparison between one who practices self-restraint and one who "walks about" spreading rumor (the slanderer literally "walks about," v. 13, NIV = **betrays**). The proverbs set up a sharp contrast between revealing and concealing. Those who "reveal" secrets, tear down the community, those who "conceal" promote solidarity. (For a more detailed treatment of the practice of pledging or going surety referred to in verse 15, see 6:1-5.)

11:16 The meaning of the text is uncertain as indicated by the verbosity of LXX, which indicates an attempt to explain the short proverb.[25] The NRSV basically follows LXX, but that is not necessary. The NIV stays close to the Hebrew.

From reading the Hebrew text, two possible meanings of this proverb emerge. First, the two parallel lines could be interpreted as complementary (i.e. synonymous). The word the NIV translates

---

[24]Ronald Clements argues that the better interpretation of רֵעַ (*rēaʿ*) is the broader word "neighbor" rather than the narrower term "friend." Ronald E. Clements "Good Neighbour," pp. 209-228. See 27:10 for a fuller development of this.

[25]The LXX reads: "A gracious woman brings honor to her husband, but a woman who hates righteousness is a throne of dishonor. The ones lacking riches become grievous, but aggressive men support themselves with riches." ("γυνὴ εὐχάριστος ἐγείρει ἀνδρὶ δόξαν θρόνος δὲ ἀτιμίας γυνὴ μισοῦσα δίκαια πλούτου ὀκνηροὶ ἐνδεεῖς γίνονται οἱ δὲ ἀνδρεῖοι ἐρείδονται πλούτῳ.")

kindhearted (חֵן, *ḥēn*, grace, favor, beauty) describes a quality that a woman can possess.[26] The word can refer to the quality of beauty (e.g., 5:19 = "a graceful doe"; i.e., a beautiful deer). In some contexts, the word refers to a "beauty" or a "charm" used for deceptive purposes. For example, the conclusion of the book of Proverbs describes a woman this way: "charm (*ḥēn*) is deceptive, and beauty is fleeting," in contrast to "a woman who fears the LORD" (31:30). In Proverbs 17:8, a bribe is compared to a "charm" or "beautiful stone" (אֶבֶן־חֵן, *'eben-ḥēn*). If the two lines in verse 16 are complementary, then the proverb means that a woman uses her beauty, like men use aggressiveness (NIV = **ruthless men**), to get what she wants. Thus the proverb observes that a beautiful woman **gains respect** and aggressive men **gain wealth** (for a picture of the latter see 1:10-19).

A second possible meaning interprets the parallel lines as contrasts (i.e., antithetic). A gracious woman is honored for her quality of kindness (*ḥēn*). In contrast, **ruthless men gain only wealth** (the NIV adds the word "only"). Supporting this interpretation is the fact that the majority of proverbs in chapters 10–15 are antithetic. In addition, the two lines make a contrast between female and male and singular (woman) and plural (men). These contrasts give some support to interpreting the two lines as antithetic. If this is the case, then the interpretation highlights the character of a woman who does not have the political power of a man. In spite of that, she gains respect because of her kindheartedness. Character is stronger than aggressive, ruthless behavior. This truth bears out in the life of such individuals as Ruth, Abigail, Esther, and the woman of noble character in Proverbs 31:10-31.

[17]**A kind man benefits himself,**
　　but a cruel man brings trouble on himself.
[18]**The wicked man earns deceptive wages,**
　　but he who sows righteousness reaps a sure reward.
[19]**The truly righteous man attains life,**
　　but he who pursues evil goes to his death.
[20]**The LORD detests men of perverse heart**
　　but he delights in those whose ways are blameless.

---

[26]H.-J. Fabry, "חָנַן," *TDOT*, ed. by G. Johannes Botterweck and Helmer Ringgren, trans. by David E. Green (Grand Rapids: Eerdmans, 1986), 5:22.

²¹**Be sure of this: The wicked will not go unpunished,**
  but those who are righteous will go free.
²²**Like a gold ring in a pig's snout**
  is a beautiful woman who shows no discretion.
²³**The desire of the righteous ends only in good,**
  but the hope of the wicked only in wrath.
²⁴**One man gives freely, yet gains even more;**
  another withholds unduly, but comes to poverty.
²⁵**A generous man will prosper;**
  he who refreshes others will himself be refreshed.
²⁶**People curse the man who hoards grain,**
  but blessing crowns him who is willing to sell.

11:17-26 Many of the proverbs in this unit continue to highlight the act or character-consequence scenario. **Life** in verse 19 does not mean eternal life.²⁷ Rather in Proverbs, "life" refers to fulfillment in the present. Verse 22 describes a **woman who shows no discretion** (lit., has "bad taste"). She displays no judgment. Thus her beauty does not fit her character. The proverb affirms a value the sages repeat constantly: internal character is more valuable than external beauty. Today one might say, "handsome is as handsome does." Character, not looks, reveals the wise person. The proverbs in verses 24 and 25 are parallel and speak of the blessings of generosity (note also verse 26).

Verse 26 is not the image of a small farmer (which Whybray claims is the context for 10–22).²⁸ A *mašbir* (מַשְׁבִּיר) is a major grain distributor like Joseph (Gen 42:6) and the greedy rich men in Amos (8:5; *mašbirim*). Fox says, "A small farmer, working just to feed his family, could not affect the market on his own, and we cannot imagine a cartel of small farmers."²⁹ The picture is of men who have control of central granaries.

²⁷**He who seeks good finds goodwill,**
  but evil comes to him who searches for it.
²⁸**Whoever trusts in his riches will fall,**
  but the righteous will thrive like a green leaf.

---

²⁷Garrett believes that it does refer to eternal life (*Proverbs, Ecclesiastes, Song of Songs*, p. 126).
²⁸Whybray, *Wealth*, p. 114.
²⁹Fox, "Social Location," p. 233.

²⁹**He who brings trouble on his family will inherit only wind,**
    and the fool will be servant to the wise.
³⁰**The fruit of the righteous is a tree of life,**
    and he who wins souls is wise.
³¹**If the righteous receive their due on earth,**
    how much more the ungodly and the sinner!

11:27-31 Verse 29 is again one of many proverbs on the family. The one who unnecessarily creates trouble in the home receives harsh warning. Such a home wrecker will lose everything he has. The phrase **he who wins souls** in the second line of verse 30 is problematic. The translation of the NIV is misleading at this point. Winning souls (נֶפֶשׁ, *nepheš*) is not a reference to evangelism. The Hebrew text says "the wise one takes (לָקַח, *lāqaḥ*) souls,"³⁰ meaning one who takes another's life or kills another. That, however, does not make sense in English. It may have the meaning here of one who promotes life (see 29:10 for a similar problem).³¹ Thus the second line would read, "a wise person promotes life." The word "take" (*lāqaḥ*) could be understood in the sense of one who takes in instruction (see 1:3). The NRSV follows the LXX in the second line, "but violence takes lives away."

First Peter 4:18 may be a loose paraphrase of verse 31. This proverb is unusual in chapters 10–15 because it demonstrates that **righteous** people experience the LORD's judgment as well. Punishment is not the exclusive domain of the wicked. The implication is that even the righteous have imperfections for which they are accountable. If that is true of the righteous, **how much more** are the wicked punished!

¹²:¹**Whoever loves discipline loves knowledge,**
    but he who hates correction is stupid.
²**A good man obtains favor from the LORD,**
    but the LORD condemns a crafty man.
³**A man cannot be established through wickedness,**
    but the righteous cannot be uprooted.

---

³⁰In Hebrew "soul" has multiple meanings. Its particular meaning must be determined by the context. It does not have the Greek sense of the eternal nature of humans.

³¹Clifford, *Proverbs*, p. 127.

⁴**A wife of noble character is her husband's crown,**
        but a disgraceful wife is like decay in his bones.
⁵**The plans of the righteous are just,**
        but the advice of the wicked is deceitful.
⁶**The words of the wicked lie in wait for blood,**
        but the speech of the upright rescues them.
⁷**Wicked men are overthrown and are no more,**
        but the house of the righteous stands firm.

12:1 Through **discipline, correction,** and reproof comes **knowledge** (v. 1). The term "knowledge" in Wisdom Literature involves more than just information. Knowledge includes wisdom, understanding, and the ability to live successfully (cf. 1:7). This knowledge comes not primarily through the visual stimulus of reading but through the oral stimulus of interaction with others. The one **who hates correction** or reproof (תּוֹכַחַת, *tôkaḥath*) is **stupid.** The term "stupid" (בָּעַר, *bā'ar*) means beastlike (cf. Ps 73:22). It is one of the terms the sage uses to describe the fool (see Characteristics of Wisdom in Introduction).

12:2-3 These verses affirm the doctrine of retribution. In Proverbs, the cause and effect principle is not always the result of natural consequences but is sometimes the result of divine intervention. The **crafty man** in verse 2 refers to the one who keeps his thoughts hidden. They are secret because he is making plans to hurt others. Sometimes, however, the word for "crafty" (מְזִמָּה, *mᵉzimmāh*) can be used in a positive sense, referring to private and independent thoughts that protect one from evil (see 1:4 and 2:11).[32] Verses 2 and 3 are linked by the catchword **wickedness** (רֶשַׁע, *reša'*, translated **condemns** in v. 2).

In verse 3, the idea of being **established** and rooted implies that something is being built. The refusal to partner with wickedness determines if what is built will last. In the sentence literature, the youth establishes a home. Here this image is used to describe the building of character.

12:4 The phrase **a wife of noble character** appears two other times in the Old Testament (Prov 31:10; Ruth 3:11). "Noble" refers

---

[32]See Fox, "Words for Wisdom," 159-160.

to strength or firmness of character. Such internal quality manifests itself in an external **crown** of public honor for the husband (the original audience was male). On the other hand, the **disgraceful wife** affects the interior health of her husband.

Though the proverb is embedded in a patriarchal culture, its application is not limited to that context. The proverb expresses the systemic relationship between two people. The actions of one spouse profoundly influence the other. There is no place for rugged individualism in wisdom's community.

12:5-7 Verses 5-7 make a contrast between the **righteous** and the **wicked**. According to verse 5, the basic difference between the righteous and the wicked is in the sphere of the **plans** and intentions. These plans can manifest themselves in **words** and **speech** (v. 6). Ultimately the household of the righteous will be established (v. 7b). Verse 7 echoes the image in verse 3. Both allude to the household metaphor.

[8]**A man is praised according to his wisdom,**
> **but men with warped minds are despised.**
[9]**Better to be a nobody and yet have a servant**
> **than pretend to be somebody and have no food.**
[10]**A righteous man cares for the needs of his animal,**
> **but the kindest acts of the wicked are cruel.**
[11]**He who works his land will have abundant food,**
> **but he who chases fantasies lacks judgment.**
[12]**The wicked desire the plunder of evil men,**
> **but the root of the righteous flourishes.**

12:8 The phrase in verse 8, **according to his wisdom**, is literally "according to the mouth of his understanding." The phrase refers to one whose words make good sense in their context. Such a person deserves praise.

12:9 The first better-than proverb in the sentence literature appears in verse 9 (see 15:16-17 for an explanation of the better-than proverbs). There are two possible ways of translating the first line. One is the way the NIV translates it. If that is correct, then the line describes a person who exhibits a modest standard of living by having just one servant. The RSV follows the LXX and translates the line, "Better is a man of humble standing who works for himself [i.e., he is his own servant]."[33] This interpretation highlights the value of those who are able to provide for basic needs from their own labor and industriousness.

Either way one chooses to translate the phrase, a fundamental meaning underlies both. The line describes one of humble means who displays integrity. "What you see is what you get." In contrast, the person in line two of the proverb puts up a façade. He pretends to be someone he is not. This person tries to impress others with his social status. His family, however, ends up starving. The point of the proverb: Being satisfied with a modest standard of living is better than trying to deceive others into believing that you are better off than you really are.

12:10-12 Verses 10 and 11 are agricultural proverbs. Verse 10b contains an oxymoron, which speaks of "cruel kindness." The **righteous** care for the most defenseless of God's creation (cf. Deut 22:6-7; 25:4). Rarely does Proverbs define the characteristics of a righteous person, but here we get a glimpse of one trait. The righteous are individuals who treat all of God's creation with care. In contrast, the **wicked** make it a practice to exploit others. The proverb in verse 11 highlights an essential quality of the wise person, and that is discipline. The wise one exercises diligence in all that he does. He is not fickle, pursuing worthless dreams.

[13]**An evil man is trapped by his sinful talk,**
     but a righteous man escapes trouble.
[14]**From the fruit of his lips a man is filled with good things**
     as surely as the work of his hands rewards him.
[15]**The way of a fool seems right to him,**
     but a wise man listens to advice.
[16]**A fool shows his annoyance at once,**
     but a prudent man overlooks an insult.
[17]**A truthful witness gives honest testimony,**
     but a false witness tells lies.
[18]**Reckless words pierce like a sword,**
     but the tongue of the wise brings healing.

---

[33]The LXX translates the line in the following way, "better to be dishonored and be a slave to self" ("κρείσσων ἀνὴρ ἐν ἀτιμίᾳ δουλεύων ἑαυτῷ").

¹⁹**Truthful lips endure forever,**
    but a lying tongue lasts only a moment.
²⁰**There is deceit in the hearts of those who plot evil,**
    but joy for those who promote peace.
²¹**No harm befalls the righteous,**
    but the wicked have their fill of trouble.
²²**The LORD detests lying lips,**
    but he delights in men who are truthful.
²³**A prudent man keeps his knowledge to himself,**
    but the heart of fools blurts out folly.
²⁴**Diligent hands will rule,**
    but laziness ends in slave labor.
²⁵**An anxious heart weighs a man down,**
    but a kind word cheers him up.

12:13-25 The majority of proverbs in this unit are concerned in one way or another with speech, a topic of special interest to the sage. Verses 13 and 14 affirm that one's speech reveals one's character. Verse 14a is duplicated in 13:2 and 18:20.

Verses 15 and 16 describe the fool as possessing two characteristics. The fool engages in self-deception (v. 15): **The way of a fool seems right to him**. That is, the fool appears "wise in his own eyes" (3:7; 26:5,12,16). This blind spot is lethal. The fool also lacks self-control, a favorite subject of sapience (v. 16). The fool cannot control his feelings (v. 16 literally reads, "a fool's anger will be made known in the day"). Crenshaw identifies the focus of the sages' pedagogy when he observes that the aim of instruction was moral formation, the building of character. The sages "praised the virtues of self-control, restraint, eloquence, and honesty."³⁴ Teaching self-control was a priority in the wisdom school. In contrast to the **wise**, the fool refuses advice from others and is quickly provoked to anger.

The most powerful resources the wise possessed were words. Words could **pierce like a sword** that maims and kills (v. 18a). Or they could bring much needed healing (v. 18b). Verse 19 contains a contrast between that which is salient and that which is evanescent: **Truthful lips endure forever, but a lying tongue lasts only a**

---

³⁴Crenshaw, *Education*, pp. 1-2.

moment. The phrase "only a moment" is literally "while I would twinkle" and emphasizes the brevity of the deceptive tongue.

It is helpful to look at verse 25 along with these two proverbs (vv. 18-19). Words have the power to transform the mental and emotional state of another human being. The contrast exists between the internal anxiety of the depressed individual and the external **word** expressed that lifts the spirits. Throughout the book of Proverbs, the function of speech is to promote social well-being within the community through the development of moral character.

[26]**A righteous man is cautious in friendship,**[a]
   but the way of the wicked leads them astray.
[27]**The lazy man does not roast**[b] **his game,**
   but the diligent man prizes his possessions.
[28]**In the way of righteousness there is life;**
   along that path is immortality.

[a]*26 Or man is a guide to his neighbor*   [b]*27* **The meaning of the Hebrew for this word is uncertain.**

12:26 The last three proverbs in this chapter contain some textual difficulties. Just perusing three or four different translations reveals a variety of nuances in the way in which they are translated. In a footnote to the first line of verse 26, the NIV provides an alternate translation: "a man is a guide to his neighbor." A literal translation of the first line reads, "the righteous one will seek out his friend," which is close to the translation the NIV has in the text, **a righteous man is cautious in friendship**. That is, one who is righteous takes care in identifying the kinds of friends with whom he or she associates. The second line literally reads "but the way of the wicked ones will wander about."[35] A subtle contrast exists between the righteous who has focused perception on what is important (friendship/neighborliness) and the wicked who has no focus (wanders aimlessly; cf. 13:16).[36]

12:27 This verse is one of many proverbs (see especially 26:13-

---

[35]BDB translate the verb תָּ֫תַע (*tāthaʿ*) "will cause to wander about," (p. 1073). See *Hebrew and English Lexicon of the Old Testament* (Oxford: Clarendon Press, 1975).

[36]The second line intensifies the first by moving from the singular "righteous one" to the plural "wicked ones."

16) that sarcastically describe the **lazy**. The indolent person cannot finish what he started. He goes all out to hunt and kill the game, but he does not have the strength to cook it (interpreting חָרַךְ, ḥārak, "to roast"). The proverb may be similar in meaning to 26:15.

12:28 The first line of verse 28 is clear. The interpretation of the second line remains debatable. The NIV translates the Hebrew phrase אַל־מָוֶת ('al-māweth, "no death") **immortality**. The sages in Proverbs, though, do not appear to have any understanding of life after death[37] (this is true with the Old Testament in general; there is no developed doctrine of the resurrection). It is best to translate the second line this way: "On the journey of her pathway is no death,"[38] meaning no "spiritual death." In Proverbs, the one who lives an immoral life is "dead."

[13:1]**A wise son heeds his father's instruction,**
   but a mocker does not listen to rebuke.
[2]**From the fruit of his lips a man enjoys good things,**
   but the unfaithful have a craving for violence.
[3]**He who guards his lips guards his life,**
   but he who speaks rashly will come to ruin.
[4]**The sluggard craves and gets nothing,**
   but the desires of the diligent are fully satisfied.

13:1 In Hebrew, there is no verb in the first line of the proverb in verse 1. The NIV provides the verb **heeds**. The idea is that an adult child publicly exhibits the **instruction** received as a youth. The saying reinforces a fundamental teaching of the book of Proverbs. A primary source of wisdom is parental instruction. And the primary responsibility of parents is the instruction of youth. Yet, as the second line reveals, youth can choose to reject instruction: **a mocker does not listen to rebuke.** The mocker (לֵץ, lēṣ) is the arrogant fool. In Proverbs, youth must take responsibility for developing moral character. The well-known proverb in 22:6 must be interpreted in this larger context.

13:2-3 One of numerous proverbs on speech surfaces once again in verse 2. One receives a blessing by the good words that come from

---

[37]All that Proverbs knows is Sheol, the place of the dead (10:28; 11:4; 13:14; 14:12; 14:27, etc). Sheol is the perspective of Proverbs.

[38]BDB, p. 677.

one's own mouth. In contrast, deceitful people are cursed with a hunger for **violence**. Both verses 2 and 3 contain the catchword "soul" (נֶפֶשׁ, *nepheš*). The word is used differently in these two verses. In verse 2, it is appropriately translated **craving**. In verse 3 it is translated **life**.

Also in verse 3, a striking contrast exists between literally "guarded mouth" in the first line and "open lips" in the second line. In English, the idioms used to describe such a contrast are between one who is tight-lipped and one who is big-mouthed. Self-control remains central to a life of wisdom.

13:4 *Nepheš* ("soul") also appears twice in verse 4 (translated **craves** and **desires**) where it means "appetite." Indolence receives much attention in Proverbs. The fool identifies sloth with a life of luxury and ease. Laziness ultimately results in barrenness, while industriousness, on the other hand, results in fullness of life.

⁵The righteous hate what is false,
>   but the wicked bring shame and disgrace.
⁶Righteousness guards the man of integrity,
>   but wickedness overthrows the sinner.
⁷One man pretends to be rich, yet has nothing;
>   another pretends to be poor, yet has great wealth.
⁸A man's riches may ransom his life,
>   but a poor man hears no threat.

13:5-6 The description of the actions of the **wicked** in verse 5b is more odious than the translation implies. The word for **shame** literally means "to cause to stink" (בָּאַשׁ, *bā'aš*). In other words, the actions of the wicked emit a bad odor. They bring **disgrace**. In verse 6, **righteousness** and **wickedness** assume qualities of personification. Righteousness provides protection for the person who lives with **integrity**. Wickedness destroys one who walks in sin (חָטָא, *ḥāṭā'*).

13:7-8 These verses contain a proverbial pair. The proverb in verse 7 contains a common topic developed within the wisdom corpus, the caution to avoid judging another based on appearance (see 11:22; 31:30). Riches and poverty in the book of Proverbs are ambiguous. One's character or the possession of righteousness determines whether or not wealth is a blessing. Even though the primary understanding of the proverb relates to the issue of appearance, in keeping with the nature of a proverb it is open ended in its interpretation. The proverb refers to those who practice self-deception in one form or another.

Verse 8 is also about wealth and poverty. The second line in the Hebrew text reads, "but the poor does not hear rebuke" (quite similar to v. 1b). This word for "rebuke" (גְּעָרָה, g^e 'ārāh) is used only three times in Proverbs (13:1,8; 17:10). Here the NIV appropriately translates it **threat** in order to make the proper contrast with the first line. The rich are vulnerable to threats in order to save their lives. The **poor** have no financial resources. No one can threaten them. In that sense, the poor are better off than are the rich. The value of wealth is relative. One translation reads, "The rich can be sued for everything they have, but the poor are free of such threats."[39] Another translation interprets the proverb, "A rich man has to use his money to save his life, but no one threatens a poor man."[40]

⁹**The light of the righteous shines brightly,**
   but the lamp of the wicked is snuffed out.
¹⁰**Pride only breeds quarrels,**
   but wisdom is found in those who take advice.
¹¹**Dishonest money dwindles away,**
   but he who gathers money little by little makes it grow.

13:9 The image of a **light** continually burning (v. 9) represents a healthy household. The image calls to mind the family of the woman of noble character in 31:18. In contrast, an extinguished **lamp** represents a life **snuffed out**.

13:10 The first line of verse 10 is somewhat vague in the Hebrew text. The line literally reads, "only in insolence will one give strife." The meaning seems to be that the main product produced by **pride** is quarreling. This is contrasted with the second line: the wise person is willing to **take advice**. Where the prideful person has contempt for others' opinions, wisdom gladly receives counsel. This proverb is apropos especially in light of 13:1 (cf., also 12:15).

13:11 With emphasis on diligence and discipline, the sage is cautious about anyone who gains wealth quickly. This is the basis of verse 11. Get rich quick schemes usually involve fraud. On the other hand, wealth that is slowly acquired will last.

---

[39]Peterson, *The Message*, p. 44.

[40]*Good News Bible: Today's English Version* (New York: American Bible Society, 1976), p. 705.

¹²Hope deferred makes the heart sick,
    but a longing fulfilled is a tree of life.
¹³He who scorns instruction will pay for it,
    but he who respects a command is rewarded.
¹⁴The teaching of the wise is a fountain of life,
    turning a man from the snares of death.
¹⁵Good understanding wins favor,
    but the way of the unfaithful is hard.ᵃ
¹⁶Every prudent man acts out of knowledge,
    but a fool exposes his folly.
¹⁷A wicked messenger falls into trouble,
    but a trustworthy envoy brings healing.
¹⁸He who ignores discipline comes to poverty and shame,
    but whoever heeds correction is honored.
¹⁹A longing fulfilled is sweet to the soul,
    but fools detest turning from evil.

ᵃ*15 Or unfaithful does not endure*

13:12-19 Many of the proverbs in this unit cluster around an interest in instruction. Verses 13 and 14 are similar in meaning. They use similar vocabulary: **instruction** (דָּבָר, *dābār*), **command** (מִצְוָה, *miṣwāh*), **teaching** (תּוֹרָה, *tôrāh*). Commands and teaching (*tôrāh*) are usually associated with Deuteronomy and the Mosaic Law, but here they do not refer to such covenantal language. The commands and teachings in the book of Proverbs refer to the instruction of the sages and the parents. The antithesis described here in verse 13 is similar to the antithesis in verse 10. One who refuses good advice only invites trouble. One who follows good advice is blessed. **Fountain of life** is a metaphor for the best of life (v. 14). The parallelism in verse 14 is a good example of synthetic parallelism in which the second line continues the thought of the first.

One of the most fundamental characteristics of the sage is described in verse 16. The sage is one who practices self-control. The **prudent** (עָרוּם, *'ārûm*) act only after acquiring the appropriate **knowledge**. In Proverbs, knowledge (דַּעַת, *dā'ath*) and wisdom (חָכְמָה, *ḥākmāh*) are most often synonymous (cf. 1:7). In contrast to the wise, the **fool** (כְּסִיל, *kᵉsîl*) demonstrates no restraint. The fool **exposes** (lit., "broadcasts" or "spreads out") his incompetence for everyone to see. A contrast exists between the prudent and the fool.

The prudent one is focused in direction. The fool has no direction (see also 12:26).

Verse 18 continues the emphasis on instruction. The proverb harks back to 12:1 and 13:1. The contrast here is between ignoring **discipline** or instruction (מוּסָר, *mûsār*) and heeding reproof (תּוֹכַחַת, *tôkaḥath*). These two words are a common word pair throughout Proverbs (see 3:11; 5:12; 6:23; 10:17; 12:1; 15:5,10,32). The word "discipline" (*mûsār*) occurs most often in the Old Testament in the book of Proverbs (more than a third of the occurrences).[41] The word translated "discipline" here and in 13:1 is the same word. Discipline (*mûsār*) is the body of knowledge necessary to manage life successfully (1:8; 4:1; 13:1). How was discipline administered? Sometimes it was dispensed with the rod, but most often it was through oral instruction. That is why discipline (*mûsār*) is frequently paired with "rebuke" and "instruction" (*tôrāh*).

The contrast between ignoring instruction and heeding reproof in verse 18 is further highlighted by the consequences. The former brings **shame** (lit., "lightweight"; i.e., superficial). The latter results in **honor** (lit., "weighty"; i.e., substantive). The person who learns from the wise becomes a person of "weight" in the community. The person who is undisciplined is strawlike (cf. Ps 1:4).

²⁰**He who walks with the wise grows wise,**
     but a companion of fools suffers harm.
²¹**Misfortune pursues the sinner,**
     but prosperity is the reward of the righteous.
²²**A good man leaves an inheritance for his children's children,**
     but a sinner's wealth is stored up for the righteous.
²³**A poor man's field may produce abundant food,**
     but injustice sweeps it away.
²⁴**He who spares the rod hates his son,**
     but he who loves him is careful to discipline him.
²⁵**The righteous eat to their hearts' content,**
     but the stomach of the wicked goes hungry.

13:20-25 In Proverbs, different reasons are given for being in a state of poverty. Verse 23 reveals that poverty is the result of **injustice**. Injustices on the part of the greedy deprive the **poor** of the fruit

---

[41]G. Johannes Botterweck, "יָסַר," *TDOT*, p. 129.

of their hard work. Sometimes, however, poverty is the result of an individual's sin, as is the case in verse 25.

In our day and time when child abuse is all too common, verse 24 creates concern for many readers. Usually **discipline** (*mûsār*) is associated with some type of rebuke or oral instruction. Here it is associated with corporal punishment (see also 22:15; 23:13-14; 29:15). It is from this proverb that we derive the contemporary saying, "spare the rod and spoil the child."

Verse 24 does not advocate child abuse. Rather the use of corporal punishment expresses a type of "tough love." The contrast in this antithetic proverb is between expressing **hate** and expressing **love**. In certain contexts, love may demand serious action. Dietrich Bonhoeffer noted that Israel did not imprison wrongdoers as a punishment.[42] They may have viewed such incarceration as a dehumanizing act.[43] Caning was the quicker and more humane punishment to use on the offender. Caning is the punishment envisioned here.

Readers, however, must understand the administration of corporal punishment in the context of the sages' emphasis on self-restraint (16:32; 25:28) and caution against excessive anger (14:17; 19:18; 19:19). One should also keep another core virtue of wisdom in mind, namely patience (12:16; 14:29; 15:1,18), in understanding how the sages implemented the use of corporal punishment.

14:1**The wise woman builds her house,**
> **but with her own hands the foolish one tears hers down.**
2**He whose walk is upright fears the LORD,**
> **but he whose ways are devious despises him.**
3**A fool's talk brings a rod to his back,**
> **but the lips of the wise protect them.**
4**Where there are no oxen, the manger is empty,**
> **but from the strength of an ox comes an abundant harvest.**
5**A truthful witness does not deceive,**
> **but a false witness pours out lies.**
6**The mocker seeks wisdom and finds none,**
> **but knowledge comes easily to the discerning.**

[42]Dietrich Bonhoeffer, *Letters and Papers from Prison* (New York: Macmillan, 1972), pp. 134, 164.
[43]See Van Leeuwen, "Proverbs," p. 136.

⁷Stay away from a foolish man,
      for you will not find knowledge on his lips.
⁸The wisdom of the prudent is to give thought to their ways,
      but the folly of fools is deception.
⁹Fools mock at making amends for sin,
      but goodwill is found among the upright.
¹⁰Each heart knows its own bitterness,
      and no one else can share its joy.
¹¹The house of the wicked will be destroyed,
      but the tent of the upright will flourish.
¹²There is a way that seems right to a man,
      but in the end it leads to death.
¹³Even in laughter the heart may ache,
      and joy may end in grief.

14:1-13 Verse 1 literally begins "the wisdom of women." The RSV
deletes "women" and makes the text identical to 9:1a, "Wisdom
builds her house." The NIV alters the text some as well. Nevertheless,
the basic image is this: A woman who practices wisdom establishes a
morally solid household. The woman of noble character in 31:10-31
demonstrates verse 1a. Verse 1b is demonstrated by the adulteress in
chapters 5–7. The temptress can destroy a **house** (27:15-16). The
image of wisdom building a house is a dominant theme in Proverbs.
Verse 2 affirms that one's moral character reflects one's relationship
to **the LORD**. The fear of the Lord is the basis of right conduct. Three
verses in this chapter refer to the "fear of the Lord" (vv. 2,26,27).

At first glance, the proverb in verse 4 appears to be quite pedantic. **Oxen** were essential to harvesting grain. The basic meaning of
the proverb is that when a farmer has no livestock, he does not have
to worry about cleaning out the cribs. He also will have no crops.
Garrett captures the essence of the meaning, ". . . one must make an
investment (obtain and feed the oxen) to get a large return."⁴⁴ The
proverb indirectly asserts the value of animals in the scheme of
God's created order. The wise treat animals responsibly (12:10).

Verses 6-8 are tied together by a common theme and vocabulary.
All three proverbs speak of **wisdom** and **folly** and **knowledge**. One

---

⁴⁴Garrett, *Proverbs, Ecclesiastes, Song of Songs,* p. 141.

of the frequently used words for fool is found in verse 6, **the mock-er** (ץ֖ל, *lēṣ*). Habitual cynicism and arrogance characterize this person. He does not have the humility necessary to acquire wisdom. Even though he **seeks wisdom**, it is a fruitless exercise. The implication here is that wisdom is not accessible to everyone (cf. 9:7-12). Verse 7 stands out as an exception to the dominant antithetic parallelism that occurs in chapters 10–15. The proverb is an admonition to leave the presence of **foolish** ones (cf. Ps 1:1-2). The admonition reminds one of the contemporary proverb, "Bad company corrupts good morals" (cf. 1 Cor. 15:33).

Wisdom gives individuals the ability to see their way more clearly through life's experiences and decisions (v. 8). Wisdom looks below the surface. In contrast, **folly** takes a shallow view of life. Folly is identified with **deception**. It actually deceives others as well as itself.

Verse 10 makes reference to the **heart**. In Hebrew thought, "heart" does not refer primarily to feelings, but to the mind and the inner self. The heart stands for the individual at a highly personal level.[45] This verse reveals a psychological perspective on personal experiences. Some experiences can never be understood by or communicated to others. Only the LORD knows a person's deepest feelings (15:11; 17:3; 21:2). The proverb confirms the limits of human ability to understand another, which should evoke humility as one enters into relationships with others. As important as community is in wisdom thought, verse 10 also affirms the uniqueness of the individual. In the mind of the sage, community does not eclipse the reality or the significance of the person.

Verse 12 presents a theology that is counter to the dominant theology found in chapters 10–15. The majority of antithetic sayings in these chapters express a simple belief: God rewards those who choose the right path, but he punishes those who deliberately choose another way. Choices in life are clear and simple. The sages seem to oversimplify life. Yet in the midst of what appears to be a dogmatic perspective, the sages themselves acknowledge their limitation (v. 12). Anyone can be misled by what appears to be the right path. Humans cannot always know what is appropriate. The end turns out to be quite different from the beginning. This is one of the

---

[45]Clifford, *Proverbs*, p. 144.

first appearances of what is known as the "limit proverbs," which dominate chapters 16–22.

Verse 13 also acknowledges the complexities of life. **Joy** and **laughter** here are not necessarily polar opposites of **grief**. They may be experienced in the same event. Things are not always as they seem. Grief is a part of any intimate human relationship.

> [14]The faithless will be fully repaid for their ways,
>   and the good man rewarded for his.
> [15]A simple man believes anything,
>   but a prudent man gives thought to his steps.
> [16]A wise man fears the LORD and shuns evil,
>   but a fool is hotheaded and reckless.
> [17]A quick-tempered man does foolish things,
>   and a crafty man is hated.
> [18]The simple inherit folly,
>   but the prudent are crowned with knowledge.
> [19]Evil men will bow down in the presence of the good,
>   and the wicked at the gates of the righteous.
> [20]The poor are shunned even by their neighbors,
>   but the rich have many friends.
> [21]He who despises his neighbor sins,
>   but blessed is he who is kind to the needy.
> [22]Do not those who plot evil go astray?
>   But those who plan what is good find[a] love and faithful-
>   ness.
> [23]All hard work brings a profit,
>   but mere talk leads only to poverty.
> [24]The wealth of the wise is their crown,
>   but the folly of fools yields folly.

[a]22 Or *show*

14:14-24 The NIV misinterprets verse 16. (The NIV adds the phrase **the LORD.**) The word **fear** (יָרֵא, *yārē'*) in this proverb is bet-ter translated "cautious." This creates a better parallelism with the second line. The sense of the proverb is that the wise are cautious of hidden danger (e.g., 7:6-27). The fool, however, lacks self-control. The meaning of the second line is similar to the contemporary proverb, "Fools rush in where angels fear to tread" (cf. 22:3).

The proverb of verse 17 employs synonymous parallelism (unlike the RSV interpretation), with the second line intensifying the first. A **quick-tempered** person does things without thinking. What is worse, however, is the **crafty** person. The former acts without reflecting. The latter acts secretive with malicious reflection.[46]

A large portion of proverbs in chapters 10–22 and 25–29 are concerned with wealth and poverty. Verses 20-21 form a proverb pair related to this subject. The word for **poor** in verse 20 is the term רָשׁ (rāš). Along with דָּל (dāl, see 14:31), they are the two most frequently used words for "poor" in Proverbs.[47] Two other common, but less frequently used words for "poor" are עָנִי ('ānî, verse 21) and אֶבְיוֹן ('ebyôn, verse 31).[48] Verse 20 makes a simple observation. The poor do not have **friends**. The **rich** have a host. However, the rich can be deceived into thinking they have genuine friends, when such friends love them only for their money. Verse 21a condemns the behavior of 20a as a **sin**. God's people, regardless of economic status, are called on to show kindness to the **needy**. Those who do will **find** as their companions **love and faithfulness** (v. 22). The word pair is found frequently in Proverbs (3:3; 16:6; 20:28).

Translations generally tend to alter verse 24 because of the repetition. The tautology is intentional, designed to highlight the ridiculous nature of **folly**. Thus the NIV appropriately translates the text **the folly of fools yields folly**.

[25]**A truthful witness saves lives,**
  but a false witness is deceitful.
[26]**He who fears the LORD has a secure fortress,**
  and for his children it will be a refuge.
[27]**The fear of the LORD is a fountain of life,**
  turning a man from the snares of death.
[28]**A large population is a king's glory,**
  but without subjects a prince is ruined.

---

[46]Ibid., p. 145.

[47]See Whybray, *Wealth*, p. 14.

[48]All four of these terms seem to be synonymous (see Ps. 82:3 where all four are used in the same context). Whybray observes, "In contrast with the plethora of words meaning poor it is remarkable that no other adjective or noun signifying 'rich' occurs, although a number of other words and phrases denoting wealth and its acquisition are used quite frequently." See Ibid., p. 22.

²⁹**A patient man has great understanding,**
　　but a quick-tempered man displays folly.
³⁰**A heart at peace gives life to the body,**
　　but envy rots the bones.
³¹**He who oppresses the poor shows contempt for their Maker,**
　　but whoever is kind to the needy honors God.
³²**When calamity comes, the wicked are brought down,**
　　but even in death the righteous have a refuge.
³³**Wisdom reposes in the heart of the discerning**
　　and even among fools she lets herself be known.^a
³⁴**Righteousness exalts a nation,**
　　but sin is a disgrace to any people.
³⁵**A king delights in a wise servant,**
　　but a shameful servant incurs his wrath.

^a*33* **Hebrew; Septuagint and Syriac** / *but in the heart of fools she is not*
known

14:25-27 Verse 26 contains the third appearance of the phrase
fears the LORD in the Solomonic sayings (see 10:27 and 14:2). Verses
26 and 27 are a pair of "Yahweh proverbs." The pair alludes to the
motto of the book in 1:7. **Fear of the LORD** is frequently associated
with practicing steadfast love and faithfulness (see 16:6; see also
14:22). Fear of God is more of an action than an emotion. Verse 27
overlaps with 13:14, where "fear of the LORD" is substituted for
"teachings of the wise." Considering these two overlapping proverbs
together, the implication is that fear of the LORD is something that
can be taught. It is not uncommon for individual proverbs to overlap like this (i.e., 13:14 and 14:27). It indicates that the sages were
flexible in their appropriation of the proverbs in daily life. The bina-
ry structure of the proverbs indicates that they were intended to be
memorized but not necessarily to be repeated verbatim. There was
more to wisdom than rote memory (see comments on 10:6-7).

　　14:28 A royal saying makes its first appearance in the book of
Proverbs.⁴⁹ This proverb follows on the heels of the Yahweh proverbs
in verses 26-27. Frequently the two are linked together (see 16:1-15).
The attachment of royal proverbs to Yahweh proverbs may be theo-
logically significant indicating the submission of the king to the LORD.

---

⁴⁹The next royal proverb is found in 14:35.

14:29-30 These verses describe the damage that results from unrestrained emotions. The wise have much to say about the self-control of emotions. Verse 29 describes the social consequences. When a **quick-tempered man** shows no control over his anger, he displays his **folly** for all to see. The quick-tempered man literally is "he who is short of breath," possibly indicating the rapid breathing of one who is angry. Verse 30 describes the physical consequences of uncontrolled feelings. Once again, **heart** refers to the mind, the inner thoughts. The Hebrew word for **peace** here is literally "healing" (מַרְפֵּא, *marpē'*). Thus "a heart at peace" is better rendered "a healthy mind." One's mental state influences one's physical health. A healthy mind brings healing to the whole **body**. By contrast, uncontrolled passions can destroy the body as quickly as a deadly disease. The wise understood the human being holistically. Thoughts and feelings affect the physical state.

14:31-35 Verse 31 is related to the thought in verse 21. The treatment of **the poor** is an ethical issue. The attitude one takes toward the poor reflects the attitude one possesses toward God. The poor are God's children as much as anyone else. Notice the personal relationship that God has with the poor. God is **their Maker**.

The second line of verse 32 is problematic. The Hebrew reads, "in his death, the righteous seek refuge." That the righteous seek refuge in death is not compatible with the theology of Scripture. Throughout Proverbs, death is associated with evil and wickedness (see 2:18; 10:2; 11:19 for just a few examples). Scripture does not speak of death as a refuge which God's people seek. That implies a form of suicide. The NIV adjusts the thought some and adds the word "even," which changes the thought from "the righteous seeking death" to "**even in death** there is refuge for the righteous." However, if the meaning here implies a reference to an afterlife, then the interpretation is improbable. Little evidence exists in Proverbs to affirm belief in an afterlife. More than likely the meaning refers to the righteous seeking refuge in God, even to the point of death (see 10:25).[50]

---

[50]Some feel that a metathesis has occurred between מוֹת (*môth*, "death") and תֹּם (*tōm*, "integrity"). The LXX understands this to be the case and transposes the consonants, thus reading "the righteous finds refuge in his integrity." The RSV and NRSV follow suit.

Verse 33b is not clear in thought. The following is a possible interpretation. The proverb compares **wisdom** in the life of both the **discerning** and the **fool**. Wisdom finds a comfortable home in the heart of those who are perceptive. And because wisdom does not find a natural home in the heart of fools, it speaks out and is easily distinguished.

A **nation** takes on a particular moral character, according to the proverb in verse 34. That means that all nations are subject to God's judgment (see Amos 1–2). God does not evaluate countries by the size of their territory or population or wealth, which is the focus of the political sphere. God evaluates societies by their **righteousness**, that is, their relationship to the LORD. The moral character of individuals shapes the political climate of a nation.

Though the proverbs in chapter 15:1-30 (I treat 15:31-33 with chapter 16) do not comprise a unified collection or form a tight cluster, there are a number of interesting features that characterize them. First, the antithetic parallelism that dominates the previous chapters becomes less frequent in this chapter. Approximately twenty of the thirty proverbs in this chapter are antithetic. Second, "Yahweh proverbs" begin to appear more frequently, making way for a major thrust in the following chapter.[51] Third, many of the proverbs in this chapter concern themselves with instruction and acquiring knowledge (vv. 2,5,7,10,12,14,22,31,32,33). A number of the proverbs reflect the language of the instruction sayings of chapters 1–9. Finally, the subject of speech is a frequent topic of the sayings.

[15:1]**A gentle answer turns away wrath,**
    but a harsh word stirs up anger.
[2]**The tongue of the wise commends knowledge,**
    but the mouth of the fool gushes folly.
[3]**The eyes of the LORD are everywhere,**
    keeping watch on the wicked and the good.
[4]**The tongue that brings healing is a tree of life,**
    but a deceitful tongue crushes the spirit.

---

[51]A total of nine Yahweh proverbs appear in chapter 15 (vv. 3,8,9,11,16, 25,26,29,33). Unlike Whybray continues to claim in his commentary, these proverbs do not function to make the "secular" proverbs more orthodox (Whybray, *Proverbs*, pp. 231, 235).

⁵**A fool spurns his father's discipline,**
    but whoever heeds correction shows prudence.
⁶**The house of the righteous contains great treasure,**
    but the income of the wicked brings them trouble.
⁷**The lips of the wise spread knowledge;**
    not so the hearts of fools.

15:1-3 Many of the sayings in these verses deal with the use of words. Roland Murphy correctly observes, "Speech is perhaps the truest indication whether one is wise or foolish."[52] The irony of verse 1 is that strength lies in *soft* not *hard* words. Verse 2 also speaks of the use of words. **The wise** person **commends knowledge**. Literally the phrase is "makes knowledge good." That is, the wise know how to communicate knowledge appropriately. They exercise restraint in dispensing it. In contrast, **the fool gushes folly**. That is, the fool does not reflect on his thoughts before speaking. He spews out whatever is on his mind. Verse 3 indicates that the **LORD** not only knows all, he is especially concerned with moral character, judging what is **wicked** and what is **good**.

15:4 In verse 4, the NIV appropriately translates the Hebrew with the phrase, **the tongue that brings healing** (the same word for "healing" appears in 14:30). Proper speech, speech that is fitting for the occasion, restores damaged relationships. **A deceitful tongue**, literally one that is crooked, damages the innermost being of another. However, the second line could mean that the deceitful tongue comes as a result of the speaker's own "broken spirit." The phrase **tree of life** appears only in Genesis and Proverbs, though it is a common image used in ancient Near Eastern art. It stands as an image for a fulfilled life.

15:5 The language of verse 5 and verse 20 reflects the language of chapters 1–9. All through Proverbs, **discipline** refers to constructive and purposeful instruction. Here the rebellious son is equated with a **fool**. In Proverbs, much of the responsibility for learning falls on the son (2:1-5). The son who **heeds correction shows prudence**. The word for "correction" is the Hebrew word תּוֹכַחַת (*tôkaḥath*, often translated "reproof") used frequently throughout Proverbs (16 times; see also verses 10,12,31,32). In Proverbs, wisdom comes

---

[52]Murphy, *Proverbs*, p. 259.

through a process of discipline. The ability to accept criticism is a mark of sapience.

15:6 Verse 6 continues to express the character-consequence scenario that dominates the theology of chapters 10–15. The **righteous** store up **treasure** for themselves. The **wicked** reap **trouble**.

15:7 The proverb of verse 7 is quite similar to verse 2. The **wise** are sensitive to sharing information that will better equip others to live successfully. In contrast, **fools** cannot be depended on for what they have to share. The word order in the second line of the Hebrew verse is "but the thought (heart) of fools—*not trustworthy.*" The sentence emphasizes the unreliability of fools. Fools possess little control over their thoughts.

⁸**The LORD detests the sacrifice of the wicked,**
   but the prayer of the upright pleases him.
⁹**The LORD detests the way of the wicked**
   but he loves those who pursue righteousness.
¹⁰**Stern discipline awaits him who leaves the path;**
   he who hates correction will die.
¹¹**Death and Destruction**ᵃ **lie open before the LORD—**
   how much more the hearts of men!
¹²**A mocker resents correction;**
   he will not consult the wise.

ᵃ*11* Hebrew *Sheol and Abaddon*

15:8-9 Verses 8 and 9 are paired together by the catchword **detest** or "abomination" (תּוֹעֵבָה, *thôʻēbāh*). Detest and **please** (רָצוֹן, *rāṣôn*) are often paired together to contrast the Lord's response to the actions of his people (cf. 11:1). The actions here involve a rare reference in Proverbs to worship activities (cf. 15:29; 21:3,27; 28:9,13). The contrast is between a costly **sacrifice**, which God abhors, and a simple **prayer** in which God takes great delight. The issue here is the character of the one sacrificing and not the sacrifice. According to verse 9, what God really wants is for his people to **pursue** ("pursue" is in the intensive form in Hebrew) **righteousness**[53] earnestly in daily living. These verses express a theological perspective the prophets so frequently proclaimed (see Amos 5:21-24).

---

[53]References to righteousness and the righteous outnumber references to wisdom and the wise in 10:1–22:16.

15:10 Stern discipline in verse 10 is an unusual description of discipline in the book of Proverbs. The word "stern" (רַע, *rā'*, literally "evil") carries with it negative connotations. In wisdom, discipline or instruction is a desired quality. One seeks after it. In this context, the phrase refers to judgment that is imposed on the wayward party.

15:11 Death and Destruction (lit., "Sheol" and "Abaddon") in verse 11 refer to the realm of the dead. The thought of the proverb is that if God knows the most hidden place in the universe, then how easy it is for him to have access to the human **heart** ("mind"). In God's eyes, humans are an "open book."

15:12 Verse 12 has a close affinity with 9:7-8. The Hebrew text of the first line literally reads, "the scoffer does not love one who reproves him." The sage in 25:12 affirms the opposite image. One of the primary ways wisdom is gained is in dialogue with others.

A couple of verbal links holds proverbs 13-17 together. "Heart" links verses 13,14, and 15 together. The word "cheerful" or "better" (טוֹב, *ṭôb*) appears in 13,15,16, and 17. Four of the five verses (vv. 13, 15-17) are concerned with creating an environment of "cheerfulness" regardless of external circumstances. Up to this point, the antithetic proverbs taught the fundamental ABCs of wisdom: one who fears the LORD will, generally speaking, prosper. The one who chooses to follow a different path will find it laden with problems. With the entry of this cluster of proverbs, however, material goods are viewed more indeterminately. Life gets a little more complicated as one moves toward chapter 16.

¹³**A happy heart makes the face cheerful,**
   but heartache crushes the spirit.
¹⁴**The discerning heart seeks knowledge,**
   but the mouth of a fool feeds on folly.
¹⁵**All the days of the oppressed are wretched,**
   but the cheerful heart has a continual feast.
¹⁶**Better a little with the fear of the LORD**
   than great wealth with turmoil.
¹⁷**Better a meal of vegetables where there is love**
   than a fattened calf with hatred.

15:13-14 In verse 13, **heart** (or "inner being") is the driving force behind the **spirit** of a person. If the heart is strong, then the spirit is energized and focused. **Happy heart** does not refer to the popular notion of positive thinking. In the context of chapter 15 and the numerous proverbs that deal with wise instruction, one develops the happy heart through submission to the instruction of the sage. Receiving wise instruction creates a happy heart (cf. Ps 1:1-2). This thought is implied in verse 14 where the **discerning heart** has a drive to discover **knowledge** and wisdom. In Proverbs, knowledge and wisdom are frequently used interchangeably. In contrast, **a fool feeds on folly**. The terms **seeks** (בָּקַשׁ, *bāqaš*) and **feeds** (רָעָה, *rā'āh*) are shepherding terms. Like a shepherd searching for good pasture, the wise seek wisdom, but fools shepherd folly.

15:15 The proverbs in verses 15-17 develop a series of paradoxes. Inner resources can overcome outward circumstances. The **cheerful heart** of verse 15 refers to the disciplined mind. Clifford makes an apropos comment, "Wisdom keeps one from being defeated by troubles that come from being poor."[54]

15:16-17 Verses 16 and 17 contain the second appearance of the better-than proverbs in the sentence literature of chapters 10–22 (the first is found in 12:9). In the book of Proverbs, there are basically two types of better-than sayings. On the one hand, some better-than proverbs make a simple comparison in which X is said to be better than Y, as for example in the second line of 19:22: ". . . it is better to be poor than a liar." On the other hand, more elaborate sayings are based on the formula, X is better with A, than Y is with B. The proverbs in verses 16 and 17 belong to the more elaborate type. Verse 17 gives the definition of the nature of a feast. A feast is a meal eaten in the context of **love**. This definition also clarifies the meaning of the **continual feast** referred to in verse 15.

Contrary to conventional wisdom (which dominates chapters 10–15), in the better-than proverbs the sages give no pat answers. Wealth and poverty are mixed blessings. These comparative-type proverbs set conventional wisdom on its head. It is by no means always true that those who practice righteousness, justice, and fairness become prosperous. These sayings make wealth's value relative. In verse 16, the point is that the scale of material prosperity (from **little** to **great**) is subordinated to the spiritual scale (from **fear of the**

---

[54]Clifford, *Proverbs*, p. 153.

LORD to **turmoil**). The conclusion that the comparative-type proverbs reach is that relationships are more important than material goods. Community and character transcend creature comforts.

Roland Murphy suggests that the three proverbs in verses 15-17 identify a different perspective on what is "good" (*ṭôb*). It is the contented mind (responsibility to self; v. 15), the fear of the LORD (responsibility to God; v. 16), and harmony with companions (responsibility to neighbor; v. 17).[55]

[18]**A hot-tempered man stirs up dissension,**
    but a patient man calms a quarrel.
[19]**The way of the sluggard is blocked with thorns,**
    but the path of the upright is a highway.
[20]**A wise son brings joy to his father,**
    but a foolish man despises his mother.
[21]**Folly delights a man who lacks judgment,**
    but a man of understanding keeps a straight course.
[22]**Plans fail for lack of counsel,**
    but with many advisers they succeed.
[23]**A man finds joy in giving an apt reply—**
    and how good is a timely word!
[24]**The path of life leads upward for the wise**
    to keep him from going down to the grave.[a]

[a]*24 Hebrew Sheol*

15:18-24 Verse 19 refers to a common image used in wisdom instruction, the two ways: **the way of the sluggard** and the way **of the upright**. There are two possibilities for understanding how the sluggard's path **is blocked with thorns**. One possibility is that the road overgrows with bushes because of the negligence of the lazy person (cf. 24:30-31). The other possibility is that the sluggard is simply offering an excuse for not working. He cannot work because there are obstacles in the way. This excuse compares closely to a later one mentioned by the sluggard, "There's a lion in the road!" (22:13). The **highway** the upright follow is not necessarily trouble free, but they can clearly see the way they need to go.

Verse 20a is identical with 10:1a. **Wise** children reflect the successful instruction of their parents. In contrast, **foolish** children

---

[55]Murphy, *Proverbs*, p. 113.

despise parental guidance. Verses 20,21, and 23 all use the catch-word **joy/delight** (שָׂמַח, *śāmaḥ*). The word order of verse 23b in the Hebrew text highlights the pleasure received from speaking a word at the right time: "a word in its time—how good!" Wisdom express-es its fundamental character in saying and doing the right thing at the right time (cf. 16:24; 18:13; 25:11,15; 24:26).

The phrase **the path of life leads upward for the wise** in verse 24a does not refer to heaven. Rather "upward" is a metaphor for suc-cess. It would be like someone today saying "onward and upward!"[56] **Down to the grave** does not refer to hell but to Sheol. In this proverb, the image of **going** down to the grave conveys failure.

²⁵**The LORD tears down the proud man's house**
    but he keeps the widow's boundaries intact.
²⁶**The LORD detests the thoughts of the wicked,**
    but those of the pure are pleasing to him.
²⁷**A greedy man brings trouble to his family,**
    but he who hates bribes will live.
²⁸**The heart of the righteous weighs its answers,**
    but the mouth of the wicked gushes evil.
²⁹**The LORD is far from the wicked**
    but he hears the prayer of the righteous.
³⁰**A cheerful look brings joy to the heart,**
    and good news gives health to the bones.

15:25-26 The material in verses 25-33 contain a series of Yahweh proverbs: 25,26,29,33. It is as though the editors are preparing the reader for the onslaught of Yahweh proverbs in the next chapter. Pride (v. 25) is public enemy number one of wisdom. Wisdom grounds itself in humility and the fear of the LORD. If **the LORD** is involved in protecting widows and the poor, then so do those who fear him. The LORD not only opposes the **proud**, he also **detests** ("abomination"; תּוֹעֵבָה, *tôʿēbāh*) **the thoughts of the wicked** (v. 26). No thought or motive is hidden from the LORD. He sees the heart.

15:27 The proverb here is illustrated in 1:8-19. Greed not only ends up hurting oneself but also one's **family** and friends. The per-son who does not succumb to such temptation, experiences deeper satisfaction in life.

---

[56]Van Leeuwen, "Proverbs," p. 151.

15:28 This verse echoes the sentiments of earlier proverbs in this chapter (see vv. 2 and 7). Verse 28b is quite similar to verse 2b. The same verb **gush** (נָבַע, *nāba'*, in the imperfect tense, which means ongoing action)[57] is used in both verses. The **wicked** lack restraint over thoughts or speech. The **righteous** think before speaking.

15:29 The thought here is similar to verse 8. The proverb speaks of the distance of God between the wicked and the righteous not spatially but relationally. He is **far from the wicked, but he hears the prayer of the righteous.**

15:30 This proverb alludes to those in verses 13-17. A pleasant look from someone else brings internal healing. External circumstances, such as **good news**, affect a person's well-being. The sage does not deny that one's environment influences physical and mental health. Such surroundings, however, do not ultimately determine the demeanor of the wise (v. 15). Verse 30 and verse 15 are examples of two proverbs expressing different perspectives on a similar event (cf. 26:4-5).

B. YAHWEH PROVERBS, LIMIT PROVERBS (15:31–22:16)

With the beginning of this section, a marked shift occurs in the theological thrust of the book. In chapters 10–15, the sage has set before the son the fundamentals of wisdom. The son must choose between two clear paths, the path of the righteous or the path of the wicked. The time now comes for the sage to reveal some of the complexities of life. The choices are not always clear. In addition, as many resources as humans have at their disposal to prepare for the future, they must also understand and accept their limitations. The son must prepare for the ambiguities of life. Unlike the previous section in chapters 10–15 in which antithetic parallelism dominated, the parallelism in chapters 16–22 is more diverse, frequently using synonymous parallelism.

In the opening unit of this new section, the series of proverbs in 15:31–16:9 cluster tightly together. Several structural and theological factors indicate this. First, the cluster consists primarily of Yahweh

---

[57]BDB define נָבַע as "bubble up," p. 615.

proverbs (proverbs that use the phrase "the LORD," 16:1-9). Except for verse 8 all the proverbs contain the catchword, "the LORD."[58]

Second, while one line in these proverbs refers to the LORD, the other line usually refers to some kind of human activity. A tension exists in many of them between the sovereignty of God and the activity of humans.

Third, a group of royal proverbs (proverbs that use the phrase "the king," 16:10-15) succeeds this text of Yahweh sayings (16:1-9). The two units are intentionally placed together. Similar terminology is used to describe God and king in both sections (e.g., v. 12).

Fourth, 15:31-33 serves as an introduction to this cluster of proverbs. With the exhortation to hear, listen, and heed instruction, the text is similar to the admonitions given to a son to listen to the instructions of his father that mark off the major units in chapters 1-9 (e.g., 1:8-9; 3:1-2; 4:1-3). This introduction encourages the son to accept instruction, which gives wisdom.

Fifth, 16:1 and 9 form an inclusion with both confirming that humans plan but God has the final say. The inclusion announces the theme of this unit of material.

[31]**He who listens to a life-giving rebuke**
    will be at home among the wise.
[32]**He who ignores discipline despises himself,**
    but whoever heeds correction gains understanding.
[33]**The fear of the LORD teaches a man wisdom,**[a]
    and humility comes before honor.

[a]*33 Or Wisdom teaches the fear of the LORD*

15:31-33 These three verses introduce the cluster of Yahweh proverbs. This introduction is quite similar to the formulaic sayings that appear throughout the first nine chapters of Proverbs: "My children, listen to your father's instruction." The text uses the familiar sapiential language of admonition (i.e., **rebuke**, v. 31; **correction**, v. 32). This is not just any kind of reproof; this is wholesome, **life-giving** (v. 31) instruction. In Proverbs, the instruction a parent offers to

---

[58]An overlapping proverb, in fact, appears in 15:16a: "Better is a little with the fear of the LORD." Considering the two proverbs together (15:16a and 16:8a), "fear of the LORD" is closely related to "righteousness."

a youth is analogous to Yahweh's admonition to his children (3:11-12). In verse 33, **fear of the LORD** is synonymous with **humility**.

The Masoretes (the scribal preservers of the Old Testament text during the medieval period) locate the middle verse in the book of Proverbs at 16:17. Thus the text of 15:31–16:9 spatially comes at a strategic point, near the center of the book of Proverbs. In regard to the sentence literature in 10:1–22:16, the thickest concentration of Yahweh proverbs occurs in chapters 15 and 16,[59] which is also spatially in the middle of this section. Chapter 15:33–16:9 represents the theological kernel of chapters 10–22.

Among other things, this cluster acknowledges human limitations. One does not need to turn to Ecclesiastes or Job to find an introduction to a theology of the limits of wisdom. The proverbs in 16:1-9 present a comprehensive picture of Yahweh as in total control of human affairs.

16:1**To man belong the plans of the heart,**
    but from the LORD comes the reply of the tongue.
2**All a man's ways seem innocent to him,**
    but motives are weighed by the LORD.
3**Commit to the LORD whatever you do,**
    and your plans will succeed.
4**The LORD works out everything for his own ends—**
    even the wicked for a day of disaster.
5**The LORD detests all the proud of heart.**
    Be sure of this: They will not go unpunished.
6**Through love and faithfulness sin is atoned for;**
    through the fear of the LORD a man avoids evil.
7**When a man's ways are pleasing to the LORD,**
    he makes even his enemies live at peace with him.

---

[59]Fifty-five Yahweh sayings are found in 10:1–22:16. Twenty of those appear in chapters 15 and 16. It is interesting to note that the highest concentration of direct references to God in the book of Proverbs is in 10:1–22:16. The lowest concentration of references is in chapters 25–29. In chapters 25–27 there are only two references to God: 25:2,22. Proverbs refers to God almost exclusively by the name Yahweh (eighty-seven times). The more generic term, "God" (*Elohim*; *Eloah*), is used only six times (2:5,17; 3:4; 25:2; 30:5,9).

⁸**Better a little with righteousness**
    than much gain with injustice.
⁹**In his heart a man plans his course,**
    but the LORD determines his steps.

16:1-3 Verses 1-3 introduce the tension that exists between the
human and the divine. The sages excel in planning (v. 1). Planning
is their area of expertise. The ability to prepare for the future is one
of the main qualities of wisdom. Yet even the most skilled plan has
limits. **The LORD** is the final arbitrator. With the first proverb, two
possible interpretations exist. On the one hand, the meaning might
be that humans have the capacity and the freedom to do their own
planning. Then God gives the gift of expression. The knack of giving the right answer, of finding the apt word for the occasion, is a
gift from God. On the other hand, the second line of the proverb
may be a figure of speech for the idea that God makes the final decision. That is to say, humans make their **plans** but God has the final
say. Eugene Peterson's translation captures the essence of its meaning: "Mortals make elaborate plans, but God has the last word."[60]
This interpretation fits more with the proverb in verse 3 and with
the inclusion verse 1 forms with verse 9. God can and sometimes
does foil an individual's plans. On the other hand, through human
plans, God can accomplish more than anyone thought possible.
After all, "man's extremity is God's opportunity."

That which gets in the way of the fulfillment of human plans is
pride, one of the deadliest sins in wisdom's dictionary. The phrase
in verse 2, "**All a man's ways seem innocent to him**" ("pure in one's
own eyes"), describes hubris.[61] The phrase depicts a person who sees
no authority or power beyond the individual, but **motives are
weighed by the LORD** (lit., "the LORD weighs the spirit"). God does
not have to wait for death in order to discern the internal motives
of a person (see Ps 139:23-24). Paul appropriated this proverb to
himself (1 Cor 4:3-5; 9:27).

Still another angle on the interaction between God and humans
comes in verse 3. The proposals that humans make are implemented

---

[60]Peterson, *The Message: Proverbs*, p. 54.

[61]This phrase, with slight variation, is used repeatedly throughout
Proverbs to describe human pride: 3:7; 12:15; 16:2; 21:2; 26:5,12,16; 28:11;
30:12.

only when in keeping with the LORD's will: **Commit to the LORD whatever you do, and your plans will succeed**. Typically humans plan and then work the plan. However, here the process is inverted. Humans *work*, but their *plans* fail unless God establishes them. The phrase "whatever you do" is inclusive of all the work that goes into accomplishing a goal. The word for "commit" (נָּלַל, *gālal*) means "to roll." Literally, the first line reads "roll on Yahweh your deeds." The phrase may be similar in thought to 1 Peter 5:7: "Cast all your cares on him." The proverb is not a formula for unfailing success but only a reminder that success does not ultimately lie in human hands. Considering the thrust of 16:1-9, verse 3 teaches that humans cannot always control their own affairs or guarantee success. Success is a gift from God.

16:4 One of the most difficult proverbs in this text to interpret is the proverb of verse 4. The NIV seems to interpret verse 4a through the theological eyes of Romans 8:28: **The LORD works out everything for his own ends**. The RSV, however, translates the verse, "The LORD has made everything for its purpose." In other words, the LORD made everything naturally to fit into the order of creation. This translation squares with the theology of wisdom and its emphasis on order and proper timing.

The phrase, **even the wicked for a day of disaster**, does not refer to predestination; it does not intimate that God has created people to be wicked. If this were the case, it would go against the whole grain of wisdom thought with its emphasis on individuals making right choices and decisions. Wisdom has high expectations of humans, their ability, and responsibility. The RSV's phrase "everything for its purpose" carries the idea that God created everything for a definite goal or end. In other words, God ensures that the ways of the wicked will not prevail because he continues to be actively involved in his creation. He reserves a day of disaster, a day of retribution and accountability, for those who refuse to make the right choices. God does not single out particular individuals for a day of disaster but a group, the wicked. All created things answer to him, including the wicked. The thought of verse 4 is illustrated in the parable of the wheat and tares, even though verse 4 does not envision the final judgment (Matt 13:24-30). One may have to wait until the end of life to separate the wicked from the righteous.

16:5 Verse 5 offers further commentary on the last line of verse

4, reassuring God's people that the punishment of the arrogant is certain. It also emphasizes a recurring theme found throughout this cluster: the sin of pride (see 15:33; 16:2).

16:6-8 The question in verse 6 is to whom does **love and faithfulness** refer? Is it God's love and faithfulness that activates atonement for **sin**? Or is it a reference to humans' love and faithfulness? If the two lines of the proverb are synonymous, then one could say the reference is to humans since the referent in the second line is humans. Nevertheless, these qualities of love and faithfulness describe fundamental attributes of God himself mentioned in Exodus 34:6-7. In addition, as mentioned earlier, the theological momentum of the cluster maintains an alternating tension between human action and divine sovereignty.

Evil is avoided by **fear of the LORD** (v. 6), but verse 8 qualifies the judgment of God in the here and now. As a better-than proverb (see 15:16-17), verse 8 implies that God's judgment is not always immediate: "Better is a little with righteousness than large income with injustice." Sometimes the righteous have **little** while unjust activities go unchecked. Moral character is not always rewarded in visible ways. This is the only proverb that does not contain the catchword "the LORD." However, when compared with the first line of 15:16 ("Better a little with the fear of the LORD"), **righteousness** appears to be synonymous with "fear of the LORD." Verse 8 is not out of place in this cluster.

16:9 The text comes full circle with verse 9: "The human mind plans the way, but the LORD directs the steps." The image of planning the way and directing the **steps** is an image of a journey. The surprise comes in discovering that in the realm of planning daily activities, where humans believe they are in control, God's will is most intimately at work. God works through the mental processes of human thought to bring about his desire. Such an arena of God's activity appears insignificant in the grand scheme of things. But if the search for wisdom is an activity of the mind, then it is in the mind of human beings that God is most directly active. Through human thought, which fears the LORD, the individual is brought into an encounter with the divine. Humans think, God directs. Even when plans are meant to do harm, God uses them to bring about good (cf. Gen 50:19-20).

[10]**The lips of a king speak as an oracle,**
    and his mouth should not betray justice.

¹¹**Honest scales and balances are from the LORD;**
    all the weights in the bag are of his making.
¹²**Kings detest wrongdoing,**
    for a throne is established through righteousness.
¹³**Kings take pleasure in honest lips;**
    they value a man who speaks the truth.
¹⁴**A king's wrath is a messenger of death,**
    but a wise man will appease it.
¹⁵**When a king's face brightens, it means life;**
    his favor is like a rain cloud in spring.

These royal proverbs intentionally follow the Yahweh proverbs in the previous section. The six proverbs are clustered into three pairs. Verses 10-11 both begin with a *segolate* noun (a particular vowel pointing in Hebrew) and contain the catchword "justice" (מִשְׁפָּט, *mišpāṭ*; the NIV translates it "honest" in verse 11). Verses 12-13 contain the catchword "kings" in the plural (מְלָכִים, *mᵊlākîm*). The proverb pair also uses a common word pair found throughout the sentence literature to describe the response of the LORD: verse 12 speaks of "wrongdoing" as an "abomination" (NIV "detest") to "kings." Verse 13, though, speaks of "honest lips" as that which is a "delight" (NIV "pleasure") to "kings." The pairing of "detest" and "pleasure" is common in describing the attitude of Yahweh (cf. 11:1). Both verses 14 and 15 describe the sovereign power of the king to announce death and give life. In both verses, "king" is singular.

16:10-11 The term rendered **oracle** in verse 10 (קֶסֶם, *qesem*; lit., divination) describes a practice that the rest of the Old Testament condemns. Only here is the word used in a positive sense. Verse 10 does not express things as they are but as they ought to be. The **king** should represent the words of Yahweh and thus he should speak words of **justice**. The king was the administrator of justice (31:1-9). Still he did not derive the principles of justice. Those principles flowed from God himself (v. 11). Verse 11 also indicates that **the LORD** is very much involved in the intricate details of life, even economic matters.

16:12-13 The NIV appropriately translates verse 12. It is not **kings** who do wrong (the NRSV could imply this meaning), but kings who **detest wrongdoing** (see also Psalm 101 which appears to be an oath the king takes to execute justice). The language of **detest**

and **pleasure** is similar to language used earlier of Yahweh (see vv. 5 and 7).

16:14-15 This pair speaks of the sovereignty of a **king**. A king has the power to curse and to bless. The only way in which one can **appease** the **wrath** of a king is by wisdom. This was what Daniel did in the case of Nebuchadnezzar (Daniel 2; see also Prov 25:15; Eccl 9:13-18).

This cluster of proverbs describes the king's role and function. That function is primarily to administer righteousness, justice, and fairness (1:3). Here there is no direct critique of the monarchy. That critique remains until later (30:1-9; see also 29:4, 14; cf. Deut 17:14-20). The primary check on the monarchy, however, resides with Yahweh who has the final say (16:1-9; 21:1). Ultimately the same requirements placed on humans are also placed on kings (16:1-9).

¹⁶**How much better to get wisdom than gold,**
    to choose understanding rather than silver!
¹⁷**The highway of the upright avoids evil;**
    he who guards his way guards his life.
¹⁸**Pride goes before destruction,**
    a haughty spirit before a fall.
¹⁹**Better to be lowly in spirit and among the oppressed**
    than to share plunder with the proud.

16:16-17 The first two proverbs echo two common themes found in the book of Proverbs. First is that of getting **wisdom**, which takes priority over everything else that humans acquire. Second is choosing the right path to follow. Verses 16 and 17 reflect the instruction literature of chapters 1–9. According to the Masoretes, these verses stand as the middle verses in the book of Proverbs. They also serve to remind the reader of what is central in life.

16:18-19 Here we have a proverb pair, both dealing with a pervasive concern of the sage: **pride**. The theme of pride is woven throughout the previous material in this chapter (15:33; 16:2,5). Verse 18a may originally have been an independent saying. It has been popularized in English, "Pride goes before a fall." The saying confirms the short-lived nature of success for the wicked.

Next is a block of sayings in which the sage acknowledges the power of words. This cluster illuminates the persuasiveness of words constructively. Duane Garrett concludes, "The overall thrust of this text is that wise teachers choose their words carefully and in so doing enhance the learning experience for their students."[62]

[20]Whoever gives heed to instruction prospers,
     and blessed is he who trusts in the LORD.
[21]The wise in heart are called discerning,
     and pleasant words promote instruction.[a]
[22]Understanding is a fountain of life to those who have it,
     but folly brings punishment to fools.
[23]A wise man's heart guides his mouth,
     and his lips promote instruction.[b]
[24]Pleasant words are a honeycomb,
     sweet to the soul and healing to the bones.

[a]*21 Or words make a man persuasive*   [b]*23 Or mouth / and makes his lips persuasive*

16:20 This verse sets the tone for what follows. Whose **instruction** is referred to in the first line, the sage's or God's? It is difficult to know. Usually in Proverbs, such instruction refers to the sages (see 13:13). Because of 20b and the description of the one who **trusts in the LORD**, the referent in the first line may be Yahweh. In Proverbs, the instruction of the sage and of God are closely connected.

16:21 Another possible translation of this verse is, "The thoughtful sage will be called perceptive, and sweetness of lips will increase persuasiveness."[63] The NRSV, NASB, and the Jerusalem Bible all translate the Hebrew word לָקַח (*lāqaḥ*) here and in verse 23 as "persuasiveness." The NIV translates it **promote instruction** (יֹסִיף לֶקַח, *yôsîph leqaḥ*). Whatever phrase one chooses, the idea is that the sage finds attractive ways to entice the listener to learn. The **wise** person does not simply throw out ideas but discovers ways of making those ideas rhetorically appealing.

16:22-24 Two images are used in these verses to highlight the rhetorical power of **words**: honey and a well (or spring) of life. Both honey and water are vital sources of health for the body. In like manner, prudent words are a source of health for the community. Like

---

[62]Garrett, *Proverbs, Ecclesiastes, Song of Songs*, p. 157.
[63]BDB translate the second line of verse 21 as "sweetness of lips increaseth persuasiveness," p. 544.

honey dripping from a **honeycomb, pleasant** words drip onto the hearer (v. 24). Because of its context in 16:20-24, the image of a **fountain** or well **of life** in verse 22 becomes a reference to the persuasive power of words: prudent speech is a well of life. **Soul** in verse 24 is a reference to a person's appetite.[64] The phrase **sweet to the soul** pertains to the satisfaction that appropriate words bring to a person.

The significance of the cluster in verses 20-24 is discovered in its holistic perspective on how words and sayings influence the self and others. First, truly effective words flow from a mind that is prudent and thoughtful (vv. 21,23). These words have substance and are able to offer guidance and instruction. Second, speech that is effective is pleasant. There is an aesthetic quality to it. This quality arises from the way in which it is formulated. The style and structure of a proverb witnesses to how words can be artfully constructed into an attractive form. In addition, their aesthetic quality stems from their appropriateness to the particular situation and individual. Finally, speech that is effective persuades. It is capable of bringing about change in others. This text affirms that when words have substance to them and are aesthetically shaped to create pleasure, their persuasive power increases.

²⁵**There is a way that seems right to a man,**
　　　but in the end it leads to death.
²⁶**The laborer's appetite works for him;**
　　　his hunger drives him on.
²⁷**A scoundrel plots evil,**
　　　and his speech is like a scorching fire.
²⁸**A perverse man stirs up dissension,**
　　　and a gossip separates close friends.
²⁹**A violent man entices his neighbor**
　　　and leads him down a path that is not good.
³⁰**He who winks with his eye is plotting perversity;**
　　　he who purses his lips is bent on evil.

16:25 This proverb is a duplicate of 14:12. According to some scholars, the duplicate proverbs indicate a transition or seam in the proverb collection. In this instance, it is difficult to see any transition in the collection.

---

[64]In verse 26, the NIV translates "soul" as "appetite."

16:26 The first line uses a word play to make a simple observation: the **appetite** of the worker **works for him**. Though the proverb is simply an observation, it carries many implications. The proverb may imply the power of greed; it may also imply the futility of work.

16:27-30 These proverbs form a distinct group. The text is a structural unit. Each line of verses 27-29 begins with the Hebrew word for "man" (אִישׁ, 'îš). In the first line of each verse, the second word is a negative modifier used to describe the man: "scoundrel," "perverse," "violent." Further, each verse is held together by a common theme: the malicious use of speech. They create a contrast to the healing words of the wise described in verses 20-24. The text has similarities with the catalog of vices mentioned in 6:16-19. It also has a number of similarities in vocabulary to 6:12-15.

In verse 27, the Hebrew text literally says of the **scoundrel** that he "digs evil." The phrase is quite unusual because one is typically described as digging a well but not digging evil. Here is a person devoted to destroying the life of the community. Verse 28 declares that **the perverse man** through his speech intends to upset friendships. Finally, the **violent man** (v. 29), through well-crafted words, persuades his friend to follow a life of injustice. What such persons say is described in more detail in 1:11-14. This is the first of the "**not good**" proverbs found in the sentence literature (see 19:2). The term appears to be a euphemism (in this case an understatement) for behavior that is disgusting or deplorable. The "not good" act is something abominable done to another fellow human.

Verse 30 may be a summary description of the evil person. Certain outward signs identify the malicious person. There are subtle and deceitful gestures, such as the winking of the eye, that indicate bad character. Youth must be alert to such signs (see also 6:13; 10:10).

³¹**Gray hair is a crown of splendor;**
   it is attained by a righteous life.
³²**Better a patient man than a warrior,**
   a man who controls his temper than one who takes a city.
³³**The lot is cast into the lap,**
   but its every decision is from the LORD.

16:31 The consensus of the sages is that wisdom comes with the experiences of life. And the longer one lives the more one attains those experiences. Thus **gray hair**, a symbol of old age, indicates a time in life when much wisdom has been accumulated. However, the sages were also aware that "there's no fool like an old fool" (Eccl 4:13). Wisdom does not automatically come with age. Wisdom **is attained by a righteous life.**

16:32 Once again, this proverb identifies a fundamental quality of wisdom, self-control. The term **patient** is literally "long of nose" (a Hebrew idiom for one who is slow to anger). This is another better-than proverb. Such proverbs usually contrast the internal with the external. This proverb is no exception. Private conquest of self is more valuable than public conquest of a **city**. The person who **controls** self has accomplished more than the one who controls others.

16:33 The final verse in this chapter echoes the very first verse. It also ties in to verse 9. The use of lots (some type of dice) is common all through Scripture. Israel chose Saul, her first king, by **lot** (1 Sam 10:17-27). After the conquest, the land was divided by lot (Num 26:55). The early church used lots to decide who would be the next apostle (Acts 1:26). The belief was that **the LORD** determines the plans of mortals. And it is the LORD who decides the outcome of the lots cast.

Chapter 17 contains several recurring thoughts. The most common thread woven here addresses the nature of the fool (vv. 2,7,10, 12,16,18,21,24,25,28). In addition, as is the case throughout the sentence literature, there is the theme of the family (vv. 1,2,6,21,25).

[17:1]**Better a dry crust with peace and quiet**
    than a house full of feasting,[a] with strife.
[2]**A wise servant will rule over a disgraceful son,**
    and will share the inheritance as one of the brothers.
[3]**The crucible for silver and the furnace for gold,**
    but the LORD tests the heart.

[a]*1 Hebrew sacrifices*

17:1 This better-than saying is quite similar to 15:17. It sets up a stark contrast between **a dry crust** of bread and a sumptuous feast. The bread was dry because the family was too poor to afford olive oil in which to dip the dry crust (cf. 19:24). On the other hand, a wealthy family has **a house full of feasting. Feasting with strife** is literally "sacrifices of strife" (זִבְחֵי־רִיב, *zibḥê-rîb*) and may refer to the meat offered at religious feasts. So here is a wealthy family who maintains the public image of religiosity all the while being privately embroiled in conflict. This image is played out in the oracle Amos preaches against the wealthy women of Samaria (see Amos 4:1-3). Van Leeuwen summarizes the picture: "Perhaps the religious activity and conspicuous consumption are a cover for family dysfunction."[65]

17:2 This verse undermines conventional customs regarding family. As strong as family ties are, wisdom has the power to transcend traditions of family inheritance. Wisdom is "thicker than blood." The proverb serves also as a warning to lazy or irresponsible sons: Do not take inheritance for granted.

17:3 This saying serves as a good example of the flexibility of proverbs. Proverbs were not simply committed to memory and then quoted verbatim. The two-line structure of the proverb ideally equips it for adaptation to different circumstances.[66] The first line of verse 3 is changed in 21:2, and in 27:21 its second line is changed. This "overlapping" phenomenon suggests that proverbs are designed for use in specific contexts. Thus the proverb user must be flexible as well as responsible in proverb use (see 10:6-7).

The content of verse 3 describes a process of purification that God puts his people through. The LORD not only sits as judge over a person's actions but also as the one who can bring about change in character. The process, which usually involves adversity, is referred to all through Scripture (see Job 23:10; 1 Pet 1:7).

[4]**A wicked man listens to evil lips;**
      a liar pays attention to a malicious tongue.
[5]**He who mocks the poor shows contempt for their Maker;**
      whoever gloats over disaster will not go unpunished.
[6]**Children's children are a crown to the aged,**
      and parents are the pride of their children.
[7]**Arrogant[a] lips are unsuited to a fool—**
      how much worse lying lips to a ruler!

[a]7 Or *Eloquent*

---

[65]Van Leeuwen, "Proverbs," p. 166.
[66]See Dave Bland, "Rhetorical Perspective on the Sentence Sayings of the Book of Proverbs," diss., University of Washington (1994), pp. 130ff.

17:4-7 Verse 5 expresses a fundamental principle of godly life, and that is that all humans, even those like the poor who seem the least worthy, deserve respect. That respect is based on the belief that the LORD created every human being. The phrase, **will not go unpunished** (occurs seven times; 6:29; 11:21; 16:5; 17:5; 19:5,9; 28:20), is central to the description of God in Exodus 34:6-7. It implies the presence of God.

The Hebrew syntax of verse 6 is "the crown of old age: sons of sons; the glory of sons: parents." The proverb implies interdependence between the generations. There is mutual respect that the younger and older have for each other. God intends individuals to find fulfillment within the family. Such fulfillment is described as a **crown** and **pride** (or "glory"). Yet the opposite is also true. One can receive grief and bitterness (see v. 25).

There is an intensification in the proverb of verse 7 as one moves from the first to the second line: If **arrogant lips are unsuited to a fool**, then **how much worse** (כִּי אַף, 'aph kî, a phrase of intensification) is a **ruler** who lies. The phrase in the first line, "arrogant lips," is literally "lips of surplus" or "lips of excellence." The NRSV renders the phrase a little clearer with "fine speech." Articulate language is not suited (נָאוֶה, nā'weh) to a fool. Elsewhere the NIV translates the word "unsuited" as "unfitting" (19:10; 26:1). If eloquent speech does not fit a fool, how much less of a fit is a leader who lies to his followers!

⁸**A bribe is a charm to the one who gives it;**
    wherever he turns, he succeeds.
⁹**He who covers over an offense promotes love,**
    but whoever repeats the matter separates close friends.
¹⁰**A rebuke impresses a man of discernment**
    more than a hundred lashes a fool.

17:8-10 Several proverbs speak favorably of concealing certain attitudes or actions (e.g., 12:23). In verse 9, the student is called on to **cover over an offense**. Such concealment is in the interest of **love** for a friend. Yet notice 27:5, where open rebuke is favored over hidden love. Again, this demonstrates the situational nature of proverbs. A friend (אַלּוּף, 'allûph) does not dwell on the faults of others. Verse 9 has close affinities to 10:12, where love calls on one to cover over offenses. Clifford concludes, ". . . one finds love by losing and loses love by finding or revealing."[67]

The word for **impresses** (תֵּחַת, *tēḥath*) in verse 10 means to go under or deeper. The act of rebuking is mentioned more often in Proverbs than in any other Old Testament book. The word used here (גְּעָרָה, *gᵊʿārāh*), however, is different than the typical one used (תּוֹכַחַת, *tôkaḥath*). Those who are wise need to be told only once: "a word to the wise is sufficient." In contrast, the characteristic of the **fool** is obstinacy. **A hundred lashes** is obviously a hyperbole. The sages advocated corporal punishment in the context of love (see comments on 13:24). They also realized that such punishment had limits and was not even the preferred form to use.

[11]**An evil man is bent only on rebellion;**
      a merciless official will be sent against him.
[12]**Better to meet a bear robbed of her cubs**
      than a fool in his folly.
[13]**If a man pays back evil for good,**
      evil will never leave his house.
[14]**Starting a quarrel is like breaching a dam;**
      so drop the matter before a dispute breaks out.
[15]**Acquitting the guilty and condemning the innocent—**
      the LORD detests them both.

17:11 Many of the proverbs in verses 11-15 address the subject of conflict. The Hebrew word for **rebellion** (מְרִי, *mᵊrî*) in verse 11 is almost always used to refer to rebellion against God, thus a person is evil because of rebellion against God. The verb **bent** is in the intensive form. Coupled with the emphatic word **only** (אַךְ, *ʾak*) that begins the sentence in Hebrew, the picture is of the intensity of one whose sole purpose is to rebel against God. The second line states the punishment for such a person.

17:12 A bear robbed of her cubs is a metaphor for a type of fury that leads to destruction. What is even worse than this kind of fury is spending time with a **fool**. The hidden damage a fool inflicts does more harm than the damage done by a natural disaster. This proverb issues a most intense statement about the effects of associating with

---

[67]Clifford, *Proverbs*, p. 165.

a fool. One might say that experiencing the folly of a fool is worse than being the victim of road rage.

17:13 Returning **evil for good** is strictly forbidden in the Old Testament. In fact, God's people are called on to do just the opposite, to return good for evil (see 25:21-22).

17:14 Two words are used for quarreling in this proverb. One is more common in Proverbs, מָדוֹן (mādôn, **quarrel**). The other was used earlier in verse 1, רִיב (rîb, "strife"; **dispute**). The latter is a legal term and implies that the dispute could lead to a court fight. Quarreling is a major enemy of the community. Like water, it erodes the foundations upon which relationships exist. It undercuts the mutual respect necessary to hold a people together.

17:15 Underlying the words for **guilty** and **innocent** is one Hebrew word, "righteous" (צַדִּיק, ṣaddîq). The term in this context has legal rather than theological connotations. The NRSV confuses the point by translating the words as "justice" and "righteousness." The NIV clarifies the meaning of the word by successively translating it "guilty" and "innocent." One who acquits the guilty and condemns the innocent is an "abomination" to the LORD (NIV **detests**).

¹⁶**Of what use is money in the hand of a fool,**
    since he has no desire to get wisdom?
¹⁷**A friend loves at all times,**
    and a brother is born for adversity.
¹⁸**A man lacking in judgment strikes hands in pledge**
    and puts up security for his neighbor.
¹⁹**He who loves a quarrel loves sin;**
    he who builds a high gate invites destruction.
²⁰**A man of perverse heart does not prosper;**
    he whose tongue is deceitful falls into trouble.

17:16 The **fool** thinks that he can buy **wisdom** with **money**. But no amount of money can attain wisdom when the fool **has no desire** (lit., "no mind"; לֵב, lēb). That is, the fool does not use his mind; no personal effort is put into attaining knowledge or wisdom. Some scholars use this proverb to prove that there were schools in Israel. Is this an indirect reference to schools? Or is it simply an assertion that wisdom cannot be bought? Elsewhere, youth are exhorted to "buy" wisdom (23:23), meaning that they are to pursue it with all their effort. Sadly, fools misunderstand the metaphor and take it literally.

17:17 The question with this proverb has to do with the parallelism. Are the two lines antithetic or synonymous? The *waw* (ו) conjunction can be translated either "and" or "but." Is there a contrast in this proverb between the **friend** and the **brother**? A friend loves all through life, "but" when one is in a crisis, call on a brother. Or are "friend" and "brother" used synonymously? If so, then "brother" is an intensification of "friend." A friend is always faithful "and" especially so in times of crisis. This second option seems more favorable, which appears to be the position of the NIV. This proverb raises the status of the friend (or "neighbor") to that of the same level as kinship, which in ancient Israel was the highest of the support systems (see 27:10).

17:18 This proverb is connected with the previous one by the catchword "friend" or **neighbor**. (The word is the same in the Hebrew text.) Not offering **security** to a neighbor is not an indication of selfishness.[68] To engage in such a venture was a precarious business practice that jeopardized the security of one's own family. Going surety (making a **pledge**) indicated a lack of forethought. That did not, however, relieve one of one's responsibilities to the neighbor. Verse 17 serves as a check on the person in verse 18 who might use the admonition against going surety as an excuse for not helping the neighbor, especially in times of crisis. See comments on 6:1-5 for the meaning of "pledge" and the practice of surety.

17:19 The question in this verse is, to what does the image **high gate** refer in the second line? The phrase appears to refer to the opening of a door. The threshold of a door that is too high will cause people to stumble. The metaphor means that if an owner raises the threshold of the house too high, people will trip over it and get hurt. The NRSV clarifies the meaning, "one who builds a high threshold invites broken bones." The image is applied to the person who looks for a **quarrel**.

²¹**To have a fool for a son brings grief;**
    there is no joy for the father of a fool.
²²**A cheerful heart is good medicine,**
    but a crushed spirit dries up the bones.

[68]See Andreas Scherer, "Is the Selfish Man Wise? Considerations of Context in Proverbs 10:1–22:16 with Special Regard to Surety, Bribery and Friendship," *JSOT* 76 (December 1997): 59-70.

²³**A wicked man accepts a bribe in secret**
    to pervert the course of justice.
²⁴**A discerning man keeps wisdom in view,**
    but a fool's eyes wander to the ends of the earth.
²⁵**A foolish son brings grief to his father**
    and bitterness to the one who bore him.

17:21 This verse is another one of the many household proverbs sprinkled throughout the sentence literature and is a variant of 10:1. It gives a contrasting image to that found earlier in verse 6. In a shame and honor society, the larger community was well aware of the **joy** and the **grief** that children brought to their parents.

17:22 This verse closely ties with 14:30 and 15:13. The sage knew that the internal psyche has the power to heal as well as to destroy the body. One's internal demeanor affects physical, mental, spiritual, and emotional health.[69] The wise have a holistic view of the individual.

17:23 Bribery is condemned, but gift-giving is not. To give a gift in some cultures is not only customary but socially mandated. There is a difference between giving a gift out of politeness, or for the sake of hastening along the social/political process, and bribery, which results in injustices (see 18:16).

17:24-25 The wise person's goals are in focus as described in verse 24. The fool cannot concentrate; he has a short attention span. According to verse 25, **foolish** children bring grief and suffering to both **father** and mother. Both parents have a stake in a child's welfare. Both hurt when a child chooses a different path.

²⁶**It is not good to punish an innocent man,**
    or to flog officials for their integrity.
²⁷**A man of knowledge uses words with restraint,**
    and a man of understanding is even-tempered.
²⁸**Even a fool is thought wise if he keeps silent,**
    and discerning if he holds his tongue.

17:26-28 As a proverb pair, verses 27 and 28 describe the quality of self-control when it comes to the use of words. The idea in the first line of verse 27 is that the one whose thought is clear uses few words to express it. The second line contains an unusual Hebrew

---

[69]גֵּהָה, *gēhāh*, "medicine," is a *hapax legomenon* (a word used only once).

phrase "cool of spirit" (קַר־רוּחַ, *qar-rûaḥ*), which the NIV translates **even-tempered**. The person who is "cool" is opposite of the "heated" one. Verse 28 suggests that silence is the first step towards wisdom. Van Leeuwen observes a pedagogical irony here in this proverb, "if you are a fool, at least act wise by keeping silent."[70] Mental and verbal restraint are qualities of wisdom.

Chapter 18 contains a variety of aphorisms that speak to a variety of subjects. One of the most prominent subjects is the fool. In addition, a number of proverbs offer advice about speaking and listening. A few sayings give attention to strife and quarreling.

[18:1]**An unfriendly man pursues selfish ends;**
        he defies all sound judgment.
[2]**A fool finds no pleasure in understanding**
        but delights in airing his own opinions.
[3]**When wickedness comes, so does contempt,**
        and with shame comes disgrace.
[4]**The words of a man's mouth are deep waters,**
        but the fountain of wisdom is a bubbling brook.

18:1 The saying in verse 1 is difficult to translate. As such, a reader will find quite a variety of meanings when comparing English translations. The NIV translates the Hebrew word פָּרַד (*pārad*, "to separate") as **unfriendly**, understanding it to refer to a person who removes him or herself from others. Literally the Hebrew text reads, "a separated person seeks his own desire." The sense is of one who goes his or her own way. Such a person does not acknowledge the value of community.

The second line intensifies the first and describes "the separated one" as breaking out against conventional wisdom. As the NIV puts it, **he defies all sound judgment** (תוּשִׁיָּה, *tûśîyāh*, or "sound wisdom"; see 2:7; 3:21; 8:14; 18:1 for use of this same phrase). The description is of persons who isolate themselves from the community because they do not need the insights or understanding of others. They are sufficient unto themselves. Clifford translates the verse, "An estranged person seeks his own will, rails against wisdom."[71] He concludes

---

[70]Van Leeuwen, "Proverbs," p. 169.
[71]Clifford, *Proverbs*, p. 168.

that ". . . excessive devotion to one's own ideas is an obstacle to prudent decision making."[72]

18:2 Verse 2 expresses a similar idea to that of the previous verse. Fools take delight in hearing themselves talk (lit., "expressing his heart"). Contrary to popular belief, wisdom is not primarily gained through meditation but through interaction with the wisdom of others.

18:3 In some ways, this saying seems to engage in overkill. Three words overlap in meaning: **contempt** (בּוּז, *bûz*); **shame** (קָלוֹן, *qālôn*); and **disgrace** (חֶרְפָּה, *ḥerpāh*). **Wickedness** and "shame" have the same results: a loss of respect.

18:4 The relationship between the two lines of this proverb is a factor in determining its meaning. Are they antithetic or synonymous? If antithetic, then the image of **deep waters** is negative. The image refers to that which is incomprehensible or stagnant. So a person pours forth words that are worthless. In contrast, the one who has wisdom **is a bubbling brook**. If the parallelism is synonymous, then the image of deep waters is positive. A wise person speaks profound words. Therefore, such wisdom is a bubbling brook. The second line intensifies the first. Wisdom is a constant source of refreshment. The NIV favors the first alternative. It adds the conjunction **but** at the beginning of the second line to show that there is a contrast. However, no conjunction appears in the Hebrew text. In light of the way the same phrase, "deep waters," is used in 20:5, it seems more reasonable to interpret it as a positive image and the parallelism as synonymous (cf. also 27:19).

⁵**It is not good to be partial to the wicked**
      or to deprive the innocent of justice.
⁶**A fool's lips bring him strife,**
      and his mouth invites a beating.
⁷**A fool's mouth is his undoing,**
      and his lips are a snare to his soul.
⁸**The words of a gossip are like choice morsels;**
      they go down to a man's inmost parts.
⁹**One who is slack in his work**
      is brother to one who destroys.

---

[72]Ibid., p. 170.

18:5 This is one of the **not good** sayings found in the proverb collection (see 19:2; also 16:29; 17:26; 24:23). **To be partial** translates the Hebrew phrase "to lift up the face." The gesture of lifting up the bowed head of another implied an act of pardon or forgiveness (see also 24:23a and 28:21a). Partiality was condemned in the law (Lev 19:15; Deut 1:17; cf. Prov 17:15).

18:6-7 This proverbial pair emphasizes the damage words do, not so much to others but to the self. A **fool's lips** and **mouth** result in unceasing trouble. It reminds one of the description of the tongue in James 3. **Soul** in verse 7 is simply another word for the person or the individual. It has nothing to do with an eternal component residing within an individual.

18:8 This same proverb is duplicated in 26:22. **Gossip** is compared to junk food. It is quite tasty. Nonetheless when absorbed into the blood stream, it remains a permanent part of the person. Once absorbed, it destroys character.

18:9 One who is slack in his work refers to the sluggard (see 6:6-11; 26:13-16). The proverb belongs to the large family of gnomic sayings that condemn laziness. The proverb is quite emphatic in associating indolence with one who destroys. Simply by negligence, individuals bring harm to the community. The counterpart of this saying calls individuals to use the gifts that God has given them for the good of others.

[10]The name of the LORD is a strong tower;
　　the righteous run to it and are safe.
[11]The wealth of the rich is their fortified city;
　　they imagine it an unscalable wall.
[12]Before his downfall a man's heart is proud,
　　but humility comes before honor.
[13]He who answers before listening—
　　that is his folly and his shame.
[14]A man's spirit sustains him in sickness,
　　but a crushed spirit who can bear?
[15]The heart of the discerning acquires knowledge;
　　the ears of the wise seek it out.

18:10-11 These two proverbs are held together by the catchword שָׂגַב (sāgab), which means "to be exalted" or "to be high." The NIV translates the word **safe** in verse 10 and **unscalable** in verse 11. The

169

two verses are also tied together by a similar military image: **strong tower** and **fortified city**. They are a good example of "conflicting" proverbs being placed side-by-side (cf. 26:4,5).[73]

The pair contrasts trust in God with trust in **wealth**. The phrase, **the name of the LORD**, appears only here in Proverbs. In contrast to the **righteous** putting their trust in the LORD, the wealthy put their confidence in their riches. They only **imagine** that it is their security. There is some debate over the translation of מַשְׂכִּית (maśkîth) as "imagination." The RSV renders the second line, "and like a high wall protecting him." If one goes with the RSV, then verse 10 contrasts verse 11. If one stays with the NIV translation, then verse 10 affirms verse 11. In both cases, the message is that God is the only one who provides ultimate and long lasting security.

18:12 The first line of the proverb overlaps with 16:18. The second line is identical to 15:33b. The proverbs were quite flexible in their use. They adjust to fit the occasion (see 10:5-6; 17:3).

18:13 The one **who answers before listening** does not regard the value of others' insights. Such a person is a fool. Wisdom is gained in mutual dialogue with another. Some understand the origin of this proverb to be in a legal setting. However, it has broader application than just to a court in Israel. Though oftentimes their images reflect a specific context, proverbs were seldom confined to a single setting.

18:14 Once again, here is a "psychological" saying. Earlier similar sayings include 15:13 and 17:22 (cf. also 12:25). In these types of proverbs, the contrast is usually between a cheerful heart and a **crushed spirit**. Here the contrast is simply between a **spirit** and a crushed spirit. The former likely implies a healthy spirit, a reference to one's mental attitude.

18:15 Two parts of the body are necessary for **the discerning** or the "understanding one" (נָבוֹן, nābôn) to acquire wisdom (wisdom and **knowledge** overlap in meaning in the sage's dictionary). One is the **heart** (or "the mind," the inner organ of reception). The other is the **ears** (the outer organs of reception). The "listening ear" is another term for the sapient (see 1 Kgs 3:9).

---

[73]Whybray says that verse 10 is an example of a Yahweh proverb commenting on an adjacent "secular" proverb (v. 11), *Proverbs*, p. 268.

Some view this next group as clustered around the legal context of the law court. Even if this is the case, these proverbs have broader application than just with the legal system.

> [16]A gift opens the way for the giver
>   and ushers him into the presence of the great.
> [17]The first to present his case seems right,
>   till another comes forward and questions him.
> [18]Casting the lot settles disputes
>   and keeps strong opponents apart.
> [19]An offended brother is more unyielding than a fortified city,
>   and disputes are like the barred gates of a citadel.

18:16 The question is: is this offering a bribe or a **gift**? If it is a bribe, then the proverb is only making an observation. It describes the positive effects of a bribe without moral evaluation. It **ushers him into the presence of the great.** If the offering is a gift, then the proverb implies an admonition.

It may be that there are different kinds of bribes. There is the kind that is a deceptive gift, which corrupts the process of justice. There is also the gift that is given for the sake of social etiquette or for the sake of accomplishing a worthy purpose (see also 17:8,23 and 21:14).

18:19 The RSV follows the LXX and translates the phrase in the first line, "A brother helped is like a strong city." The problem centers on how the word **offended** (נִפְשָׁע, *niphšā‘*) is understood. It appears to refer to someone who has been snubbed or hurt.[74] Thus the NIV appropriately translates it as **an offended brother.** The second line of the proverb expands the first: once a friend is offended it is like trying to break down **the barred gates of a citadel.** Clifford translates it, "A brother offended is more unyielding than a fortified city; such quarrels are more daunting than castle gates."[75] The general meaning is that it is more difficult to repair the relationship of a friend who has been offended than to conquer a city (cf. 16:32).

> [20]From the fruit of his mouth a man's stomach is filled;
>   with the harvest from his lips he is satisfied.
> [21]The tongue has the power of life and death,
>   and those who love it will eat its fruit.

---

[74]McKane, *Proverbs,* p. 520.
[75]Clifford, *Proverbs,* p. 169.

²²**He who finds a wife finds what is good**
    and receives favor from the LORD.
²³**A poor man pleads for mercy,**
    but a rich man answers harshly.
²⁴**A man of many companions may come to ruin,**
    but there is a friend who sticks closer than a brother.

18:20-21 This proverb pair describes the power of the organs of speech: **mouth, lips,** and **tongue** (see 10:18-21).

18:22 The first line of the proverb appears to be a popular saying based on its structure: **find a wife, find good.** The first line describes the human responsibility or role to find. The second line intensifies the first and describes the LORD's role: **and receives favor from the LORD.** Both the human and the divine are involved in finding a good spouse (see 19:14). How they work together to do this, the sages never say. It is simply assumed. As 16:9 affirms, "In his heart a man plans his course, but the LORD determines his steps." No explanation is needed.

18:23 The saying offers an observation about the **poor** and the **rich.** This Proverb reveals that one's speech betrays one's social class.

18:24 The first line of this proverb is unclear. The Hebrew begins, "a man of friends."[76] The root meaning of the last verb in the first line, **may come to ruin,** is "to break" (רָעַע, rā'a').[77] It is also possible that the root means "to associate with" (רָעָה, rā'āh).[78] Clifford translates it, "There are friends who spend time with you."[79]

Regardless of the decision one makes in translating the first line, there is an obvious contrast between the first and second lines. In the first line, **companions** is plural. In the second line, **friend** (אֹהֵב, 'ōheb; "he who loves") is singular. The contrast is between casual friends on the one hand and a close friend on the other; it is a contrast between the appearance of friendship and real friendship. The **friend who sticks** (דָּבַק, dābaq) **closer than a brother** reminds one of

---

[76]Some would like to emend the text to read יֵשׁ (yēš, "there is") rather than אִישׁ ('îš, "man"). Thus the RSV reads, "There are friends." But such emendation is not necessary.
[77]See BDB, p. 950.
[78]Ibid., p. 946.
[79]Clifford, *Proverbs*, p. 169.

the story of Ruth, who "clings" (*dābaq*) to Naomi. The friend/neighbor took on new meaning for the Jews during the postexilic period when the clan (extended families with a common ancestor) no longer lived in close proximity. A neighbor became more important than even a brother for the sake of support and moral development of the community (see 27:10).

[19:1]**Better a poor man whose walk is blameless**
        than a fool whose lips are perverse.
[2]**It is not good to have zeal without knowledge,**
        nor to be hasty and miss the way.
[3]**A man's own folly ruins his life,**
        yet his heart rages against the LORD.

19:1 This is a better-than saying which simply compares the **poor** who walks in integrity and the **fool** who lives by lying. One would expect a reference to a rich man in the second line to parallel the poor man in the first line. Because of that and because of a parallel proverb in 28:6, some would emend the text to read "rich man" rather than a fool.[80] Such emendation is not necessary to make sense of the proverb.

19:2 Here is another **not good** proverb (for others see 16:29; 17:26; 18:5; 20:23; 25:27; 28:21). The **not good** proverbs relate to a dominant wisdom theme woven throughout Proverbs which has to do with what is or is not appropriate. What is inappropriate is to possess **zeal without knowledge**. The word נֶפֶשׁ (*nepheš*, "soul") is used here in a special sense to refer to a person's desire or energy or appetite.[81] The NIV translates it "zeal."[82] Zeal or enthusiasm must ground itself in reflective thought. Otherwise one engages in activism that has no reality base. Such a person is like chaff blown about by the wind (Ps 1:4). Enthusiasm without understanding is misguided.

Line two intensifies the first line: **nor to be hasty and miss the way**. The Hebrew text reads, "feet that hasten, miss the mark."

---

[80]Ibid., p. 174.

[81]See 16:24,26; 21:10; 23:2; and 24:14 where נֶפֶשׁ is used in this sense. In 28:25 there is reference to the greedy man, literally the one who has "a wide soul." Clifford is correct in translating the word "throat," *Proverbs*, pp. 176, 193, 196, 215, 247. See H. Seebass, "נֶפֶשׁ," *TDOT*, p. 504ff.

[82]The RSV inappropriately translates נֶפֶשׁ as man.

"Haste" is highly suspect in wisdom's list of vices (cf. 20:25; 21:5; 28:20; 29:20). The two lines complement each other. Line one speaks of the inner desires (soul) and thoughts. Line two speaks of the outer actions (feet). When internal desires and external actions are not informed by reflective thought (wisdom), they will not achieve their goals. This is a fitting proverb for an anti-intellectual climate, which sometimes exists in the church (cf. also 17:16).

19:3 One of the marks of a fool is that he blames others, especially God, for the mess that he has made of his own **life**. Here the foolish man **rages against the LORD**. The lament psalms often express anger against God. However, this proverb does not speak to the righteous who cry out, but to the fool.

⁴**Wealth brings many friends,**
　　but a poor man's friend deserts him.
⁵**A false witness will not go unpunished,**
　　and he who pours out lies will not go free.
⁶**Many curry favor with a ruler,**
　　and everyone is the friend of a man who gives gifts.
⁷**A poor man is shunned by all his relatives—**
　　how much more do his friends avoid him!
Though he pursues them with pleading,
　　they are nowhere to be found.ᵃ
⁸**He who gets wisdom loves his own soul;**
　　he who cherishes understanding prospers.
⁹**A false witness will not go unpunished,**
　　and he who pours out lies will perish.

ᵃ**7 The meaning of the Hebrew for this sentence is uncertain.**

19:4 Verses 4,6, and 7 focus on the relationship between wealth and friendship. Verse 4 asserts that **wealth brings many friends**. In contrast, the one friend the **poor man** has will leave him. Note the intentional contrast between "many friends" and a single "friend" (cf. 18:24). Though the proverb simply makes an observation, its subtle intention is to side with the poor. It also warns the rich to practice caution in identifying those who are their true friends.

19:5 In the oral culture in which Israel lived, giving true testimony was a matter of grave importance. Here is a proverb that speaks of the character-consequence sequence that dominates chapters

10-15. The **false witness** will receive his just deserts. The phrase **not go unpunished** is used to describe the nature of God in Israel's creedal statement in Exodus 34:6-7. It is possible that the punishment envisioned in the proverb will come from the LORD himself (see 17:5).

19:6-7 The first line of verse 6 in the Hebrew text reads, "many will entreat/appease the face of a noble." The phrase carries with it a nuance of flattery. The proverb is an indirect reproof of those who, out of self-interest, seek out the rich.

Verse 7 follows closely in thought, only coming from the angle of the **poor**. If a poor person's family shuns him, **how much more** will a friend distance himself! It is a proverb of intensification. The plural **friends** in the NIV is singular in the Hebrew text (cf. v. 4b). This is the only three-line proverb in chapters 10:1–22:16. As such some scholars believe it is a later addition. The NIV makes the second sentence part of the first line, thus avoiding three lines to the proverb.

19:8 He who gets wisdom is literally "he who acquires heart." The heart or mind is one of the main storehouses of wisdom. Such a person **loves his own soul**. "Soul" (*nephesh*) is simply another word for the self. Acquiring wisdom leads to a genuine respect of self. Such individuals are good stewards of what God has given them. The second line affirms the first: **he who cherishes understanding prospers**. This proverb acknowledges a character-consequence scenario to life: One who seeks wisdom will succeed (see chapters 10–15).

19:9 This verse is a duplicate of verse 5.

¹⁰It is not fitting for a fool to live in luxury—
>   how much worse for a slave to rule over princes!
¹¹A man's wisdom gives him patience;
>   it is to his glory to overlook an offense.
¹²A king's rage is like the roar of a lion,
>   but his favor is like dew on the grass.

19:10 In line with the sages' concern for doing that which is appropriate, this proverb speaks of what is **not fitting** (see also 17:7 and 26:1). The proverb is also a first cousin to the "not good" proverbs (see verse 2 above). The proverb employs the common "less to greater" argument. If a fool is out of place living in luxury, then **how much worse for a slave to rule over princes!** Though the specific images used here relate to a monarchic society, by design the proverb is intended to be adapted to other contexts. Wherever honor and position are bestowed on those who do not deserve it, this proverb speaks a word.

19:11 Literally, "a prudent man is slow to anger, and his glory is to pass over (עָבַר, *ʿābar*) a transgression." The NIV captures the meaning of the proverb. The second line expands on the first by insisting that it is to a person's credit to **overlook an offense**. This thought is quite similar to that of 10:12 and 17:9 where the seeker of wisdom is called on to "cover over" an offense that he has experienced. The proverb does not refer to continuing sin that a person engages in, or to a criminal act. This proverb is suitable advice for the quarrelsome man (26:21) and the quarrelsome woman (19:13). One gains respect by not being contentious.

19:12 The first line of the proverb overlaps with 20:2a. The second line overlaps with 16:15b. The proverb offers an observation about the king that also serves as a warning to his subjects.

¹³**A foolish son is his father's ruin,**
and a quarrelsome wife is like a constant dripping.
¹⁴**Houses and wealth are inherited from parents,**
but a prudent wife is from the LORD.
¹⁵**Laziness brings on deep sleep,**
and the shiftless man goes hungry.
¹⁶**He who obeys instructions guards his life,**
but he who is contemptuous of his ways will die.
¹⁷**He who is kind to the poor lends to the LORD,**
and he will reward him for what he has done.

19:13-14 The proverbs come from a male perspective because that is the primary audience being addressed. The image in verse 13 depicts a dysfunctional home environment. The two main sources of domestic strife in Proverbs are children and spouses. The image of **a constant dripping** more than likely refers to a perpetual leaky roof that eventually makes the house uninhabitable (see 27:15-16).

Verse 14 forms a counter image to verse 13. By custom and law, **parents** passed on **houses and wealth**. It was what children expected. In contrast, **a prudent wife** was a gift **from the LORD**. There is an increase in intensity developed in this proverb. The material goods that children inherit from their parents influence their future. However, what has a far greater influence is the spouse one marries.

A prudent spouse is a gift from God (cf. 18:22). Parents did not always arrange marriages, as was the case of Samson in Judges 14.

19:15 Laziness is a frequent topic of the sage. The **deep sleep** that laziness **brings on**, reminds one of the "deep sleep" God brought upon the first man, Adam (Gen 2:21). Ironically, this sleep does not energize the indolent, but rather debilitates and exhausts him.

19:16 The first line literally says, "He who keeps commandments is he who keeps his life" (*nephesh*; soul). The reference here is primarily to the **instructions** the parent gives, even though these are ultimately based upon the commands of God. The RSV emends the second line to read "his word" (cf. 13:13) rather than **his ways** ("his ways" is the reading of the Hebrew text). Such a translation would make it easier for the proverb to refer to Yahweh's commands. However, the emendation is not necessary. Ultimately the proverb speaks to the respect that youth must have for parental authority and advice.

19:17 How one treats the poor reflects one's relationship and respect for God (cf. 14:31; 17:5). The idea of the proverb serves as the basis for Jesus' parable of the sheep and goats (Matt 25:31-46).

[18]**Discipline your son, for in that there is hope;**
    do not be a willing party to his death.
[19]**A hot-tempered man must pay the penalty;**
    if you rescue him, you will have to do it again.
[20]**Listen to advice and accept instruction,**
    and in the end you will be wise.
[21]**Many are the plans in a man's heart,**
    but it is the LORD's purpose that prevails.
[22]**What a man desires is unfailing love[a];**
    better to be poor than a liar.
[23]**The fear of the LORD leads to life:**
    Then one rests content, untouched by trouble.

[a]*22 Or A man's greed is his shame*

19:18 This proverb is an admonition (one that states its case in the imperative), which is quite unusual in chapters 10:1–22:16. The issue in 18a is how to translate the conjunction (כִּי, *kî*). Is it *causal*, which is the way the NIV translates it, **for** or "because"? Or should one translate it as *temporal*, "while"? The word can be taken either way. If it is the *causal* sense, then the meaning is that in the activity of disciplining a child, one creates hope for a productive life. If it is the *temporal*, then the sense is that a parent has a small window of opportunity in which a child is more receptive to discipline. Do not neglect that opportunity (see 4:3). The issue is one of seizing the moment. With either of the above interpretations, the motive for discipline is not revenge or venting anger. The motive is that discipline brings about the possibility of change.

Verse 18b is not certain. There are two possibilities. First, the admonition here may address excessive use of corporal punishment. In other words, do not go to extremes in the use of punishment so that it results in **death**. Israelite law set limits on the corporal punishment of a son. Lethal punishment was a corporate decision made by the community and not an option parents could exercise (Deut 21:18-21). Second, "death" may refer not to physical death but to a metaphorical death. That is, refusal to discipline a child will lead to an unproductive life for that child. This is the same thought expressed in verse 16. The second interpretation seems more fitting since Proverbs often uses the term "death" to refer to living a futile life (see 21:16 and 9:18).

19:19 Here is another character-consequence proverb. Certain attitudes lead to inevitable consequences: **A hot-tempered man must pay the penalty**. The second line builds on this and admonishes that in the case of the habitual anger of an out-of-control person, intervention will not help. The admonition is to let the individual suffer the consequences. Van Leeuwen says this is "a warning against enmeshment in another person's dysfunctional life."[83]

19:20 This is the staple admonition of the sage. The one who is open to **advice** (עֵצָה, *'ēṣāh*) and **instruction** (מוּסָר, *mûsār*) will **in the end be wise**.

19:21 This "limit proverb" has affinities with a number of other proverbs in the sentence literature (14:12; 16:1,2,9,33; 20:24; 21:1; 27:1). As capable as humans are, they are ultimately limited by the purpose of God. A contrast is set up between the two lines of the proverb. Verse 21a speaks of the multiple plans of mortals. Verse 21b speaks of a single divine **purpose** that will **prevail**. The same word translated "purpose" in 21b is the same word translated "advice" in verse 20a.

---

[83]Van Leeuwen, "Proverbs," p. 81.

19:22 A person's deep longing is for **unfailing love,** or "genuine faithfulness" (חֶסֶד, *ḥesed*). One's **desires** should be focused on this kind of faithfulness and not on deceitfulness or lying. Poverty with loyalty is better than money with deceit (v. 22b). Character is more important than possessions.

19:23 The fear of the LORD is the foundation, that is, the beginning of wisdom, which leads to a fulfilled **life.** It is this foundation that enables one to experience true contentment.

²⁴**The sluggard buries his hand in the dish;**
       he will not even bring it back to his mouth!
²⁵**Flog a mocker, and the simple will learn prudence;**
       rebuke a discerning man, and he will gain knowledge.
²⁶**He who robs his father and drives out his mother**
       is a son who brings shame and disgrace.
²⁷**Stop listening to instruction, my son,**
       and you will stray from the words of knowledge.
²⁸**A corrupt witness mocks at justice,**
       and the mouth of the wicked gulps down evil.
²⁹ **Penalties are prepared for mockers,**
       and beatings for the backs of fools.

19:24 The sage loves to satirize the lazy person. Here is a comical picture of those who are so lazy they do not have the energy to feed themselves. For a more detailed treatment of the lazy, see 26:13-16.

19:25 Three characters often referred to in wisdom are mentioned in this proverb. The **mocker** (לֵץ, *lēṣ*) is the one beyond instruction; he thinks he knows it all (9:7,8,12). The **simple** (פֶּתִי, *pethî*) is the one who is inexperienced, naïve, but open to instruction (1:4). The simple learns from observing what happens to the mocker. The **discerning man** (נָבוֹן, *nābôn*, "the understanding one") is the one who is already wise but continues to grow (1:5) from listening to wise reproof (25:12). To restate verse 25b using a contemporary proverb, we would say, "A word to the wise is sufficient." A parallel proverb is found in 21:11.

19:26 The proverb describes how the conduct of children can bring disgrace on the whole house (cf. 28:24).

19:27 The proverb makes its case in the form of an admonition (an imperative), which is uncommon in the sentence literature of

10:1–22:16. The language used reminds one of the formal addresses given to the son in chapters 1–9.

19:28-29 This proverb pair describes those pathetic individuals
that feed on and perpetuate the evils of society. They offer nothing of
value to the community. In verse 29, the **penalties** and **beatings**
reserved for the **mockers** and **fools**, seem not to be instructional in
nature but are simply a deterrent to others. The mockers and fools
are themselves beyond help. The main concern is to put them in their
place so that harm to the community can be kept to a minimum.

Chapter 20 contains a potpourri of proverbs on various subjects.
Few connections exist between the individual sayings. Whybray
claims that the proverbs in verses 5-12 are all concerned with the
issue of discerning character. He maintains, "This is a particularly
clear example of a group of proverbs with thematic unity."[84] It is difficult, however, to see how this unit is clearly clustered together.

The chapter contains six "Yahweh proverbs" (vv. 10,12,22,23,24,
27). Whybray maintains that later editors sprinkled in Yahweh sayings to make the collection more theological.[85] The editors clustered
the "secular" proverbs around the Yahweh sayings. It is still difficult
to see how the remaining proverbs in this chapter gravitate around
these sayings as Whybray asserts. The chapter also contains four
royal proverbs (proverbs about the king; vv. 2,8,26,28; see 16:10-15).
Verses 22-28 contain the majority of Yahweh and royal proverbs and
emphasize the authority of the LORD and the king to judge the character of others.

[20:1]**Wine is a mocker and beer a brawler;**
    whoever is led astray by them is not wise.
[2]**A king's wrath is like the roar of a lion;**
    he who angers him forfeits his life.
[3]**It is to a man's honor to avoid strife,**
    but every fool is quick to quarrel.
[4]**A sluggard does not plow in season;**
    so at harvest time he looks but finds nothing.

---

[84]R.N. Whybray, *The Composition of the Book of Proverbs* (Sheffield: JSOT
Press, 1994), p. 115.
[85]R.N. Whybray, *Proverbs*, p. 291.

⁵The purposes of a man's heart are deep waters,
   but a man of understanding draws them out.
⁶Many a man claims to have unfailing love,
   but a faithful man who can find?
⁷The righteous man leads a blameless life;
   blessed are his children after him.

20:1 In the first line of the proverb, **wine** is personified. It is characterized as a **mocker** (לֵץ, *lēṣ*) and a **brawler**. These are the qualities the inebriated exhibit. The effects of such drink lead to treating others with disrespect. The **wise** avoid such a state. It is possible to translate **is led astray** as "staggers," which is how the LXX translates the verb in Isaiah 28:7. Woman Wisdom served **wine** at her table (9:5), but the sages condemn overindulgence (23:29-35).

20:2 The king had the power of life and death in his hands. The righteous king used such power with wisdom (see vv. 26,28). Even the wise king was to be feared. His **wrath is like the roar of a lion**. The lion was a common royal symbol. The **king's** wrath was a lethal weapon that, when provoked, could kill. Such anger, however, can be deflected by wisdom (16:14; Eccl 9:13-18).

20:3 It is the nature of **fool**s to gravitate to a **quarrel**. The wise man **avoids strife**. The sage has much to say about the divisive nature of quarreling and strife in the community (15:18; 17:1,14,19; 26:17-26).

20:4 God's creation models the orderliness of wisdom. One can count on seedtime and harvest, cold and heat, summer and winter, day and night (Gen 8:22). And those who observe creation learn about wisdom and order their lives accordingly. A farmer who takes responsibility for his crops and livestock models wisdom, but the fool and the **sluggard** do not fall into step. Rather than keeping with God's timing, they follow their own calendar. The results are disastrous.

20:5 Purposes (עֵצָה, *'ēṣāh*) is the same word used in 19:21 to describe God's work. **Deep waters** is a positive image of that which is profound (see comment on 18:4). Such profound insights often lie buried within an individual. However, in the company of **a man of understanding**, such insights are **drawn out**. In other words, it takes wisdom to expose the valuable insights of others. This saying affirms a fundamental principle of wisdom: wisdom is not gained in isolation but in relationship with others.

20:6 This proverb is based on an antithesis between those who proclaim **unfailing love** (חֶסֶד, *ḥesed*; cf. 19:22) or friendship and those who practice genuine friendship. The rhetorical question in the second line expects a negative answer (cf. 31:10 for the same question asked about a woman of noble character). The question is a way of expressing the rarity of such **a faithful man**. The proverb contrasts friendship that is proven with that which is unproven (actions over words).

20:7 This proverb might be characterized as a "beatitude" because it contains the word **blessed**. Other beatitude-type proverbs include 8:32,34; 16:20; 29:18. Parents who lead **a blameless life** will pass on that lifestyle to their children, who in turn will be blessed by such an example. "Blameless" does not mean "perfect" but a life of "integrity" (תֹּם, *tōm*). Children imitate parents. The epigram affirms the interconnectedness of the generations (see 17:6). One generation benefits from another. The process results in the solidarity of values.

⁸**When a king sits on his throne to judge,**
      he winnows out all evil with his eyes.
⁹**Who can say, "I have kept my heart pure;**
      I am clean and without sin"?
¹⁰**Differing weights and differing measures—**
      the LORD detests them both.
¹¹**Even a child is known by his actions,**
      by whether his conduct is pure and right.
¹²**Ears that hear and eyes that see—**
      the LORD has made them both.
¹³**Do not love sleep or you will grow poor;**
      stay awake and you will have food to spare.
¹⁴**"It's no good, it's no good!" says the buyer;**
      then off he goes and boasts about his purchase.
¹⁵**Gold there is, and rubies in abundance,**
      but lips that speak knowledge are a rare jewel.

20:8 The wise **king** practices justice, which is the meaning of the phrase, **sits on his throne**. The king is the Lord's appointed authority. The king's function as it is described in this saying is primarily negative, that of **winnowing out all evil**.

20:9 Verse 9 expresses the universal nature of **sin**. Every life has roots in sin (Ps 51:5). In this regard, wisdom is realistic about human nature. On the one hand, it sees humans with great potential accomplish much through wise planning and implementing. On the other hand, wisdom sees every human involved in sin. No one escapes its clutches. Through this rhetorical question, the sage affirms the complex nature of human beings. While chapters 10–15 affirm clear differences between right and wrong and distinguish between the righteous and the wicked, in general humans are a mixed bag. Even the life of the most righteous person is shrouded in ambiguity. Only through the fear of the LORD can God enter to forgive.

20:10 The Hebrew text reads, "Stone and stone, ephah and ephah, both are an abomination of the LORD." Deuteronomy 25:13-16 helps to clarify the meaning of this proverb by exhorting individuals engaged in trade not to have two different stones in their bags, one large and one small. Nor should they have two ephahs of differing sizes (an ephah is similar to but smaller than a bushel basket). The buyer and seller should be fair in how they weigh the product. **The LORD detests** deceptive measures; they are an "abomination" to him. The proverb affirms that God is very much involved in the routine affairs of business, money, and trade. Verse 10 "overlaps" with verse 23.

20:11 Two possible interpretations exist in understanding the aphorism. One possibility, advocated by Clifford, maintains that the word for **known** (נָכַר, *nākar*) can be translated "disguise." Thus he translates the first line as, "even a boy can playact."[86] That is, a youth can fake his or her true character. This meaning is more unusual. The other possibility is to translate the root נָכַר as "to reveal or make known."[87] This is the choice the NIV makes. The thought conveyed is that the early behavior of a **child** or youth reveals the direction that youth will go. This thought is expressed in the statement, "What you are today largely determines what you will become tomorrow." Another nuance of this thought might be that the early childhood training sets the tone for later character development. If that is the idea, then this proverb is in line with the meaning of 22:6.

In all actuality, this saying may not be directed primarily to the youth but to adults. The proverb begins with the Hebrew particle

---

[86]Clifford, *Proverbs*, p. 180. Clifford goes on to conclude, "character is not always revealed by actions" (p. 184).

[87]BDB, p. 648.

even (□, *gam*), indicating that the focus is on adults. The proverb implies an "all the more reason" type of argument (*a fortiori*). The sense is this: if **even a child is known by his actions, by whether his conduct is pure and right**, how much more should adults!

20:12 Clifford identifies two possibilities for interpreting this verse.[88] First, God created **ears** and **eyes** for us to **hear** and see. If humans can see and hear with what God **made** for them, then how much more can God hear and see in us and in our world. The second possible interpretation is that God gave humans **ears that hear and eyes that see** in order to use those senses to gain wisdom. In light of how the sage calls upon youth to engage all the senses to seek wisdom (4:20-27), it seems more reasonable to assume the second interpretation (consider also Exod 4:10-16).

20:13 If the fool is known for the ability to engage in quarreling (v. 3), the indolent is known for the ability to **sleep**. Such "activity" brings the lazy person nothing but poverty. His activity also adversely affects family and community. **Stay awake** in Hebrew is "open your eyes." The phrase connects this verse with the previous verse. One uses the senses and abilities that are given by God for the betterment of self and others.

20:14 In Hebrew the adage in this verse has a sharp edge to it that is not immediately captured by the NIV: "bad, bad, says the one who buys; he goes, then he boasts." The context is the bartering practice of the marketplace. The buyer pretends to view the goods as worthless, thus driving down the price. Once the price is down, he buys the product. Upon leaving, he praises himself for the great deal he made. Though the initial context was the marketplace, the proverb has broader application. It describes people who do not say what they really think in order to get what they want.

20:15 In the book of Proverbs, the value of wisdom always surpasses that of **gold** and precious metals (3:14; 8:10,19; 16:16). The sage does not discount the value of wealth. As the better-than proverbs continually point out, wisdom is more valuable. To adorn oneself in wisdom is more beautiful than the adornment of jewelry. Proverbs 25:11-12 pictures this phenomenon.

---

[88]Clifford, *Proverbs*, p. 184.

¹⁶Take the garment of one who puts up security for a stranger;
  hold it in pledge if he does it for a wayward woman.
¹⁷Food gained by fraud tastes sweet to a man,
  but he ends up with a mouth full of gravel.
¹⁸Make plans by seeking advice;
  if you wage war, obtain guidance.
¹⁹A gossip betrays a confidence;
  so avoid a man who talks too much.
²⁰If a man curses his father or mother,
  his lamp will be snuffed out in pitch darkness.
²¹An inheritance quickly gained at the beginning
  will not be blessed at the end.
²²Do not say, "I'll pay you back for this wrong!"
  Wait for the LORD, and he will deliver you.
²³The LORD detests differing weights,
  and dishonest scales do not please him.
²⁴A man's steps are directed by the LORD.
  How then can anyone understand his own way?

20:16 Three individuals are involved in this transaction: the poor **stranger** who receives the financial help, the guarantor who promises to pay if the stranger is unable, and finally the guarantee who holds the purse. The saying addresses the third person, the guarantee who, if the stranger defaults and the guarantor does not back it up, must pay the price. This verse has a duplicate in 27:13.[89] The proverb demands that the guarantee get some security, **the garment of one who puts up security**, to ensure that the pledge will be kept. The sage had little tolerance for the practice of surety (see 6:1-5).

20:17 Food gained by fraud (Hebrew reads, "bread of deceit") initially **tastes sweet**. Later, however, such food leaves a bitter taste; it seems like **a mouth full of gravel** (see Job 20:12-16). Engaging in fraudulent behavior does not ultimately satisfy but disappoints. Satisfaction gained through deceptive means is short lived. The sage rarely favors taking short cuts in life. Impatience is a vice (14:29).

20:18 The phrase, **make plans by seeking advice**, affirms that the ability to plan is one of the main resources of the wise (see 16:1-

---

[89]The Hebrew text says "strangers" (masculine). But an alternate reading is "strange woman." The NIV follows the alternate reading because of the duplication in 27:13.

9). If the ability to plan flows out of wisdom's respect for order, then to seek out others in establishing those plans is a necessary part of the community nature of wisdom. Verse 18b offers one example of application: **if you wage war, obtain guidance**. When making important decisions seek out the counsel of others.

20:19 The reason a **gossip** must be avoided is because of the damage he or she does to the solidarity of the community. The RSV translates the Hebrew word פֹּתֶה (*pāthah*) as one who speaks "foolishly." The NIV translates the word as **a man who talks too much** (from the root meaning "to be open"; i.e., he opens wide his lips). This is more in keeping with how the gossip **betrays a confidence**. The bottom line is that the gossip is one who speaks irresponsibly.

20:20 If a son does not honor **his father or mother** (Exod 20:12) but instead **curses** them (Exod 21:17), **his lamp will be snuffed out in pitch darkness**. The last phrase may be a metaphor for describing parents as a primary resource for attaining wisdom. Those who dishonor parents, extinguish the lamp that first gave them light. The phrase "pitch darkness" is from the Hebrew which reads "pupil of eye."[90]

20:21 Wisdom is suspicious of anything attained **quickly** or in haste. This maxim reminds one of the Prodigal Son who too quickly gained his inheritance. The results were disastrous. It also recalls Ahab's plan to acquire illegitimately Naboth's inheritance from him (1 Kings 21).

20:22 A number of proverbs begin with the "Do not" formula (3:27-31; 20:13; 26:4) or the "Do not say" formula (3:28; 24:29). This saying begins, **Do not say, "I'll pay you back for this wrong!"** Instead the youth is to **wait for the LORD, and he will deliver you**. What the proverb asks is that one suspend the traditional wisdom belief in the act-consequence mind set. Conventional wisdom taught that those who mistreat others will reap the consequences of their behavior. In contrast, biblical wisdom understood that the world did not operate mechanistically. God has his own timetable that is different from that of humans. The proverb calls on individuals to exercise patience, trust, and spiritual maturity as they face the injustices of life. David is a good example of this in refusing to take Saul's life (1 Samuel 24–26).

---

[90]The pupil was the darkest part of the eye.

20:23 The saying is a variant of verse 10. See comments there.

20:24 This is another "limit proverb," one that limits human achievement. Wisdom affirms the great potential that humans have. At the same time, it holds that potential in check with God's purpose. The cluster of proverbs in 16:1-9 addresses the perspective in more detail (see also Jer 10:23). Like the dominant metaphor portrayed in chapters 1–9, the saying imagines life as a journey. Verse 24a overlaps with Psalm 37:23.

²⁵**It is a trap for a man to dedicate something rashly**
    and only later to consider his vows.
²⁶**A wise king winnows out the wicked;**
    he drives the threshing wheel over them.
²⁷**The lamp of the LORD searches the spirit of a manᵃ;**
    it searches out his inmost being.
²⁸**Love and faithfulness keep a king safe;**
    through love his throne is made secure.
²⁹**The glory of young men is their strength,**
    gray hair the splendor of the old.
³⁰**Blows and wounds cleanse away evil,**
    and beatings purge the inmost being.

ᵃ27 Or *The spirit of man is the LORD's lamp*

20:25-26 One question of interpretation in verse 26 is to what does "wheel" (אוֹפָן, *'ôphān*) refer? Does this refer to some wheel of torture?[91] Or does it refer to, as the NIV interprets it, a **threshing wheel**? In light of the agrarian image in 26a, the NIV correctly translates the figure. The picture is of a threshing machine being run over the shocks of grain to separate or loosen the kernel from the husks. Then the grain is thrown in the air in order to separate the chaff from the grain as the wind blows away the chaff. **A wise king** functions this way among his people. He **winnows out the wicked** and **drives the threshing wheel over them** (see reference to threshing sledges in Amos 1:3).

---

[91]Daniel C. Snell identifies parallels in Hittite laws where the wheel is used as an instrument of torture and execution by the king. He feels that this understanding of "wheel" in 20:26 is more probable than seeing the wheel as an agricultural instrument. See Snell "The Wheel in Proverbs XX 26," *VT* 39 (1989): 503-505.

20:27 The spirit of a man could also be translated "the breath of man." Two possibilities exist for interpreting the phrase. First, the "breath" that God has put into humans is his **lamp** for searching them out and understanding their innermost thoughts. In other words, breath or spirit is God's instrument for knowing us. It is his lamp. The second possible interpretation is that "breath" and "lamp" are tools that God has given humans to understand themselves. Breath is the God-given conscience the LORD has put in individuals. With the first interpretation, God is the one who does the searching. With the second, humans are given instruments to search themselves. Clifford translates the verse so that it can be interpreted either way: "The lifebreath of a mortal is the lamp of Yahweh, searching through all the chambers of the stomach."[92] The NIV seems to favor the first interpretation. However, the nature of a proverb enables it to carry the possibility of multiple meanings.

20:28 This is the final of four royal proverbs that appear in chapter 20. **Love** and **faithfulness** guard a king's throne and are what qualify him to be a servant of God.

20:29 The NIV translates the verse in such a way as to render an evenhanded compliment to both the **young** and the **old**. Each offers a contribution to the community. In some ways, each depends on the other. All of this is well and good. However, the Hebrew text does not just abut the two lines against each other. The text contains the *waw* conjunction ("but" or "and"). A heightening effect is intended with the second line. The purpose of the second line is to assert the wisdom (**gray hair**) of the old over the **strength** of young **men**. Such an interpretation is in keeping with the overall theology of wisdom.

20:30 As a number of proverbs show, the sage did not shy away from corporal punishment. Such punishment was a way of purging the heart and mind. The external **wounds cleanse away** the internal dross or **evil**. Such was always administered in the context of love (see 13:24 for further comment on corporal punishment). While wisdom calls for rigorous discipline, wisdom does not sanction physical abuse. Wisdom involves the ability to know what is the appropriate discipline for the occasion and the person.

---

[92]Clifford, *Proverbs*, p. 181.

²¹:¹**The king's heart is in the hand of the** LORD;
    he directs it like a watercourse wherever he pleases.
²**All a man's ways seem right to him,**
    but the LORD **weighs the heart.**
³**To do what is right and just**
    is more acceptable to the LORD **than sacrifice.**
⁴**Haughty eyes and a proud heart,**
    the lamp of the wicked, are sin!
⁵**The plans of the diligent lead to profit**
    as surely as haste leads to poverty.
⁶**A fortune made by a lying tongue**
    is a fleeting vapor and a deadly snare.ᵃ
⁷**The violence of the wicked will drag them away,**
    for they refuse to do what is right.
⁸**The way of the guilty is devious,**
    but the conduct of the innocent is upright.

ᵃ**6 Some Hebrew manuscripts, Septuagint and Vulgate; most Hebrew
manuscripts** *vapor for those who seek death*

21:1 The LORD not only directs the steps of ordinary humans, he
is also sovereign over the **king** who has the power to grant life or
death. God not only directs the course of major historical events, he
exercises sovereignty over that sphere where humans believe they
exercise the most freedom: the **heart** (i.e., the mind; see 16:1-9).

The image of **a watercourse** is a positive one. It is an agrarian
picture of irrigation channels used to fertilize parched wilderness
land (cf. 5:16). God uses the decisions of kings to bring about his
will. Water is usually difficult to control. It has its own will. Humans
build large dams to control and harness its power. God, however,
manages both water and kings with little effort.

21:2 A contrast is made between what humans see and what God
sees. The phrase rendered **right to him** is literally "right in his own
eyes" (see 16:2). Thus there is a contrast between the external view
of human eyes and the internal view God has of **the heart**. The sage
continually reminds youth of the ever-present danger of self-deception. The first line overlaps with 16:2,25 and 30:12. The second line
overlaps with 17:3b.

21:3 This is one of only a few proverbs in wisdom material that
deals with the theme of Israel's sacrifice or worship. The proverb

carries a tone reminiscent of a prophetic voice (see Amos 5:24). The worshiper's **sacrifice** is not rejected (with the exception of wicked sacrifices, v. 27). Rather doing **what is right and just is more acceptable to the LORD**. The saying carries the flavor of a better-than proverb. Sacrifices have their place, but better is a life lived in righteousness and justice. Right living transcends the offering of sacrifices. The core wisdom virtues that the sage teaches are righteousness, justice, and fairness (1:3; 2:9; 8:20).

21:4 Proud heart in the Hebrew text reads "wide or broad heart." A contrasting phrase used in Proverbs to describe the fool is "needy of heart" (חֲסַר־לֵב, ḥăsar-lēb; see 10:13), which the NIV usually translates "lacks judgment." Both terms are used in a pejorative sense. "Lamp" has already been mentioned earlier in 20:20,27 and refers to the internal makeup of humans. The question that arises with this maxim concerns the relationship of the second line to the first. How does **the lamp of the wicked** relate to **haughty eyes and a proud heart**? It may be that pride results in the lamp of the wicked "failing" (חָטָא, ḥāṭā').[93] Or it may be that haughty eyes, a proud heart, and the lamp of the wicked are examples of **sin**.

21:5 The verse contrasts those who **plan** with those who do not plan. One gift that God gave to humans was the ability to use their minds to plan for the future (16:1-9). Those who do not are doomed. Usually they are characterized by impetuousness. In an agrarian culture, no farmer could afford to be hasty. The truly wise know that "haste makes waste."[94]

21:6 The **lying tongue** received utmost attention in an oral community that relied on the faithful witness of others to do business and pass fair judgments. The **fortune** or rewards of practicing deceitfulness are twofold. The fortunes made are **a fleeting vapor** (הֶבֶל, hebel, Ecclesiastes' favorite term) and **a deadly snare** (lit., "the seeking of death").

21:7 Those who **refuse** to practice the virtues of wisdom (righteousness and justice, v. 3), will reap what they sow. Those who live by the sword will die by the sword.

---

[93]This alternative translates חָטָא as "failing" rather than "sin."

[94]Or in terms of the axiom that Van Leeuwen suggests, "make haste slowly," "Proverbs," p. 192.

21:8 The adage contrasts underhanded deception and open honesty. The **guilty** work on the sly. The **innocent,** or righteous, are straightforward.[95]

⁹Better to live on a corner of the roof
　　than share a house with a quarrelsome wife.
¹⁰The wicked man craves evil;
　　his neighbor gets no mercy from him.
¹¹When a mocker is punished, the simple gain wisdom;
　　when a wise man is instructed, he gets knowledge.
¹²The Righteous One[a] takes note of the house of the wicked
　　and brings the wicked to ruin.
¹³If a man shuts his ears to the cry of the poor,
　　he too will cry out and not be answered.
¹⁴A gift given in secret soothes anger,
　　and a bribe concealed in the cloak pacifies great wrath.
¹⁵When justice is done, it brings joy to the righteous
　　but terror to evildoers.
¹⁶A man who strays from the path of understanding
　　comes to rest in the company of the dead.

[a]*12 Or the righteous man*

21:9 This better-than proverb is duplicated in 25:24 and, except for the image used, is quite similar to verse 19. The **corner of the roof** could refer to a small room or a "cramped attic" in the upper chambers of the house, such as the Elisha room described in 2 Kings 4:10.[96] More than likely, the corner room refers to dwelling on the corner of a roof exposed to the elements. This makes the contrast sharper and more extreme. There are several suggestions for rendering the phrase **share a house** (בֵּית חָבֵר, *bêth ḥāber*). The term could be translated "noisy house." The critical notes in the Hebrew text suggest the text be emended from חָבֵר (*ḥāber*) to רְחָב (*rāḥāb*, "broad" or "spacious"), thus meaning "spacious house." It is best to stay with the Hebrew text, as does the NIV, and translate the word,

---

[95]Clifford argues for a different translation of this verse, "A person's path may zigzag and be strange, but his actions are blameless and right," see *Proverbs*, p. 187.

[96]McKane, *Proverbs*, p. 553. The cramped room serves a nice contrast to the spacious house in the second line.

"shared house." Actually neither of the above alters the general meaning of the proverb. It is better to make oneself vulnerable to the stormy blasts of nature on the outside, than to expose oneself to the storms of a **quarrelsome wife** on the inside. For counterdescriptions of the "quarrelsome man," see 26:17-28.

21:10 The verb "desire" (אָוְּתָה, *'āwāh*) is in the intensive form and thus appropriately translated by the NIV as **craves**. One can allow a desire or appetite to gain such control that it takes over a person's whole life. Amnon's rape of Tamar shows how lust can overpower an individual and destroy another person's (sister, friend, or neighbor) life (2 Sam 13:1-19). The priest and the Levite in the parable of the Good Samaritan may have been so caught up in fulfilling their religious appetites that they failed to show mercy to their neighbor (Luke 10:25-37).

21:11 The question behind this apothegm is, who is the recipient of the **wisdom** and **knowledge**? Is the **simple** the subject in both lines? If so, then the proverb means that by observing **a mocker** when he **is punished**, the simple gain wisdom. And when the simple observes **a wise man** when he **is instructed**, he (the simple) **gets knowledge**. In other words, the simple learn by the negative example of the mocker and by the positive example of the wise. The other way to interpret the proverb is to see two different subjects in each line. In the first line, the simple learns by watching what happens to the mocker. In the second line, the wise one learns from instruction (see 1:4-5;19:25).

21:12 If the NIV is correct in interpreting **Righteous One** (צַדִּיק, *ṣaddîq*) as referring to Yahweh, then this is the only text in the Old Testament that describes the LORD as the Righteous One (see the NIV footnote and the RSV for an alternate translation). The translation of the NIV is quite valid, however, because it is the LORD who **brings the wicked to ruin** and not a "righteous person" (*ṣaddîq*).

21:13 The proverb makes one of the most rhetorically powerful arguments for accepting one's responsibility to **the poor** of any statement found in the Old Testament. If a person refuses to help the poor, then others will refuse to help this one in time of distress. Because of the precarious economic state of the ordinary citizen, one could easily fall victim to difficult times. Poverty always lurked in the shadows of the farmer and the merchant.

21:14 This is simply an observation. The statement does not pass judgment on the practice of bribery. It acknowledges that bribery works, but that does not mean that it is to be practiced. The wise condemned bribery as a tool of injustice (15:27; 17:23). It is possible that this refers to a form of plea-bargaining. The one who injures provides secret compensation for the one injured in order to appease.

21:15 When **the righteous** observe that **justice is done** (one of wisdom's virtues; 1:3), **it brings** them **joy.** When the wicked observe justice, it brings them nothing but **terror** and pain.

21:16 The company of the dead (the "Raphaim") refers to the inhabitants of Sheol (see Ps 88:10). The one **who strays from the path of understanding** will experience premature death. In other words, such a person will not experience a fulfilling life (see 9:18). Van Leeuwen says that this saying summarizes chapters 1–9.[97]

[17]**He who loves pleasure will become poor;**
  whoever loves wine and oil will never be rich.
[18]**The wicked become a ransom for the righteous,**
  and the unfaithful for the upright.
[19]**Better to live in a desert**
  than with a quarrelsome and ill-tempered wife.
[20]**In the house of the wise are stores of choice food and oil,**
  but a foolish man devours all he has.
[21]**He who pursues righteousness and love**
  finds life, prosperity[a] **and honor.**
[22]**A wise man attacks the city of the mighty**
  and pulls down the stronghold in which they trust.
[23]**He who guards his mouth and his tongue**
  keeps himself from calamity.

[a]*21* **Or** *righteousness*

21:17 Chapters 1–9 set forth three primary temptations that youth face as they move into adulthood: lust, laziness, and luxury. Verse 17 describes the one, usually the lazy person, who is tempted by luxury. The proverb could also be a fitting summary to the instruction saying in 1:10-19 where the youth is tempted to gain the comforts of life through the violence of gang activity. The proverb serves as an affirmation of the popular maxim, "you can't have your

---

[97]Van Leeuwen, "Proverbs," p. 194.

cake and eat it, too." The one **who loves pleasure, wine and oil** will sacrifice the more substantive riches of life.

21:18 The word כֹּפֶר (*kōpher*) throughout the Old Testament is usually translated "atonement," "substitute," or, as appropriately rendered here by the NIV, **ransom**. The thought of the verse is that the punishment **the wicked** receive serves as compensation for **the righteous** who are now immune from such discipline. Why the righteous need a ransom is not stated.

21:19 This verse is quite similar to verse 9 (see comments there). The main difference is that the image used there was "the corner of the roof." The picture here is **a desert**. It is far **better** to be exposed to the harsh elements the arid desert-land hurls at one, than to the harsh words a **wife** hurls (see 26:17-28 for a picture of the male verbal abuser).

21:20 The **wise** practice conservation (recall the ant in 6:6-11). **A foolish man** is the consummate consumer. Like a bottomless pit, he is never satisfied (see v. 10 on the appetite of the wicked). The foolish man is a poor steward of the resources God gives. By its metaphoric nature, this proverb does not confine itself exclusively to material resources. The resources also include spiritual and mental, especially the resource of wisdom.

21:21 The sapiential virtues of **righteousness and love** (חֶסֶד; *ḥesed*) simply serve as a summary statement of the trio mentioned at the very beginning of the book in 1:3: righteousness, justice, and fairness. When one pursues such virtues, the serendipity is **life, prosperity and honor**.[98] The Hebrew text reads "life, righteousness, and honor." Since "righteousness" already appears in the first line, the NIV omits it and substitutes "prosperity." When a person makes the sapiential virtues a priority, then everything else in life is put in perspective (Matt 6:33).

21:22 The saying is not to be taken literally. Rather it expresses a thought woven in the wisdom literature that wisdom is greater than physical strength (see 16:32; Eccl 9:13-16).

21:23 The person who practices self-control in speech **keeps himself from calamity**. The proverb is an expansion of the first line in 13:3.

---

[98]Woman Wisdom promises these rewards (8:18).

²⁴**The proud and arrogant man—" Mocker" is his name;**
    he behaves with overweening pride.
²⁵**The sluggard's craving will be the death of him,**
    because his hands refuse to work.
²⁶**All day long he craves for more,**
    but the righteous give without sparing.
²⁷**The sacrifice of the wicked is detestable—**
    how much more so when brought with evil intent!

21:24 The saying is stacked with synonyms of **pride** which seem overly repetitive. Actually, the sage uses the rhetorical strategy of intensification. The focus of the intensification is on the **"Mocker."** The ultimate way of describing such a character is arrogance. The "Mocker" is the one who is always "right in his own eyes" (another phrase wisdom uses to describe the insolent; see 26:5).

21:25 The ones the wise most love to make fun of are the lazy. Once again, they do it here. For the **sluggard,** an unfulfilled **craving** does nothing but drain his or her energy. The wise use their desires as motivation for healthy action.

21:26 The first line of the Hebrew text reads, "All the day he desires desire." It is not a scribal gloss but a rhetorical strategy for describing the emptiness of the lazy person's cravings. Who is the one who **craves for more?** Some would say it refers to the sluggard in verse 25. Thus verses 25 and 26 are a proverb pair. At any rate, the basic contrast in verse 26 is between the greedy and the generous. Those who are **righteous** demonstrate it by their unselfish behavior.

21:27 The **sacrifice the wicked** offer serves as a cover for an ulterior motive. According to Ronald Clements, there is little if any distinction between the general reference to actions that are **detestable** (תּוֹעֲבַת, *tô'ăbath,* "abomination") and the more specific reference to actions that "the LORD detests" (תּוֹעֲבַת יהוה, *tô'ăbath YHWH*; refer to 15:8). In other words, the proverb assumes Yahweh as the one who is offended. Clements concludes, ". . . the very idea of abomination has taken on a kind of absolute quality that implies that such actions are contrary to the very order of life and creation as a whole."[99] The sages used the idea of "abomination" as a moral sanction against those attitudes and behaviors that were difficult to cover under the law.

---

[99]Clements, "Abomination," p. 219.

²⁸**A false witness will perish,**
     and whoever listens to him will be destroyed forever.^a
²⁹**A wicked man puts up a bold front,**
     but an upright man gives thought to his ways.
³⁰**There is no wisdom, no insight, no plan**
     that can succeed against the LORD.
³¹**The horse is made ready for the day of battle,**
     but victory rests with the LORD.

^a*28 Or / but the words of an obedient man will live on*

21:28 The first line is clear enough in the Hebrew text: **a false witness will perish**. It is the second line that is somewhat problematic. The Hebrew text is difficult to decipher. It reads, "But a man who listens will speak forever." The NIV, with slight change in pointing, translates יְדַבֵּר (*y^ədabbēr*) as יְדֻבָּר (*y^ədubbār*), "to drive out or destroy." Thus the second line reads, **and whoever listens to him will be destroyed forever.**

Such a change may not be necessary. The thought of the Hebrew may be to contrast the false witness with the one who really listens to all sides of the argument.[100] The NRSV translates the verse, "A false witness will perish, but a good listener will testify successfully." If this translation is the preferred one, then the meaning is close to the thought of 18:17. False witnesses receive a lot of attention from the wise. Oral testimony was the primary means for determining the truth in a court case. The abuse of legal power (lying, bribes, false witnessing) is not to be tolerated.

21:29 The **wicked** are those who stubbornly conceal their plans. They consult no one. In contrast, **an upright man gives thought to his ways**. The wicked put up a **front**, while the upright are straightforward with their plans. The righteous consider the advice of others and take great care in discerning the right course of action to take.

21:30-31 Like many of the proverbs in 16:1–22:16, this proverb pair holds in check the more fundamental belief described in chapters 10–15. Life is more ambiguous than at first glance. The righteous do not always prosper. This proverb pair acknowledges human limitation and calls on the wise to accept such limitations. Such is

---

[100]See J.A. Emerton, *The Interpretation of Proverbs 21:28*, ZAW Supp. 100 (1988), pp. 161-170.

the nature of true **wisdom**. No human wisdom can ultimately triumph over God's plans. Wisdom does not guarantee success. Contrary to popular opinion, the sages of Proverbs do not believe in a rigid, moralistic world where everything always works out nicely for the prudent. God often has other plans that even the wisest cannot immediately discern.

Verse 31 follows up on the thought of verse 30. In this proverb, **horse** serves as a metonymy for **battle** preparations. The first line conjures images of the detail, energy, time, and strategy that go into the preparations for an encounter with the enemy. Both horse and rider are trained and outfitted for war in order to ensure a successful campaign. The proverb concludes, in the second line, with the element of surprise. A third party enters the picture, Yahweh. He is the one who really determines the result. This surprise ending is intensified because the second line contains only two words in Hebrew, which are difficult to translate into two words in English. A close rendering might be, "**victory** is Yahweh's."

The horse was a powerful technological weapon of war. However, it was easy to become overconfident in such "technology." The Philistines learned this when they brought their superior technology to battle against David and the Israelites in 1 Samuel 17. What they discovered was that **no wisdom, no insight, no plan can succeed against the LORD**.

²²⁺¹**A good name is more desirable than great riches;**
    to be esteemed is better than silver or gold.
²**Rich and poor have this in common:**
    The LORD is the Maker of them all.
³**A prudent man sees danger and takes refuge,**
    but the simple keep going and suffer for it.
⁴**Humility and the fear of the LORD**
    bring wealth and honor and life.
⁵**In the paths of the wicked lie thorns and snares,**
    but he who guards his soul stays far from them.
⁶**Train**ᵃ **a child in the way he should go,**
    and when he is old he will not turn from it.

ᵃ6 Or *Start*

22:1 The proverb does not issue a disparaging remark about wealth. Rather wisdom believes that in and of itself, wealth has no value. It is only in the context of a person's character that wealth assumes worth. Two monosyllabic nouns similar in sound highlight the contrast in this proverb: **Name** (שֵׁם, *šēm*; pronounced *shame*) and **to be esteemed** (חֵן, *ḥēn*; pronounced *hane*) are **better than silver or gold**. If one must choose between a **good name** and **great riches**, the former is **better**. This proverb is quite similar to the one found in Ecclesiastes 7:1.

22:2 The first line of the Hebrew text reads, "rich and poor meet together." The line can be understood in two possible ways. One, it means that the **rich and poor** live in close proximity to each other. Two, it means that the rich and poor have something **in common**. The second possibility makes more sense in light of the second line. The NIV understands, **Rich and poor have this in common: The LORD is the Maker of them all**. Humans do not relate to one another on the basis of their possessions but upon their value as people created in the image of God (cf. 14:31; 17:5; 29:13).

22:3 The aphorism contrasts the prudent one who is seasoned by the experiences of life with the **simple** ones who have little experience. In the first line, **a prudent man** is singular. In the second line, **the simple** is plural. The simple tend to be led by the curiosity of the group and thus be less cautious. A duplicate proverb is found in 27:12. A contemporary proverb parallels this thought: "Fools rush in where angels fear to tread" (cf. 14:16).

22:4 This Yahweh proverb equates **fear of the LORD** with **humility** (see 1:7). One who fears the LORD understands and humbly accepts his place under God's rule.[101] The result of such a posture is **wealth and honor and life**. One will receive material, social, physical, and spiritual blessings. Such blessings are not automatic or predictable because God as the source does what he sees fit in his good time.

22:5 The **paths of the wicked** (lit., "twisted man") are lined with all kinds of traps. He intentionally walks an unceasing obstacle course. **But he who guards his soul stays far from them**. The term for "soul" is better translated here as "life." The person who keeps focused on that which is most important will avoid the snares of life.

22:6 In the context of the book of Proverbs, **child** (נַעַר, *na'ar*) generally refers to a youth or young adult. The instruction to avoid gangs (1:8-19) and the temptress (chapters 5, 6, and 7), not to be lazy (6:6-

---

[101]Whybray, *Proverbs*, p. 318.

11), and to learn to speak words appropriate to the occasion (25:11) is advice suited for young adults and not young children. However, this does not preclude the implication that the proverb exhorts parents to start early in the training process (see 4:3; 19:18).

What does the phrase **in the way he should go** mean?[102] In Hebrew, the phrase is more closely rendered "according to his way." Several possibilities exist. First, "according to his way" refers to the vocation or life work of the youth. This is highly unlikely since youth had little option but to follow in the vocational guilds of their fathers. In addition, Proverbs focuses on training for character, not vocation. Second, the phrase refers to the personal aptitude of the youth. That is, the youth's individual nature, his or her likes and dislikes, talents and abilities must be considered in the process of training.[103] This proverb, however, as well as wisdom in general, does not emphasize individualism. Rather, the emphasis is on how the individual best fits into the community. The sages show little interest in discovering a child's hidden potential or personal bent. Third, "according to his way" is an ironic statement. In a satirical sense, the emphasis is on *his* way. Let youth do what they want, and they will grow into self-indulgent adults.[104] Fourth, the phrase refers to the moral training that youth are to receive early in life. "According to his way" is not to be taken individualistically as his unique way but collectively. As a youth he should be trained, like other youth, in the fear of the LORD. Parents offer instruction to youth in the fundamental principles of right and wrong.

Considering the whole context of the book of Proverbs, the fourth option is the best. The primary goal of the sage was the moral education of youth. In many ways, this proverb is best interpreted in light of the instruction poem in 2:1-11, which speaks of

---

[102]For a more detailed treatment of this verse see Ted Hildebrandt, "Proverbs 22:6a: Train Up a Child?" *Grace Theological Journal* 9, no. 1 (1988): 3-19.

[103]Ellen Davis argues that the emphasis should be "according to *his* way." She writes, "Educating each child according to her own way means that we must relax our theories and pay attention to this particular child, adjust our methods to the way in which she may best learn, nurture her particular gifts, respect her interests," (p. 120). See Ellen Davis, *Proverbs, Ecclesiastes, and the Song of Songs* (Louisville, KY: Westminster John Knox Press, 2000).

[104]This is the position of Richard Clifford, *Proverbs*, p. 197.

the collaborative effort of youth, parents, and Yahweh in the task of moral education.

⁷**The rich rule over the poor,**
    and the borrower is servant to the lender.
⁸**He who sows wickedness reaps trouble,**
    and the rod of his fury will be destroyed.
⁹**A generous man will himself be blessed,**
    for he shares his food with the poor.
¹⁰**Drive out the mocker, and out goes strife;**
    quarrels and insults are ended.
¹¹**He who loves a pure heart and whose speech is gracious**
    will have the king for his friend.
¹²**The eyes of the LORD keep watch over knowledge,**
    but he frustrates the words of the unfaithful.

22:7 A simple observation is made on a fact of life: **The rich rule over the poor, and the borrower is servant to the lender**. The adage serves as a warning about the folly of borrowing and indebtedness. Such a warning continues to speak a relevant word in a credit card world. Whybray says that this proverb is a good example of the economic status of the writer.[105] He was neither rich nor poor (see also 14:20; 18:23; 30:7-9).

22:8 The one **who sows wickedness reaps trouble** appears to refer to the wealthy who have the power to rule. **The rod** the individual holds may be some kind of farm implement used as a hand thresher. The wealthy are pictured as exercising excessive punishment to keep their workers in check. Yet such uncontrolled anger will lead to the owner's own destruction: **the rod of his fury will be destroyed.**

22:9 A generous man is literally "a good eye." The ability to see others with compassion leads to expressions of generosity. For the sage, the opposite of the one with "a good eye" is the person with "a bad eye" (23:6; 28:22). This stingy, avaricious person has blurred vision that affects his ability to share with others. Paul may allude to this proverb in 2 Corinthians 9:7: "God loves a cheerful giver."

22:10 The mocker who feeds on **strife** is one of the main enemies of the sage. The mocker is another name for a fool. The maxim

---

[105]Whybray, *Proverbs*, p. 320.

is in the form of an admonition (an imperative): **drive out** the mocker. Some individuals are clearly to be excluded from the community for the sake of solidarity (cf. 9:7-8).

22:11 The syntax of the verse is difficult to translate. Literally, the verse reads, "He who loves, pure in heart, his gracious lips, a king's friend."[106] The NIV appropriately interprets the text to refer to those qualities a **king** looks for in a confidant: **a pure heart** and one **whose speech is gracious**. The thought is similar to that in 16:13. The verse indirectly describes two qualities a **friend** or "neighbor" possesses: integrity and gracious speech.

22:12 The LORD guards **knowledge**. He cares for those who are good stewards of the gifts of wisdom. In his own way and time, **he frustrates the words of the unfaithful.**

¹³**The sluggard says, "There is a lion outside!"**
   or, "I will be murdered in the streets!"
¹⁴**The mouth of an adulteress is a deep pit;**
   he who is under the LORD's wrath will fall into it.
¹⁵**Folly is bound up in the heart of a child,**
   but the rod of discipline will drive it far from him.
¹⁶**He who oppresses the poor to increase his wealth**
   and he who gives gifts to the rich—both come to poverty.

22:13 The lazy person is a favorite target of the sage's sarcasm (20:4). The **sluggard** imagines the most bizarre disasters occurring in order to keep from working. By adding the conjunction **or**, the NIV interprets the proverb in such a way that the sluggard has two ready-made excuses: **There is a lion outside!** and **I will be murdered in the streets!** However, it seems that the second line simply describes what the lion will do to the sluggard. What makes the excuse so ridiculous is that lions did not roam the streets in ancient Israel. A parallel proverb is found in 26:13.

22:14 Outside of chapters 1–9, reference to the **adulteress** (זָרוֹת, *zārôth*; "strange women") occurs only here and in 23:27. The adulteress was known for her seductive speech (2:16; 5:3; 6:24; 7:5). God uses her speech and its consequences as a way of punishing those who are disobedient.

---

[106]The LXX adds "Lord" as the subject of love in the first line, "The Lord loves a man of pure mind."

22:15 In Proverbs, **child** usually refers to a young adult (see 22:6). Youth are not innately wise. In fact, foolishness characterizes more of their nature. Youth must learn the ways of wisdom (2:1-5). To do that, the parent sage believed that corporal punishment was sometimes necessary. **The rod** may refer to a threshing rod that served to separate the hull covering the seed from the seed itself. In the same way, the rod **of discipline** separates the folly that surrounds the heart and mind of the youth and opens the way for wisdom to take root. Through the process of discipline, youth develop morally and spiritually (see discussion of corporal punishment in 13:24).

22:16 The aphorism contains an interesting paradox. The one **who oppresses the poor** does so to **increase his wealth**. Those who **give gifts to the rich** will temporarily become poor until they win the favor of the wealthy. The real irony is that, in the end, **both come to poverty**. Greed destroys oneself. Here is a call for justice against those that oppress the poor and against a system (tax, business, or otherwise) that gives special favors or breaks to the rich. This proverb concludes the Solomonic collection that began in 10:1.

PROVERBS 22:17–24:34

OVERVIEW

It is quite obvious that a new section begins at this point in the collection. Chapter 22:17-21 introduces the section and contains a type of title: sayings of the wise. The introduction admonishes the son to listen, much like the admonitions found in chapters 1–9. This new section consists of a different rhetorical form than the previous chapters. Where the previous chapters (10:1–22:16) consisted primarily of individual sentence literature, the material now primarily consists of instruction sayings (instruction in the form of poems—usually couplets—similar to but briefer than those found in chapters 1–9). The instruction poems are frequently couched in the form of admonitions (commands), something rarely found in 10:1–22:16.

During the past century, much scholarly debate centered on the relationship of 22:17–24:22 to the "Thirty Sayings" of the Egyptian sage Amenemope (ca. 1100 B.C.). No consensus exists as to the degree to which this unit in Proverbs depends on the Egyptian. That there are similarities is clear.[1] Similarities are found primarily in 22:17–23:11. However, the Israelite sage did not slavishly copy from Amenemope. His work exhibits obvious independence, yet the Israelite sage did see the Egyptian document as a resource from which to glean wisdom. The Israelite sage filtered the insights he gained from the document through the Yahwistic lens and then creatively appropriated the reinterpreted material into his work for Israelite youth. The material served as an ethical guidebook for those seeking professional careers in the existing bureaucracy.

The NIV divides 22:17–24:22 into thirty units to correspond with the reference to the "thirty sayings" in verse 20. It is difficult always

---

[1] For a detailed survey of the issues involved see R.N. Whybray in *The Book of Proverbs: A Survey of Modern Study* (New York: Brill, 1995), pp. 6-18, 78-84.

to identify the smaller units of material in this section, thus it is hard to know if there actually are "thirty sayings." One could also divide this material on the basis of the admonition formula "my son" or "listen to your father" or "apply your heart to instruction,"[2] which is the way the instruction sayings are divided in chapters 1–9.

IV. THE INSTRUCTIONS OF THE WISE (22:17–24:34)

A. INITIAL INSTRUCTIONS OF THE WISE (22:17–24:22)

[17]**Pay attention and listen to the sayings of the wise;**
　　apply your heart to what I teach,
[18]**for it is pleasing when you keep them in your heart**
　　and have all of them ready on your lips.
[19]**So that your trust may be in the LORD,**
　　I teach you today, even you.
[20]**Have I not written thirty[a] sayings for you,**
　　sayings of counsel and knowledge,
[21]**teaching you true and reliable words,**
　　so that you can give sound answers
　　to him who sent you?

[a]*20 Or not formerly written; or not written excellent*

22:17-21 The extended introduction introduces all of 22:17–24:22. The court sage, speaking directly to the youth in the second person, admonishes him to **pay attention and listen to the sayings of the wise**. The phrase, "the sayings of the wise," is taken to refer to the title of this unit of material.

Clifford identifies the process of growing in wisdom that is subtly embedded in verses 17 and 18.[3] The initial phase involves the ear: "pay attention and listen," says the teacher. Then the student engages the mind, **apply your heart to what I teach** (the heart or "mind" was the center of thought and reflection for the Israelite). That which is reflected on is also committed to memory, **keep them**

---

[2]See Leo Perdue, *Proverbs*, Interpretation (Louisville: John Knox Press, 2000), p. 200.
[3]Clifford, *Proverbs*, p. 206.

in your heart (lit., "keep them in your belly/innermost being"). Finally, the lips are brought into service: **and have all of them ready on your lips.**[4] Wisdom involves hearing, memorizing, reflecting, and speaking with rhetorical sensitivity.

What is the purpose of the instruction the youth receives? Verse 19 specifies: **So that your trust may be in the LORD.** The explicit religious goal of the teaching is to infuse and strengthen one's trust in the LORD (cf. 3:5-8). Later in verse 21 the sage also says it is to instruct in the truth: **teaching you true and reliable words.**

The Hebrew text of verse 20 contains a word that has given commentators much difficulty. It is the word שִׁלְשׁוֹם (šilšôm, meaning "three days ago"). Since the discovery of the Instruction of Amenemope and its affinity with 22:17-24:22, commentators have emended the text in light of this Egyptian text. At the conclusion of the Instruction, Amenemope refers to the "thirty sayings" he has just written. The reference sheds light on what the scribes may have meant by the word. The majority of commentators and translations, including the NIV, emend the text to read **thirty sayings** (שְׁלֹשִׁים, šᵊlōšîm). Though one could not make a definitive argument for 22:17-24:22 containing exactly thirty sayings, it is not unreasonable to divide the material in this way. The NIV does this, and this commentary follows these divisions.

> [22] **Do not exploit the poor because they are poor**
>   **and do not crush the needy in court,**
> [23] **for the LORD will take up their case**
>   **and will plunder those who plunder them.**

22:22-23 Do not crush the needy in court (lit., "in the gate"). The gate was the place where legal and business matters were conducted. The main reason the poor were not to be exploited is theological: **the LORD** is their protector. Yahweh brought Israel out of oppression in Egypt. Israel must remember what God did for them and treat the poor and oppressed in like manner. What God did in Egypt was the reason for keeping the Sabbath (Deut 5:15). It was the basis for how they were to treat strangers (Exod 22:20-26). **Do not**

---

[4]McKane suggests that 18b means that the thoughts "are poised for shapely utterance" (*Proverbs*, p. 375). Such a meaning is in keeping with the sage's appreciation for the aesthetic beauty of oral discourse (cf. 25:11).

exploit the poor because the LORD is their defender. **The LORD will take up their case** (כִּי־יהוה יָרִיב רִיבָם, *kî-YHWH yārîb rîbām*).

²⁴**Do not make friends with a hot-tempered man,**
   do not associate with one easily angered,
²⁵**or you may learn his ways**
   and get yourself ensnared.

22:24-25 What is it that is ensnaring about **a hot-tempered man** (lit., "the lord of rage")? Such a person does not sound attractive to be around. A person might find himself or herself **ensnared** because the man's anger may not be readily apparent. Or when he express-es anger, he seems to get quick results. Whatever the attraction, one must avoid such a companion. As do a number of proverbs, this one admonishes youth not to get in with the wrong crowd (cf. 1:8-19). "Evil companions corrupt good morals" (cf. 1 Cor 15:33).

²⁶**Do not be a man who strikes hands in pledge**
   or puts up security for debts;
²⁷**if you lack the means to pay,**
   your very bed will be snatched from under you.

22:26-27 For the figure **strikes hands**, see 6:1; 11:15; 17:18. This is one of many sayings addressing the problem of surety or a **pledge** (see 6:1-5). In the making of a pledge, three parties were involved. The first was the poor person who found himself indebted to anoth-er party. The law protected the indebted person. The second was the wealthy owner who had to give back the cloak he took as a pledge from the poor by nightfall so that the poor would not be without covering (Exod 22:25-27; Deut 24:10-13). A third party, how-ever, could step in and protect the poor from loss of property or enslavement. This third party had no protection under law. The sage seems to think such a person was foolish to step in. Whatever the details were of practicing surety, it seems to have created more prob-lems than it resolved.

²⁸**Do not move an ancient boundary stone**
   set up by your forefathers.

22:28 In ancient Israel, land was not only a means for a family to survive, it was also a part of one's identity and heritage. So **moving an ancient boundary stone** destroyed the social order and well-being of individuals in the community. Basically it involved stealing another's property. Such was the case of Naboth in 1 Kings 21:4.

²⁹Do you see a man skilled in his work?
> **He will serve before kings;**
> **he will not serve before obscure men.**

22:29 The emphasis is on the **man skilled in his work**. Such a man prepares himself in acquiring appropriate skills (מָהִיר, *māhîr*). The result is that opportunities will come his way to **serve**.

^{23:1}When you sit to dine with a ruler,
> **note well what^a is before you,**
²and put a knife to your throat
> **if you are given to gluttony.**
³Do not crave his delicacies,
> **for that food is deceptive.**

^a*1 Or* who

23:1-3 Restraint in behavior and activities occupies much of wisdom's instruction. Self-restraint enables the wise to carry out responsibilities in an orderly manner and gain the respect of others. That is the issue in this instruction saying. The phrase **note well what is before you** (lit., "consider that which is before your face") refers to the food that is placed in front of you. It can also be translated, "note well *who* is before you," which refers to the host. However, both food and host may be in mind.

The admonition to **put a knife to your throat** if your appetite gets out of hand seems rather severe (v. 2), but this is not a death threat as the English sense conveys. Rather to pick up a knife and bring it to the throat is a figure for restraining the appetite. The phrase **if you are given to gluttony** literally reads "if your are a man of soul" ("soul" here refers to one's appetite; see 19:2).

How is it that the ruler's **food is deceptive** (v. 3)? **Do not crave** the ruler's **delicacies** appears to mean that the luscious food set before the youth becomes an enticement to eat too much. So do not crave his delicacies. At all costs, restrain your appetite. This instruction on proper etiquette seems rather trivial, but politeness is a manifestation of respect. Respect for those in authority is an important dimension of wisdom.

⁴**Do not wear yourself out to get rich;**
　　have the wisdom to show restraint.
⁵**Cast but a glance at riches, and they are gone,**
　　for they will surely sprout wings
　　and fly off to the sky like an eagle.

23:4-5 Restraint must be shown, not only in one's appetite (vv. 1-3), but also in the accumulation of wealth. Wealth can quite easily **sprout wings and fly off to the sky like an eagle.** Wealth has an unpredictable, evanescent quality to it: "here today, but gone tomorrow." Do not let wealth become all consuming. Proverbs has much to say about wealth. More than any other book in the Bible, it portrays wealth in a balanced way. Riches are not bad. But many other things are more important, mainly acquiring wisdom.

⁶**Do not eat the food of a stingy man,**
　　do not crave his delicacies;
⁷**for he is the kind of man**
　　who is always thinking about the cost.ᵃ
"Eat and drink," he says to you,
　　but his heart is not with you.
⁸**You will vomit up the little you have eaten**
　　and will have wasted your compliments.

ᵃ7 Or *for as he thinks within himself, / so he is*; or *for as he puts on a feast, / so he is*

23:6-8 The phrase **do not crave his delicacies** was used in 3a. In verses 1-3 the emphasis was on the behavior of the youth sitting at table; here the emphasis is on the host (not a ruler as in vv. 1-3). This host is **a stingy man.** The phrase literally means "bad of eyes," the opposite of the phrase "good of eyes" (i.e., one who is generous) used in 22:9.

The translation and interpretation of 7a remains uncertain. The KJV translates the line "for as he thinketh in his heart, so is he," which has become a well-known proverb in the English language. The NIV translates it **for he is the kind of man who is always thinking about the cost.** The NRSV translates it, "for like a hair in the throat, so are they." These are quite diverse translations. The problem centers around how to translate the phrase שָׁעַר בְּנַפְשׁוֹ (*šāʻar bᵊnaphšô*).⁵ Some have proposed to emend שָׁעַר (*šāʻar*, "reckon" or "think"?) to שֵׂעָר (śē'ār, "hair"). In this context, soul (נֶפֶשׁ, nepheš) may mean "throat" (see 19:2). McKane's solution is to follow the LXX, which he translates: "Eating and drinking (with him) is as if one should swallow a hair." Following the LXX at this point appears to be the best solution to the enigmatic verse. This is the basic approach the NRSV takes in its translation, "for like a hair in the throat, so are they." Hair in the throat makes one gag. In like manner, eating and drinking with a stingy man will cause you to **vomit up the little you have eaten**. That is not literally what will happen. Once the duplicity of the stingy man's character is discovered, you will be sick to your stomach.

Regardless of whether one goes with the NIV or the NRSV, the thought of the instruction remains basically the same. The host is one who puts on a nice front, pretending to be a friend. While outwardly he says cordially, **"Eat and drink,"** inwardly **his heart is not with you.** He gives the appearance of generosity, but in reality he is a greedy man. Discovering such a sham makes one nauseous. The image in this instruction is just the opposite of that found in 22:9: "A generous man will himself be blessed, for he shares his food with the poor."

**⁹Do not speak to a fool,
      for he will scorn the wisdom of your words.**

23:9 The proverb gives similar advice to that offered in 26:4. One must not waste wise words on the fool. Know your listeners and speak only words of wisdom to those who can appreciate it. Jesus put it this way: "Do not cast your pearls before swine" (Matt 7:6).

**¹⁰Do not move an ancient boundary stone
      or encroach on the fields of the fatherless,
¹¹for their Defender is strong;
      he will take up their case against you.**

---

[5]The use of the triliteral root שָׁעַר as a verb in the *qal* (i.e., the basic root meaning) does not exist in the Bible except in Gen 26:12 where it means "a measure of grain." BDB defines the meaning of the word as "to calculate, reckon" (p. 1045). Amenemope uses the phrase, "a poor man's goods are a block in the throat" in one of his Thirty Sayings. For further treatment of the word see also Kenneth L. Barker, "Proverbs 23:7–'To Think' or 'To Serve Food'?" *The Journal of the Ancient Near Eastern Society* 19 (1989): 3-8.

23:10-11 One does not **encroach on the fields of the fatherless** because the land is a part of their inheritance. Primarily, though, the LORD is **their Defender** (נֹאֲלָם, gō'ălām). "Defender" refers to the next of kin who is also mentioned in the book of Ruth. See 22:28 regarding the **ancient boundary stone.**

Verse 11 concludes the section that contains parallels found in the Instruction of Amenemope. The sage continues, though, to construct his own "Thirty Sayings" that equip Israelite youth to trust in the LORD (22:19).

¹²**Apply your heart to instruction**
    and your ears to words of knowledge.

23:12 This verse serves to introduce what follows. It is an admonition to the youth to heed the instructions found throughout this unit. Similar admonitions were given the youth in chapters 1–9.

¹³**Do not withhold discipline from a child;**
    if you punish him with the rod, he will not die.
¹⁴**Punish him with the rod**
    and save his soul from death.^a

^a*14* Hebrew *Sheol*

23:13-14 All through Proverbs, the parent sages encourage the use of corporal punishment. However, this admonition to parents seems rather harsh with the observation, **if you punish him with the rod, he will not die.** The expression is a hyperbole and may be similar to today's parents exhorting teenagers to complete a difficult work task, "It's not going to kill you." The goal of the punishment is not the venting of parental anger and frustration but the saving of a youth's life from untimely death (see 13:24; Eph 6:4).

In Proverbs, the rod is always administered in the context of a loving family environment (13:24b). This admonition to parents should be read in light of the succeeding instruction in verses 15-16, which speaks of the affection a father has for his son.

¹⁵**My son, if your heart is wise,**
    then my heart will be glad;
¹⁶**my inmost being will rejoice**
    when your lips speak what is right.

23:15-16 The saying overflows with affection and joy for a son who manifests a life of wisdom. It is difficult for parents to express the joy and satisfaction they feel from seeing a youth grow in wisdom and in stature and in favor with God and fellow humans. This parent expresses the pleasure he will experience in his son's moral development.

> [17]**Do not let your heart envy sinners,**
>   **but always be zealous for the fear of the LORD.**
> [18]**There is surely a future hope for you,**
>   **and your hope will not be cut off.**

23:17-18 More than likely, one comes to **envy sinners** because of their apparent success. A more detailed description of such envy is found in Psalm 73:3-12. Not to envy sinners means that the righteous do not incorporate them into their circle of close friends. This, along with other instructions, admonishes youth to be wary of the company they keep (see 1:9-19; 22:24-25). Verse 17b in Hebrew contains no verb. The NIV rightly understands the verb "envy" (קָנָא, *qānā'*) in the first line to double also as the verb in the second line where it is appropriately translated **zealous**. The verb can be used in either a negative or a positive sense (as in the English words jealous or zealous; see S of S 8:6). For example, Phinehas is described in Numbers 25:13 as one "zealous (*qānā'*) for the honor of his God." The advice given in verse 17 is that zeal (*qānā'*) must focus on **the fear of the LORD** and not on sinners.

Such focused zeal for the LORD results in **a future hope**, a **hope** that **will not be cut off** (the same phrase is used in 24:14c). The last phrase does not refer to the afterlife, rather to a long and fulfilling life in the here and now.

> [19]**Listen, my son, and be wise,**
>   **and keep your heart on the right path.**
> [20]**Do not join those who drink too much wine**
>   **or gorge themselves on meat,**
> [21]**for drunkards and gluttons become poor,**
>   **and drowsiness clothes them in rags.**

23:19-21 Verse 19a is a standard formulaic introduction: **Listen, my son, and be wise.** Chapters 1–9 introduced the reader to three temptations to which youth find themselves vulnerable: lust, laziness, and leisure. This instruction addresses the third: the tempta-

tion to enjoy the good life. Gluttony and drunkenness are examples
of conspicuous consumption undertaken to flaunt status. What is
the result of such a lifestyle? **For drunkards and gluttons become
poor, and drowsiness clothes them in rags**.

²²**Listen to your father, who gave you life,**
        and do not despise your mother when she is old.
²³**Buy the truth and do not sell it;**
        get wisdom, discipline and understanding.
²⁴**The father of a righteous man has great joy;**
        he who has a wise son delights in him.
²⁵**May your father and mother be glad;**
        may she who gave you birth rejoice!

23:22-25 To **buy the truth** (v. 23) does not mean to pay money
for it. Rather it means for one to invest mental, emotional, and spiritual resources in pursuing it (see 17:16). Even though the primary
referent of this instruction is the youth, the admonition describes
the reciprocal relationship that exists in healthy families. Parents
bestow **life** in its fullest sense (biological, spiritual, and moral) on
children. In return, children bestow honor on **father** and **mother**.
After children have spent years pursuing **wisdom, discipline and
understanding**, parents experience the final reward of satisfaction
and **joy** (v. 24). It is only in the context of such healthy reciprocity
and mutual respect that sages envisioned the use of corporal punishment (vv. 13-14).

²⁶**My son, give me your heart**
        and let your eyes keep to my ways,
²⁷**for a prostitute is a deep pit**
        and a wayward wife is a narrow well.
²⁸**Like a bandit she lies in wait,**
        and multiplies the unfaithful among men.

23:26-28 The parent sage admonishes the youth to **give me your
heart** (v. 26). The request is for the youth to submit his will to the
ways of the older and wiser adult. Such submission will keep one
focused on the right path and prevent one from falling into the
deep pit and **narrow well** of the **wayward wife** (נָכְרִיָּה, *nākrîyāh*). The
mention of the wayward (or "foreign") woman echoes chapters 1–9.
The wayward wife is described like a **bandit** who waits to ambush

inexperienced youth (cf. 7:12). One means of protection against such an ambush is to keep to the ways of wisdom. The wise display restraint when it comes to expressing sexual energy.

²⁹**Who has woe? Who has sorrow?**
   Who has strife? Who has complaints?
   Who has needless bruises? Who has bloodshot eyes?
³⁰**Those who linger over wine,**
   who go to sample bowls of mixed wine.
³¹**Do not gaze at wine when it is red,**
   when it sparkles in the cup,
   when it goes down smoothly!
³²**In the end it bites like a snake**
   and poisons like a viper.
³³**Your eyes will see strange sights**
   and your mind imagine confusing things.
³⁴**You will be like one sleeping on the high seas,**
   lying on top of the rigging.
³⁵**"They hit me," you will say, "but I'm not hurt!**
   They beat me, but I don't feel it!
 When will I wake up
   so I can find another drink?"

23:29-35 The sage paints a graphic picture of the effects of alcohol on the human body. Verse 29 includes a series of six questions, which set up the instruction as a type of riddle. Subtly, the questions portray the consequences of inebriation in the fashion of a litany: **woe, sorrow, strife, complaints, needless bruises,** and **bloodshot eyes**. The obvious answer to the "riddle" comes in verse 30. The consequences describe **those who linger over wine**. Then the sage gives the admonition in verse 31: **Do not gaze at wine when it is red, when it sparkles in the cup, when it goes down smoothly!** A striking word play occurs in verse 31 on the image of "eye." The phrase **when it sparkles in the cup** literally reads "when it gives its eye" (a type of personification). **Do not gaze at wine** because it will stare back at you with alluring eyes. So whatever you do, do not make eye contact with wine.

Verses 32-35 describe the consequences of overindulgence. The drink releases deadly venom into the bloodstream and an individual experiences hallucinations, motion sickness, and disorientation. All the while, the drunkard remains oblivious to the dangers. Such persons find themselves caught in a vicious cycle: **when will I wake up so I can find another drink?**

Besides the important admonition to refrain from intoxication, the poem presents a great rhetorical model for how to instruct. The poem uses rhetorical questions and a riddle-type form. It makes use of colorful concrete language. It includes a mock monologue of the inebriated. It employs vivid word plays and personification. The poem incorporates a host of instructional devices that serve as a model for teaching moral values today.

²⁴:¹**Do not envy wicked men,**
  do not desire their company;
²**for their hearts plot violence,**
  and their lips talk about making trouble.

24:1-2 The admonition is a common one in this part of the Proverb collection. Similar advice is given on two other occasions (23:17-18; 24:19-20). Common to all three of these admonitions is the verb **envy** (קָנָא, *qānā'*). The envy that one feels for another person's success destroys the inner self (14:30). At first the motive given in verse 2 for not envying the **wicked** seems rather shallow: what the wicked do is morally wrong. However, a youth who has been instructed in righteousness, justice, and fairness needs no further reason (1:3).

The proverbs in verses 3-9 resemble more closely the sentence literature in 10:1–22:16. They do not admonish; they simply make observations.

³**By wisdom a house is built,**
  and through understanding it is established;
⁴**through knowledge its rooms are filled**
  with rare and beautiful treasures.

24:3-4 Does **house** (v. 3) refer to a physical building or metaphorically to a home or family? The latter seems to be the case as indicated by the tools used to build it: **wisdom** and **understanding** and **knowledge**. The building of a familial home and community is the goal of wisdom, which is ultimately described in 31:10-31 (allusions are made earlier in 9:1 and 14:1). It is noteworthy to contrast the house that wisdom built with the house the gang builds in 1:10-19.

The gang brags about getting "all sorts of valuable things" and filling "our houses with plunder" (1:13). In contrast, wisdom offers to fill the house **with rare and beautiful treasures** that result from knowledge and understanding. This house will stand.

⁵**A wise man has great power,**
   and a man of knowledge increases strength;
⁶**for waging war you need guidance,**
   and for victory many advisers.

24:5-6 The Hebrew text of 5a reads, "A man of wisdom is strong." The idea of verse 5 is clear. True **power** resides not in brute physical strength, but in **knowledge** or understanding. It is this kind of power one seeks in time of war (v. 6; cf. 11:14 and 21:22).

⁷**Wisdom is too high for a fool;**
   in the assembly at the gate he has nothing to say.

24:7 Clifford points out that verses 3-6 describe the advantages of wisdom and verses 7-9 speak of the disadvantages of folly.[6] Verse 7a observes that wisdom is **too high,**[7] that is, out of the reach of the **fool**. As a result, the fool has no contribution to make **at the gate** where issues are discussed and decisions made.

⁸**He who plots evil**
   will be known as a schemer.
⁹**The schemes of folly are sin,**
   and men detest a mocker.

24:8-9 The one who **plots evil** has lost his reputation in the community and now has a new name: **schemer.** In Proverbs certain conduct is described as detestable to God or "an abomination to the LORD." Verse 9b is unusual in that it describes the **mocker** as being someone whom **men detest** or who is "an abomination to men."

¹⁰**If you falter in times of trouble,**
   how small is your strength!

24:10 The Hebrew contains a word play between **trouble** (צָרָה, ṣārāh) and **strength** (צַר, ṣar). The adage affirms a difficult but true

---

[6]Clifford, *Proverbs,* p. 214.
[7]The Hebrew word is רָאמוֹת (*rā'môth,* "coral") and probably should be emended to רָמוֹת (*rāmôth,* "to be high").

principle: adversity tests the strength of one's character (cf. Jer 12:5-6; Jas 1:2-4).

[11]**Rescue those being led away to death;**
   hold back those staggering toward slaughter.
[12]**If you say, "But we knew nothing about this,"**
   does not he who weighs the heart perceive it?
 Does not he who guards your life know it?
   Will he not repay each person according to what he has
      done?

24:11-12 The question that arises with this proverb is, who are **those being led away to death**? Several possibilities have been suggested. (1) It could be prisoners unjustly accused. (2) It could refer to those who are morally blind, the naïve youth described in Proverbs. (3) It could be ones being robbed by bandits or victimized by oppressors. Whoever they are, they are innocent victims of the plight in which they find themselves. That is why **rescue** or some kind of intervention is necessary. The ones who are being asked to intervene do not appear to have special power to stop an unjust juridical decision made in court. Instead those called on to rescue seem to be citizens who have observed some kind of injustice in the ordinary affairs of life. Thus options 2 and 3 seem to be the best alternatives.

The admonition calls on them to step in. However, the temptation is not to respond. Ignorance, though, is no excuse. To say **we knew nothing about this** is unacceptable. It seems that those who were present chose to ignore the problem and plead ignorance. The sage responds, "The LORD **who weighs the heart** sees the problem and your indifference and will respond accordingly." Failure to act is also the characteristic of the sluggard.

The instruction identifies the primary realm of God's rule emphasized all through Proverbs. It is his intimate and daily involvement in the hearts and minds of his people: **Does not he who weighs the heart perceive it? Does not he who guards your life know it?** The LORD discerns our thoughts and intentions (16:2).

[13]**Eat honey, my son, for it is good;**
   honey from the comb is sweet to your taste.
[14]**Know also that wisdom is sweet to your soul;**
      if you find it, there is a future hope for you,
      and your hope will not be cut off.

24:13-14 Is verse 13 an admonition to eat healthy food? The sages were concerned about maintaining healthy physical bodies. However, the admonition here to **eat honey** is metaphoric. It is a figure for finding **wisdom** (v. 14). The student must also know that wisdom, like honey, **is sweet to your soul**. "Soul" (נֶפֶשׁ, *nepheš*) would be better rendered here as "appetite" (see 19:2). In Proverbs, the quest is to **find** (מָצָא, *māṣa'*) wisdom (1:28; 3:13; 8:17; 8:35) or to find that which is good (16:20; 17:20) or to find a good wife (18:22; 31:10) or to find a good man (20:6). In verse 14, if one finds wisdom, then **there is a future hope for you**. For the phrase **your hope will not be cut off**, see 23:18.

¹⁵**Do not lie in wait like an outlaw against a righteous man's house,**
   do not raid his dwelling place;
¹⁶**for though a righteous man falls seven times, he rises again,**
   but the wicked are brought down by calamity.

24:15-16 Do not bother to bring about the downfall of the **righteous man's house** because it will only be a waste of time. The **righteous** are a hardy bunch. They will continually recover from adversity or temptation (**seven times**) and be even stronger (notice a different scenario in 25:26). In contrast, **the wicked are brought down** when they face a single crisis.

¹⁷**Do not gloat when your enemy falls;**
   when he stumbles, do not let your heart rejoice,
¹⁸**or the LORD will see and disapprove**
   and turn his wrath away from him.

24:17-18 It could be quite tempting to develop a self-righteous attitude and **gloat when your enemy falls**. To do so circumvents God's justice. Instead, youth are admonished to leave judgment to God. All through Proverbs, those who are wise learn to respect their enemies (17:13; 20:22; 24:29). The enemy must not only be respected, he is to be treated with kindness (25:21-22). This is a principle taught in the Old Testament (Exod 23:4-5).

¹⁹**Do not fret because of evil men**
   or be envious of the wicked,
²⁰**for the evil man has no future hope,**
   and the lamp of the wicked will be snuffed out.

24:19-20 This is the third of three instructions regarding **envy** of the prosperous **wicked** (see 23:17-18; 24:1-2).

²¹**Fear the LORD and the king, my son,**
and do not join with the rebellious,
²²**for those two will send sudden destruction upon them,**
and who knows what calamities they can bring?

24:21-22 To **fear the LORD and the king** is an unusual association, but it should come as no surprise. God had ordained the king to be his ambassador for justice on the earth. The proverb does not put the king on equal ground with Yahweh. There are other proverbs that clearly describe the subordinate role of the king (e.g., 21:1; 16:1-15).

The precise meaning of verse 21b is unclear. The text literally reads "do not associate with the ones who change." The NIV basically follows this meaning, interpreting "the ones who change" as rebels. Following the LXX, the NRSV reads, "do not disobey either of them." Whichever reading one chooses, the underlying message remains the same. One respects not only God, but also government officials who exercise responsible authority.

B. FURTHER INSTRUCTIONS OF THE WISE (24:23-34)

²³**These also are sayings of the wise:**

To show partiality in judging is not good:
²⁴**Whoever says to the guilty, "You are innocent"—**
peoples will curse him and nations denounce him.
²⁵**But it will go well with those who convict the guilty,**
and rich blessing will come upon them.

24:23-25 A new heading is found in verse 23a: **These also are the sayings of the wise**. The first instruction that follows concerns **showing partiality**. The phrase used in Hebrew, "to recognize faces," means to play favorites. The same phrase is used in 28:21a. Verse 23b is another **not good** proverb (see 16:29; 18:5; 19:2).

In court, whoever pronounces the guilty innocent perverts justice. Courtroom injustice is a universal crime. All **peoples and nations** will **denounce** such activities.

[26]An honest answer
    is like a kiss on the lips.

24:26 Uncertain of its context (some would place the proverb with the previous verses and in the setting of the court), the axiom remains ambiguous. When one "returns honest words" (so the Hebrew) or gives an **honest answer**, the experience **is like a kiss on the lips**. The phrase is some type of idiom that expresses affection or love.

[27]**Finish your outdoor work**
    and get your fields ready;
    after that, build your house.

24:27 The specific image is that of a farmer and an agricultural context. Whatever the sequence of events refers to (first **outdoor work**, then **build your house**), the advice is vintage wisdom as it admonishes the farmer to do his work in an orderly way. Even though the specific context is agrarian, the proverb has broader application. The underlying concern calls on individuals to establish priorities and do things in their proper time. Once a person has prioritized, then the rest of life falls into place.

[28]**Do not testify against your neighbor without cause,**
    or use your lips to deceive.
[29]**Do not say, "I'll do to him as he has done to me;**
    I'll pay that man back for what he did."

24:28-29 Another of the many warnings in Proverbs about false witnessing and perjury (see 21:28). On the theme of revenge, see 25:21-22.

[30]**I went past the field of the sluggard,**
    past the vineyard of the man who lacks judgment;
[31]**thorns had come up everywhere,**
    the ground was covered with weeds,
    and the stone wall was in ruins.
[32]**I applied my heart to what I observed**
    and learned a lesson from what I saw:
[33]**A little sleep, a little slumber,**
    a little folding of the hands to rest—
[34]**and poverty will come on you like a bandit**
    and scarcity like an armed man.[a]

[a]*34* Or *like a vagrant / and scarcity like a beggar*

24:30-34 Here is an instruction story told in the first person. Contrary to the field of the wise in verse 27, which is kept in an orderly manner, **the field of the sluggard** is in total disarray. The "house" of the lackadaisical person manifests no focus or discipline, as does the "house" of the wise in 24:3-4.

Like 23:29-35, here is another good model for teaching moral principles. It is out of personal experience that the instructor begins. He sees the field of the sluggard. Then he **applied** his **heart to what** he **observed**. That is, he reflects on the experience. Out of that reflection, he **learned a lesson**. Finally, he expresses the lesson or principle in a creative rhetorical form (a proverb) to the student: **A little sleep, a little slumber, a little folding of the hands to rest—and poverty will come on you like a bandit and scarcity like an armed man**. That this was a well-known proverb is evident from the fact that it is also quoted in 6:10-11.

With this instruction story, the instruction literature, found in 22:17–24:34, closes. The next section of the collection moves back to the more familiar sentence literature.

PROVERBS 25–29

OVERVIEW

The heading in 25:1 clearly marks off the beginning of a new collection from the preceding one. The next heading is found in 30:1. Thus it appears that chapters 25–29 form another collection. This collection is made up of sentence literature much like that found in chapters 10:1–22:16. Within this second Solomonic collection, there are two distinct subunits: chapters 25–27 and 28–29. Chapters 25–27 are made up of "analogic" proverbs that use rich images and metaphors. Chapters 28–29 are dominated by antithetic proverbs, which revert to the form that dominated the first Solomonic collection in chapters 10–15.

The proverbs in chapters 25–27 usually contain a comparison in the first line and then in the second line, the referent, or the object of comparison. The comparison is simply laid alongside the referent without the use of the particle "like" or "as."[1] However, the NIV typically adds the particle and also sometimes reverses the order of the two lines, stating the referent first and then making the comparison. This takes away from the anticipation that the proverb intends to create by stating the comparison first. For example, the following is my translation of the proverbs in 25:11 and 12 that tries to follow closely the sequence of the Hebrew text:

> [11]Apples of gold in settings of silver,
>   a word well turned.
> [12]A ring of gold and a trinket of fine gold,
>   one who gives wise reproof to a listening ear.

---

[1]When a comparison is simply laid alongside the object of comparison without the use of "like" or "as," the proverb is said to have an asyndetic arrangement.

Compare the way in which the NIV translates these same two proverbs:

> [11]A word aptly spoken
> is like apples of gold in settings of silver.
> [12]Like an earring of gold or an ornament of fine gold
> is a wise man's rebuke to a listening ear.

With verse 11, the NIV reverses the order of the lines, putting the analogy last. And while it keeps the order of lines in verse 12, the NIV adds "like." While the NIV communicates the meaning of the proverbs, their rhetorical power and the function are diminished. Throwing a common image or experience alongside a moral statement without explanation requires the reader to do the satisfying work of making the connection between the two.

The comparisons used in these chapters come from the everyday experiences of life. When such images are placed alongside the virtue or vice in the second line, the meaning intensifies, and the thought penetrates the mind of the reader, such as in the following proverb: "Iron sharpens iron, and a man sharpens his friend" (27:17).

Chapters 25–27 are distinct because of their heavy use of analogic proverbs. These chapters also are virtually absent of any references to Yahweh. Chapter 25:2 contains a reference to the more generic term "God" (אֱלֹהִים, 'ĕlōhîm). However, this does not mean that these proverbs are secular in nature. Underlying the whole of Proverbs is the fundamental belief in the God, Yahweh, who created the heavens and earth.

Some scholars have argued for an overarching structure to chapter 25.[2] Even if one takes issue with the existence of a larger structure at work, at the least the reader can identify couplets that have been placed together as well as the pattern of alteration between "admonitions" and "sayings."[3] I will identify the couplets as they arise.

---

[2]See Glendon E. Bryce, "Another Wisdom-'Book' in Proverbs," *JBL* (1972): 145-157. Also see Raymond C. Van Leeuwen, *Context and Meaning in Proverbs 25–27* (Atlanta: Scholars Press, 1988), p. 70. Van Leeuwen devotes chapter two in his book to explicating Bryce's work (pp. 21-28).

[3]"Sayings" are proverbs that make a simple observation on life. They offer descriptions of experiences or teach a moral. "Admonitions" are stated in the imperative. They issue a moral command to the reader.

V. SENTENCE LITERATURE OF THE SECOND
SOLOMONIC COLLECTION (25:1–29:27)

A. COMPARATIVE PROVERBS (25:1–27:22)

[1]These are more proverbs of Solomon, copied by the men of
Hezekiah king of Judah:

25:1 The scribes in Hezekiah's court (715–687 B.C.) **copied** the
proverbs of Solomon. The responsibility of copying probably
involved collecting and transmitting the proverbs that circulated
among the culture of the day. This heading seems to apply to the
collection found in chapters 25–29.

Verses 2-7b express some type of concern for the king. Verses 2-5
are a narrative dealing with the responsibility of the king. Verses 6-7b
are a vignette addressing the relationship a young man is to have in the
king's court. And verses 7c-10 are a narrative about ethical responsibilities to one's neighbor. In all, verses 2-10 contain a series of couplets.

[2]**It is the glory of God to conceal a matter;**
to search out a matter is the glory of kings.
[3]**As the heavens are high and the earth is deep,**
so the hearts of kings are unsearchable.

25:2-3 In verse 2, wisdom describes the close relationship that
exists between **God** and **kings**. A fundamental difference distinguishes the two. The very nature of God means that his character is
shrouded in mystery. That God conceals relates to his inscrutable
ways (see Isa 55:8-9). Such inscrutability creates a sense of wonder in
his creation. In contrast, kings are praised for their ability to uncov-
er secrets. The Contemporary English Version translates verse 2 as
follows: "God is praised for being mysterious, rulers are praised for
explaining mysteries."

Verse 3 describes the **hearts** (i.e., "minds") **of kings** as unfath-
omable resources for dealing with the problems and affairs of state.
The king's mental resources are not predictable, but creative and
ingenious.

[4]**Remove the dross from the silver,**
and out comes material for[a] the silversmith;

⁵**remove the wicked from the king's presence,**
> **and his throne will be established through righteousness.**

ª*4 Or comes a vessel from*

25:4-5 As the **silversmith** who separates the impurities of metal
in the smelting process, the **king** separates **the wicked**. The couplet
describes the responsibility of the king as that of establishing **righteousness**. The responsible king does not surround himself with the
wicked but with those who, through the fear of the Lord, live righteous lives.

⁶**Do not exalt yourself in the king's presence,**
> **and do not claim a place among great men;**
⁷**it is better for him to say to you, "Come up here,"**
> **than for him to humiliate you before a nobleman.**

25:6-7b Here is an admonition to a young man aspiring to have a
prominent role in the royal court regarding the dangers of self-promotion. The advice is offered in the form of a better-than proverb that
urges the youth to express a posture of humility in the presence of the
king. Jesus' parable in Luke 14:7-11 expands on this proverb.

What you have seen with your eyes
⁸   **do not bring hastilyª to court,**
for what will you do in the end
> **if your neighbor puts you to shame?**

ª*7,8 Or nobleman / on whom you had set your eyes. / ⁸Do not go*

25:7c-8 Whether the dispute described is public or private, the
admonition is against making a hasty judgment. A person can easily
jump to conclusions about what he or she has witnessed and bring
litigation against another that is frivolous.

⁹**If you argue your case with a neighbor,**
> **do not betray another man's confidence,**
¹⁰**or he who hears it may shame you**
> **and you will never lose your bad reputation.**

25:9-10 Continuing the advice given in verses 7c-8, the admonition is to keep the quarrel between you and the neighbor. **Do not**
slander another. The cost for violating another's **confidence** is a loss
of **reputation**. In the book of Proverbs, the sages are quite reluctant

to resolve disputes in court. They prefer that matters be settled face-to-face outside a legal context.

¹¹A word aptly spoken
    is like apples of gold in settings of silver.
¹²Like an earring of gold or an ornament of fine gold
    is a wise man's rebuke to a listening ear.

25:11-12 Verses 11 and 12 are a proverb pair because both use the image of precious metal as an analogy for proper speaking and listening. In both proverbs, the **gold** is crafted into something aesthetically pleasing. The analogy **apples of gold in settings of silver** comes in the first line in the Hebrew text (not in the second line, as in the NIV) and is intended to engage the reader actively in wondering what it is about. The first line intentionally withholds the reference. The line simply alludes to some beautiful piece of artwork, jewels, or precious stones that are inlaid on a silver frame. The second line discloses the referent. Such a masterpiece of human art is compared to the artistic use of words: **a word aptly spoken**. The meaning of "aptly" (אֹפֶן, *'ōphen*) is uncertain because this is the only time the word appears in the Old Testament.[4] McKane suggests that the phrase "aptly spoken" (עַל־אׇפְנָיו, *'al-'āphnāyw*) might literally allude to a word "upon its two wheels."[5] That is, the "two wheels" refer to the two parallel halves of a proverb. Without a doubt, proverbs themselves model artful speech. In any event, the second line (in the Hebrew text), "a word aptly spoken," speaks to the artful and appropriate use of speech. When used aptly, words are a beautiful piece of artwork (cf. 15:23).

In verse 12, the image is stated first, **like an earring of gold or an ornament of fine gold**. The artwork here is jewelry, a gold earring. The reader then anticipates the second line, **a wise man's rebuke to a listening ear**. Such attractive jewelry is compared to advice that is seasoned with correction given to one (a student or a youth) who has a listening ear. Notice the team effort necessary to

---

[4]BDB take it to mean "circumstance" (p. 67).

[5]McKane, *Proverbs*, p. 584. He suggests that the image of two wheels refers to the two lines of the proverb that stand in balanced relationship to one another.

acquire wisdom, "wise rebuke"[6] and "a listening ear." The process of offering reproof that is in good taste to one who is receptive to it is described as a work of art.

**[13]Like the coolness of snow at harvest time
is a trustworthy messenger to those who send him;
he refreshes the spirit of his masters.
[14]Like clouds and wind without rain
is a man who boasts of gifts he does not give.**

25:13-14 Verses 13 and 14 are also a pair of proverbs. While verses 11-12 speak of nature that has been artistically molded and shaped by humans, verses 13-14 speak of another kind of nature that is beyond human control: the weather. Some translators question the reality of the image, **coolness of snow at harvest time**, (v. 13a) and the high improbability of snow during harvest. It is possible that what the phrase implies is servants who bring down snow from the mountains in the north to harvesters (or even more probable, to the wealthy; note that the verse contains *three* lines rather than the usual two).

However, the image does not have to be a reality or an actual event but simply a figure, an intentional exaggeration, depicting unexpected and pleasurable refreshment.[7] The proverb imagines the relief harvesters receive from the heat of the day by something cold and refreshing. That image is used as an analogy to describe a **master** who receives refreshment simply from knowing he can depend on his **messenger** to relay the message faithfully. The message will be handled with integrity.

Where verse 13 described the reliable messenger, verse 14 describes the unreliable boaster. The focus is on the person who makes empty promises. Such promises are **like clouds** that appear on the horizon over a parched country that bring no **rain**.

**[15]Through patience a ruler can be persuaded,
and a gentle tongue can break a bone.**

25:15 The maxim has to do with the control of speech. **Through**

---

[6]In Proverbs "rebuke" or "reproof" refers to offering sound advice like that given by a father to his son in 1:9-19. Reproof does not refer to scolding or constant nagging.

[7]Think about contemporary beverage commercials depicting a snowstorm during the summer.

patience (one who is literally "slow to anger") **a ruler can be persuaded**. By the proper use of discourse, someone of a lesser status can exercise influence over someone of a greater status. Through the controlled use of speech, a person who has political clout can literally be "opened"[8] (**persuaded**) to considering other ideas and perspectives. The second line uses figurative language to express the power of such persuasion: **and a gentle tongue can break a bone**. As Van Leeuwen astutely observes, ". . . the softest organ, the tongue, breaks the hardest organ, the bone."[9] In this proverb, the power of speech is put to positive use as it influences people in powerful positions (the proverbs in 16:21,23-24 are closely related in thought to v. 15). An example of this proverb in action is found in the story of the poor wise man in Ecclesiastes 9:13-16. At the conclusion of that story, the writer observes, "The quiet words of the wise are more to be heeded than the shouts of a ruler of fools" (Eccl 9:17). The observation is similar in meaning to this proverb (see also 16:14).

[16]**If you find honey, eat just enough—
   too much of it, and you will vomit.**
[17]**Seldom set foot in your neighbor's house—
   too much of you, and he will hate you.**

25:16-17 These verses form a couplet. Both use the key word "sated" (שָׂבַע, śbʿ; the NIV translates it, **too much of**). Both proverbs refer to something valuable becoming harmful because it is not controlled. In the Old Testament, **honey** is viewed as a health food with medicinal qualities. However, too much honey can make one ill. The proverb of verse 17 picks up on this image and becomes the center of gravity for the pair. Friendship (the NIV translates it **neighbor**), like honey, has medicinal value for the mental health of an individual. However, overstaying one's welcome can harm the relationship.

[18]**Like a club or a sword or a sharp arrow
   is the man who gives false testimony against his neighbor.**

---

[8]The Hebrew word פָּתָה (*pāthāh*) means "to be simple" or "open." BDB translates it "be persuaded" (p. 834). It is the root from which the noun פֶּתִי (*pethî*, the "simple" or "naïve" one) comes. McKane remarks, "By patience a prince . . . can be . . . 'made to act like a *peti*,' a youth who is untutored and innocent of affairs" (*Proverbs*, p. 584).

[9]Van Leeuwen, *Proverbs*, p. 219.

[19]**Like a bad tooth or a lame foot**
     is reliance on the unfaithful in times of trouble.
[20]**Like one who takes away a garment on a cold day,**
       or like vinegar poured on soda,
     is one who sings songs to a heavy heart.

25:18-20 Verses 18,19, and 20 are closely related in thought and image. All the images used are in some way negative. The analogies have to do with something natural being transformed into something abusive or harmful. The first line of verse 18 lists a series of instruments of war: **club, sword, sharp arrow.** The common denominator underlying them is that they are all like an individual who speaks out falsely against a "friend" or **neighbor.** Here is an image of the destructive force of speech. Each of the three weapons of war listed may symbolize the different ways in which words destroy. A club smashes or splits open its victim. A sword instantly kills its opponent. And an arrow can destroy its enemy at a great distance. All three lethal weapons highlight the destructive power of speech.

This destructive nature is pressed even further in verse 19. Teeth and feet are two parts of the body necessary for survival. One automatically assumes that the body parts will perform their functions. Here, these natural allies have betrayed the body and are now, because of impotence, used to defeat the individual. This betrayal is compared to one who places confidence in an unreliable person at a critical moment in time. At all costs, avoid the slanderer (v. 18) and **the unfaithful** (v. 19).

Verse 20 is the climax to the trio (vv. 18-20) and highlights the use of outside forces to defeat the internal character.[10] The Hebrew text of verse 20 juxtaposes two analogies before identifying the referent in the third line:

> Removing a garment on a cold day
> vinegar on a wound[11]
> and singing songs to a sad heart.[12] (my translation)

---

[10]Like verse 13, verse 20 is unusual in construction because it is composed of three rather than two lines.

[11]The Hebrew text reads "vinegar on soda." The idea is that the two are incompatible, adding one bitter thing to another. However, the word can also be translated "wound." See McKane *Proverbs,* p. 588.

[19]Since the LXX adds another line after the last one, McKane translates the

One of the issues pertaining to this verse has to do with whether the **heavy heart** belongs to the one who is doing the singing or to the one to whom the **songs** are being sung. If the former, it would be analogous to the image of a clown entertaining an audience when the clown himself or herself is sad. More than likely, the force of the verse resides with the latter interpretation. The images in the previous lines support this reading. The first two lines describe an external force being used to shock a person: cold air hitting one's body and applying vinegar to an open wound.[13] The reference of these images appears in the third line and describes the shock of someone singing a lighthearted song to another who possesses a heavy heart. The heavy-hearted person who hears the lighthearted songs may feel like he or she has just received a club to the head or a sword thrust or an arrow in the heart (see v. 18). The one who does the singing has no sensitivity to what is appropriate for the grieving person.

²¹**If your enemy is hungry, give him food to eat;**
   if he is thirsty, give him water to drink.
²²**In doing this, you will heap burning coals on his head,**
   and the LORD will reward you.

25:21-22 If your enemy (lit., "the one who hates you") **is hungry, give him food to eat**. The saying imagines an occasion when the enemy is vulnerable, hungry or **thirsty**. On the occasion when it is easiest and most tempting to get back at "the one who hates you," you are to do the opposite of what your natural instincts call on you to do. Demonstrate acts of kindness.

The difficulty in this couplet lies in what is meant by the phrase, **heap burning coals on his head**. At least four possibilities exist. (1) The phrase envisions a form of punishment or torture (cf. 2 Esd 16:53). When one returns good for evil, one is bringing a self-inflicted punishment on the enemy.[14] (2) Van Leeuwen suggests that the imagery might be that of dehydration and fever due to heat. When

---

proverb, "As vinegar is bad for a wound, so a pain which afflicts the body afflicts the heart. As a moth in a garment and worm in wood, the pain of a man wounds the heart" (ibid., p. 588). See also NRSV translation of this verse.

[13]Elizabeth Faith Huwiler, "Control of Reality in Israelite Wisdom," dissertation, Duke University (1988), pp. 220-221.

[14]This appears to be McKane's position (*Proverbs,* p. 592).

a person gives the thirsty enemy water to drink, the dehydration is cured: "then you will be snatching coals (from) upon his head."[15] (3) R.B.Y. Scott offers the possibility that "the figure was derived from an Egyptian repentance ritual, i.e., 'you will make your enemy repent.'"[16] (4) The burning or fiery coals represent the red-faced humiliation of the enemy. Thus the enemy is brought to shame.

The fourth alternative seems the most likely in light of the honor and shame culture in which Israel lived. The more fundamental difficulty in this couplet, however, is not the meaning of burning coals but the admonition to actually practice doing good to those who hate you. To love one's enemies is a recurring theme found in Proverbs (10:12; 17:13; 20:22; 24:17-18; 24:29; see also Rom 12:19-21).

**[23]As a north wind brings rain,
    so a sly tongue brings angry looks.**

25:23 The basic meaning of the verse is clear, but the mention that the **north wind brings rain** is perplexing, particularly since the west wind in Palestine brings rain, not the north wind. Whybray offers four different possibilities.[17] First, the saying has its origins in Egypt, where the north wind does bring rain. Second, "north" really means northwest, which sometimes brings rain with it. Third, the word for **north** (צָפוֹן, ṣāphôn) should really be emended to the verb "to hide" (צָפַן, ṣāphan). Thus the hidden or unanticipated wind brings rain. This complements nicely the image in the second line of the **sly** (lit., "secret") **tongue**.[18] Fourth, the word rendered "brings" has another nuance, which means "to hold back." Thus the north wind holds back the rain. Whybray opts for the third alternative. Whatever alternative one chooses, the meaning of the verse is that gossip or slander **brings angry looks**. The focus of attention is on the unexpectedness of what the wind and the tongue produce. The hidden tongue of gossip is destructive.

---

[15]Van Leeuwen, *Context,* p. 60.

[16]Scott, *Proverbs, Ecclesiastes,* p. 156.

[17]Whybray, *Proverbs,* pp. 368-369.

[18]Van Leeuwen proposes the following connection between the two lines of verse 23: "The thought seems to be that as the North wind is an unanticipated (hidden) source of rain contrary to the observer's expectation, so talk in secret suddenly produces outrage from an unexpected—perhaps trusted (cf. v 19b!)—corner," in *Context,* p. 60.

²⁴Better to live on a corner of the roof
than share a house with a quarrelsome wife.

25:24 Just as gossip is destructive (v. 23), so is a contentious and
quarrelsome wife. It is better to be exposed to nature's elements **on
a corner of the roof** than to share the comforts of a house with the
verbal fury of a wife (see 21:9).

²⁵Like cold water to a weary soul
is good news from a distant land.
²⁶Like a muddied spring or a polluted well
is a righteous man who gives way to the wicked.

25:25-26 These verses are paired because they use the image of
water to illustrate their message. In verse 25, **cold** water revives a
parched throat (**weary soul**); it brings refreshing relief to the whole
person. In like manner, pleasant words that come unexpectedly
from a distant land refresh the mental and emotional well-being of
an individual.

In verse 26, the image is of refreshing water that has become **polluted** by animals or humans. Something that is good has been abused
and wasted. According to the second line, a righteous person can be
polluted by the work of the wicked: The **righteous man gives way to
the wicked**. How this is done is not specified. Did the righteous act
cowardly? The proverb itself is quite open ended. Contrast this statement with that made in 24:15-16, where the "righteous man falls
seven times, yet he rises again." One proverb does not say it all. The
righteous are durable. Yet even they can succumb to temptation.

²⁷It is not good to eat too much honey,
nor is it honorable to seek one's own honor.

25:27 Even though the second line of verse 27 is difficult to
translate and interpret,[19] there is good evidence for understanding it
to refer to the overuse of complimentary words.[20] So the RSV trans-

---

[19]See Raymond Van Leeuwen, "Proverbs xxv 27 Once Again," *VT* 36
(1986): 105-114.
[20]The Hebrew reads "and searching out their glory [honor] is glory [honor],"
which is a nonsensical phrase. McKane translates the phrase "so be sparing
with eulogizing words" (*Proverbs*, p. 588). Glendon E. Bryce supports a similar
idea in his 1972 article. See Bryce "Another Wisdom-'Book,'" 148-150.

lates the second line, "So be sparing of complimentary words." The NIV tries to stay as close to the literal rendering of the Hebrew as possible: **nor is it honorable to seek one's own honor.** Does the verse advocate seeking honor in moderation or expressing honor to another in moderation? Either way, the point is that even something that is good, if misappropriated, can do harm.

²⁸Like a city whose walls are broken down
   is a man who lacks self-control.

25:28 The first line of the proverb contains the analogy: **a city whose walls are broken down.** The second line reveals the subject: **a man who lacks self-control.** External defenses of a city are compared to the internal defense of self-control that humans must develop. Lack of self-restraint leaves one vulnerable to emotions and desires that wage war within (cf. 16:32).

Sometimes the collections of sentence literature in Proverbs are not just randomly assembled but are intentionally clustered together. This was true, for example, of the cluster in 16:1-15. It is also true of three clusters found in chapter 26:1-12,13-16, and 17-28.

The proverbs in verses 1-12 are deliberately grouped together. First, all the proverbs, except for verse 2, contain the catchword "fool" (כְּסִיל, *kᵉsîl*). This subunit of sayings looks at the qualities of a fool and how one should relate to such a character. Second, these proverbs are also united by a common theme. The underlying theme is about that which is fitting or appropriate, a favorite topic of wisdom: the use of malicious words that are not fitting (v. 2), knowing how to give the appropriate "answer" (vv. 4-5), the proper care in sending "messages" (lit., "words"; v. 6), the proper use of "proverbs" (vv. 7,9), and the giving of respect that is fitting to the person (vv. 1,8).

²⁶:¹Like snow in summer or rain in harvest,
   honor is not fitting for a fool.
²Like a fluttering sparrow or a darting swallow,
   an undeserved curse does not come to rest.
³A whip for the horse, a halter for the donkey,
   and a rod for the backs of fools!
⁴Do not answer a fool according to his folly,
   or you will be like him yourself.

⁵Answer a fool according to his folly,
　　or he will be wise in his own eyes.
⁶Like cutting off one's feet or drinking violence
　　is the sending of a message by the hand of a fool.
⁷Like a lame man's legs that hang limp
　　is a proverb in the mouth of a fool.
⁸Like tying a stone in a sling
　　is the giving of honor to a fool.
⁹Like a thornbush in a drunkard's hand
　　is a proverb in the mouth of a fool.
¹⁰Like an archer who wounds at random
　　is he who hires a fool or any passer-by.
¹¹As a dog returns to its vomit,
　　so a fool repeats his folly.
¹²Do you see a man wise in his own eyes?
　　There is more hope for a fool than for him.

26:1-3 These verses compare phenomena in the natural world with words and actions in the community that are either appropriate or not appropriate. Verse 1 introduces an important word that ties the message of the whole unit together. It is the word **fitting** (נָאוֶה, *nā'weh*). Certain things in nature do not fit at certain times of the year. This proverb compares disorder in nature with disorder that occurs in society. Those elements that are in and of themselves good can be harmful because they are not suited to the occasion. **Snow** does not fit the season of **summer**, nor **rain** the season of **harvest** (during harvest, rain can be quite destructive; see 1 Sam 12:16-18). Neither in the realm of the community is **honor fitting for a fool**. What is described is a person put in a position for which he or she is not suited. The proverb could also relate to a politician, an athlete, an executive, or a preacher who receives accolades even though such a person is known to live an immoral life.

Verse 2 is the only verse that does not contain the catchword "fool," but it still relates to the overall theme developed in this cluster. The first line uses the image of a bird that flitters aimlessly around without ever landing. Such a phenomenon is compared to someone receiving an **undeserved curse**. To express a curse to an innocent party is out of place. Yet because the curse is inappropriate, it will not take root in the life of the innocent person.

233

Finally, verse 3 describes what really is *fitting* to **fools**: physical
punishment. The way an owner communicates with **the horse** or **the
donkey** is to get physical and beat them. In the same way, fools are
like dumb beasts of burden. They do not learn from wise reproof
(17:10; 19:25). The only language fools understand is the language
of brute force.

26:4-12 These verses describe the contextual nature of words
and actions. According to Van Leeuwen, such a concern is a hermeneutical one: "Wisdom, to a very large extent, is a matter of interpreting people, events, situations, actions in relation to norms for
existence."[21]

Verses 4-5 are two admonition proverbs that highlight the *relative*
nature of discourse. They appear to give contradictory advice. Their
first lines overlap, except for the addition of the prohibition **not** in
verse 4. The admonition of verse 4 is not to **answer** the **fool** so that
one will not stoop to his level. The admonition in verse 5 is to
answer the **fool** so that he will see his faults and be able to make corrections. So which is it? Kenneth Aitken says that the rabbis solved
the problem by making verse 4 refer to worldly matters and verse 5
to spiritual matters.[22] However, the problem is not one of contradiction, but of fittingness.

Verse 4 admonishes one, **do not answer a fool according to his
folly**, otherwise **you** (emphatic in the Hebrew text) **will be like him
yourself**. Van Leeuwen points out that this seems to be the more
customary advice given. One was not to respond or even associate
with a fool (23:9; 17:12).[23] Verse 5 states the "minority" advice:
Answer a fool according to his folly. Sometimes the occasion may
call for one to respond to the fool on his own level, putting him in
his place lest **he be wise in his own eyes**. The fool needs to hear just
how foolish he really sounds.

These two admonitions bring to light a common dilemma: when
to speak and when not to speak. Strikingly and intentionally they
contain no criteria for deciding the matter. It is the responsibility of
the wise to evaluate the situation, event, and person involved in

---

[21]Van Leeuwen, *Context*, p. 100.

[22]Kenneth T. Aitken, *Proverbs*, The Daily Study Bible Series (Philadelphia:
Westminster Press, 1986), p. 104.

[23]Van Leeuwen, "Proverbs," p. 224.

determining the best response to make. Those who are truly wise, do not offer "canned" responses.

The first line of verse 6 describes someone who **cuts off** his **feet** and who **drinks violence**. The image activates the reader to question who in their right mind would do this. The answer comes in the second line: it is the one who sends **a message by the hand of a fool**. The person who relies on the unreliable fool actually cuts his or her own feet off and experiences the destructive consequences ("drinks violence"). The person who does this has not properly evaluated the situation and the circumstances.

Verse 7 overlaps with verse 9. The second line of both is a duplication: **a proverb in the mouth of a fool**. The image in the first line, however, is different. In verse 7, the image depicts the uselessness of the proverb: **like a lame man's legs that hang limp**. Like legs that are impotent, proverbs in the mouth of fools who do not know how to use them are also impotent. Fools may be able to recite proverbs, but they do not know how to appropriate them for the proper occasion (cf. 25:11 for a counterimage).

In verse 9, the image intensifies and depicts proverbs as dangerous. They are **like a thornbush in a drunkard's hand**. The issue raised here is, is the thorn (חוֹחַ, *ḥôaḥ*) a wound inflicted on the drunk or is it a weapon ("thornbush") used by the drunk?[24] If the former is correct, then the image portrays a drunken man who, having no control over his faculties, falls down and runs a thorn into his hand. In like manner, a **proverb** that is used by one who has no sensitivity to the situation inflicts harm to himself.[25] If the latter is the case, then the image is of a drunken man who picks up a thornbush and thrashes it about uncontrollably. The result is bodily harm to anyone who arbitrarily comes in his way. So a proverb that is used by one who does not know how to appropriately use it becomes destructive. I favor the NIV interpretation, "thornbush," rather than "thorn" as does the RSV. The emphasis in this cluster is the rhetorical effect that words have on others (this is also the thrust of 26:17-28). In either case, the idea is related to the proper and improper use of a proverb.

---

[24]See McKane, *Proverbs*, p. 599.

[25]The *Today's English Version* gives the action of the fool in this proverb a benign meaning in its translation: "A fool quoting a wise saying reminds you of a drunk man trying to pick a thorn out of his hand."

Simply having the "knowledge of a stock of proverbs does not ensure their wise application."[26] The wise are not wise because they have memorized a lot of proverbs. They are wise because they know how and when to use them.

Verse 8 is closely linked in thought to verse 1 in speaking of the **honor** bestowed upon a fool. The image in the first line describes the absurdity of **tying a stone in a sling** that is about to be thrown. Similarly, when one gives honor to another who does not deserve it, it is absurd. The term for "honor" (כָּבוֹד, *kābôd*) is related to one's position, status, or reputation in a community. When a **fool** is placed in a position for which he is not suited, both he and the community suffer.

The same kind of indiscretion is spoken of in verse 10. **Like an archer who** goes berserk and randomly shoots passersby[27] is one who takes a **fool** or someone unknown and presses him or her into a service for which he or she is not competent. The one who has not evaluated the situation well and placed such an incompetent person into a service role in the community will hurt even innocent bystanders.[28] The results of his poor judgment and lack of understanding are far reaching.

Verse 11 contains a rather vivid image: **As a dog returns to its vomit, so a fool repeats his folly**. Fools develop entrenched habits that they cannot automatically change (cf. 1:15-19). That this saying became a popular adage is confirmed by the use of it in 2 Peter 2:22. A contemporary proverb continues the thought, though without the vivid imagery: "fool me once, shame on you; fool me twice, shame on me."

---

[26]Van Leeuwen, *Context*, p. 104.

[27]The first line of this proverb is quite problematic. Daniel Snell translates it this way: "A great one makes a fool of everyone, but a drunkard is a fool (even of) passers-by" (p. 353). See Snell, "The Most Obscure Verse in Proverbs: Proverbs XXVI 10," *VT* 41 (1991): 350-356.

[28]In summing up the theme of this group of proverbs, Van Leeuwen makes this important observation: "the *sine qua non* of wise judgment is a sense of fittingness, of how the realia of life are good only when properly applied. That is, the wise person perceives the larger, tacit context of norms and circumstances in terms of which persons, a saying (vv. 7,9), a word (v 2b), a rod (v 3), a message (v 6), status (vv. 1,8), or a job (v. 10b) are fitting." See Van Leeuwen, *Context*, p. 105.

Verse 12 concludes this first subunit of proverbs. It concludes with a warning not to the **fool** but to the **wise**. The proverb follows the same form as others like 22:29; 29:20 with the phrase, **"Do you see . . . ?"** To the person who claims wisdom, the question is posed, **Do you see a man wise in his own eyes?** The expression "wise in his own eyes" is not limited to fools (cf. 3:7; and 28:11). This person claiming wisdom for himself or herself is in worse condition than the fool who has been set up as a negative model in the previous eleven verses. **There is more hope for a fool than for** the one who claims wisdom as his possession. As a conclusion to this cluster, the proverb serves as a form of self-evaluation. It is a check on the wise regarding their posture: first deal with your own arrogance before evaluating the fool.

¹³**The sluggard says, "There is a lion in the road,**
   a fierce lion roaming the streets!"
¹⁴**As a door turns on its hinges,**
   so a sluggard turns on his bed.
¹⁵**The sluggard buries his hand in the dish;**
   he is too lazy to bring it back to his mouth.
¹⁶**The sluggard is wiser in his own eyes**
   than seven men who answer discreetly.

26:13-16 This is the second subunit found in chapter 26. The catchword found in all four verses is **sluggard** (עָצֵל, 'āṣēl). These adages contain some of the most sarcastic and humorous images found in the book of Proverbs. Along with the fool, the sluggard is one of the characters the sage most enjoys ridiculing. Two previous instruction poems dealt with this character (6:9-11; 24:30-34). Both verses 13 and 15 are duplicates of proverbs already a part of earlier collections in the book (see 22:13; 19:24). Placed together in this collection, the cluster paints a holistic picture of total immobility. The sluggard uses none of the faculties that God has given him. Thus he refuses to get out of the house (v. 13). He refuses to get out of bed (v. 14). He even refuses to eat (v. 15).²⁹ Along with lust and leisure, laziness was one of the biggest temptations youth faced, according to the sages (chapters 1–9).

---

²⁹See Van Leeuwen, "Proverbs," p. 225.

Next comes the third and final cluster found in chapter 26. Wisdom counsels against using certain kinds of speech, not because it is ineffective but because of its harmful influence on others. This subunit centers on such a negative influence.

Structurally, this text is held together by a common theme, imagery, and vocabulary.[30] First, the theme that holds the cluster together is the malicious use of discourse. The second structural element holding the text together is related to imagery. Because most of the proverbs in this subunit are proverbs that use analogies (as are most of the proverbs in chapters 25–27), the imagery is rich.[31]

One image used in 26:17-28 to describe malicious speech is that it is a lethal weapon. Such speech is like a madman shooting arrows; it is like an angry dog, like coal or wood fueling a fire, like a pit into which one can fall.

Another image involves a psychological dimension: malevolent discourse is portrayed as externally attractive, but it is bent on internal destruction. So the slanderer's words are like tidbits of tasty finger foods, like a time-release capsule that goes down easily but later delivers its deadly poison. His words are like a smooth mouth (flattery), impure silver overlaid on clay pots, and like a disguise or a trap. Such speech gives the appearance of being amusing, but its destructiveness is far reaching.

The third structural factor that holds this text together is a common vocabulary that describes the verbal abuser. The verbal abuser is a man of strife, a slanderer, a deceiver and a madman.[32] This person is depicted as one who verbally wounds.

In addition to the above elements, it should be noted that the text begins and ends with a reference to the consequences facing the

---

[30]Van Leeuwen, *Context*, pp. 111-122.

[31]In the analogic proverbs, an image has been selected in order to make a particular point. The second line of each proverb interprets the image in the first line. However, there are a couple of variations of this in 26:17-28. In 21a there are two images instead of the normal single image. Verse 22a interprets the image in the first line. Verse 27 contains two images, one in the first and one in the second. But the referent is not specified.

[32]The word for "strife" used in this text is רִיב (*rîb*; vv. 17,21), its synonym in this passage is מָדוֹן (*mādôn*; vv. 20,21). The word for slanderer is נִרְגָּן (*nirgān*; vv. 20,22). The word for deception is מִרְמָה (*mirmāh* from *rāmāh*; vv. 19,24).

verbal wounder. Thus an inclusion envelops the text. Verse 17 implicitly states the consequences the verbal wounder faces. Anyone knows that the person who grabs a passing dog by the ears will be hurt. Verses 26-28 are more explicit, and thus more emphatic, bringing the poem to a climax. The verbal abuser will be exposed by the community (v. 26), and his deceptiveness will lead to his own ruin (vv. 27-28). Such an inclusion knits these proverbs into a structural unit.

[17]**Like one who seizes a dog by the ears**
　　is a passer-by who meddles in a quarrel not his own.
[18]**Like a madman shooting**
　　firebrands or deadly arrows
[19]**is a man who deceives his neighbor**
　　and says, "I was only joking!"
[20]**Without wood a fire goes out;**
　　without gossip a quarrel dies down.
[21]**As charcoal to embers and as wood to fire,**
　　so is a quarrelsome man for kindling strife.
[22]**The words of a gossip are like choice morsels;**
　　they go down to a man's inmost parts.
[23]**Like a coating of glaze[a] over earthenware**
　　are fervent lips with an evil heart.
[24]**A malicious man disguises himself with his lips,**
　　but in his heart he harbors deceit.
[25]**Though his speech is charming, do not believe him,**
　　for seven abominations fill his heart.
[26]**His malice may be concealed by deception,**
　　but his wickedness will be exposed in the assembly.
[27]**If a man digs a pit, he will fall into it;**
　　if a man rolls a stone, it will roll back on him.
[28]**A lying tongue hates those it hurts,**
　　and a flattering mouth works ruin.

[a]*23* **With a different word division of the Hebrew Masoretic Text** *of silver dross*

26:17 According to verse 17, those who get involved in quarrels that are none of their business provoke retaliation and will suffer injury.[33] Here the subject of strife and quarreling is introduced.

---

[33]The NIV maintains the *athnach* (an accent that divides a verse into two

26:18-19 Verses 18 and 19 are one proverb. The proverb introduces the verbal abuser. He is one who is deceptive, a characteristic
that is developed all through the text. He is deceptive because he puts
on the appearance of simply wanting to have fun, to amuse. However,
there is a hidden agenda, which is to undermine the order of the community for the sake of accomplishing his own selfish desires.

The proverb in verses 18 and 19 contains a hypothetical quote
from the lips of the deceiver who lightheartedly defends his actions
by saying, "was I not joking?" Elizabeth Huwiler refers to this as
"reported speech" and concludes, after surveying the use of all such
speech in the sentence proverbs, that such "[r]eported speech is
overwhelmingly negative."[34] Positive reported speech is found only
in chapters 1–9 and is closely associated with wisdom and with parents. The conclusion is that speech that is not connected with sapiential figures should be viewed with suspicion.

26:20-22 Having been introduced to the verbal seducer and the
lethal word games he plays in verses 17-19, verses 20-25 detail his
effect on the community. In verse 20, the slanderer's role in society
is described as destructive; he destroys the trust which produces solidarity.[35] Such a slanderer, according to verse 21, feeds and fans the
flames of dissension (**kindling strife**).[36] He piles on more verbal fuel
in order to keep the fires of contention burning. The quarreler has
developed a long-established habit of disregarding the best interest

---

logical parts) in its present position in the Hebrew text thus reading the
verse as follows: "Like one who seizes a dog by the ears is a passer-by who
meddles in a quarrel not his own." My translation of this proverb moves the
athnach from under "passing" to the next word in the proverb thus keeping
the term for "passing" with the first line: "He who seizes the ears of a passing dog; one who insinuates himself in a quarrel not his own."

[34]Huwiler, "Control," p. 236. She includes the following examples of
reported speech: 1:11-14; 3:28; 5:12-14; 7:14-20; 9:16-17; 20:14,22; 22:13;
23:7,29,35-36[sic]; 24:12,24,29; 26:13,19; 28:24; 30:9,15,16,20 (p. 237). She
says that examples of positive reported speech include the speech of wisdom (1:22-33) and of parents (4:4). She concludes that outside of chapters
1–9, there is little positive reported speech.

[35]R.B.Y. Scott maintains that the "rhyme and structure of the second line
suggests that it is a popular proverb of the type: No-this, No-that" (*Proverbs,
Ecclesiastes*, p. 160). He tries to capture the rhyme and structure by translating it: "No calumny, no quarrel" (p. 158).

[36]The Hebrew word חָרַר (*ḥārar*) means "to be hot" and is in keeping with
the image of fire portrayed in this verse.

of the community. The techniques the slanderer uses are alluring but camouflaged, which make them quite effective. Verse 22 makes this clear (cf. 18:8).

Verse 22 also speaks of the long-lasting impression such discourse has on the psyche. Like tasty finger food that goes to the inner chambers of the body, so the words of the verbal wounder remain indelibly etched on the mind of the listener. The **gossip** is a person artistically skilled in using discourse for destructive ends. His speech is by no means impotent. Gossip has the power to shape one's perception of others and thus the way in which one behaves in community.

26:23 Verse 22 is transitional because it not only reminds the reader of the deceptive nature of appearance, already alluded to in verses 18-19, but it also anticipates this motif in verses 23-25. The proverbs of verses 23-25 are all concerned with the thought that an attitude of deep, settled malice may be cloaked by civility of speech and charming manner. The polished exterior is not what it appears to be (v. 23). The image used in verse 23 is of a clay pot lacquered over with silver to give the earthen vessel an appearance of something it is not.

26:24-26 Verses 24-26 are a narrative vignette specifying and elaborating on the image of verse 23 in a more detailed fashion. With verse 25 comes the first imperative and the first offer of advice on how to deal with the verbal wounder. The counsel is straightforward: **do not believe him**. Such a person, according to McKane, "has no respect for words, and language as used by him is always prostituted to evil ends and made the servant of deceit. . . ."[37] McKane correctly explains that the phrase **seven abominations** in the second line of verse 25 "has no precise numerical significance and means something like 'any number of'. . . ."[38] The number seven is used in the verse just preceding the subunit in 26:17-28 (v. 16). Aitken comments that "behind a veneer of friendly words 'seven abominations' lurk; while he smiles to your face he will stab you in the back."[39] Seven abominations may reflect on the numerical proverb of 6:16-19, which begins with the formulaic phrase, "There are six things which the LORD hates / seven which are an abomination to him. . . ." The idea is that hatred spawns a number of wicked thoughts and

---

[37]Ibid., p. 604.
[38]Ibid., p. 601.
[39]Aitken, *Proverbs*, p. 175.

actions. In verse 25, the verbal manipulator breeds continual disorder in the community.

Verse 26 concludes the narrative vignette and also serves as a transition into the final subsection (vv. 26-28), which specifies the consequences the verbal abuser will face. Those who use their organs of speech to harm the community will themselves suffer the evil they intended for others. The one who schemes against another will himself suffer the repercussions. The reference in verse 26 to **the assembly** (קָהָל, *qāhāl*) is not a reference to a formal judicial body. Whybray affirms this in his remark on the proverb: "It can have the meaning of a religious meeting, but here it probably means an informal gathering of citizens, in which reputations could be made or destroyed."[40]

26:27-28 Verse 27 further illustrates the consequences: **if a man digs a pit, he will fall into it**. In the context of this cluster, the phrase has specific application to the verbal wounder. The proverbial phrase is alluded to in various parts of Scripture.[41] Here it refers to the consequences faced by one who uses his discourse to disrupt community life and solidarity. In light of this, verse 28 is also to be interpreted with the same referent in mind: the self-destructive tendencies of the verbal seducer. R.B.Y. Scott translates this verse, "A lying tongue is a man's own worst enemy, And smooth talk leads to downfall."[42]

The verbal abuser described in verses 17-28 stands as the male counterpart to the quarrelsome woman (see Prov 19:13; 27:15-16; 21:9; 25:24; 21:19) as well as to the temptress, the character that looms largest in Proverbs 1–9. The temptress used words to entice her unwary prey: "With persuasive words[43] she led him astray[44]; she

[40]R.N. Whybray, *The Book of Proverbs* (Cambridge: University Press, 1972), p. 154.

[41]Compare Psalms 7:15f; 9:15f; Ecclesiastes 10:8f; Proverbs 28:10.

[42]Scott, *Proverbs, Ecclesiastes*, p. 158.

[43]The Hebrew word לֶקַח (*leqaḥ*) is the same one used and translated "instruction" in 16:21 and 16:23.

[44]BDB say that the *hiphil* (causative form) of נָטָה (*nāṭāh*) carries the idea of influence or persuasion (p. 640). Elsewhere in Proverbs there are descriptions of the temptress's persuasive powers: "For the lips of a temptress drip honey, and her speech is smoother than oil" (5:3). The instruction of the sage is "to preserve you . . . from the smooth tongue of the adventuress" (6:24). The young man who is wise ". . . will be saved from the temptress, from the adventuress with her smooth words . . ." (2:16).

seduced him with her smooth talk" (7:21). Like the temptress, this male counterpart seduces with words. The speech of the male seducer is charming (v. 25); he will allure the innocent person as one is allured by tasty food (v. 22). He is the one with the **flattering mouth** (v. 28). Persuasive speech in the mouth of the wrong person destroys the solidarity of the community. In this text, the verbal abuser brings disorder, creates division, and spreads chaos among friends and community. His character is the epitome of all that one should *not* be.

Like chapters 25 and 26, chapter 27 contains a number of analogic proverbs. The chapter is basically divided into two subunits. The first is verses 1-22 and the second verses 23-27. The former subunit is made up primarily of proverbial pairs. It also contains a large number of proverbs about the friend/neighbor (vv. 5,6,9,10,14,17,19). The latter subunit is a brief proverb poem admonishing the farmer to diligence in maintaining his flocks and fields.

²⁷:¹**Do not boast about tomorrow,**
        for you do not know what a day may bring forth.
²**Let another praise you, and not your own mouth;**
        someone else, and not your own lips.

27:1-2 The couplet is united by the catchword **boast/praise** (הָלַל, *halal*). Both sayings set limits on what humans can accomplish. Verse 1 speaks of human limitations on the future. No one can control what will happen tomorrow. Contrary to popular opinion, wisdom does not promise that the righteous will always prosper and the wicked suffer. True wisdom knows its own limits. The narrative counterpart to this saying is found in James 4:13-15.

Verse 2 speaks of the limitations of self-promotion. Respect is a quality that is given, not taken. Rather than praising self, the proverb implies that individuals seek out opportunities to praise others.

³**Stone is heavy and sand a burden,**
        but provocation by a fool is heavier than both.
⁴**Anger is cruel and fury overwhelming,**
        but who can stand before jealousy?

27:3-4 Both of these verses have a common structure. Compare the structure of the first lines:

3a **Stone is heavy and sand a burden,**
4a **Anger is cruel and fury overwhelming.**

Both verses argue from the lesser to the greater. Verse 3 moves from the physical realm to the moral: from heaviness of stone and weightiness of sand to the anger or **provocation** of a **fool** being **heavier than both.** Verse 4 moves from the harsh emotions of **anger** and **fury** to that which is worse, **jealousy.** Anger is clearly harmful, but jealousy serves as its catalyst (see 6:34). Jealousy erodes the moral and spiritual fiber of an individual (according to 14:30, it "rots the bones").

⁵**Better is open rebuke**
    than hidden love.
⁶**Wounds from a friend can be trusted,**
    but an enemy multiplies kisses.

27:5-6 The catchword that ties the pair together is the word **love** (אַהֲבָה, *'ahăbāh*), translated **friend** in verse 6 (lit., "he who loves"). As in most of the better-than proverbs, an element that is normally undesirable is placed with that which is good. The result is a reversal. Normally, **rebuke** is less desirable than love, but when one is **hidden** and the other is **open,** a reversal occurs. Thus open rebuke is better than hidden love. Love that is hidden becomes undesirable because it is dormant love, a love that fails honestly to express itself (cf. 28:23). To keep silent is not always a sign of love. Open rebuke (or "reproof") in the book of Proverbs is an important tool in the process of moral instruction (see 1:20-33; cf. also Eccl 7:5-6; 12:11). The one who offers rebuke does so wisely (25:12) and never demeans another (11:12).

Though verse 6 is not a better-than proverb, it follows the same format: that which is undesirable is placed alongside that which is desirable and a reversal occurs. So in verse 6, a cut is better than a kiss because the cut, or **wound,** comes from a friend (lit., "one who loves"). The **enemy** (lit., "one who hates") gives all the appearances of being a friend with his flattering words, but he practices deception. The one who offers honest and open critique that initially hurts (we might say "tough love") is the true friend who **can be trusted.**

⁷**He who is full loathes honey,**
    but to the hungry even what is bitter tastes sweet.

244

27:7 The mention of **honey** is common in Proverbs (cf. 16:24; 24:13; 25:16). As a health food, it was highly prized. Even that which is good, however, can be overdone. In contrast, to those who are starving, **even what is bitter tastes sweet.** In Clifford's words, "Hunger is the best sauce."[45] The saying has application not only to the physical realm, but also to the mental and spiritual, that is, to those who seek wisdom.

⁸**Like a bird that strays from its nest**
    is a man who strays from his home.

27:8 The word translated **home** is literally "place" (מָקוֹם, *māqôm*). Humans find their identity in community. To live life like a "rolling stone," continually shifting and moving, is to sentence a person to despair and loneliness. Cain was punished for his crime by being required to wander throughout the remainder of his life (Gen 4:12-16).

⁹**Perfume and incense bring joy to the heart,**
    and the pleasantness of one's friend springs from his
        earnest counsel.
¹⁰**Do not forsake your friend and the friend of your father,**
    and do not go to your brother's house when disaster
        strikes you—
    better a neighbor nearby than a brother far away.

27:9-10 Verse 9b is problematic, as comparing various translations will indicate. The text literally reads "sweetness of his friend from the counsel of soul." The LXX does not believe the line stands in good antithetic relationship to 9a and so emends the text to read, "but the inner being is torn down by trouble," which the NRSV adopts as its reading. But the NIV offers a good interpretation in trying to make sense of the text as it stands: **and the pleasantness of one's friend springs from his earnest counsel.** The verse is an analogy. The enjoyment received from the sweet aroma of **perfume** is compared to the pleasant counsel received from a friend.[46] The

---

[45]Clifford, *Proverbs*, p. 238.

[46]In the second line, the מִן (*min*) can be taken either as source ("springs from," as the NIV) or comparison (better-than). If the latter, then the line might read "the sweetness of his friend is better than his own counsel." McKane offers the following translation as a possibility: "The sweetness of friendship strengthens the spirit" (*Proverbs*, p. 613).

Hebrew word can be translated either "friend" or "neighbor." During postexilic times, with the extended family no longer living in close proximity, the "neighbor" took on new significance for Israel.

Verse 10 pairs nicely in thought with verse 9. The verse contains three lines, which is unusual in the sentence literature. The first two lines seem unrelated. What does the injunction to maintain the loyalty of old family friends/neighbors have to do with the advice not to go to **your brother's house** in times of trouble? The third line helps clarify the relationship. The one who practices the ideals of neighborliness, will also demonstrate dependability in times of crisis. The good **neighbor** is just as supportive as the family member (the brother).[47]

The reader should take care not to impose a contemporary understanding of "friend" on the sage's understanding. The sages did not use the term "friend" primarily to refer to an individual personally chosen as a companion. Rather the term implies the broader concept of "neighbor." Neighbors are more numerous; they encroach upon one's life through living in close proximity and the chance encounters of work and travel. To learn to love the neighbor is more challenging than to love the friend.[48]

In Proverbs, the immediate family and neighborhood are more of the focus than the clan and the extended family that no longer lived close by. It is in the context of the former that moral character and solidarity are developed. Thus for the sage, the friend/neighbor was chosen not for the sake of self-fulfillment but on the basis of need. The story of the Good Samaritan in the New Testament illustrates who really is one's neighbor. As a more contemporary proverb says, "A friend in need is a friend indeed."

[11]Be wise, my son, and bring joy to my heart;
    then I can answer anyone who treats me with contempt.

27:11 The sentence literature strongly emphasizes the reciprocity that exists in a healthy family environment. When children develop responsible character, they **bring joy** to both father and mother (see 17:6). The LORD designed family members to treat each other with mutual respect.

---

[47]Clements "Good Neighbour," p. 216.
[48]Ibid., pp. 210-211.

¹²**The prudent see danger and take refuge,**
    but the simple keep going and suffer for it.
¹³**Take the garment of one who puts up security for a stranger;**
    hold it in pledge if he does it for a wayward woman.

27:12-13 Verse 12 is a duplicate of 22:3 (see that verse for comments). Verse 13 expresses the contempt the sages had for individuals who practiced surety. Except for the word **stranger** in the second line, this verse is a duplicate of 20:16 (see that verse for comments).

These next verses are not an intentionally clustered group of proverbs, but they do share some affinity in speaking of various types of relationships, namely that of the wife and the neighbor, and the interaction that ensues.

¹⁴**If a man loudly blesses his neighbor early in the morning,**
    it will be taken as a curse.
¹⁵**A quarrelsome wife**
    is like a constant dripping on a rainy day;
¹⁶**restraining her is like restraining the wind**
    or grasping oil with the hand.
¹⁷**As iron sharpens iron,**
    so one man sharpens another.
¹⁸**He who tends a fig tree will eat its fruit,**
    and he who looks after his master will be honored.
¹⁹**As water reflects a face,**
    so a man's heart reflects the man.

27:14 The word for **neighbor** can also be translated "friend," but in most cases, as here, "neighbor" better communicates the individual the sage had in mind (see v. 10). When does a blessing become a **curse?** When the blessing is insincere, apparently done only for show. That seems to be the implication of the one who gives the blessing **loudly**. He does it for show, going to great lengths to demonstrate an amiable spirit. Like the multiple kisses of the enemy in verse 6, the blessing is nothing more than flattery.

The blessing is also a curse when it is given at the wrong time, **early in the morning**. Because of the poor timing, the words become abusive. He greets when it is convenient for him, not for the recipient. The proverb has broader application than just to early morning risers. Underlying the image of the early morning riser is an attitude of inconsideration toward others. Cheerful words are used to disguise what is really insulting. Rudeness is one of the vices the sage cannot tolerate (cf. 23:1-2).

27:15-16 Once again the **quarrelsome wife** is pictured with a heavy dose of sarcasm (cf. 21:9,19). This proverb expands the image in 19:13b. The imagery of **a constant dripping on a rainy day** is similar to that used in Ecclesiastes 10:18 to describe a leaky roof that can erode a whole house. In his modern paraphrase, Eugene Peterson misses the gravity of the constant dripping image when he translates the proverb, "A nagging spouse is like the drip, drip, drip of a leaky faucet; You can't turn it off, and you can't get away from it."[49] The image is not about something that is simply a nuisance with which one must learn to live. It is about a habit that can destroy a whole house.

Verse 16 elaborates further on the problem. Such a woman cannot be restrained. The Hebrew says, "to hide her is to hide the wind." In other words, there is no way to confine her fury to the private sector. The quarrelsome woman not only wreaks havoc on a household, but also on the larger community.

27:17 The first line contains a popular folk saying, **iron sharpens iron**. The image is that of a farm implement or sword or knife being sharpened by another metallic piece. The metaphor of metal rubbing against metal in the first line is applied in the second line to the relationship between two friends: **so one man sharpens another**. The text literally reads, "so a man sharpens the face of his friend." The phrase "face of his friend" may simply be carrying over the image from the first line in which one sharpens the "face" or edge of a farm tool (Eccl 10:10 describes iron as having a "face"). The proverb describes the abrasion or friction necessary for growth in one's personal character and moral development. The friend/neighbor plays a primary role in the demanding process. Being a friend is not an idyllic relationship.

27:18 The text offers a simple image in the first line and the corresponding relationship in the second line. The first line describes a very simple process, **he who tends a fig tree will eat its fruit**. The second line applies the agrarian figure to the master/slave relationship. The one who takes care of his daily farming responsibilities will eat the fruit

---

[49]See Peterson, *The Message*.

of his labor. In the same way, the worker who looks after and protects his master's interests will also receive honor.[50] Even those who engage in the most menial tasks will in some way receive honor.

27:19 Because of their poetic nature, many proverbs are intentionally ambiguous. This proverb, however, is more cryptic than most. The following is a literal translation of the text: "As water, the face unto the face, so the heart of man to man." The text appears to make an analogy between a natural phenomenon and a human experience. When looking in **water**, one sees the reflection of his or her **face**. In like manner, the **heart** of a **man reflects** a **man**.

The question is, into whose heart is one looking (the NIV keeps the second line ambiguous)? There are two possibilities. First, some understand the second line to refer to a single individual who is reflecting on his own thoughts.[51] Through *introspection* a person comes to a better understanding of the self. The second possibility is that the second line refers to two people engaged in reflecting on each other's ideas.[52] Through *interaction* a person comes to a better understanding of the self (see NRSV).

Because of the unusual number of proverbs in chapter 27 about the friend/neighbor, it seems most natural to interpret the second line of verse 19 as describing the *interaction* between two individuals challenging each other and not simply private reflection on one's thoughts. This is the thought not only of verse 17 but of verses 5-6

---

[50]John Eaton sees 27:17-18 as a proverbial pair. He claims the referent of both is a tutorial debate that takes place between a teacher and student. See John Eaton, *The Contemplative Face of Old Testament Wisdom in the Context of World Religions* (Philadelphia: Trinity Press, 1989), p. 26.

[51]The second line, McKane says, "has to do only with one man whose self is mirrored in his *lev* [heart], and the meaning . . . is that it is through introspection . . . that a man acquires self-knowledge" (*Proverbs,* p. 616).

[52]Robert Alter's analysis of the imagery is especially apropos: "The terseness makes you work to decipher the first verset. Once it dawns on you that what is referred to is the reflected image of a face in water, further complications ensue: Does each man discover the otherwise invisible image of his own heart by seeing what others are like, or, on the contrary, is it by introspection (as we say, "reflection"), in scrutinizing the features of his own heart, that a person comes to understand what the heart of others must be? And is the choice of water in the simile merely an indication of the property of reflection, or does water, as against a mirror, suggest a potentially unstable image, or one with shadowy depths below the reflecting surface?" (Robert Alter, *The Art of Biblical Poetry* [Basic Books, 1985], p. 178).

and 9 as well.[53] When one engages in rigorous interaction with another, such a person discovers new insights. The proverb confirms other statements made by the "good neighbor" proverbs in chapter 27. The neighbor is a vital link to the health and well-being of the whole community especially in the absence of extended family.

²⁰Death and Destruction[a] are never satisfied,
    and neither are the eyes of man.
²¹The crucible for silver and the furnace for gold,
    but man is tested by the praise he receives.
²²Though you grind a fool in a mortar,
    grinding him like grain with a pestle,
    you will not remove his folly from him.

[a]*20 Hebrew Sheol and Abaddon*

27:20 In verse 20, **Death and Destruction** are personified. They have an unquenchable thirst. In the same way, the human eye is **never satisfied**. **The eyes of man** refer to human desires, which are the basis of greed. It is a description of the conspicuous, consumptive lifestyle into which humans so easily fall.

27:21-22 The couplet describes the process by which people are tested. Unlike 17:3, which overlaps with verse 21, the one who does the testing is not the LORD but other people. The test comes **by the praise he receives**. The reputation one attains in the community indicates the kind of character a person possesses. McKane comments that "the point of the simile . . . is that the processes at the disposal of the community for testing a man's reputation are as rigorous and reliable as those employed for testing silver and gold. . . . A man will enjoy such public esteem as he deserves."[54]

Once again in verse 22, we are reminded that the **fool** is unteachable (see 9:7-8). One can use extreme force on the character, **grinding him like grain with a pestle**, but to no avail. You cannot rid the fool of **folly**. In Proverbs, the fool is set up as a foil in order for youth to see what happens to those who do not follow wisdom (see 1:20-33).

---

[53]Van Leeuwen writes, "The idea is of water as a mirror: man comes to self-knowledge through confrontation with the other" (*Context*, p. 125).

[54]McKane, *Proverbs,* p. 608.

B. INSTRUCTION POEM (27:23-27)

[23]Be sure you know the condition of your flocks,
    give careful attention to your herds;
[24]for riches do not endure forever,
    and a crown is not secure for all generations.
[25]When the hay is removed and new growth appears
    and the grass from the hills is gathered in,
[26]the lambs will provide you with clothing,
    and the goats with the price of a field.
[27]You will have plenty of goats' milk
    to feed you and your family
    and to nourish your servant girls.

27:23-27 An instruction poem concludes the chapter. The text is addressed to the farmer who is admonished to care for his **flocks** and **herds**. When properly tended, his farm will provide enough to feed and clothe his **family** with possibly enough extra to buy **the price of a field**. A flock, a field, and a farm, though, need constant care (v. 24), otherwise the land will end up like the field of the sluggard (24:30-34). This farmer does not appear to be wealthy because he has just what is necessary to care for his family with only a little left over to purchase a little plot of land.

Chapter 27 began with the admonition, "do not boast about tomorrow," an acknowledgment of the limitations of human wisdom and the uncertainty of human affairs. Human life is lived in a constant state of change. The sages, however, did not respond with a fatalistic attitude; they did not live in a state of anxiety, wringing their hands in despair. Instead they offer a vignette of a hard-working farmer who goes about his task responsibly and carefully in the face of an uncertain tomorrow. The farmer cares for the creation over which God has placed him. He cares for his family and loved ones. Through such responsible caring, he finds wisdom, satisfaction, and fulfillment in life.

C. SAYINGS ON THE RIGHTEOUS AND THE WICKED
(28:1–29:27)

Chapters 28 and 29 form a new subsection in the sentence literature of 25–29. The material is set apart from the previous chapters by reverting to the use of antithetic parallelism so prevalent in chapters 10–15. These two chapters contain several Yahweh proverbs (see 16:1-9) and a number of other proverbs that contain religious overtones. A contrast between the righteous and the wicked also dominate chapters 28–29. The quality emphasized about the righteous is that they are socially responsible. The wicked are those who manifest antisocial behavior, behavior that destroys community life.

Four overlapping proverbs serve as a refrain to emphasize this theme (28:12,28; 29:2,16).[55] When the wicked and wickedness reign, a society is thrown into chaos. When the righteous and righteousness reign, a society thrives. These chapters, especially in 28:13-27, describe in detail those who are socially irresponsible. They are the ones who hide transgressions (v. 13); they are oppressors (v. 16); they are guilty of murder (v. 17); they follow worthless pursuits (v. 19); they pursue get-rich-quick schemes (v. 20); they show partiality (v. 21); they are greedy (v. 22); they disregard parents (v. 24); and they are selfish (v. 27).

In contrast, those who are socially responsible exhibit the following traits: they confess sins (v. 13); they fear the LORD (v. 14); they are diligent workers (v. 19); they manifest faithfulness and integrity (v. 20); they are fair in their treatment of others (v. 21); they are giving (vv. 22,27); they engage in the process of moral instruction (v. 23); and they walk in wisdom (v. 26).

The lines are clearly drawn between those who contribute to society and those who dehumanize society. There is no middle ground. In a pluralistic culture, such clear demarcations do not sit well, but to make such distinctions is essential to the health of the nation in which one lives. God calls his church to represent these qualities of righteousness in its body life.

---

[55]Bruce Malchow identified the relationship that exists between these four proverbs. See Bruce V. Malchow, "A Manual for Future Monarchs," *CBQ* 47 (April, 1985): 238-245.

¹The wicked man flees though no one pursues,
  but the righteous are as bold as a lion.
²When a country is rebellious, it has many rulers,
    but a man of understanding and knowledge maintains
      order.
³A ruler^a who oppresses the poor
    is like a driving rain that leaves no crops.
⁴Those who forsake the law praise the wicked,
    but those who keep the law resist them.
⁵Evil men do not understand justice,
    but those who seek the LORD understand it fully.
⁶Better a poor man whose walk is blameless
    than a rich man whose ways are perverse.
⁷He who keeps the law is a discerning son,
    but a companion of gluttons disgraces his father.
⁸He who increases his wealth by exorbitant interest
    amasses it for another, who will be kind to the poor.
⁹If anyone turns a deaf ear to the law,
    even his prayers are detestable.
¹⁰He who leads the upright along an evil path
    will fall into his own trap,
    but the blameless will receive a good inheritance.
¹¹A rich man may be wise in his own eyes,
    but a poor man who has discernment sees through him.
¹²When the righteous triumph, there is great elation;
    but when the wicked rise to power, men go into hiding.

ª*3 Or A poor man*

28:1 The wicked man flees though no one pursues probably because fear and guilt rule his entire life. It is a classic case of paranoia governing the life of the wicked. In contrast, **the righteous are as bold as a lion.** In this context, "bold" (בָּטַח, *bāṭaḥ*) might better be translated "confidence." The righteous have the confidence of a lion.

28:2 The NIV brings out well the contrast between the plural and the singular. When a **country** is characterized by transgression (**is rebellious**), **rulers** fight over control and position (for a description of such a chaotic society see Hos 4:1-3). Such a society is marked by instability. A single individual of wisdom and **understanding,**

though, is more efficient than several wicked rulers. Such a person can bring about stability.

28:3 The Hebrew text reads, "the poor man oppresses the poor." The NIV emends the text to read **ruler** on the grounds that it does not make sense for the **poor** to oppress their own kind. However, the emendation is not necessary. It was not uncommon for the poor to take advantage of other poor people.

A metaphor is placed in the second line of this proverb to inten-sify the observation:[56] **a driving rain that leaves no crops**. Normally, rain is a welcome sight, nourishing crops, but a hard driving rain can also destroy a grain field and erode the soil. Such an image high-lights the catastrophe that results when the poor prey on their own kind. All one needs to do is observe inner city life in urban centers across this country to see that such an erosive phenomenon still exists in abundance.

28:4 A contrast is noted between **those who forsake the law** and **those who keep the law**. Distinctions exist in these chapters between those who contribute to the well-being of society and those who tear it down.

The word "law" (תּוֹרָה; *tôrāh*) appears twice in this proverb and introduces a theme that is woven throughout chapters 28–29. The question is, to what does *torah* refer? Does it refer to the "instruction" of the parents and the sages? Or does it refer to the "law" of God (Mosaic Law)? In Proverbs, the NIV translates *torah* "instruction" or "teaching" or "learning," referring to the instruction of parents and the wise (cf. 1:8; 3:1; 4:2; 6:20; 7:2; 13:14). This verse is the first time that the NIV translates *torah* "law," implying that the reference is to the law of the LORD.[57] Given the context of the word in Proverbs, it is best to understand it referring primarily to the instruction given by parents and the wise. However, the sages, in part, based their instruc-tion upon God's law, so in a secondary sense, "law" could refer to the Mosaic Law. The keeping of the instruction of the sages is funda-mental to the well-being of a community.

28:5 The phrase **evil men** is emphatic and refers to those who

---

[56]Usually such comparisons are placed in the first line (see chapters 25–27).

[57]The NIV translates *torah* as "law" six times. All but one are in chapters 28 and 29 (28:4[2×],7,9; 29:18; 31:5).

have devoted their entire lives to wickedness. In contrast, **those who seek the LORD** "**understand** all" or "**understand** everything." That is, they have been trained in the fundamental virtues stated in 1:3: righteousness, justice, and fairness. Those who seek the LORD know how to treat fellow human beings.

28:6 Like all of the better-than proverbs, this one also contains a reversal (see 15:16-17). That which initially appears less than desirable becomes more desirable. In this case, poverty is **better than** wealth when poverty is accompanied by "integrity" or one who possesses strong moral character (i.e., one **whose walk is blameless**). The sages do not live by a strict system of the prospering righteous and the suffering wicked. Sometimes, as here, those who are people of integrity live in poverty.

28:7 Especially in the familial context, **law** (*torah*) is better translated "instruction of the wise/parents" (see v. 4). The **discerning son** is the one who sees the big picture of life. The **companion of gluttons** takes a more myopic view. As a result, he **disgraces his father**. The phrase "companion of gluttons" is related to the language used in Deuteronomy 21:18-21 to describe a rebellious son. One quality of such a son is that he is "a glutton and drunkard." He is like the prodigal son who wastes the resources that the father has given him.

Wisdom continually shows paramount concern for the kind of company one keeps. It is within community that morals are shaped for good or for ill. In turn, the moral character formed enables individuals to contribute either to the good or to the ill of society.

28:8 Israel was forbidden to charge interest for the sake of the **poor**. Money loaned to the poor could not be for profit (Exod 22:25; Lev 25:35-37). The first line literally reads, "He who increases his wealth with interest and interest." The two terms used (וּבְתַרְבִּית בְּנֶשֶׁךְ, *bᵊnešek ûbetharbîth*, "interest and interest") are a set pair found in other Old Testament texts (Lev 25:36; Ezek 18:8,13,17). The phrase is a type of figure in which two words are used for one, a way of highlighting. Thus the NIV translates it **exorbitant interest**. The one who engages in such antisocial activity will in the end lose. His or her money will be given to another **who will be kind to the poor**. There is a play on word sounds between the one who adds to **his wealth** (הוֹנוֹ, *hônô*) and the one "who will be kind" (חוֹנֵן, *hônēn*).

28:9 The one who does not hear instruction (i.e., **turns a deaf ear to the law**) is the one who does not obey. The prayer of such a disobedient youth is **detestable** ("an abomination") to the LORD. One is reminded of the prophet's rebuke to Israel in Isaiah 1:10-17.

28:10 One is reminded of Jesus' statement in Matthew 18:6-7 about causing one of the "little ones" (a reference to disciples of Jesus) to sin. The word **blameless** does not refer to perfection, rather to one whose overall life is characterized by integrity.

28:11 Wise in his own eyes is a common phrase used in Proverbs (16:2). Often, but not always, it refers to the fool. In 26:12 it appears to serve as a warning to the wise themselves. Here it refers to **a rich man**. The one who is wise in his own eyes is the one who feels little dependence on others. A reversal of social positions is envisioned. The inferior **poor man** is actually better off than the superior rich man because he possesses **discernment** ("wisdom"). Once again, the sage grants that prosperity does not always come to the wise (cf. v. 6).

28:12 This is the first of four thematic sayings found in chapters 28–29. A stark contrast is shown between the consequences of **righteous** rule and **wicked** rule. With the former, the country celebrates: **there is great elation** (lit., "glory"). "Glory" can refer to material well-being (Ps 49:16), but here it probably refers to the triumph of sapiential virtues. When it comes to the wicked, **men go into hiding**. Perhaps this means that in a degenerate society, people are dehumanized. So they find all possible ways they can to escape the injustices.

[13]**He who conceals his sins does not prosper,**
> **but whoever confesses and renounces them finds mercy.**
[14]**Blessed is the man who always fears the LORD,**
> **but he who hardens his heart falls into trouble.**
[15]**Like a roaring lion or a charging bear**
> **is a wicked man ruling over a helpless people.**
[16]**A tyrannical ruler lacks judgment,**
> **but he who hates ill-gotten gain will enjoy a long life.**
[17]**A man tormented by the guilt of murder**
> **will be a fugitive till death;**
> **let no one support him.**
[18]**He whose walk is blameless is kept safe,**
> **but he whose ways are perverse will suddenly fall.**
[19]**He who works his land will have abundant food,**

> but the one who chases fantasies will have his fill of
>   poverty.
> [20]A faithful man will be richly blessed,
>   but one eager to get rich will not go unpunished.
> [21]To show partiality is not good—
>   yet a man will do wrong for a piece of bread.
> [22]A stingy man is eager to get rich
>   and is unaware that poverty awaits him.
> [23]He who rebukes a man will in the end gain more favor
>   than he who has a flattering tongue.
> [24]He who robs his father or mother
>   and says, "It's not wrong"—
>   he is partner to him who destroys.
> [25]A greedy man stirs up dissension,
>   but he who trusts in the LORD will prosper.
> [26]He who trusts in himself is a fool,
>   but he who walks in wisdom is kept safe.
> [27]He who gives to the poor will lack nothing,
>   but he who closes his eyes to them receives many curses.
> [28]When the wicked rise to power, people go into hiding;
>   but when the wicked perish, the righteous thrive.

28:13 Sometimes it is appropriate to conceal. When one is hurt by another's actions, the sage advocates concealing or covering over (cf., 10:12 and 17:9). When it is one's own **sins**, concealing is disastrous. There is a time to **conceal**; there is a time to reveal. Knowing the appropriate thing to do is a hallmark of wisdom. Regarding one's personal sins, the sage says **whoever confesses and renounces them finds mercy** (here primarily referring to God's mercy). This is the only proverb in the book to speak of confessing sins. A good commentary on the thought is found in Psalm 32.

28:14 Blessed is the man who always fears the LORD. The NIV adds "the LORD," which in this proverb is appropriate. The fear of the LORD was a sign of submission and humility. The opposite of humility is **harden**ing one's **heart**. This does not mean one who lacks compassion, but rather one who is stubborn, who lacks humility.

28:15 The NIV translates this as a simile when it is actually a metaphor: "a growling lion and a running bear, a wicked one ruling over poor people." A **lion** and a **bear** are animals that can destroy when provoked. In the same way, a **wicked** ruler can easily take advantage of the disenfranchised, like the poor. It is the primary responsibility of rulers to protect the poor. When that does not happen, a whole society is thrown into chaos.

28:16 To **lack judgment** (another term for "fool;" see Characteristics of Wisdom Literature in the Introduction, p. 16) is to be less than human. That trait distinguishes humans from animals. A lack of judgment leads to dehumanizing others, which is why gaining understanding and wisdom is so essential for the sage. A paradox exists: those who have *little* understanding "*increase* violence" (רַב מַעֲשַׁקּוֹת, *rab maʿăšaqqôth*; cf. the NRSV translation). In contrast, **long life** (i.e., fulfilling or satisfying) waits for those who gain understanding.

28:17 The one guilty of killing (**murder**; lit., "the blood of another") will be burdened with a life of **guilt**. A warning is extended to anyone who might want to help a killer to escape.

28:18 The image of the two ways so frequent in wisdom underlies the thought of this verse. The phrase **whose ways are perverse** is also found in 6b.

28:19 The theme of diligence in work is woven into the book of Proverbs (e.g., 6:6-8). **The one who chases fantasies** in the Hebrew text reads, "the one who pursues emptiness." The picture is of frenetic activity, busybodies who lack purpose and direction in life. The psalmist describes these kinds of people "like chaff that the wind blows away" (Ps 1:4).

28:20 A faithful man represents a person of integrity (the phrase is closely related to one who "fears the LORD"); he is the one who exemplifies steadiness. Such an individual **will be richly blessed**. The **one eager to get rich** is "the hasty one," of which the wise are so skeptical (see v. 22; also 19:2; 21:5). To act hastily means to act without thinking, without reflecting. Reflection is a fundamental resource of the wise.

The saying contrasts the one who sees the larger picture and who carefully plans what is done in terms of its effect on the community and the one who acts impetuously for the sake of personal gain. Any society that promotes "get rich quick" schemes (e.g., gambling and casinos) unravels the moral fiber which maintains its solidarity.

28:21 This is the last of the several **not good** proverbs found sprinkled through the collections (for others see 16:29; 17:26; 18:5;

19:2; 20:23; 24:23; 25:27). Three of the proverbs, including this one, are related to the issue of showing partiality (the other two are 18:5 and 24:23). This proverb affirms that **to show partiality is not good**, which is closely related to the fundamental virtues of wisdom instruction: righteousness, justice, and fairness (1:3). It does not take much for humans to distort justice and fairness: **yet a man will do wrong for a piece of bread**. Because of human nature, it is quite easy to be lured into sin.

28:22 The **stingy man** is the one who has the "bad eye" (cf. 23:6). The generous one has the "good eye" (cf. 22:9). Because of the "bad eye," he is unable to think and reflect, he loses perspective, and thus he **is eager** (lit., "hastens") **to get rich** (see v. 20). With the "bad eye," the stingy man cannot see the future. He is totally **unaware that poverty awaits him**.

28:23 Rebuke or reproof is one of the main resources the wise use to instruct (cf. 9:8; 25:12; 27:5-6). Reproof includes warning, exhortation, and instruction. The bottom line is that reproof involves the interaction of two individuals in a healthy exchange of ideas. (That is why one is to avoid the fool. He is unable to carry on this kind of exchange; see 29:9.) At first, the one who **rebukes** seems to do harm. Later, it will become clearer that it was in the best interest of the student, and the teacher will receive honor (cf. Heb 12:11).

On the other hand, the **flattering tongue**, which at first appeared beneficial, is not (26:28). The flattering (or "smooth") tongue is the same image used to describe the temptress in 2:16; 5:3; and 7:5,21. Such speech is ultimately a trap, especially for the inexperienced.

28:24 Because of the number of related proverbs, it appears that abuse of parents was not uncommon (see 19:26; 20:20; 30:17). As parents grew older, children could take advantage of them, such as in manipulating the family inheritance (19:14).

Certain instructions and sayings in Proverbs incorporate what is referred to as "reported speech." This is speech that is reported within the confines of the proverb (e.g., 1:11-14; 7:14-20; 20:14; 22:13; 26:13,19). In the present case, the youth is quoted as saying, **"It's not wrong."** The youth is either completely blind to the crime or, more than likely, covering it with a profession of innocence.[58]

---

[58]Elizabeth Huwiler observes that within chapters 10–29 all reported speech is negative (see *Control of Reality*, p. 236).

28:25 The **greedy man** is one who is literally "wide of throat or appetite." He is never satisfied. The result of his greed is that he wreaks havoc on the community by stirring **up dissension**. But the one **who trusts in the LORD** will be satisfied. Riches are not always a blessing from the LORD. The value of wealth depends on the one who possesses it and on what or in whom that person places trust.

28:26 The phrase **he who trusts in himself** means that one trusts his own judgment. It may be similar to the common wisdom phrase "wise in his own eyes" (see v. 11; also 26:12).

28:27 The principle is woven throughout Scripture: the generous will never be in want. Those who close their **eyes** to the **poor** will ultimately receive punishment.

28:28 This is the second of four thematic verses that appear in chapters 28 and 29 (see 28:12).

[29:1]**A man who remains stiff-necked after many rebukes**
      will suddenly be destroyed—without remedy.
[2]**When the righteous thrive, the people rejoice;**
      when the wicked rule, the people groan.
[3]**A man who loves wisdom brings joy to his father,**
      but a companion of prostitutes squanders his wealth.
[4]**By justice a king gives a country stability,**
      but one who is greedy for bribes tears it down.
[5]**Whoever flatters his neighbor**
      is spreading a net for his feet.
[6]**An evil man is snared by his own sin,**
      but a righteous one can sing and be glad.
[7]**The righteous care about justice for the poor,**
      but the wicked have no such concern.
[8]**Mockers stir up a city,**
      but wise men turn away anger.
[9]**If a wise man goes to court with a fool,**
      the fool rages and scoffs, and there is no peace.
[10]**Bloodthirsty men hate a man of integrity**
      and seek to kill the upright.
[11]**A fool gives full vent to his anger,**
      but a wise man keeps himself under control.
[12]**If a ruler listens to lies,**
      all his officials become wicked.

[13]**The poor man and the oppressor have this in common:**
   The LORD gives sight to the eyes of both.
[14]**If a king judges the poor with fairness,**
   his throne will always be secure.

29:1 The **stiff-necked** person has received **many rebukes**. The image of the stiff-necked is a familiar description of the Israelites in the Old Testament (Deut 31:27). We might speak of persons in the face of confrontation as "bowing their backs." The sense is of individuals who have become recalcitrant to reproof (see v. 23). A stiffened neck is more susceptible to "breaking," which is the word the NIV translates **be destroyed**. Woman Wisdom continually pleads with the youth to heed reproof because she knows the deadly consequences of not doing so (1:20-33).

Continued obstinacy leads to **sudden** destruction, to a point of no return, when there are no more opportunities. The NIV tries to capture the heightening effect of the proverb with the hyphenated pause followed by the succinct phrase **without remedy** (the second line in the Hebrew text contains only two words). The recalcitrant has no hope for being healed (see 9:7-8).

29:2 This is the third of the thematic verses found in chapters 28–29 (see 28:12,28). Clifford points out that the response of the people is expressed in sound.[59] **The people rejoice** when **the righteous thrive**, but they **groan** when **the wicked rule**. The way in which a society is governed manifests itself not only visibly but verbally as well.

29:3 This verse reflects the language common in chapters 1–9. Clifford astutely observes that, "wise adult children have a profound effect upon their parents."[60]

29:4 A visual contrast exists in this verse between causing a country to "stand" (**gives a country stability**) and **tearing it down**. The qualities by which a leader rules either build up or tear down a community. The leader can either contribute to the well-being of the nation or take from it for personal gain. Samuel spoke of the ruler who would "take" from the people and ultimately leave them demoralized (1 Sam 8:10-18).

---

[59]Clifford, *Proverbs*, p. 250.
[60]Ibid.

29:5 On flattering see 28:23. For whose foot is the **net** spread? Is it for the one who **flatters** or for the **neighbor**? The text is ambiguous. If the former, then the flatterer will eventually fall into his own trap. If the latter, then the maxim serves as a warning to the naïve neighbor against being deceived by the smooth words (cf. 1:17).

29:6 A contrast is set up between the **evil** and the **righteous**. The evil find themselves entrapped by their own destructive lifestyle. But the righteous face the snares and temptations of life confidently, knowing that they will overcome.

29:7 Though hidden by the paraphrase of the NIV, a stark contrast exists between the **righteous** and the **wicked** in these two lines. The righteous are the ones who "know the rights of the poor" (the NIV translates **care about justice for the poor**). The wicked "do not understand such knowledge" (NIV, **the wicked have no such concern**). The issue is who has "knowledge" and "understanding." Lack of understanding leads to the dehumanization of others. Those who have knowledge of others, namely the poor, will take up their cause (see 28:16).

29:8 The image in the first line is of the words of **mockers** setting on fire a whole city (cf. 26:21; think of the fiery tongue James speaks of in Jas 2:6). The **wise** are able to repel and control the **anger** they experience.

29:9 The NIV assumes a legal context, the **court**, but a more general context of debate and argument is also possible. One of the reasons for not engaging a **fool** in conversation or discussion is the futility of it (recall 26:4). The fool does not know how to interact. In order to gain wisdom, the student must be willing to engage in lively dialogue (27:17).

The object of **rages and scoffs** is not specified in the second line in the Hebrew text. It could be either **a fool** or **a wise man**. The NIV supplies the object by assuming it is the fool (the NIV adds this to the text), which seems likely.

29:10 The main issue in the verse comes in the second line. The NIV translates it **and seek to kill the upright**. The Hebrew text reads, "but the upright will seek his life." The phrase "seek his life" in the Old Testament usually means, "seek to kill" (see, e.g., Jer 19:7,9; Ps 35:4; 40:14). However, here the **upright** are the ones seeking to kill the **man of integrity**. Since this cannot be, the NIV changes the syntax of the verse so that it makes more sense. The

RSV takes a similar view, translating the line "and the wicked seek his life."

Another way of approaching the issue is to give the phrase "seek his life" some kind of positive rather than a negative connotation (for a similar phrase that is positive, see 11:30). **Bloodthirsty men** seek to destroy people of integrity, but the upright seek out the life of the person of integrity to set things right and form camaraderie.

29:11 In Proverbs, the fool is the foil used by the sage to instruct youth. The common characteristic of the fool is lack of control. The fool is volatile, unpredictable, a "loose cannon." Once again this quality is highlighted: **a fool gives full vent to his anger**. The Hebrew text reads, "all a fool's anger will go forth." The word for anger (רוּחַ, *rûaḥ*) carries a variety of nuances. The word can be translated "wind," "spirit," "breath," or "anger." The context determines the meaning. Here the word is best translated "anger." The image created by this word is of one who is taking short quick breaths due to perturbation or agitation.[61]

In contrast, **a wise man keeps himself under control** (lit., "stills it backwards," i.e., keeps it in the background or holds it back). The text does not specify whose anger is held back. Does the wise hold back the anger of the fool (15:1,18), or does he hold back his own anger (16:32; 14:29)? The NIV interprets it in the latter sense, which seems most likely since the wise have little control over the fool.

29:12 The principle of "a little leaven leavens the whole lump" not only applies to the community at large but also to leadership administrations. The same principle is found in 25:5.

29:13 The first line places two phenomena together that normally would never be seen together: **the poor man and the oppressor**. (This is a common rhetorical device found in the sentence literature [17:12; 21:9; 19:26; 20:10]). Of all things, the line maintains that they possess a **common** bond! The proverb builds anticipation for the second line where the reader discovers what brings the two together: **The LORD gives sight to the eyes of both**. The phrase refers to the LORD who sustains life for both the poor and the oppressor. The same phrase is used in Psalm 19:8 to describe the effects of God's law: "The precepts of the LORD are right, giving joy

---

[61]Ibid., p. 252; רוּחַ is the word used for anger in 16:32 and 25:28 as well.

to the heart. The commands of the Lord are radiant, giving light to the eyes."

29:14 A basic and universal responsibility of government is to treat **the poor with fairness** (אֱמֶת, *'ĕmeth*). The goal of wisdom is not only to train the inexperienced and the wise (1:4-5) in "righteousness, justice, and fairness" (1:3), but also rulers and kings. These virtues do not come naturally to kings; they too must be taught fairness.

[15]The rod of correction imparts wisdom,
    but a child left to himself disgraces his mother.
[16]When the wicked thrive, so does sin,
    but the righteous will see their downfall.
[17]Discipline your son, and he will give you peace;
    he will bring delight to your soul.
[18]Where there is no revelation, the people cast off restraint;
    but blessed is he who keeps the law.
[19]A servant cannot be corrected by mere words;
    though he understands, he will not respond.
[20]Do you see a man who speaks in haste?
    There is more hope for a fool than for him.
[21]If a man pampers his servant from youth,
    he will bring grief[a] in the end.
[22]An angry man stirs up dissension,
    and a hot-tempered one commits many sins.
[23]A man's pride brings him low,
    but a man of lowly spirit gains honor.
[24]The accomplice of a thief is his own enemy;
    he is put under oath and dare not testify.
[25]Fear of man will prove to be a snare,
    but whoever trusts in the Lord is kept safe.
[26]Many seek an audience with a ruler,
    but it is from the Lord that man gets justice.
[27]The righteous detest the dishonest;
    the wicked detest the upright.

[a]*21 The meaning of the Hebrew for this word is uncertain.*

29:15 The Hebrew text reads, "the rod and reproof give wisdom." The NIV combines the two disciplines into one and translates the line, **the rod of correction imparts wisdom**. The "rod" and "reproof" were two primary means of instruction for the sage; the one physical, the other verbal. In the overall context of Proverbs, the wise relied primarily on the verbal instrument more than corporal punishment (see 25:12; 27:5-6; 28:23 for the meaning of "rebuke"). Refer to 13:24 for a treatment of the use of **the rod**.

The second line of the proverb reads **but a child left to himself disgraces his mother**. A child left to himself has no constraints or guidelines. The result brings shame to **his mother**. In an ancient Near Eastern culture, honor and shame were powerful social forces. This is the only verse in Proverbs that mentions mother without reference to father.

29:16 This verse is the fourth and final appearance of the refrain found in chapters 28–29. Once again the stark contrast between the **righteous** and the **wicked** is affirmed (see 28:12; 29:2).

29:17 In Proverbs, the primary responsibility assigned to parents is the education of youth. Parents have the responsibility for the moral and spiritual **discipline** of children. Discipline refers to the educational process involved in instruction, which includes physical and verbal instruction (v. 15). Such instruction results in bringing **peace** and **delight** to the parents.

29:18 The language of the KJV has made this verse popular: "Where there is no vision the people perish." The proverb is interpreted to mean that where people have not created a clear vision or a dream for which they can strive, then they have nothing for which to live. They will perish for lack of a goal. That misses the meaning of the proverb. The NIV captures well its idea: **Where there is no revelation, the people cast off restraint**. The word for "revelation" (חָזוֹן , ḥāzôn) is the term often used to describe a prophetic vision, that is, the word that God spoke through the prophets (cf. Ezek 7:26). In other words, where there is no instructional word from God (by way of the sages), people will lack **restraint** (פָּרַע , pāra').[62] For a picture of such a society, read Romans 1:18-32.

But blessed is he who keeps the law. Once again the NIV translates *torah* as "law" (see 28:4). The NIV interprets both lines of the

---

[62]The same word is used in Exodus 32:25 to describe Israel "running wild." The word is often used to describe hair that is not cut or combed (Lev 10:6; 13:45; Num 6:5). Lamentations 2:9 describes a culture that has lost its moorings because "her prophets no longer find visions from the LORD." Amos speaks of a famine for the word of the LORD in 8:11-12.

proverb to refer to the two parts of the Old Testament canon, the prophets and the law, which is not unreasonable. It is also reasonable to interpret "revelation" and "law" as referring more specifically to the revelation and law (i.e., instruction) received from the sages. However, the teachings of the sages build on the revelation received from the law and the prophets.

Notice the contrast between the collective plural, "people," in the first line with the singular individual in the second line. Even though a nation may live in moral chaos, the individual who keeps God's instruction does not have to be influenced by the larger culture. In the same way, in 1:8-19 the father advises the son not to follow the way of the gang. Such a way will lead to chaos and destruction. The son can choose to yield to the instruction of the father and be blessed.

29:19 When taken in conjunction with verses 15 and 21, the verse may be contrasting verbal discipline with physical. This is the way the NIV interprets it. The Hebrew text, however, could imply a little different nuance of meaning: "With words a servant will not be disciplined, though he understands, there is no answer (response)." Because of the inequity that existed in the master/slave relationship, true interactive discourse cannot take place. The servant will remain silent, so it is futile to enter into serious conversation with him.

29:20 The same rhetorical form used here is found in 26:12 ("Do you see"). The wise not only looked with suspicion upon wealth gotten in haste (28:20) and hasty actions (19:2), but also upon **a man who speaks in haste**. Such a person is even worse than a **fool**.

29:21 The difficulty in understanding this verse is that the last word in the Hebrew text (מָנוֹן, *mānôn*) appears nowhere else in the Old Testament.[63] The NIV makes an educated guess in translating it **bring grief**. Whatever the meaning of the word is, it appears that there is some kind of negative consequence related to **pampering** a **servant from youth**.

29:22 Anger and **dissension** ("strife") go hand in hand. Anger is a virtual hot-house for sin. Proverbs repeatedly dwells on this theme (14:17,29; 15:1,18; 19:19; 22:24; 29:8,11).

---

[63] A *hapax legomenon*, that is, something said only once. BDB interprets the word as "thankless one" (p. 584). The critical notes of the Hebrew text suggest emending the word to מָנוֹד (*mᵊnôd*) which means something like "bring shame."

29:23 The classic reversal statement is affirmed in the saying: **A man's pride brings him low, but a man of lowly spirit gains honor.** The NIV captures nicely the wordplay found in the Hebrew text between the proud being brought *low* and the *low* of spirit brought to honor. All through Scripture, the LORD promises to humble the proud and exalt the humble (1 Sam 2:2-10; Luke 1:46-55).

29:24 Typically commentators refer to Leviticus 5:1 as the background to understanding the meaning of these two lines. The issue seems to be of someone who is aware of the wrongdoing of a **thief**, but who refuses to **testify** when asked. Such a person becomes an **accomplice** and will suffer the consequences.

29:25 The basic contrast is between the person who **trusts in the LORD** and the one who does not. **Fear of man** could refer to either fear of other human beings or the fears that humans experience that threaten their security.

29:26 While a person cannot always count on receiving **justice** from a **ruler**, one can always count on justice from God.

29:27 The dichotomy between the **righteous** wise and the unrighteous **wicked** is a fitting conclusion to chapters 28–29 in which antithetic parallelism dominates. Distinctions are well defined between those who contribute to the well-being of society and those who tear down its moral fiber. Such a stark contrast between good and evil does not sit well in a pluralistic culture like ours. When it comes to the moral and spiritual health of the community, lines are clearly drawn. There is no middle ground.

PROVERBS 30–31

VI. THE SAYINGS OF AGUR (30:1-9)

With chapter 30, a new unit begins as indicated by the heading. The majority of the chapter is made up of numerical sayings beginning with verse 15. However, one could also speak of a type of numerical saying that appears earlier in verses 7-9 and 11-14. Chapters 30–31 are reminiscent of the form of the instruction literature found in chapters 1–9.

One issue surrounding the sayings of Agur is where do they end? Commentators are divided over the boundaries.[1] Some conclude the sayings at verse 4, others at verse 9, and still others at verse 14. There is no way to be certain, but the position I take is that the unit concludes at verse 9. Verses 1-6 and 7-9 appear to have some logical coherence to them.[2] Verses 11-14 are set apart by the numerical listing of four worthless characters, a listing that points to the numerical sayings that follow in verses 15-33.

[1]The sayings of Agur son of Jakeh—an oracle[a]:

This man declared to Ithiel,
     to Ithiel and to Ucal:[b]
[2]**"I am the most ignorant of men;**
     I do not have a man's understanding.
[3]**I have not learned wisdom,**
     nor have I knowledge of the Holy One.
[4]**Who has gone up to heaven and come down?**
     Who has gathered up the wind in the hollow of his hands?

---

[1]The LXX places the contents of this chapter in a completely different location. The following is the sequence of verses followed by that Greek translation: 22:17–24:22; 30:1-14; 24:23-34; 30:15-33; 31:1-9; 25:1–29:27; 31:10-31.

[2]See Clifford, *Proverbs*, p. 257.

Who has wrapped up the waters in his cloak?
    Who has established all the ends of the earth?
What is his name, and the name of his son?
    Tell me if you know!
⁵"Every word of God is flawless;
    he is a shield to those who take refuge in him.
⁶Do not add to his words,
    or he will rebuke you and prove you a liar.
⁷"Two things I ask of you, O LORD;
    do not refuse me before I die:
⁸Keep falsehood and lies far from me;
    give me neither poverty nor riches,
    but give me only my daily bread.
⁹Otherwise, I may have too much and disown you
    and say, 'Who is the LORD?'
Or I may become poor and steal,
    and so dishonor the name of my God.

ᵃ1 Or *Jakeh of Massa*   ᵇ1 Masoretic Text; with a different word division
of the Hebrew *declared, "I am weary, O God; / I am weary, O God, and
faint.*

Are these sayings the words of a skeptic? Or are they expressions
of a humble believer in the presence of God? Those who view them
as the words of a skeptic typically interpret the difficult line in verse
1, "There is no God! There is no God!"[3] Those who interpret the
sayings as the words of a pious believer sometimes interpret verse 1,
"I am weary, O God. I am weary, O God" (see v. 1 below). The

---

[3]See R.B.Y. Scott, *Proverbs, Ecclesiastes,* p. 175. James Crenshaw takes a similar view. He understands the sayings of Agur to include verses 1-14. Within
these verses there are several speakers and views expressed. Agur, the skeptic, speaks in verses 1-4. Then beginning with verse five a new speaker, an
orthodox Jew, "takes a sacred scroll and beats Agur over the head with it."
The two competing perspectives of the skeptic and the religious devotee col-
lide with each other. Then in verses 7-9 the religious devotee shifts his attention from speaking to Agur to addressing God in prayer. Finally, in verses
10-14 an unknown individual rushes to Agur's defense and rebukes the
defender of traditional spirituality. Crenshaw demonstrates how the text
brings together a variety of conflicting perspectives, which he refers to as
"clanging symbols." See James Crenshaw, "Clanging Symbols," in *Justice and
the Holy,* eds. D.A. Knight and P.J. Paris (Philadelphia: Fortress Press, 1989),
pp. 51-64.

tentative position that I take is that the sayings reflect humble submission to God in light of the great divide that exists between
human ignorance and divine knowledge.

30:1 The heading in verse 1 is plagued with difficulties. First, the
question is whether to translate the word *hamassa* (הַמַּשָּׂא, *hammaśśā'*)
as a type of speech, **oracle** (so NIV), or as a reference to a place,
"Massa" (so RSV).[4] The very next word in the text is another techni-
cal term for "oracle." It seems odd to have the two words side by
side, so it is better to translate the word as a proper noun, "Massa."
A similar phrase is also used in 31:1 and makes better sense there to
translate it as a place, "The words of King Lemuel of Massa" rather
than "The words of King Lemuel—an oracle."

Second, how does one translate 1b?[5] The NIV chooses a literal
rendering of the Hebrew text (a transliteration), which takes the
words as proper nouns: **Ithiel, to Ithiel and to Ucal.** This translation
makes no sense (notice the NIV footnote). What makes better sense,
and what fits the context of one expressing humble submission to
God, is to translate the second line: "I am weary, O God. I am weary,
O God. I am exhausted."[6]

Massa (Gen 25:14) was a tribe in north Arabia, so **Agur** appears
to be a non-Israelite sage. However, he was one who seems to have
been in relationship with Israel's God, Yahweh (v. 9 uses the name
Yahweh).

30:2-3 Agur's speech continues in verses 2-3. He confesses his
ignorance in the presence of God (reminiscent of Ps 73:22). In keeping with wisdom's perspective on human limitations (16:1-9; 21:30-
31), Agur acknowledges that he has **not learned wisdom** or **knowledge of the Holy One.** In other words, he is not "wise in his own
eyes" (see 26:12). The confession acknowledges a stark contrast
between his exhaustive but futile efforts and God's all knowing wisdom. The confession actually serves as a way of expressing rever-

---

[4]The latter calls for emending the text (the addition of a particle) from
הַמַּשָּׂא (*hammaśśā'*) to מִמַּשָּׂא (*mimmaśśā'*).

[5]For a list of the different options, see R.N. Whybray, *Composition of the
Book of Proverbs*, p. 150, fn 3.

[6]Emending from לְאִיתִיאֵל לְאִיתִיאֵל (*l'ithî'ēl l'ithî'ēl*) to לָאִיתִי אֵל לָאִיתִי אֵל
(*lā'ithî 'ēl lā'ithî 'ēl*) and to take וָאֵכָל (*w'ukāl*) from the root כלה (*kālāh*,
"exhausted"). See the critical notes of the Hebrew text.

ence before the Holy One.[7] To proclaim human helplessness is a way of acknowledging divine power.

30:4 This verse contains four **who** questions and a final **what** question. The questions demand a negative answer in terms of the human realm. They are intended to highlight the huge gulf that exists between human ignorance and divine understanding, which further serves to express wonder and reverence to the Creator God. These questions are also reminiscent of the dialogue between God and Job (Job 38–39).

The final question posed in the litany is, **What is his name, and the name of his son?** In other words, who is it that is equal in wisdom and understanding to the LORD of the universe? What is his name? Do you know his son's name? That is, is his offspring present among us? The question demands a negative response.

The first four verses of the oracle declare the tremendous gulf that exists between humans and God. Agur's confession of weariness and ignorance is a way of expressing amazement, awe, and homage to the God who created the world.

30:5 While verses 1-4 describe the ignorance of humans, verses 5-6 speak of God's revelation. The NIV translates the first line, **Every word of God is flawless**. The word for "flawless" (צָרַף, ṣāraph) is the word which means "to refine" and refers to the testing experiences of life.[8] The line would be better translated, "**Every word of God** has stood the test of life." In the experiences of life, God's word stands sure. In contrast to humans, God's word is reliable. Verse 5 is a quote from Psalm 18:30 (cf. 2 Sam 22:31).

30:6 Do not add to his words. The phrase alludes to the words in Deuteronomy 4:2 (also Deut 12:32). There is no need to speculate about the word of God; it is sufficient. That word is all that is necessary to address the ignorance of human beings. So trust in God's word.

30:7-9 In an act of reverence, the pious one turns his face to God in prayer. This is the only prayer recorded in the book of Proverbs. The inquirer prays, **two things I ask of you, O LORD**. Even though the Hebrew text does not have the words "O LORD," it is not inappropri-

---

[7]The term is plural in Hebrew, a plural of majesty (cf. 9:10).

[8]The word is used to describe the smelting process of a refiner's fire (Prov 25:4; Mal 3:2). Isaiah 48:10 uses the word in the following way: "See, I have refined you, though not as silver; I have tested you in the furnace of affliction."

ate for the NIV to add them. The worshiper requests two things. First, **keep falsehood and lies far from me**. And second, to be kept from extreme economic conditions: **give me neither poverty nor riches**.[9] The reason he requests no **riches** is that, **I may have too much and disown you and say, 'Who is the LORD?'** Living a life of luxury was one of the temptations of youth, highlighted in chapters 1–9. Such a life leads one to forget God, which was the temptation Israel faced as they entered into the land flowing with milk and honey (Deut 8:11-17).

On the other hand, the worshiper prays that neither will the LORD give him poverty, lest he **steal and so dishonor the name of God**. The poverty referred to here is abject poverty, a desperate hunger. This is not the poverty described in the sentence literature that speaks of a modest existence: "Better a little with the fear of the LORD than great wealth with turmoil. Better a meal of vegetables where there is love than a fattened calf with hatred" (15:16-17). The worshiper simply asks the LORD, **give me only my daily bread**.[10] The way the NIV translates it reminds one of Jesus' model prayer to the disciples in Matthew 6:11.

Verses 1-9 reflect a worshipful reverence to God. In the face of the uncertainties of life, the worshiper comes to rely on God's word (vv. 5-6) and on God for the necessities of life (vv. 7-9). Trusting in God enables the worshiper ultimately to accept human limitations.

VII. THE NUMERICAL SAYINGS (30:10-33)

Most of the material in this unit is characterized by its use of a numerical formula to introduce the instruction. There are five sub-units that use the numeration in one way or another, typically in the formula of x, x + 1. Such a numerical formula is used throughout the Old Testament (see Amos 1–2). Earlier, in Proverbs 6:16-19, the sage begins with the formula: " There are six things the LORD hates, seven that are detestable to him." The graded numbering serves a rhetorical function to create a heightening effect. In a sense, it is Hebrew parallelism at work with numbers.

---

[9]Duane Garrett says the two requests are 1) poverty and 2) wealth. The falsehood and lies refers to the deceptiveness of poverty and wealth. See Garrett, *Proverbs, Ecclesiastes, Song of Songs*, p. 238.

[10]The phrase "only my daily bread" means a prescribed portion of food, BDB, p. 348.

[10]"**Do not slander a servant to his master,**
    or he will curse you, and you will pay for it.

30:10 This verse does not contain the numerical introduction and may be an isolated proverb that warns against interfering in domestic affairs, which should be kept between the **servant** and the **master**.

[11]"**There are those who curse their fathers**
    and do not bless their mothers;
[12]**those who are pure in their own eyes**
    and yet are not cleansed of their filth;
[13]**those whose eyes are ever so haughty,**
    whose glances are so disdainful;
[14]**those whose teeth are swords**
    and whose jaws are set with knives
  to devour the poor from the earth,
    the needy from among mankind.

30:11-14 Even though the subsection does not begin with the numerical formula common to the rest of the chapter, it may still be classified with it because of its cataloging of vices. It highlights four classes of people that are especially destructive to community life. Each verse begins with the Hebrew word דּוֹר (*dôr*, usually translated "generation" or "class"). The NIV translates it as **those**. In this context the term highlights the collective nature of sin; sin can infect a whole generation. Sin usually works within a cluster of people. It cannot remain isolated. Four classes of wrongdoers are singled out: the disrespectful (v. 11); the self-righteous (v. 12); the arrogant (v. 13); and the oppressor (v. 14).

[15]"**The leech has two daughters.**
    'Give! Give!' they cry.
  "**There are three things that are never satisfied,**
    four that never say, 'Enough!':
[16]**the grave,**[a] **the barren womb,**
    land, which is never satisfied with water,
    and fire, which never says, 'Enough!'

[a]*16* Hebrew *Sheol*

30:15-16 This is the first of the five instructions that specifically uses the x, x + 1 formula. The image in verse 15a serves as the introduction: **The leech has two daughters. 'Give! Give!' they cry.** The leech had two suckers on each end of its body with which it could attach itself. The two suckers are the names of its daughters: Give and Give. The phrase "they cry" is not in the Hebrew text. This image introduces the numerical saying that follows: **There are three things that are never satisfied, four that never say, 'Enough!'** The first two, **the grave** and **the barren womb**, are given no explanation. Maybe because they need no explanation. The grave (Sheol; see 27:20) never gets its fill of death. The barren womb is never satisfied with barrenness (this was especially true in Israelite culture). The last two are succeeded by a brief explanation. **Land, which is never satisfied with water** refers to the arid desert land of the region. **And fire, which never says, 'Enough!'** indicates that fire is an all consuming phenomenon of nature.

The instruction speaks of the power of greed to consume the life of a person. Once it takes control, it ravages one's mental and spiritual resources. The individual assumes the life of a parasite. The picture painted in this instruction is just the opposite of the worshiper in verses 7-9 who prays for a modest lifestyle.

[17]"**The eye that mocks a father,**
    that scorns obedience to a mother,
  will be pecked out by the ravens of the valley,
    will be eaten by the vultures.

30:17 There may be no harsher punishment envisioned for those who dishonor their parents in all of Scripture than what is visualized in this isolated proverb. The proverb pictures the corpse of the guilty party exposed to the elements, their eyes **will be pecked out by the ravens** and **the vultures**. In other words, it is death without burial. Especially for Israel, failure to bury the body of the deceased was a most dehumanizing act. From the number of sayings in Proverbs, it appears that disrespect of parents was not an uncommon occurrence in Israel (15:20; 17:25; 19:26; 20:20; 23:22; 28:24). Recall that one of the four classes of scoundrels mentioned in verses 11-14 was those who dishonor parents.

[18]"**There are three things that are too amazing for me,**
    four that I do not understand:
[19]**the way of an eagle in the sky,**
    the way of a snake on a rock,

the way of a ship on the high seas,
   and the way of a man with a maiden.
[20]"This is the way of an adulteress:
   She eats and wipes her mouth
   and says, 'I've done nothing wrong.'

30:18-20 This is the second of the five numerical sayings. The wise were keen observers of nature. They were especially attentive to the ordinary affairs of life. Once again the sages acknowledge and accept their own human limitations as they stand in awe of creation (cf. 16:1-9; 21:30-31). As a result, they express adoration to God.

Four things remain a mystery to the observer: the way of an **eagle**, a **snake**, a **ship**, and a **man with a maiden** (probably meaning young woman). The medium that each uses is different: air, land, water, and communication. The instruction moves from the animal world to the human world.

What is the mystery about each of these? Is it that with each there is the absence of a visible means of movement? Or is it that after they pass over their respective media, they leave no trace? No one can tell they have passed this way. The key lies in the repetition of the word **way** in verse 19. The word is repeated with each of the four items. The mystery lies in the way they travel through life. What is it that moves them forward (in the form of motivation or attraction) along their path? The focus of the instruction is on the last item, a man and a maiden (or woman). What attracts the two and brings them together? Whatever one understands the mystery to be between these four elements, the sage stands in awe of them all, especially of the relationship between a man and a woman.

Verse 20 contains the catchword, **way**, which loosely connects it with the preceding verses. If it is taken in this context, then it is a picture of the mystery of love, namely sexual love that has gone awry. The verse echoes the image of the temptress in the first nine chapters of Proverbs.

[21]"Under three things the earth trembles,
   under four it cannot bear up:
[22]a servant who becomes king,
   a fool who is full of food,
[23]an unloved woman who is married,
   and a maidservant who displaces her mistress.

30:21-23 The third numerical saying holds together by the word **under** (תַּחַת, *tāḥath*), used as an anaphora in each of the successive lines of the poem. The instruction pictures a world upside down in a negative sense.[11] That is, social hierarchical relations intended to maintain the order of society are inverted (cf. Eccl 10:6-7). Such an inversion disrupts the stability of a people which was designed to enable them to function properly in community. Two of the examples used are male and two are female.

It would be disastrous for a **servant** to become a **king** (v. 22a). In a similar vein, a **fool** who lives a life of luxury disrupts the work ethic on which a society is built (v. 22b). Verse 22 is closely related to the sentence saying in 19:10.

Such disruption occurs not only in the public realm, but also in the home where a competitive spirit reigns. **An unloved woman who is married** might have reference to a polygamous marriage in which one of the wives receives less favor from the husband than the other (e.g., Elkanah, Peninnah, and Hannah in 1 Samuel 1; or Jacob, Rachel, and Leah in Genesis 29–36; see also Deut 21:15-17). The second line of verse 23 expands on the familial context: **a maidservant who displaces her mistress**. Such a displacement, for example, resulted in a series of problems between Sarah and her handmaid Hagar (Gen 16:1-6).

Such is the instability that results when the institutions, political or familial, are disrupted. This instruction is designed to affirm the hierarchical role of those in power by imagining the world upside down in a negative sense. However, sometimes a society's institutions become corrupt and require change, a reversal of roles. The song of Hannah in 1 Samuel 2:1-10 pictures a world upside down in a positive sense, where God intervenes to humble the proud and exalt the humble.

[24]**"Four things on earth are small,**
        yet they are extremely wise:
[25]**Ants are creatures of little strength,**
        yet they store up their food in the summer;
[26]**coneys[a] are creatures of little power,**
        yet they make their home in the crags;

---

[11]See Raymond C. Van Leeuwen, "Proverbs 30:21-23 and the Biblical World Upside Down," *JBL* 105 (1986): 599-610.

²⁷**locusts have no king,**
      yet they advance together in ranks;
²⁸**a lizard can be caught with the hand,**
      yet it is found in kings' palaces.

ᵃ*26* **That is, the hyrax or rock badger**

30:24-28 The fourth numerical saying (which does not strictly hold to the x, x + 1 pattern) sets up a paradox between those things that are **small** (meaning insignificant; cf. 1 Sam 9:21) yet **extremely wise** (or more closely with the Hebrew, "wisest of the wise"). Four insignificant creatures are singled out for observation. **Ants are creatures** who have the wisdom to **store up their food** during the good days so they will have something during the bad days. **Coneys** (possibly rock badgers) have the wisdom to **make their homes in** inaccessible places (**crags**) out of reach of their enemies. **Locusts** have the ability to organize themselves into vast destructive swarms, without the aid of a leader. Finally, **a lizard** is easily caught, yet it finds its way into **kings' palaces** where ordinary humans seldom go, but long to dwell.

The sage uses a series of examples from the natural world to make an implied application to the human world: those who are insignificant, who acquire wisdom, can accomplish amazing tasks. A dominant theme in sapiential teaching is that wisdom is more powerful than physical strength.

²⁹**"There are three things that are stately in their stride,**
      four that move with stately bearing:
³⁰**a lion, mighty among beasts,**
      who retreats before nothing;
³¹**a strutting rooster, a he-goat,**
      and a king with his army around him.ᵃ

ᵃ*31* **Or** *king secure against revolt*

30:29-31 This is the fifth and final numerical saying. Unfortunately, verse 31 lacks clarity, which makes the meaning of the saying uncertain. The first phrase in verse 31, which the NIV translates **a strutting rooster**, is in the Hebrew text "girded of loins."[12] The last

---

[12]The first word in the verse, "girded" appears to be a *hapax legomenon*, the only time the word appears in the Old Testament.

phrase, which the NIV translates **his army around him**, is also unclear.[13] However, the idea of a king leading "his people," (עִמּוֹ, *'immô*) **army**, fits with the overall movement of the saying.

[32]**"If you have played the fool and exalted yourself,**
> **or if you have planned evil,**
> **clap your hand over your mouth!**
[33]**For as churning the milk produces butter,**
> **and as twisting the nose produces blood,**
> **so stirring up anger produces strife."**

30:32-33 The final instruction in chapter 30 is not one of the numerical sayings. However, it serves as a fitting summary to the chapter, highlighting the sin of arrogance, so frequently condemned by the sages, that leads to producing strife (cf. vv. 9,12,13). The final instruction contrasts with the humble posture described by Agur in verses 1-9.

The NIV appropriately translates the second line of verse 32, **if you have planned evil, clap your hand over your mouth** (lit., "if you have been plotting—hand to mouth!"). The figure of covering the mouth with the hand is an image of a person who is horrified by the consequences of his behavior. Pride and plotting evil do nothing but destroy the solidarity of the community. That is what the analogies demonstrate in verse 33.

Verse 33 contains an interesting wordplay with the repetition of two key terms (מִיץ [*mîṣ*] and יוֹצִיא [*yôṣî'*], "press" and "produce"). The NIV uses a variety of words to highlight the repetition of the expression "press" or "squeeze:" **churning**, **twisting**, and **stirring up**. The NRSV best captures the wordplay: "For as *pressing* milk *produces* curds, and *pressing* the nose *produces* blood, so *pressing* anger *produces* strife."[14] The analogy of **churning milk** to **produce butter** sets the tone for what follows in the next two images.

---

[13]The next to the last word also appears to be a *hapax legomenon*. BDB translates it "band of soldiers," p. 39. Clifford makes a guess that it means "not stand" (p. 265). Either way it is difficult to make sense of it. Notice the NIV footnote offers an alternate reading which follows the translation of the Vulgate.

[14]A further wordplay is found here. The same word for "anger" is also the same word in Hebrew for "nose" (the symbolic source of anger).

The virtue highlighted in this instruction is central to the life of the wise, and that is self-control. The specific thought is that foolish behavior, especially uncontrolled speech, will produce nothing but negative consequences. Trouble follows those who create it.

VIII. THE SAYINGS OF KING LEMUEL (31:1-9)

[1]The sayings of King Lemuel—an oracle[a] his mother taught him:
[2]"O my son, O son of my womb,
    O son of my vows,[b]
[3]do not spend your strength on women,
    your vigor on those who ruin kings.
[4]"It is not for kings, O Lemuel—
    not for kings to drink wine,
    not for rulers to crave beer,
[5]lest they drink and forget what the law decrees,
    and deprive all the oppressed of their rights.
[6]Give beer to those who are perishing,
    wine to those who are in anguish;
[7]let them drink and forget their poverty
    and remember their misery no more.
[8]"Speak up for those who cannot speak for themselves,
    for the rights of all who are destitute.
[9]Speak up and judge fairly;
    defend the rights of the poor and needy."

[a]1 Or *of Lemuel king of Massa, which*   [b]2 Or / *the answer to my prayers*

This passage forms a distinct unit with verse 1 introducing the sayings and with verse 10 introducing another instruction poem. The admonition in these verses comes from a mother to a son. The instruction serves as an example of one who offers wise reproof to a receptive ear (25:12), even though we do not know the degree to which Lemuel was receptive. The instruction possibly comes on the occasion of a new king transitioning into office. Rites of passage often make one more open to receiving advice. The underlying theme of the advice calls the king to administer justice among the poor and marginal of society. For another example of a royal instruction, see 1 Kings 2:1-12.

31:1 The NIV translates the Hebrew word מַשָּׂא (*maśśā'*), **an oracle**, but it is better to translate it as a proper noun, "Massa," the home of **King Lemuel** (see the NIV footnote; see also 30:1 for the same issue). Clifford observes that whenever a king is introduced, usually the editor gives the name of the country where he rules.[15]

31:2 The NIV translates the Hebrew interrogative "what" with the exclamation **O**. The interrogative in this context functions as a call for attention, such as when someone exclaims, "What are you doing?" The queen **mother** expresses shock that her son would even consider violating her instruction.

The phrase **O son of my vows** reflects a promise the mother made before her son was born, something similar to what Hannah made when she asked God to give her a son (1 Sam 1:9-11). Interestingly, the name Lemuel may be a long form of the phrase, "to God," that is, one who is dedicated to God. The vow indicates that, for this queenly mother, the spiritual and moral responsibilities began before her son was even born.

31:3-5 With these verses the specific advice begins. The admonition (or reproof) is that the king not give his **strength** to **women**. Here the term "strength" refers to the king's moral character, similar to the meaning of the woman of strength described in 12:4 and 31:10. The king must not allow his moral integrity to be compromised by his relationship to women. The king was especially vulnerable to all kinds of sexual temptation in the context of the harem that lived in his court. Solomon serves as a witness to that (1 Kgs 11–12). Samson's relationship with women also led to his undoing (Judges 16). Just as the youth in chapters 1–9 wrestle with sexual temptation, those in power are equally vulnerable to the temptation, perhaps more so.

The second admonition the mother gives relates to alcohol: **It is not for kings to drink wine, not for rulers to crave beer**. The Old Testament frequently warns about the misuse of wine. The mother's advice to the king on the occasion of his inauguration is that he completely abstain. Verse 5 gives two reasons for the abstinence: wine affects memory and judgment. The mother's admonition focuses on the responsibilities of the king and not his privileged position. The primary duty is to administer justice.

---

[15]Clifford, *Proverbs*, p. 269.

31:6-7 Verses 6-7 set up a stark contrast with verses 4-5 (contrasting proverbs are frequently found in the Proverbs collection; cf. 26:4-5). In the previous verses, the admonition called for abstinence from drinking alcohol. These verses call for the king to **give beer to those who are perishing, wine to those who are in anguish**. Alcohol is reserved for the dying and those experiencing great pain, serving as an anesthetic. However, simply giving alcohol to those experiencing great suffering does not fulfill the king's obligation to them as the next verses explain.

31:8-9 The queen mother calls for her son to take action for the cause of the **poor**. He must speak out **for the rights of all who are destitute**. Once again, the focus of the admonition is not on the privileges the son receives as king, but on his responsibilities.

IX. THE WOMAN OF NOBLE CHARACTER (31:10-31)

This poem serves as a fitting climax to the book. As an acrostic, each verse of the hymn of praise begins with the succeeding letter of the Hebrew alphabet. The twenty-two verses of the poem correspond to the twenty-two letters of the alphabet. The acrostic may convey a message of completeness, that is, this is what wisdom looks like from A to Z.

The hymn is grounded in realistic components of Israelite life.[16] Women in Israel made a vital contribution to the health and well-being of the community. Many contributed to the economic security of their households. And yes, a young man should seek out and marry this kind of woman. But is the primary function of this poem to advise young men to find the ideal wife? Very little information that is found in chapters 10–29 prepares the reader for the arrival of this kind of advice at the end, if all that the poem is concerned about is finding a hardworking wife.

In this poem, the husband remains in the background (vv. 11-12, 23,28-29). He is portrayed as doing nothing more than sitting in the city gate praising his wife. The woman comes across as superhuman (can any one woman achieve all of this?) while the man remains

---

[16]See Ellen Louise Lyons, "A Note on Proverbs 31:10-31," in *The Listening Heart: Essays in Wisdom and the Psalms in Honor of Roland E. Murphy*, ed. by Kenneth G. Hoglund et al. (Sheffield: JSOT Press, 1987), pp. 237-245.

quite passive. So does the woman exist only to serve the husband? Is the poem advocating that young men find industrious, hardworking wives so they can simply lounge around in the Town Square? Something more is at stake.

Chapter 31:10-31 complements the Woman Wisdom described in chapters 1-9. Placed at the beginning and the end of Proverbs, chapters 1-9 and chapter 31 serve as the interpretive framework for understanding the sentence literature of chapters 10-29.[17] In fact, the poem in 31:10-31 echoes a number of the same images of chapters 1-9.[18] That the woman is worth far more than rubies echoes an earlier description of personified Wisdom (3:15). The woman provides food, like Wisdom does (9:1-6). She speaks wisdom and offers instruction as does Wisdom in 4:5-6. The woman described here is most likely Wisdom incarnated. This passage does not depict an "all in a day's work" scene, rather this is the culmination of a life lived in the pursuit of wisdom.

The interpretive "bookends" of chapters 1-9 and 31 place the sentence literature in a narrative context. At the beginning of Proverbs (chapters 1-9), Woman Wisdom invites youth to her banquet. Those who accept her invitation and sit at her table are served a feast of insight and understanding. The substance of this feast comes in the content and form of the pithy proverbs found in chapters 10-29. After a lifetime of feasting at wisdom's table, chapter 31:10-31 describes what mature wisdom looks like. The home that wisdom builds displays love and service for others. It is a home that expresses compassion, that possesses emotional and financial security, and that receives honor and praise among the community. Placed at the end of the book, the "woman of noble character" represents the culmination of a life lived by wisdom. She is wisdom incarnate. The house she builds is the goal toward which all strive (cf. 9:1; 14:1; 24:3-4).[19]

---

[17]This is the perspective of Claudia Camp in her work, *Wisdom and the Feminine in the Book of Proverbs*.

[18]Camp identifies the parallels between the two units, (ibid., pp. 179ff). Specifically, on pages 188-189 she lists the similar language and metaphors used.

[19]For a strong case in favor of interpreting the woman of noble character symbolically see Thomas P. McCreesh, "Wisdom as Wife: Proverbs 31:10-31," *Revue Biblique* 92 (1985): 25-46.

^{10ᵃ}A wife of noble character who can find?
    She is worth far more than rubies.
¹¹Her husband has full confidence in her
    and lacks nothing of value.
¹²She brings him good, not harm,
    all the days of her life.
¹³She selects wool and flax
    and works with eager hands.
¹⁴She is like the merchant ships,
    bringing her food from afar.
¹⁵She gets up while it is still dark;
    she provides food for her family
    and portions for her servant girls.
¹⁶She considers a field and buys it;
    out of her earnings she plants a vineyard.
¹⁷She sets about her work vigorously;
    her arms are strong for her tasks.
¹⁸She sees that her trading is profitable,
    and her lamp does not go out at night.
¹⁹In her hand she holds the distaff
    and grasps the spindle with her fingers.
²⁰She opens her arms to the poor
    and extends her hands to the needy.
²¹When it snows, she has no fear for her household;
    for all of them are clothed in scarlet.
²²She makes coverings for her bed;
    she is clothed in fine linen and purple.
²³Her husband is respected at the city gate,
    where he takes his seat among the elders of the land.
²⁴She makes linen garments and sells them,
    and supplies the merchants with sashes.
²⁵She is clothed with strength and dignity;
    she can laugh at the days to come.
²⁶She speaks with wisdom,
    and faithful instruction is on her tongue.
²⁷She watches over the affairs of her household
    and does not eat the bread of idleness.
²⁸Her children arise and call her blessed;
    her husband also, and he praises her:

²⁹"Many women do noble things,
   but you surpass them all."
³⁰Charm is deceptive, and beauty is fleeting;
   but a woman who fears the LORD is to be praised.
³¹Give her the reward she has earned,
   and let her works bring her praise at the city gate.

ᵃ*10* Verses 10-31 are an acrostic, each verse beginning with a successive letter of the Hebrew alphabet.

31:10-20 In verse 10 the NIV translates the Hebrew phrase אֵשֶׁת־חַיִל (*'ēšeth-ḥayil*) **a wife of noble character**. Literally, the phrase means "woman of strength" or "woman of worth." The term may involve economic connotations. Elsewhere, the phrase refers to one's character (12:4; Ruth 3:11; 1 Kgs 1:42,52). The NIV captures the essence of the phrase. A woman of such noble character, like wisdom itself (1:28; 8:35; Job 28:12-13), is hard to find (so is a faithful man; see 20:6). A good wife and wisdom are both a gift from the Lord (19:14; Job 28:20-27).

Only a casual mention is made in verses 11 and 12 and at the end of the poem (vv. 23,28-29) of the **husband**. Beginning with verse 12, the description of the woman's work focuses primarily on her economic activity. The **good** that she **brings** her husband is primarily economic good. She acquires and provides for her household. The routine activity she faithfully carries out ultimately expresses her reverence to God (v. 30). The woman engages in all kinds of trade and commerce. She **selects wool and flax** (v. 13). She acts **like the merchant ships, bringing her food from afar** (v. 14). **She considers a field and buys it** (v. 16). **She sees that her trading is profitable** (v. 18). The woman demonstrates a high degree of initiative and industry.

Verses 19 and 20 display a striking chiasmus. Four times the Hebrew text uses the word "hand."[20] For the sake of variety, the NIV alternates the words by translating them **hands**, **fingers**, and **arms**. Roland Murphy translates the two verses in the following way:

> She puts her hand to the distaff;
>   her palms grasp the spindle.
> Her palms she extends to the poor;
>   her hands she reaches to the needy.

---

[20]Twice it uses the word יָד (*yod*) and twice the word כַּף (*kaph*).

The woman works with her hands to provide for her household. She also opens her hands to provide for the needs of the poor. The phrase **opens her arms** ("hands") **to the poor** reflects the language of Deuteronomy 15.

31:21-31 Some ancient versions emend 21b to read "all have double coverings" in order to fit more with the first line which describes cold weather. In other words, the woman puts a double layer of clothing on her family as they leave the house. The argument for emendation was that **scarlet** could not protect one from the cold and the snow during winter. In actuality, scarlet probably refers to clothing of the highest quality that protects one from the harsh elements.[21]

Verse 26 describes her use of language, something that characterizes wisdom. **She speaks with wisdom, and faithful instruction is on her tongue.** "Faithful instruction" literally is "*torah* of kindness." *Torah*, here as elsewhere in Proverbs, refers to instruction the wise gives. Does this mean that the woman instructs in kindness (חֶסֶד, *ḥesed*), or that she gives instruction about kindness? Or does the term "kindness," as the NIV translates it here, refer more to the quality of faithfulness? No definitive answer can be given. However, the NIV offers a viable option.

The word translated **watches over** in verse 27 is the Hebrew word צוֹפִיָּה (*ṣôphîyāh*, a transliteration of the Greek word for wisdom, *sophia*). This subtle poetic touch may be an indirect way the author uses to associate this woman of character with Woman Wisdom.

The poem ends in verses 28-31 on a note of praise. The **children** and her **husband** praise her. The whole community knows about this wife of noble character and joins in honoring her. The author of the poem offers a final perspective: **Charm is deceptive, and beauty is fleeting; but a woman who fears the LORD is to be praised** (v. 30). The wisdom teachers were not opposed to charm and beauty, but in perspective they held limited value. Charm can easily mislead. Beauty is fleeting (הֶבֶל, *hebel*), the favorite word in Ecclesiastes, sometimes translated "vain." Here the NIV appropriately translates it "fleeting." Beauty is like a vapor; it does not last very long. Only those qualities that endure should receive praise. What endures is a

[21]McKane, *Proverbs,* pp. 668-669.

woman who fears the LORD. The description echoes the fundamental quality of wisdom itself, which was first mentioned in 1:7: "The
fear of the LORD is the beginning of wisdom." The ending of the
book thus forms an inclusion with the beginning.

The hymn in verses 10-31 praising the wife of noble character
ultimately serves as a praise of wisdom itself.[22] Those who construct
their lives by the principles of wisdom manifest the kind of home
built by the wife of noble character. The poem pictures the culmination of a life lived by wisdom.

---

[22]Naphtali Gutstein offers a paraphrastic translation of this text in which
he interprets it not as a description of an Israelite woman but of "Wisdom
incarnate." See Gutstein, "Proverbs 31:10-31: The Woman of Valor as
Allegory," *The Jewish Bible Quarterly* 27 (1999): 36-39.

ECCLESIASTES

INTRODUCTION

When one enters into wisdom's world, one embarks on a journey. In the book of Proverbs, this journey leads a person to seek out the order by which creation and society live. In the book of Job, wisdom's journey leads one on a quest for the presence of God. In Ecclesiastes, the journey leads to the search for meaning in life. Underlying all of these quests is the desire to manage the complexities of life and the "messes" that one encounters along the way. If individuals can find order or God or meaning in life, then they can navigate life's rocky shoreline.

As readers enter into the journey in the book of Ecclesiastes, they are introduced to a face of wisdom that they have not seen before, especially if they are just leaving the world described in the book of Proverbs. The book of Ecclesiastes engages the reader in a quest for the meaning of life. As the writer (referred to as "the Teacher" or Qoheleth; see below) faces the reality of the fragile nature of life and the decaying body (12:1-7), he asks the question, Does life make any sense? He observes contradictions (3:16; 10:7) and injustices (4:1; 8:9) in the world. He decides that what is crooked cannot be straightened (1:15; 7:13).

Because of its eccentric nature, some have referred to Ecclesiastes as the "resident alien" of Scripture.[1] Qoheleth (pronounced ko-*hell*-it) questions the traditional instruction of the sages. He questions conventional wisdom that says that the righteous will live well and securely through all of life and the unrighteous will receive their just deserts. However, he is not, as it is sometimes thought, revolting against the book of Proverbs per se. Though Proverbs does contain a healthy dose of traditional wisdom instruction (see Proverbs chapters 10–15),

---

[1]Duane Garrett, *Proverbs, Ecclesiastes, Song of Songs*, The New American Commentary, vol. 14 (Nashville: Broadman Press, 1993), p. 254.

it also acknowledges the complexities of life and the limits of wisdom (see Proverbs chapters 16–22). Rather, Qoheleth questions traditional wisdom that oversimplifies or ignores the realities of life, which was a part of the oral culture of the day.

All the while Qoheleth challenges traditional wisdom's teaching, he uses wisdom's method to do so. That is, as Qoheleth tests wisdom he uses wisdom's tools, which include observation, reflection, experience, and proverbial lore. Wisdom is both a method[2] and a body of instruction.[3] As Qoheleth embarks on a journey to understand the meaning of life in the face of its uncertainties, he relies on the resources of wisdom to guide him along the way.

NAME

The Hebrew name of the book is Qoheleth, which occurs seven times in the text (1:1; 1:2; 1:12; 7:27; 12:8; 12:9; 12:10). Grammatically, Qoheleth is a feminine participle from the verb קָהַל (qāhal), "to assemble." From this name derives the Greek title with which English readers are most familiar, "Ecclesiastes" (i.e., "Assembly"). In its broadest sense, Qoheleth has something to do with "assembly" or "congregation." It is not a proper name, but a job description. The traditional understanding has been that Qoheleth was one who spoke to an assembly, thus Qoheleth is often translated as "the Preacher" (see KJV, RSV, NASB). Nowhere in the book, however, does Qoheleth preach or deliver a sermon. Others argue that, as a sage, Qoheleth was one who assembled students for study. Or in keeping with the description of the editor in 12:9-10, Qoheleth was one who assembled proverbs and wisdom material. Because it appears that Qoheleth assembles wisdom material in order to teach young adults about the meaning of life (11:9–12:1), a better translation of the participle is "Teacher," which is how the NIV consistently renders it.

---

[2]Qoheleth inquired about life through the use of wisdom. That is, he "guided" and "tested" by wisdom (2:3; 7:23).

[3]See 1:16; 8:16.

AUTHORSHIP

Solomon is traditionally understood to be the author of Ecclesiastes. Several reasons appear to lead to this conclusion. First, the author is described as the "son of David." Second, the author is also described as being "king over Jerusalem." Third, chapters 1 and 2 describe the life of a king and the experiments he undertook to attempt to find meaning. Only a wealthy king could embark on the experiences described in these two chapters. The composite of all of these seems to point to Solomon as author.[4]

Many scholars question this conclusion and argue for a later date for the book. After chapter 2, the image of kingship virtually disappears from the book, and the writer appears to look upon the monarchy with critical eyes (3:16; 4:1-3,13-16; 5:8-9). The king was responsible for executing righteousness and justice. He was the one who could take action to alleviate wrongs. Qoheleth, however, cannot do anything about the injustices he witnesses. He can only mourn that the oppressed have no comforter (4:1-3).[5] In later sections of the book, the perspective appears to be that of an outsider giving advice about how to relate to a king rather than from one who actually is a king giving advice on the monarchy (8:2-4; 10:4-7,16-17,20).

Those who hold to non-Solomonic authorship argue that the author makes no attempt to deceive the reader into believing he is the historical Solomon. Rather, for the sake of developing his message, he identifies himself as being *like* Solomon. That is, taking on the persona of Solomon, he bases his life on the life of the king; he writes this royal testament *as though* he were Solomon. This enables

---

[4]There are, however, a couple of unusual characteristics regarding the description of the author. In several places the author exclaims that he increased in wisdom "more than anyone who has ruled over Jerusalem before me" (1:16; 2:7,9). The phrase indicates that a number of kings ruled over Jerusalem before this king came to the throne. In the case of Solomon, only one Israelite king reigned in Jerusalem before him, and that was David.

In 1:12 the author comments, "I, the Teacher, *was* king over Israel in Jerusalem." Even though not a strong argument, the perfect tense (indicating completed action) is used, indicating that the one writing no longer reigned as king. But Solomon remained king until his death.

[5]Solomon, in fact, contributed to injustices (see 1 Kings 11).

him in the first two chapters to engage in an extravagant mental experiment on the meaning of life.[6]

Clearly, an editor plays a role in the process of compiling the work. This is seen at the beginning with the editorial comment, "The words of the Teacher, son of David, king in Jerusalem" (1:1). Once again, the editor's voice is heard in 7:27, "'Look,' says the Teacher, 'this is what I have discovered.'" His voice is heard one final time at the conclusion, "Not only was the Teacher wise, but also he imparted knowledge to the people. He pondered and searched out and set in order many proverbs. The Teacher searched to find just the right words, and what he wrote was upright and true" (12:9-10). Through the work of this editor, God communicates his message to those who fear God and seek to be faithful to him.

PESSIMISTIC OR OPTIMISTIC MESSAGE

The message of Ecclesiastes is closely related to how one interprets the frequently used word *hebel*. It is also related to how one understands the passages in the book that affirm enjoyment of life. I would like to explore these two dimensions as a way of introducing the reader to the message of Ecclesiastes.

The key word most frequently used is הֶבֶל (*hebel*, lit., "breath" or "vapor"). Ecclesiastes uses the word thirty-eight times, more than the rest of the Old Testament put together. Usually it appears as the summary statement of a section of material. It appears as a superlative that brackets the book at the beginning (1:2) and end (12:8): "'Meaningless! Meaningless!' says the Teacher. 'Utterly meaningless! Everything is meaningless'" (NIV translation). Therefore *hebel* becomes a very important word for the writer.

What remains troublesome is that no consensus exists on the word's meaning. Many translations render it "vanity" (KJV, RSV,

---

[6]Some scholars argue that the language of the book also gives an indication that the time period is not during the United Monarchy. A number of Aramaisms appear in the text, possibly indicating a postexilic rather than a preexilic period. For a brief treatment of this see Michael V. Fox, *Qohelet and His Contradictions* (Sheffield: Almond, 1989), pp. 154-155. However, the history of the development of the Hebrew language is uncertain. One cannot use it to determine the book's date. See Tremper Longman, *The Book of Ecclesiastes*, NICOT (Grand Rapids: Eerdmans, 1998), p. 15.

NRSV, JB). The New English Bible translates it with the word "emptiness." The Good News Bible prefers "useless." Michael Fox argues for
"absurd" or "senseless" as an appropriate translation.[7] Without exception, the NIV always translates *hebel* as "meaningless."[8]

To translate the word "meaningless," however, is problematic since
Qoheleth does not understand everything in the world to be meaningless. He frequently commends certain ways of living to the reader
(e.g., 2:24-26; 9:7-10). In actuality, the word carries nuances of different meanings in different contexts of Ecclesiastes. The basic meaning
of *hebel* is "vapor," or "breath" or "mist." The name Abel in Genesis 4
derives from the word. Abel himself, whose life signifies brevity, represents the fundamental meaning of the word. Other texts of Scripture
use *hebel* to describe that which is ephemeral or short lived:

> Man is like a breath [*hebel*];
> > his days are like a fleeting shadow (Ps 144:4).

> Charm is deceptive, and beauty is fleeting [*hebel*]
> > but a woman who fears the LORD is to be praised
> > (Prov 31:30).

> A fortune made by a lying tongue
> > is a fleeting vapor [*hebel*] and a deadly snare
> > (Prov 21:6).

In Ecclesiastes, the frequent association of *hebel* with the phrase
"chasing after the wind" (רוּחַ, *rûaḥ*) indicates a connection with
"breath." C.L. Seow suggests that one should not dismiss too quickly the literal meaning of the word "breath" or "vapor."[9] Sometimes
in the book the word carries the meaning of "vapor" as it refers to
the brevity of life. For example, in 6:12 *hebel* is associated with the
words "few" and "shadow." In 11:10, the writer concludes, "So then,

---

[7]Michael V. Fox, *A Time To Tear Down & A Time To Build Up: A Rereading
of Ecclesiastes* (Grand Rapids: Eerdmans, 1999), p. 31.

[8]This is the preferred meaning that Longman assigns to the word in the
prologue and epilogue. He argues that outside Ecclesiastes in the Old
Testament *hebel* is frequently used to characterize idol worship (Deut 32:21;
2 Kgs 17:15; Ps 31:6; Jer 2:5; 8:19; Jonah 2:8; Zech 10:2). The passages attribute *meaninglessness* and not *brevity* to idols (63).

[9]C.L. Seow, *Ecclesiastes*, The Anchor Bible (New York: Doubleday, 1997),
p. 47.

banish anxiety from your heart and cast off the troubles of your body, for youth and vigor are meaningless" (NIV). Qoheleth does not believe that the time of youth is a time when life is "meaningless" (cf. also 9:9). In the very next verse (12:1), he admonishes youth to remember their Creator, "before the days of trouble come." Youth is a time when life offers the most promise, but the time of youth is brief. Therefore, it is better to translate the word in 11:10 as "brief" or "transient" rather than "meaningless" (cf. also 7:15 and 9:9). Following the poem in 12:1-7 that describes aging and the transitory nature of life, the writer concludes with his signature epigram, "Meaningless, meaningless . . . Everything is meaningless" (v. 8). In its context here, *hebel* seems to refer to the fleeting nature of life.

At other times *hebel* carries a different nuance. Not infrequently it refers to that which is incomprehensible to the human mind or that which is beyond human control.[10] For example, in 8:14 the writer describes with perplexity the experience of the righteous being punished and the wicked receiving rewards. It is better to translate *hebel* in this context not as "meaningless" but as that which humans cannot fully comprehend.[11] The writer observes the experience of a person receiving wealth from God but then not being able to enjoy it. He pronounces that as a *hebel* experience, an experience that does not make sense. In a later article, Seow concludes that *hebel* most often means "everything is beyond mortal grasp."[12] This is the conclusion the writer reaches in the "catalog of occasions" in 3:1-8. That is, humans cannot fathom what God does from beginning to end (3:11).

The writer often speaks of the limitations of human understanding. The phrases "who knows," "do not know," and "cannot find out" are repeated in chapters 7 through 11. Such undercurrent supports the idea that on numerous occasions *hebel* refers to that which is enigmatic, unknowable. In addition, the phrase frequently connected with *hebel*, "chasing after the wind," not only implies transience but also

---

[10]Ibid., p. 59.

[11]An event may have meaning without that meaning being comprehended by those experiencing it. I may not understand the game of rugby, but that does not mean that the game has no meaning. Humans may not understand why many things happen in life but that does not mean that those experiences have no meaning.

[12]Choon-Leong Seow, "Beyond Mortal Grasp: The Usage of Hebel in Ecclesiastes," *ABR* 48 (2000): 1-16.

this elusive dimension (1:14,17; 2:11,17,26; 4:4,6,16; 6:9). The writer concludes that humans must learn to accept their limited understanding of life, so much remains beyond human understanding.

All through the book, the NIV consistently translates *hebel* as "meaningless." While there may be times when Qoheleth pronounces certain experiences as void of meaning, that does not appear to be the dominant sense of the word. The more prevalent sense involves two ideas: 1) that which is fleeting or transitory, and 2) that which is hard to comprehend or enigmatic. Eugene Peterson captures the essence of these two ideas in the image he consistently uses to translate *hebel*, "smoke."[13]

However one translates *hebel*, the word evokes a realistic view of life. Life is but a brief, fleeting moment; humans cannot fully grasp it. Only emphasizing the word *hebel*, however, could leave the reader with a skeptical outlook on life. So is that Qoheleth's perspective? Many scholars would say, "Yes." Representative of this group is James Crenshaw, who reaches the following conclusion about the book: "No discernible principle of order governs the universe, rewarding virtue and punishing evil. . . . In short, Qoheleth examined all of life and discovered no absolute good that would survive death's effect. . . . Qoheleth bears witness to an intellectual crisis in ancient Israel."[14] Crenshaw views Qoheleth's message as thoroughly pessimistic. Longman also views Qoheleth's message as cynical.[15] Longman, however, distinguishes between the message of Qoheleth and the message of the editor of the book who frames Qoheleth's thought in 1:1-11 and 12:8-15.[16] In the end, the editor basically refutes the message of Qoheleth (given in 1:12–12:7) in 12:8-15. Qoheleth himself, though, is basically a "confused wise man."[17]

Other scholars, however, emphasize a different perspective of Ecclesiastes. Sprinkled throughout the book are exhortations to enjoy life. R.N. Whybray refers to these as the "joy passages,"[18] which

---

[13]Eugene H. Peterson, *The Message: The Old Testament Wisdom Books* (Colorado Springs: Navpress, 1996).

[14]James L. Crenshaw, "Ecclesiastes, book of," in *Anchor Bible Dictionary*, vol. II, ed. by David N. Freedman (New York: Doubleday, 1992), p. 277.

[15]Longman, *Ecclesiastes*, p. 36.

[16]Ibid., pp. 36-37.

[17]Ibid., p. 207 (see also pp. 184, 188, 231).

[18]R.N. Whybray, "Qoheleth, Preacher of Joy," *JSOT* 23 (1982): 87-98.

include 2:24-26; 3:12-13; 3:22; 5:18-20; 8:15; 9:7-10; 11:7-10. They typically contain an admonition to enjoy life, to eat and drink, and to find satisfaction in one's work (e.g., 2:24). They understand the enjoyment of life as a gift from God (2:24-26; 3:12; 5:19; 9:7; 11:9).

Usually the joy passages abut a declaration that life is *hebel*. So do the joy passages cancel out the *hebel* texts? Some, like Whybray, appear to emphasize these texts to the neglect of the *hebel* passages and thus conclude that Qoheleth is ultimately a "preacher of joy." Ecclesiastes contains an optimistic message.

A key to understanding the message of Ecclesiastes lies in considering the relationship between these two components. The history of the interpretation of Ecclesiastes demonstrates the tendency to come down either on the side of the *hebel* conclusion or on the side of the joy passages, one eclipsing the other.[19] Thus the reader comes away deciding that Ecclesiastes is either pessimistic or optimistic in outlook.

These two poles, however, do not cancel out each other. There are times when God tears down, and there are times when he builds up (3:3b). The poles remain in tension with one another all through the course of the book. Qoheleth clings tenaciously to both. Life is *hebel*. But in the midst of *hebel*, God gives enjoyment. In the face of the uncertainties of life, contentment is possible.

In addition to the joy passages, elsewhere in Ecclesiastes Qoheleth also acknowledges the good in life. In many of the better-than proverbs, Qoheleth observes at least some provisional good (4:6; 7:1-2; 9:17-18). He sees good in companionship (4:9-12). He also praises the goodness of the day (11:7). As Seow concludes, enjoyment is realizing life in its fullest sense.[20] It is approaching life not fatalistically, but realistically. It is to recognize human limitations and to learn contentment with what comes one's way, leaving the rest to the sovereign LORD.[21]

---

[19]Craig Bartholomew, "Qoheleth in the Canon?! Current Trends in the Interpretation of Ecclesiastes," *Themelios* (May, 1999): 4-20.

[20]Choon-Leong Seow, "Theology When Everything Is Out of Control," *Interpretation* 55, no. 3 (2001): 246.

[21]Longman argues that the "joy" passages do not present a positive view of life but simply concede that people have nothing better to do than eat and drink and toil. That is, these passages express *resignation* and not *affirmation* toward life (*Ecclesiastes*, p. 34). Roland Murphy holds to the same

QOHELETH'S VIEW OF GOD

What does this book have to say about God and who he is? Strikingly Qoheleth never uses the name Yahweh. He uses the more generic term *Elohim* (which is also true of most of the book of Job).

Qoheleth describes an active God. He is active in creation, in heaven, and in the cosmos. And even though God is active on earth, Qoheleth does not portray his activity in a personal sense (7:13-14). Qoheleth says very little about God's imminence. Qoheleth describes a transcendent God who is inscrutable, sovereign. Ecclesiastes stresses the distance between humans and the divine. God is in heaven. Humans are on earth (5:2). God does not seem to spend much time in intimate interaction with mortals.

This inscrutable God determines the future; he alone controls the direction of history. Humans have limited control over the course that events take. They cannot change the future. However, as William Brown puts it, the world is "not so much a theatre of the absurd as the arena of God's mystery."[22] A transcendent God controls everything, determines the future, and remains a mystery to finite beings.

Thus humans remain ignorant about much of life. We cannot understand the course of events in the world. Nonetheless, and even in the face of divine sovereignty, humans still exercise freedom and responsibility. Divine sovereignty and human freedom stand in tension in Ecclesiastes (as they do in Proverbs; see 16:1-9). Moreover, within its pages, Scripture holds tenaciously to both affirmations. The fact that God will judge humans for how they live (11:9; 12:14) testifies to their freedom and responsibility.

In the presence of an inscrutable God, Qoheleth admonishes his readers to fear him. Qoheleth does not use the noun form "the fear of the LORD" but only the verbal form, "fear God" (3:14; 5:7; 7:18; 8:12; 8:13; 12:13). The one who fears God is the one who accepts

---

view. See Murphy, *Ecclesiastes*, Word Biblical Commentary (Dallas: Word, 1992), p. 27. If, however, Qoheleth takes a resigned, defeatist attitude, then why does he advise individuals to work with all their might (9:10) and to take aggressive action in the face of uncertainty (11:1-6)?

[22]William Brown, *Ecclesiastes*, Interpretation (Louisville: John Knox Press, 2000), p. 15.

God's transcendent power and at the same time acknowledges his or her own limitations as a mortal human being (3:14). To fear God means that humans do not approach God in a casual way. He is in heaven, and we are on earth (5:2). Therefore we "stand in awe of" (fear) him (5:7). Humans live their lives acknowledging the mysteries of God and accepting their limitations.

The admonition that introduces the final poem on aging and death (12:1-7) is particularly relevant at this point: "Remember your Creator in the days of your youth" (12:1). This admonition is followed by the threefold repetition of "before . . . " (12:1,2,6). As the poem is read, the repetition serves as a reminder to the reader of the initial exhortation to "remember your Creator." The exhortation stands analogous to the command to "fear God."[23] It calls on the reader to keep a particular perspective on life in the face of death. This perspective does not eliminate the struggles, frustrations, and uncertainties of life. It does, as Craig Bartholomew affirms, "provide one with a place to stand amidst the struggle so that the 'light is sweet, and it is pleasant for the eyes to see the sun (11:7).'"[24] When readers understand the call to remember their Creator, the final imperative in the book is not an afterthought tacked on, but quite in line with the message of Qoheleth, "Fear God, and keep his commandments, for this is the whole duty of man."

Mortals stand with fear in the presence of an inscrutable God who determines the course of events. Once again, however, that does not take away from human freedom. In light of the incomprehensible nature of the world, humans have the responsibility to enjoy life when those opportunities come their way (see above on "Pessimistic or Optimistic Message"). Enjoyment, though, is not something that humans seek. Enjoyment comes as a gift from God. So in the face of accepting God's control, humans also accept the opportunities that God gives to enjoy life.

In chapters 5:8–6:9, Qoheleth observes life. All he sees is oppression, greed, discontentment, futility, frustration, affliction, and anger. Nonetheless, this whole unit appears to gravitate around the joy passage in 5:18-20, where Qoheleth concludes, "When God gives any man wealth and possessions, and enables him to enjoy them, to

---

[23]Bartholomew, *Ecclesiastes*, p. 16.
[24]Ibid.

accept his lot and be happy in his work—this is a gift of God" (v. 19). The result is that the individual no longer reflects on the grievous evil that lies all around but on the good that "God keeps him occupied with" (v. 20). Even though Qoheleth emphasizes over and over the futility of human effort and ignorance, ultimately Qoheleth is not pessimistic. What Qoheleth calls for is a change in attitude on life. He calls on the reader to look at wealth and possessions and wisdom differently. Seow says, "Enjoyment is possible only when people accept that God has made the world just so and that mortals have been given a *heleq*, that is, a portion.[25] Mortals have the responsibility to enjoy the life that God gives to them. Those who do not enjoy this gift, God holds accountable (11:9).

STRUCTURE

The book lacks a clearly defined structure as evidenced by the number of different proposals suggested in the commentaries. Its literary structure, however, is not completely void and without form. The book's beginning and ending provide a fairly tight symmetrical framework in which to explore various themes. The superlative "meaningless, meaningless, utterly meaningless" brackets the work. The refrain is first stated in 1:2 and then repeated at the conclusion in 12:8. Ecclesiastes begins with an introductory poem on the weary cycle of creation, which results in despair (1:4-11). It concludes with a poem on the demise of the human body, which also leads to despair (12:1-7). In between these two poetic bookmarks, the author experiments with different lifestyles and explores a variety of life-related issues. The book appears as a kind of journal of reflections on life's experiences which the writer jots down as they come to mind. No sequential story line is tightly developed.

Seow proposes a two-part structure to the book (1:2–6:9 and 6:10–12:8). Each part consists of two major blocks of material. The first block reflects on the human condition. The second block offers practical advice for dealing with that situation.

> 1:2–4:16 — Reflection: Everything Is Ephemeral and Unreliable
> 5:1–6:9 — Ethics: Coping with Uncertainty

---

[25]Seow, *Ecclesiastes,* p. 58.

6:10–8:17 — Reflection: Everything Is Elusive
9:1–12:8 — Ethics: Coping with Risks and Death[26]

Overall, as Brown has observed, the book moves from self-reflective language (1:16; 2:1,15; 3:17-18) to more directive language (11:9).[27] Couple this with the fact that the last half of the book contains a greater density of proverbs than the first, and the indications are that the writer moves into a pedagogical mode near the end.[28] I offer the following outline as a way of organizing the book. It is the outline that organizes this commentary.

---

[26]Ibid., pp. 46-47.
[27]Brown, *Ecclesiastes,* p. 15.
[28]Ibid., p. 16.

OUTLINE

BIBLIOGRAPHY

Bartholomew, Craig G. "Qoheleth in the Canon?! Current Trends in the Interpretation of Ecclesiastes." *Themelios* 24, no. 3 (1999): 4-20.

_____. *Reading Ecclesiastes: Old Testament Exegesis and Hermeneutical Theory*. Analecta Biblica, 1.39. Rome: Editrice Pontificio Istituto Biblico, 1998.

Brown, William P. *Ecclesiastes*. Interpretation. Louisville: John Knox Press, 2000.

Clifford, Richard. *The Wisdom Literature*. Interpreting Biblical Texts. Nashville: Abingdon, 1998.

Crenshaw, James. *Ecclesiastes*. Old Testament Library. Philadelphia: Westminster Press, 1987.

_____. "Ecclesiastes, book of." In *Anchor Bible Dictionary*, vol. II. Ed. by David N. Freedman. New York: Doubleday, 1992.

_____. "Qoheleth in Current Research." *Hebrew Annual Review* 7 (1983):41-56.

_____. "The Shadow of Death in Qoheleth." In *Israelite Wisdom: Theological and Literary Essays in Honor of Samuel Terrien*. Ed. by John G. Gammie. New York: Scholars Press, 1978.

Farmer, Kathleen A. *Proverbs & Ecclesiastes: Who Knows What Is Good?* International Theological Commentary. Grand Rapids: Eerdmans, 1991.

Fox, Michael V. "Aging and Death." *Journal for the Study of the Old Testament* 42 (1988): 55-77.

_____. *Qohelet and His Contradictions*. Sheffield: Almond, 1989.

_____. *A Time to Tear Down & a Time to Build Up: A Rereading of Ecclesiastes*. Grand Rapids: Eerdmans, 1999.

Garrett, Duane. *Proverbs, Ecclesiastes, Song of Songs.* The New American Commentary, vol. 14. Nashville: Broadman Press, 1993.

Longman, Tremper. *The Book of Ecclesiastes.* New International Commentary on the Old Testament. Grand Rapids: Eerdmans, 1998.

Murphy, Roland E. *Ecclesiastes.* Word Biblical Commentary. Dallas: Word, 1992.

Ogden, Graham S. "The 'Better'-Proverb (Tob-Spruch), Rhetorical Criticism, and Qoheleth." *Journal of Biblical Literature* 96, no. 4 (1977): 489-505.

——————. *Qoheleth.* Sheffield: Sheffield Academic Press, 1987.

——————. "Qoheleth's Use of the 'Nothing Is Better'-Form." *Journal of Biblical Literature* 98, no. 3 (1979): 339-350.

Peterson, Eugene H. *The Message: The Old Testament Wisdom Books.* Colorado Springs: Navpress, 1996.

Provan, Iain. *Ecclesiastes, Song of Songs.* The NIV Application Commentary. Grand Rapids: Zondervan, 2001.

Rudman, Dominic. *Determinism in the Book of Ecclesiastes.* Sheffield: Sheffield Academic Press, 2001.

Salyer, Gary D. *Vain Rhetoric: Private Insight and Public Debate in Ecclesiastes.* Sheffield: Sheffield Academic Press, 2001.

Seow, Choon-Leong. "Beyond Mortal Grasp: The Usage of *Hebel* in Ecclesiastes." *Australian Biblical Review* 48 (2000): 1-16.

——————. *Ecclesiastes.* Anchor Bible Series. New York: Doubleday, 1997.

——————. "Theology When Everything Is Out of Control." *Interpretation* 55, no. 3 (2001): 237-249.

Sneed, Mark. "The Social Location of the Book of Qoheleth." *Hebrew Studies* 55, no. 3 (2001): 41-51.

Taylor, J. Patton. "A Time to Dance: Reflections on the Book of Ecclesiastes." *Irish Biblical Studies* 18 (1996): 114-135.

Towner, W. Sibley. "The Book of Ecclesiastes: Introduction, Commentary, and Reflections." *The New Interpreter's Bible*, Vol. 5. Nashville: Abingdon, 1997.

Whybray, R.N. *Ecclesiastes.* New Century Bible. Grand Rapids: Eerdmans, 1989.

_____ . "Qoheleth, Preacher of Joy." *Journal for the Study of the Old Testament* 23 (1982): 87-98.

Wright, A.G. "The Riddle of the Sphinx: The Structure of the Book of Qoheleth." *Catholic Biblical Quarterly* 30 (1968): 313-334.

ECCLESIASTES 1:1–6:9

I. HEADING AND MOTTO (1:1-2)

¹**The words of the Teacher,ᵃ son of David, king in Jerusalem:**

ᵃ*1* Or *leader of the assembly*; also in verses 2 and 12

1:1 The term **the Teacher** (Qoheleth; pronounced ko-*hell*-it) occurs seven times in Ecclesiastes: three times in the beginning (1:1,2,12); three times at the conclusion (12:8,9,10); and once in the middle (7:27). Qoheleth is the one who "set in order many proverbs" (12:9) and adds "one thing to another to discover the scheme of things" (7:27). Thus he appears to be a person who collects wisdom material. He is **son of David, king in Jerusalem** (see Authorship in Introduction).

²**"Meaningless! Meaningless!"**
    says the Teacher.
  "Utterly meaningless!
    Everything is meaningless."

1:2 The word the NIV translates **meaningless** is the Hebrew term הֶבֶל (*hebel*). The NIV consistently translates it as "meaningless." *Hebel* contains a variety of meanings (see Introduction), yet no corresponding English word covers its range of meaning. The range of possibilities in Ecclesiastes includes "brief," "incomprehensible," "worthless," and "absurd." The context helps to determine the particular nuance. The two most common meanings ascribed to it by the writer have to do with the brevity of life and the inability of humans to comprehend all of life's experiences.

As the book begins, Qoheleth uses the word as a superlative: **Meaningless! Meaningless!** It carries the same sense as the phrase "king of kings" (Ezek 26:7) or Song of Songs. Verse 2 summarizes the book and is once again stated at the conclusion (12:8). As a summary, it makes a generalization about life: **Everything is meaningless**. Ecclesiastes uses *hebel* to describe human experiences in general. The generalization, however, is not intended to include every act, every experience, or every occasion in a person's life. In addition, Qoheleth never assigns the *hebel* quality to God's activity (though 6:1-2 might imply this).

II. INTRODUCTORY POEM (1:3-11)

[3]What does man gain from all his labor
      at which he toils under the sun?
[4]Generations come and generations go,
      but the earth remains forever.
[5]The sun rises and the sun sets,
      and hurries back to where it rises.
[6]The wind blows to the south
      and turns to the north;
 round and round it goes,
      ever returning on its course.
[7]All streams flow into the sea,
      yet the sea is never full.
 To the place the streams come from,
      there they return again.
[8]All things are wearisome,
      more than one can say.
 The eye never has enough of seeing,
      nor the ear its fill of hearing.
[9]What has been will be again,
      what has been done will be done again;
      there is nothing new under the sun.
[10]Is there anything of which one can say,
      "Look! This is something new"?
 It was here already, long ago;
      it was here before our time.
[11]There is no remembrance of men of old,
      and even those who are yet to come
 will not be remembered
      by those who follow.

1:3 The verse states the question Qoheleth explores all through the book. Is there any **gain** that mortals receive from all their **toils under the sun?** The verse contains several key words and phrases that recur in the book. The word for "gain" (יִתְרוֹן, *yithrôn*) occurs ten times and only in Ecclesiastes carrying with it economic overtones. Such a person looks at life from a consumer-oriented perspective. Still the word is broader than that in meaning. It concerns that which has advantage or profit.

Is there any advantage to human toil (עָמָל, *'amāl*)? In Ecclesiastes, toil suggests a sense of weariness, that which is burdensome. For Qoheleth, life basically is filled with toil. The toil with which humans toil (the word is repeated twice in the verse) takes place under the sun. The final phrase in the verse is a favorite of Qoheleth. It appears nowhere else in the Old Testament, but is used twenty-nine times by this writer. "Under the sun" is not used to contrast this life with heaven or the afterlife.[1] Ecclesiastes gives little if any indication of awareness of an afterlife. That remains for New Testament writers to develop. Rather, the phrase is a way of referring to all of human life and experience. "Under the sun" contrasts the realm of the living with the realm of the dead (9:5-6).

The obvious answer to the question, **What does man gain from all his labor at which he toils under the sun?** is a resounding "nothing." What follows in verses 4-11 is a poem that uses an analogy to confirm the answer in verse 3.

1:4-7 The poem describes the weariness that the writer observes in the world. The weariness revolves around four components: **generations, sun, wind**, and water (**streams**). Verse 4 describes generations coming and going in contrast to **the earth**, which **remains forever.** "The earth" refers not just to the physical realm but also to humanity at large. Qoheleth's use of "the earth" is in the same sense as the psalmist who declares in 33:8, "Let all the earth fear the LORD; let all the people of the world revere him." So generations will come and go, but humanity as a whole remains the same.

The second element of the cosmos Qoheleth describes is the sun. He says it **rises** and **sets and hurries back to where it rises.** The writer

---

[1] Graham Ogden argues that all through the book, Qoheleth gives hints that he believes in an afterlife (*Qoheleth* [Sheffield: JSOT Press, 1987], pp. 22-26).

describes the unending cycle of the rising and setting of the sun. The weariness of this cycle is highlighted by describing the sun as literally "panting" (שָׁאַף, ša'āph) back to where it rises. This stands in stark contrast to the psalmist's description of the sun in Psalm 19:4b-5: "In the heavens he has pitched a tent for the sun, which is like a bridegroom coming forth from his pavilion, like a champion rejoicing to run his course." The psalmist sees purpose and energy to the sun's activity. Qoheleth sees no purpose, only perpetual motion.

This is all that he sees in the wind as well (v. 6). **Round and round it goes, ever returning on its course**. The motion of the wind described here sets up the reader for another favorite phrase of Qoheleth that he constantly repeats: "chasing after the wind." The fourth and final component is water. The streams continually **flow into the sea, yet the sea is never full** (v. 7). Verses 4-7 depict a lot of activity and energy exerted, but no progress. The components of the universe (generations, sun, wind, and water) are all entities in themselves. There is no interaction taking place. Each element exists unto itself and thus becomes a pointless activity. The overall picture of the cosmos is a universe without beginning or end. Life and history are cyclical, which is quite in contrast to the rest of Scripture with its linear understanding of the world. There was clearly a beginning point to the world. There will also be a profound conclusion (the Alpha and the Omega), but not here in this introductory poem.

1:8-11 These verses round out the poem by describing the human realm of the cosmos. Human **eyes** and **ears** never experience satisfaction or contentment with the world around them (v. 8). Nothing ever occurs that is **new**. Life remains monotonously predictable. **There is nothing new under the sun**. The statements in verses 9-10 do not deny that certain events remain unique. No other war had the technological resources used by Americans to fight in the Gulf War. The Gulf War, however, is representative of a broader phenomenon that is not new, and that is war. The verses do not speak of specific incidents but of larger types or patterns of life such as birth, death, love, hate, suffering, joy, etc. These human experiences are not new, even though they may be expressed differently in different times and by different generations.

Verse 11 speaks literally of not remembering the "beginnings or the endings," possibly because life remains one monotonous cycle. In this predictably monotonous life, what is especially surprising is that even the accomplishments of previous individuals and generations will not be remembered. In Hebrew thought, the way in which immortality expressed itself was in the posterity that remained after one's death. Much weight was given to one's name being passed on through one's offspring. Posterity perpetuates the life of the deceased. Qoheleth claims that **there is no remembrance of men of old** (v. 11). It is like the people of the Tower of Babel who tried to create a "name for themselves" yet failed to do so (Gen 11:4).

The cumulative effect of the poem in verses 3-11 is the portrayal of a cosmos that exhibits constant motion but no purpose; it has no beginning and no culmination. The poem makes no mention of God or of human interaction. Therefore there is nothing to provide purpose or solidarity to the individual components. Each component remains independent. This poem about the cosmos and the weariness of its cycle serves as an analogy for what also takes place in the human realm. Nature in its cyclical movement does not produce any surplus, so why should humans think there ought to be profit for them (v. 3)? Qoheleth devotes the rest of the book to investigating this phenomenon in the human sphere.

III. THE HUMAN EXPERIMENT (1:12–2:26)

¹²**I, the Teacher, was king over Israel in Jerusalem. ¹³I devoted myself to study and to explore by wisdom all that is done under heaven. What a heavy burden God has laid on men! ¹⁴I have seen all the things that are done under the sun; all of them are meaningless, a chasing after the wind.**

¹⁵**What is twisted cannot be straightened;**
    what is lacking cannot be counted.

¹⁶**I thought to myself, "Look, I have grown and increased in wisdom more than anyone who has ruled over Jerusalem before me; I have experienced much of wisdom and knowledge." ¹⁷Then I applied myself to the understanding of wisdom, and also of madness and folly, but I learned that this, too, is a chasing after the wind.**

¹⁸**For with much wisdom comes much sorrow;**
    the more knowledge, the more grief.

1:12-15 Verses 12-15 and 16-18 appear as two symmetrically parallel units that introduce Qoheleth's quest. Verse 12 signals a clear break with the preceding poem, with the writer once again introducing himself (v. 1). As **king, the Teacher** was the wisest in Israel. His role as king qualifies him for undertaking his intense search for wisdom.

The Teacher says, **I devoted myself** ("my heart" or "mind"; the same phrase is used in v. 17a and 8:9,16). He undertook an investigation that required him to engage all of his mental resources. His task is to **study . . . all that is done under heaven**. The phrase "under heaven" (2:3; 3:1) is similar in meaning to the more favored expression of Qoheleth, "under the sun." It is a spatial figure referring to the whole world. Qoheleth was not going to leave any stone unturned in his search.

He conducts his search for meaning **by** using the *instrument* of **wisdom** (v. 13). Qoheleth distinguishes between the *content* of wisdom and wisdom as a *method of investigation*. Here he highlights wisdom as a method. Qoheleth often questions the content of traditional wisdom. In his search, Qoheleth expresses confidence in the methodology of wisdom (2:3,9; 7:23). He uses the tools of observation (**I have seen**; v. 14),[2] experience, critical thinking, and reflection to investigate. Qoheleth is not antiwisdom when it comes to wisdom as a process of inquiry. He is subversive when it comes to some of the traditional teachings of wisdom.

About this investigation he exclaims, **What a heavy burden God has laid on men!** "Heavy burden" is the NIV's rendition of the literal phrase "evil task." This is evil not in the sense of a moral judgment but in the sense of misery. The same phrase is used in 4:8 where the NIV translates it "miserable business." For the first time in the book, the name of God is mentioned (אֱלֹהִים, *'ĕlōhîm*, used forty times). God is said to "give" or to have "laid on men" a wearisome task. Qoheleth does not say why the task has been given to humans. This God-given desire drives humans to investigate life's meaning. The name of God will not be mentioned again until the conclusion of this larger unit in 2:24-26, where, interestingly, Qoheleth says that God gives wisdom and happiness.

---

[2]Notice how often Qoheleth uses the phrase "I saw" (1:14; 2:13,24; 3:10,16,22; 4:1,4,7,15; 5:13,18; 6:1; 7:15; 8:9,10,17; 9:13; 10:5,7).

Qoheleth states his conclusion for the first time in the body of the book in verse 14. In using the process of wisdom, Qoheleth has observed **all the things that are done under the sun**. The verdict is that everything is *hebel* (**meaningless**). Life is ephemeral, its meaning unknowable. Frequently paired with the *hebel* judgment is the phrase **a chasing after the wind**. The phrase is used nine times and found only in Ecclesiastes. It is a phrase that expresses frustration; it describes the pursuit of something that is futile. "Wind" represents that which has no lasting value. Proverbs 11:29 describes the person who brings trouble to the family as "inheriting the wind." Trying to control a quarrelsome person is described as an attempt to "restrain the wind" (Prov 27:16). Trying to experience and understand life is like pursuing after the wind.

Qoheleth quotes a proverb in verse 15 to emphasize the point: **What is twisted cannot be straightened; what is lacking cannot be counted** (cf. 7:13). The proverb is a humble acknowledgment of human wisdom. Even the wisest of all sages like this king cannot straighten out the world's problems (cf. Prov 25:2).

1:16-18 These verses reaffirm the message of the previous paragraph. Qoheleth announces his superiority over all of his predecessors. Here is a man steeped in **knowledge** (16b; the root word יָרַע, *yāra'*, is used five times in these verses!). Qoheleth quickly learns that his superiority does not matter. In verse 17, the search for **understanding** intensifies as he investigates the shadowy side of **wisdom**: **folly**. He hopes that by exploring wisdom's shady side he can better understand wisdom, but to no avail. **This, too, is a chasing after the wind**. The conclusion is once again capped with a proverb: **For with much wisdom comes much sorrow; the more knowledge, the more grief**. Sorrow (or "irritation"; cf. 7:3,9) and grief are the result of wisdom. That is, pursuing wisdom not only brings pain, but so does possessing wisdom.

²:¹**I thought in my heart, "Come now, I will test you with pleasure to find out what is good." But that also proved to be meaningless. ²"Laughter," I said, "is foolish. And what does pleasure accomplish?" ³I tried cheering myself with wine, and embracing folly—my mind still guiding me with wisdom. I wanted to see what was worthwhile for men to do under heaven during the few days of their lives.**

[4]I undertook great projects: I built houses for myself and planted vineyards. [5]I made gardens and parks and planted all kinds of fruit trees in them. [6]I made reservoirs to water groves of flourishing trees. [7]I bought male and female slaves and had other slaves who were born in my house. I also owned more herds and flocks than anyone in Jerusalem before me. [8]I amassed silver and gold for myself, and the treasure of kings and provinces. I acquired men and women singers, and a harem[a] as well—the delights of the heart of man. [9]I became greater by far than anyone in Jerusalem before me. In all this my wisdom stayed with me.

[10]I denied myself nothing my eyes desired;
    I refused my heart no pleasure.
My heart took delight in all my work,
    and this was the reward for all my labor.
[11]Yet when I surveyed all that my hands had done
    and what I had toiled to achieve,
everything was meaningless, a chasing after the wind;
    nothing was gained under the sun.

[a]*8 The meaning of the Hebrew for this phrase is uncertain.

2:1-3 These verses describe the experiment that Qoheleth undertook. The king is the ideal character to choose to undertake this experiment because of his wisdom, wealth, and reputation. This indulgence in **pleasure** was not done impulsively. It was undertaken with deliberate planning. The testing used "qualitative research" with the king as the participant observer. The king thoroughly immersed himself in the pleasures[3] of life. This is not a mindless indulgence but a serious quest for enjoyment. Before Qoheleth details the experiment, however, he states the conclusion up front. It all **proved to be meaningless** (v. 1b). In this particular context, *hebel* ("meaningless") carries the nuance of "fleeting," that which does not last, which will become clearer as the passage unfolds.

The purpose of the in-depth experiment was **to see what was worthwhile for men to do under heaven during the few days of their lives** (v. 3b). Life consists of only a few days (the same phrase is used in 5:18; cf. 5:20; 6:12). The emphasis in Ecclesiastes is on the

---

[3]The word for "pleasure" is the same one used in the summary "joy passages" sprinkled through the book (2:24; 3:12,22; 8:15; 9:7-9; 11:7-10).

transitory nature of life. This gives support to *hebel* in verse 1 at least in part, including the idea of brevity. Since life is so brief, the key question is what is it that is worthwhile ("good"; v. 3)?

2:4-8 Verses 4-8 describe the endeavor. These verses are basically a royal résumé. It is the king's catalogue of accomplishments based on 1 Kings 3–11. The king immerses himself in building projects, horticultural endeavors, and sexual exploits. He explores happiness in possessing people and property and livestock and riches. He did not go about this frivolously. Seven times in these verses (vv. 4-8) the preposition "for me" (לִי, *lî*) is repeated: "I built for myself," "planted for myself," "made myself," and "acquired for myself." It emphasizes the personal investment in the ventures.

The most attention is paid to describing the palace gardens (vv. 4-6). The horticultural enterprise demonstrated the king's ability to conquer not only nations but also the arid land in which the people lived. Verses 3-8 describe the king indulging in the pleasures of all five senses. Striking similarities exist between this text and the parable of the Rich Fool in Luke 12:13-21. The parable contains a heavy concentration of the first person singular as the rich man speaks of "my crops," "my grain," and "my barns." He worries over what "I'll do" and what "I'll say." Jesus concludes, "A man's life does not consist in the abundance of his possessions" (12:15).

2:9 In all his endeavors, the king says, **my wisdom stayed with me** (v. 9b). That is, his wisdom served him well. It served him well as an *instrument* for investigating life (see 1:13). It also served him well in his dealings with other people to acquire his possessions.

2:10-11 Verses 10 and 11 give the results of the experiment. The two stand in tension with one another. On the one hand, something positive was produced: **My heart took delight in all my work, and this was the reward for all my labor.** In other words, pleasure was produced. The word for "reward" ("portion," חֵלֶק, *ḥālaq*)[4] conveys a positive sense in referring to one's portion or "lot" in life. The "portion" he received was pleasure or delight (both come from the same root "joy," שָׂמַח, *śāmaḥ*). The idea of enjoyment or pleasure will be developed a little later at the conclusion of this unit (2:24-26).

---

[4]The triliteral root is used eight times in Ecclesiastes and almost always carries a positive meaning (2:10,21; 3:22; 5:18,19; 9:6,9; 11:2). The word refers to both the possibilities and the limitations of human life.

The shift from verse 10 to verse 11 is jolting. Qoheleth moves from saying that he received enjoyment from his pursuits to concluding that he experienced nothing of lasting value. Verse 11 formally answers the question first asked in 1:3: "What does man *gain* from all his labor . . . ?" **Nothing was gained under the sun** (v. 11b). In both verses, the NIV translates the Hebrew word יִתְרוֹן (*yithrôn*) as **gain**. That is, when the king **surveyed** ("faced") all that he had accomplished, did he achieve any advantage or surplus? His answer resonates his earlier conclusion in verse 1: **everything was meaningless**. However, *hebel* does not convey the thought of being without meaning. His endeavors did produce enjoyment and pleasure, but it was short-lived. It was only a small "portion" or "lot" (v. 10) that he had been given.[5] But when looked at in the grand scheme of things, the king's experiment was like **chasing after the wind**.

[12]**Then I turned my thoughts to consider wisdom,**
    and also madness and folly.
What more can the king's successor do
    than what has already been done?
[13]**I saw that wisdom is better than folly,**
    just as light is better than darkness.
[14]**The wise man has eyes in his head,**
    while the fool walks in the darkness;
  but I came to realize
    that the same fate overtakes them both.

   [15]**Then I thought in my heart,**

"The fate of the fool will overtake me also.
    What then do I gain by being wise?"
I said in my heart,
    "This too is meaningless."
[16]**For the wise man, like the fool, will not be long remembered;**
    in days to come both will be forgotten.
Like the fool, the wise man too must die!

   [17]**So I hated life, because the work that is done under the sun was grievous to me. All of it is meaningless, a chasing after the wind.**

---

[5]This position is also developed by Seow, *Ecclesiastes*, p. 152.

2:12 Qoheleth turns his attention from pleasure **to consider wisdom**. These verses wrestle with the tension between wisdom and folly. When Qoheleth says **I turned my thoughts,** he is employing the *method* of wisdom to investigate the *contents* of wisdom (see 1:13). Along with wisdom he explores the opposite phenomenon: **madness and folly.** He leaves no stone unturned. In 12b he maintains that because he has scrutinized the whole range of life experiences, there is nothing more that anyone who comes after him could discover.

2:13 What he concludes is that **wisdom is better than folly just as light is better than darkness.** The word for "better" is "advantage" (*yithrôn*), one of the unique words that Qoheleth likes to use. In this verse, the reader is introduced to one of the many contrasts Qoheleth sets up in the book. In verse 11, he concluded that "nothing was gained (no "advantage") under the sun." In verse 13, though, he claims that wisdom is an "advantage" over folly, a significant advantage! It is like the contrast between light and darkness, like comparing day and night. Wisdom has always guided Qoheleth; it has never let him down (vv. 3,9).

2:14-16 Then he **came to realize that the same fate overtakes** both the **wise man** and the **fool** (v. 14). The wise do have a significant advantage over fools, but that advantage is limited by fate (מִקְרֶה, *miqreh*). Qoheleth always uses this word in reference to death (2:14,15; 3:19; 9:2,3). Qoheleth does not use "fate" in the sense of chance or luck. Nowhere in Scripture do the writers affirm a belief in events just happening by accident. In the case of Qoheleth, God himself controls the fate he speaks of, and that is death. The most nagging problem that Qoheleth faces is death. When one puts up both wisdom and folly against the face of death, death equalizes the two. Here again is a contradiction that Qoheleth works with. In life wisdom is superior to folly, yet in the face of death, it does not have an advantage. Neither the wise nor the fool is immune to death. Neither one will **be long remembered; in the days to come both will be forgotten** (v. 16).

2:17 One of the harshest statements the writer makes in the book is the conclusion he reaches in verse 17: **so I hated life, because the work that is done under the sun was grievous to me.** The reader must interpret this verse, as all the verses, in the context of the whole book. When Qoheleth makes the pronouncement that he hated life, he is neither making an absolute statement nor generalizing about life. At that particular moment in his quest for meaning, Qoheleth comes to this personal conclusion. In verses 12-17, Qoheleth is reflecting. His quest has not ended at this point, so his proclamation is tempered by other discoveries he will make.

The investigation of wisdom and folly ended up being grievous ("evil"; see 1:13) for him. It was grievous or disturbing because of the contradictions that seemed inherent in life. Once again, he concludes the paragraph with the refrain **All of it is meaningless** (*hebel*), **a chasing after the wind**. In this context, *hebel* refers to that which is incomprehensible because of the contradictions that abound. Qoheleth is true to life as well as true to the wisdom tradition which, contrary to popular understanding, does not envision life as simple and clear cut. Wisdom acknowledges the complexities of life (Prov 16:1; 21:30-31; 26:4,5).

¹⁸I hated all the things I had toiled for under the sun, because I must leave them to the one who comes after me. ¹⁹And who knows whether he will be a wise man or a fool? Yet he will have control over all the work into which I have poured my effort and skill under the sun. This too is meaningless. ²⁰So my heart began to despair over all my toilsome labor under the sun. ²¹For a man may do his work with wisdom, knowledge and skill, and then he must leave all he owns to someone who has not worked for it. This too is meaningless and a great misfortune. ²²What does a man get for all the toil and anxious striving with which he labors under the sun? ²³All his days his work is pain and grief; even at night his mind does not rest. This too is meaningless.

2:18-23 In these verses Qoheleth trains his thoughts on toil (עָמָל, *'āmal*). The word occurs ten times in verses 18-23. Qoheleth laments the inability he has to control how others will use his assets after his death. Death levels any advantage a person had in the accumulation of material goods through hard work. You cannot take it with you, neither can you leave it with anyone who follows. There is no way to know their character and whether or not they will use it wisely (v. 19). The phrase **who knows** (v. 19) is a favorite one of Qoheleth's (see especially chapters 9–11). It lies at the heart of what Qoheleth means by *hebel*.

Verse 22 echoes the initial question asked in 1:3: **What does a man get for all the toil and anxious striving with which he labors**

under the sun? His answer once again is "nothing." During the day, he experiences nothing but **pain and grief**. Night brings no relief. At night the overachiever tosses and turns. Qoheleth ends with the typical refrain: **this too is meaningless**. In the face of all the contradictions, life is *hebel*. Humans cannot understand or control the course of events.

[24]A man can do nothing better than to eat and drink and find satisfaction in his work. This too, I see, is from the hand of God, [25]for without him, who can eat or find enjoyment? [26]To the man who pleases him, God gives wisdom, knowledge and happiness, but to the sinner he gives the task of gathering and storing up wealth to hand it over to the one who pleases God. This too is meaningless, a chasing after the wind.

2:24-26 This short paragraph concludes the long unit that began in 1:12 with Qoheleth using wisdom to explore in depth "all that is done under heaven." He observed and experienced all the vicissitudes of human life. He has made conclusions along the way, mainly that all is *hebel*. Now, at the end of this unit, he steps back and makes an overarching observation. There is something good in the midst of *hebel*.[6] **A man can do nothing better than to eat and drink and find satisfaction in his work** (v. 24). The "good"[7] consists of enjoying the routine experiences of this life: eating and drinking and finding satisfaction in work. The last phrase literally reads "and see good [טוֹב, *ṭôb*] in his toil [*'āmal*]." Contradictions once again stand out in stark reality: "good" against *hebel*; work as satisfying against work as "pain and grief" (v. 23). In regard to work, in verses 24-26 Qoheleth has a change of perspective as he literally "*sees* good in his toil*." He "sees" the good of life coming **from the hand of God**. That is, it is a gift. Finally Qoheleth brings God into the picture. The only previous mention of the name of God was at the beginning of this unit in 1:13, where God is said to "give" humans a "heavy burden." Without God no human being can enjoy life (v. 25).[8]

---

[6]Longman takes this text, and others like it, as Qoheleth's statement of resignation (*Ecclesiastes*, p. 106). The "good" Qoheleth speaks of is a resigned good and not an affirming good (p. 183). See 2:24-26.

[7]"Good" (טוֹב) is used twice in this verse. It is the word the NIV translates "better" and "satisfaction."

[8]Verse 25 contains a couple of textual problems. For one, it is difficult to

Verse 26 contrasts the one who finds favor (*ṭôb*) in the presence of God and the **sinner** who displeases God. This verse gives the specifics of what it is that is from the hand of God: **To the man who pleases him, God gives wisdom, knowledge and happiness** ("happiness" = שָׂמַח, *śāmaḥ*, same word as in 2:1). Qoheleth contrasts this with what he gives **to the sinner.** "Sinner" does not refer to one who is a transgressor but to one who is synonymous with a fool. The sinner is the one who always makes mistakes, who offends, and who displeases God. To such a person, God **gives the task of gathering and storing up wealth** simply to give it to someone else. This is the toil that is futile; it results only in "pain and grief" (v. 23). The final *hebel* judgment applies to the toil of the fool.

In verses 24-26, Qoheleth does not describe the task of pursuing pleasure as he has described in 2:1-11. There is no compulsive or obsessive attitude about enjoyment at this point. Rather than pursuing enjoyment, Qoheleth accepts it as a gift. Brown concludes, "Neither achieved nor planned, neither grasped nor produced, the gifts of true pleasure are simply received from God."[9] This is the first of seven passages in which Qoheleth pauses in the thick of the *hebel* action to reflect on the enjoyment of life (the other six include 3:12-13; 3:22; 5:18-20; 8:15; 9:7-10; 11:7-10).

IV. THE ISSUE OF TIME AND GOD'S PURPOSES (3:1-22)

This chapter forms a fairly tight development of thought. The dominant motif is on the sovereignty of God. In 3:1-15, God deter-

---

know how to translate the word יָחוּשׁ (*yāḥûš*, "enjoyment," NIV). Seow argues for translating it "glean." He maintains that verses 25-26 consist of a series of contrasts between the one who eats and the one who gleans, the one who is favored and the one who offends (sinner), (*Ecclesiastes*, pp. 139-140). Fox translates the word "worry" or "fret," (*A Time*, p. 189). Still others argue that it comes from the root חוּשׁ (*ḥûš*) meaning "to hasten." So the KJV translates the verse, "Or who can eat, or who else can hasten hereunto, more than I?" Its meaning remains uncertain. But the overall thought of the verse is clear: God is the source of human experiences.

For another, the Hebrew text reads "who will eat . . . outside me (חוּץ מִמֶּנִּי, *ḥûṣ mimmennî*)?" Some wish to emend the text to its reference to God "outside him" (חוּץ מִמֶּנּוּ, *ḥûṣ mimmennû*). This emendation seems obvious in light of the context.

[9]Brown, *Ecclesiastes*, p. 37.

mines the events of human life. In 3:16-22, God determines the ulti-mate destiny of human beings.

This poem is probably the most well known passage in all of Ecclesiastes. Its meaning is dependent on at least two considera-tions. On the one hand, does the poem stand alone as an inde-pendent unit? On the other hand, is this poem interpreted in light of its context in 3:1-15? An argument could be made for both possi-bilities. The issue here is similar to the issue in New Testament scholarship regarding the parables of Jesus. Do they stand on their own, or do they need to be interpreted in context? Scripture con-tains various levels of interpretation depending on how broad a con-text is included in the interpretive process.

If this poem in Ecclesiastes is interpreted as an independent unit (as is often done at funerals or in popular songs), the poem provides a word of comfort or reassurance. The poem affirms what wisdom teaches elsewhere, that humans must discern the appropriate times to act. The wise person is the one who knows the right time (Prov 15:23; 25:11). As the wise reflects on the opposite experiences described, they know that life consists of good times as well as bad times. The wise learn that humans cannot accept one without the other. The poem by itself focuses on human activity.

If the poem is interpreted in light of the commentary that fol-lows in verses 9-15, then the primary focus is on God. The issue no longer is human timing but God's activity and the human response to it. God controls everything that happens in life. Humans cannot change that which God sets in motion. Instead, they learn to make themselves open to the seasons of life as they come and ultimately enjoy that which God gives (3:12-13).

[1]There is a time for everything,
    and a season for every activity under heaven:
[2]   **a time to be born and a time to die,**
    a time to plant and a time to uproot,
[3]   **a time to kill and a time to heal,**
    a time to tear down and a time to build,
[4]   **a time to weep and a time to laugh,**
    a time to mourn and a time to dance,
[5]   **a time to scatter stones and a time to gather them,**
    a time to embrace and a time to refrain,

6   **a time to search and a time to give up,**
     a time to keep and a time to throw away,

7   **a time to tear and a time to mend,**
     a time to be silent and a time to speak,

8   **a time to love and a time to hate,**
     a time for war and a time for peace.

3:1-8 The poem consists of twenty-eight items paired together in fourteen antitheses. The poem contains no discernible pattern in its overall movement, just a catalog of activities and their opposites that represent common occasions in human experience. The catalog of occasions pairs positives and negatives, constructive and destructive activities. The list affirms an overall order to life. Life is not random. However, the catalog does not describe moral categories, like a time for righteousness and a time for wickedness. Rather these activities are simply part and parcel of the vicissitudes of human life.

Some commentators point to verse 2a as setting a strict deterministic tone for the whole poem: **a time to be born and a time to die**. Humans have no control over when they are born and when they die. However, the point of these two pairs is not that God predestines individuals to a specific day, month, and year when they will be born and when they will die. Rather, Qoheleth speaks in broader terms. The readiness for birth remains essentially the same for all humans. It takes about nine months for the fetus to mature. There **is a time to be born.**[10] The time period is set for the human species but a specific date is not predetermined for the individual.

There is also **a time to die**. That time is essentially the same for all people. The psalmist says it usually is seventy or eighty years (Ps 90:10). This poem does not advocate a strict deterministic perspective on life.[11]

Some of the antithetic pairs are clear in their meaning while other pairs remain more ambiguous. **A time to plant and a time to uproot** (v. 2b) speaks of agricultural activity. However, a time to uproot does not refer to harvest but to the activity of pulling up unwanted weeds in the process of cultivation. The pair in verse 3b, **a time to tear down and a time to build,** seems to refer not to

---

[10]When various animals give birth remains a mystery to human beings and a source of awe at what God has created. See Job 39:1-4.

[11]See Fox, *A Time*, pp. 201-204.

agricultural activities but more to architectural activities, that is, business or building ventures.

The most ambiguous pair of all is the reference to **a time to scatter stones and a time to gather them** (v. 5a). Some commentaries understand it to be a euphemism for sexual relations, tying the pair closely to the reference in the second line, which speaks of **a time to embrace**. No other pair in the catalog, however, is interpreted metaphorically. In all likelihood, the obscurity of meaning enables the pair to refer to several events. It could refer to casting stones on the field of an enemy in time of war (2 Kgs. 3:19,25). It may refer to the preparation of a field for cultivating. Or it may refer to the building of a stone fence.

Like verse 5a, verse 6 as well may allude to a number of different experiences. The categories of searching and giving up, of keeping and throwing away are general categories in which many specific human activities could fit. Verse 7a may be a reference to the mourning process in which garments were torn to express grief. Those garments were mended when the grieving process ceased.

How do humans live with the parameters God has set? God does not force humans to keep with his time frame. As Michael Fox says, humans can ignore them and God can even decide on occasions to override them.[12] But those who are wise live within the range of possibilities God has set in motion. Within the boundaries, humans discern the appropriate moment and then respond accordingly. They take advantage of opportunities as they arise. The message of 3:1-8 is reinforced in 11:1-6 but is approached from a slightly different angle, exhorting the reader to take the initiative in acting responsibly even in the face of life's uncertainties.

When the poem in verses 1-8 is interpreted in light of the commentary that follows, a somewhat different emphasis appears. God, not humans, becomes the principal actor (vv. 11,13,14). God determines the seasons of human life; humans can do nothing to change that. Some interpreters understand the whole unit together to teach a gloomy theology about life. Humans have no control. Life is completely in God's hands. Mortals can do nothing to change the course of events that occur in life. Humans cannot even begin to understand

---

[12]Ibid., p. 204.

life. Therefore the best response is resigned acceptance. What happens will happen, and humans simply must roll with the punches God doles out. A rigid theology of determinism overrides chapter 3:1-15.

The poem (vv. 1-8) along with the commentary that follows (vv. 9-15), however, does not teach rigid determinism.[13] God does not determine specific times nor does he prearrange every little detail in human life. Rather God determines the broad order of human events and experiences. He has created general occasions and appropriate opportunities, such as times to build up and times to tear down. Even though, according to Qoheleth, God gives wealth and wisdom and work (2:26; 6:1-2), he does not predetermine every specific incident that occurs. Within the framework of God's order, humans are called to act responsibly, to seize opportunities as they arise. God will hold humans accountable for their choices (9:7-10; 11:9; 12:14). As Fox concludes, "Time as fate . . . is foreign to Qoheleth."[14] God does not lock humans into a deterministic mode, but within the larger fixed framework God sets, humans are given opportunities to choose. Humans can ignore the time of planting or harvesting. They can choose to ignore the time of mourning or dancing. God does not force anyone to keep within his occasions.

[9]What does the worker gain from his toil? [10]I have seen the burden God has laid on men. [11]He has made everything beautiful in its time. He has also set eternity in the hearts of men; yet they cannot fathom what God has done from beginning to end. [12]I know that there is nothing better for men than to be happy and do good while they live. [13]That everyone may eat and drink, and find satisfaction in all his toil—this is the gift of God. [14]I know that everything God does will endure forever; nothing can be added to it and nothing taken from it. God does it so that men will revere him.

[15]Whatever is has already been,
     and what will be has been before;
     and God will call the past to account.[a]

[a]15 Or God calls back the past

---

[13]See Fox's Excursus on "Time in Qohelet's 'Catalogue of Times,'" in *A Time*, pp. 194-206.
[14]Ibid., p. 202.

3:9-10 Verse 9 echoes the question raised in 1:3 (cf. 2:22; 5:16; 6:11). There the question was raised at the beginning of a poem describing the monotonous cycle of creation. Here the question is raised at the conclusion of a poem cataloging common patterns in human life. The writer envisions God laying a **burden** (עִנְיָן, *'inyan*)[15] on mortals: an intense desire to understand the world (v. 10).

3:11 As Qoheleth reflects on the "catalog of occasions" God set in order, he concludes **he has made everything beautiful in its time** (v. 11a). The word for "beautiful" (יָפֶה, *yāpheh*) does not describe an aesthetic evaluation on human events but describes that which is suitable for the occasion. God has made everything (all human activities as described in 3:1-8, not creation) right or appropriate in its time. Qoheleth seems to stand in awe of this dimension of God's work. Yet the most perplexing part of the verse and of this whole chapter is the meaning of the word "eternity" (הָעֹלָם, *hā'ōlām*). What does Qoheleth mean when he says, God **has also set eternity in the hearts of men**? Some argue that the reference is to eternal life, but Qoheleth does not have an understanding of the afterlife in the New Testament sense. Some emend the text to read "the world." That does not clarify the meaning of the text. Others suggest interpreting the word from its root עָלַם (*'ālām*), meaning "darkness" or ignorance." This meaning appears in Ecclesiastes 12:14. Probably the best way to interpret "eternity" is in the sense of "that which transcends time."[16] This same word is used with the same meaning in verse 14. It refers to that which is timeless. God has put eternity (*hā'ōlām*) into the minds of mortals. The idea of timelessness stands in contrast to the "times" in which humans live. This is the burden mentioned in verse 10 that God has put on human beings. People know that God has made everything appropriate for its time. Humans can deal only with the moment; they can understand only in the sense of their own time. They have a compulsive drive to understand the larger scope of things but they cannot (the verse is similar to 8:17). Humans have a longing to step out of time and see the overarching picture in order to understand how all the pieces fit together. This was Job's desire, but he was never granted that perspective. Qoheleth concludes verse 11 by confirming that humans

---

[15]The word עִנְיָן is used eight times in the book. It is one of several words and phrases that appears only in Ecclesiastes.

[16]Seow, *Ecclesiastes*, p. 163.

cannot fathom what God has done from beginning to end. This is the burden of having *hāʻōlām* (eternity) placed in one's mind.

3:12-13 Since human beings cannot grasp God's larger scheme, they must live within the parameters of their own time frame. In the midst of all the uncertainties, Qoheleth states a certainty, **I know** (v. 12). The one thing he knows is **that there is nothing better for men than to be happy and do good while they live**. The same description is used here as was used earlier in 2:24-26: **That everyone may eat and drink, and find satisfaction in all his toil** (v. 13). Qoheleth calls on individuals to enjoy the common experiences of life, which include the catalog of occasions described in the poem. Qoheleth's instruction calls on individuals to "seize the moment," to take advantage of life's little pleasures along the way. This enjoyment that comes to humans **is the gift of God**. The phrase is synonymous with the clause earlier used "from the hand of God" (2:24).

3:14 Still Qoheleth has a problem. Even though he advocates the *carpe diem* philosophy (seizing the day), he wants an understanding of the larger picture. There remains something else with which he can exclaim with certainty: **I know that everything God does will endure forever; nothing can be added to it and nothing taken from it**. He knows that what God does is "eternal" (*hāʻōlām*), that which transcends time (see v. 11). Consequently, humans cannot change what God has set in motion. God's activity is not bound by human time frame. In Ecclesiastes, human activity is set against divine activity. A major gap exists between the two. God intentionally creates this hiatus in order **that men will revere** (i.e. "fear") **him** (v. 14). To "fear God" emphasizes the transcendence of God and his distance from human beings (5:7; 7:18; 8:12-13).

3:15 Verse 15 recalls the words of 1:9, except this time the name of **God** is brought into the scenario. The poem in 1:3-11 was void of any reference to the Deity, but here the message seems to be that God takes responsibility for what lies beyond human control.

> [16]**And I saw something else under the sun:**
>
> **In the place of judgment—wickedness was there,**
> **in the place of justice—wickedness was there.**
>
> [17]**I thought in my heart,**
>
> **"God will bring to judgment**
> **both the righteous and the wicked,**

for there will be a time for every activity,
a time for every deed."

[18]I also thought, "As for men, God tests them so that they may
see that they are like the animals. [19]Man's fate is like that of the animals; the same fate awaits them both: As one dies, so dies the
other. All have the same breath[a]; man has no advantage over the
animal. Everything is meaningless. [20]All go to the same place; all
come from dust, and to dust all return. [21]Who knows if the spirit
of man rises upward and if the spirit of the animal[b] goes down into
the earth?"

[22]So I saw that there is nothing better for a man than to enjoy
his work, because that is his lot. For who can bring him to see what
will happen after him?

[a]*19 Or spirit   [b]21 Or Who knows the spirit of man, which rises upward, or
the spirit of animal, which*

3:16-17 Having affirmed the complete sovereignty of God over
all the occasions of human life, Qoheleth turns his attention to the
problem of injustice. By the method of observation (**I saw**; v. 16), a
tool he relies on through all his investigation (see 2:13,24; 3:10,22;
4:1,4,15; 5:13,18; 6:1; 8:9,10; 10:5,7), Qoheleth discovers that justice
has miscarried. In the place of **judgment** and **justice** (lit., "righteousness"), **wickedness** reigned. Nevertheless, God is not to blame
for the miscarriage, because eventually, **"God will bring to judgment both the righteous and the wicked, for there will be a time
for every activity, a time for every deed"** (v. 17). The judgment
mentioned is not the eschatological judgment but the judgment that
God exercises in this life on his own time frame. Some argue that
this verse is a later addition because the book's dominant thought is
that conventional wisdom, with its belief in a just universe and the
law of retribution, has failed (see 7:15; 8:14). Qoheleth never denies
that God is just. His quandary is that he does not understand how
God exercises it (cf. 5:6; 11:9).

Verse 17 repeats the phrase found at the beginning of the poem
in 3:1: "for there will be a time for every activity." Just as God has
established occasions for every human activity (3:1-8), he has also
established an occasion for justice to occur. The main frustration is
that Qoheleth does not witness God's judgment at work and does
not know how or when God will activate it.

3:18-19 How verses 16-17 are connected in the train of thought with verses 18-21 is unclear. Qoheleth moves from speaking of the dominance of injustice to the common fate that both humans and animals experience. Perhaps the deferred judgment of God leads to the opportunity for humans to understand themselves better. At any rate, verses 18-21 describe the relationship between humans and animals. One question arises in verse 18 as to the purpose of the **test** (from the root בָּרַר, *bārar*). The test appears to be for the sake of proving to mortals that they share a common fate with animals, that both will die. The ultimate reason was to emphasize the chasm that exists between human beings and God.

From this, Qoheleth does not conclude that humans are no better than animals. Rather, humans share a solidarity with animals in that they both die (Ps 49:10-12,20). Qoheleth made a similar argument earlier when he compared wisdom to folly (2:12-17). At first he claimed that the difference between the two was like night and day (2:13). When both came face to face with death, however, neither one could escape (2:14-15). So in verse 19, Qoheleth claims **man's fate is like that of the animals**. The word for "fate" (מִקְרֶה, *miqreh*, used three times in v. 19a) was used earlier to describe the solidarity the wise had with the fool. In Ecclesiastes, the word does not mean "chance" or "luck" but is always used by Qoheleth to speak of "death." The result: **man has no advantage** (מוֹתַר, *môthar*) **over the animal**. Then Qoheleth adds the common refrain: **everything is meaningless**. This is the only time the refrain occurs in chapter 3. Everything is *hebel*, that is, enigmatic, beyond comprehension.

3:20-21 Echoes of the creation account in Genesis 1 and 2 reverberate in verses 20-21. Does the **spirit** (רוּחַ, *rûaḥ*) or breath of humans rise **upward**? Does the **spirit** (*rûaḥ*) or breath of the animal descend **down into the earth?** In the creation account, God "breathed" into both humans and animals the "breath" or "soul of life." With his exclamation **who knows** (2:19; 6:12; 8:1), Qoheleth implies that at death the life-breath of both returns to God. Ecclesiastes maintains a dark cloud of ambiguity over what happens to humans after death (12:7). It appears that Qoheleth comes down on the side of affirming that death is final (9:10).

3:22 In the midst of a sea of ambiguity, Qoheleth carves out a space for enjoyment. For the third time in the book, he concludes **that there is nothing better for a man than to enjoy his work.** Such enjoyment is a part of the human **lot**. "Lot" (חֵלֶק, *ḥeleq*) is one of those words that the writer of Ecclesiastes uses mostly in a positive sense. It includes both the "limitations and possibilities" with which humans live.[17] The human lot is like a plot of land that one inherits. A natural part of receiving the land is that it requires hard work to maintain it. Along with the toil, the worker receives enjoyment in seeing the land produce. The implication is that the lot humans possess is God-given (3:13). The enjoyment experienced is not the pursuit of material goods but appreciating the moment.

Qoheleth's final statement once again affirms the ambiguity with which human beings live: **For who can bring him to see what will happen after him?** To what does "after him" refer? In light of the whole context of Ecclesiastes and his agnostic stance on the afterlife, it would appear that it refers to what happens in this life after the person dies (cf. 2:12; 2:18; 7:14; 9:3).

V. GOOD IN THE PRESENCE OF COMPANIONSHIP (4:1-16)

Chapter 4:1-16 contains the first of two clusters of better-than sayings (the second cluster is in 7:1-12). The better-than sayings are a common proverbial form used by the sage. A number of these sayings are sprinkled in Proverbs 15–20 (e.g., 15:16-17). The form enables the sage to describe the conditional nature of life. The irony in Ecclesiastes results from Qoheleth earlier announcing that there is no "advantage" (2:11) to now declaring that certain things are advantageous or "better."

The material in chapter 4 is loosely connected. Formally, it is held together by the better-than sayings (1-3,4-6,7-8,9-12,13-16). Thematically, the unit focuses on the individual in isolation against the individual in community. The key word woven through the chapter is the numeral "two" (vv. 3,8,9,10,11,12,15).

4:1Again I looked and saw all the oppression that was taking place under the sun:

**I saw the tears of the oppressed—
and they have no comforter;**

---

[17]Ibid., p. 176.

power was on the side of their oppressors—
    and they have no comforter.
²And I declared that the dead,
    who had already died,
are happier than the living,
    who are still alive.
³But better than both
    is he who has not yet been,
who has not seen the evil
    that is done under the sun.

4:1 Qoheleth investigates another dimension of life, one that is unfortunately all too pervasive. He begins by saying, **Again I looked and saw** (lit., "I turned and I saw"). The same phrase is used in verse 7 (cf. 1:14; 2:13,24; 3:10,16,22). What he saw was **all the oppression that was taking place under the sun**. Clearly he is stating a hyperbole. The idea is that he observed the widespread existence of oppression. Qoheleth does not identify the source of the oppression. One thing seems certain: he does not explicitly put the blame on God, as his counterpart Job did (Job 10:3). Actually Qoheleth's main concern is not with the oppression that runs rampant, rather he laments that those oppressed **have no comforter**. He repeats the phrase twice in verse 1: **and they have no comforter**. This was the same cry repeated in the first poem in Lamentations (1:2,9,16,17,21).

4:2 Because the oppressed suffer alone, without a comforter, Qoheleth concludes that **the dead, who had already died, are happier than the living, who are still alive**. Death is not better than life, but it is better than having to witness people suffering in solitude. Later, however, Qoheleth concludes that a "*living* dog is better than a *dead* lion" (9:4-5). Further, he maintains that death serves as a motivating force to enjoy life in the present (9:10). Once again, Qoheleth lives with a contradiction within his own experience.

4:3 Still better than **both** (the NIV appropriately translates the Hebrew word, which literally means "two," as "both"; see 4:7-8) the living and the dead, **is he who has not yet been, who has not seen the evil that is done under the sun**. Experiencing affliction without consolation is so troublesome for Qoheleth that the best state is never to have been born! Qoheleth does not make a definitive statement here. Rather his outcry comes in a moment of heavy burden and grief. Just as earlier he had announced "I hated life" (2:17), he now makes another "irrational" statement in a moment of intense pain.

⁴And I saw that all labor and all achievement spring from man's envy of his neighbor. This too is meaningless, a chasing after the wind.
⁵The fool folds his hands
and ruins himself.
⁶Better one handful with tranquillity
than two handfuls with toil
and chasing after the wind.

4:4 From the oppression described in the first three verses, Qoheleth moves to a closely related topic: toil (עָמָל, 'āmāl). The underlying question is, When does one work too much and when does one not work enough? Qoheleth states another hyperbole, **And I saw that all labor and all achievement**[18] **spring from man's envy of his neighbor**. Qoheleth claims that all the effort humans put into their work is the result of "envy" (קִנְאָה, qin'āh). The point is that competitiveness drives people to put pressure on themselves to accomplish more. The results become destructive not only to others but to the self as well. In wisdom material, envy is always self-destructive (Prov 6:34; 14:30; 27:4; Job 5:2). The verse describes just the opposite of Jesus' command to "love your neighbor." So Qoheleth concludes, **This too is meaningless, a chasing after the wind**. It is *hebel* in that it is a worthless pursuit.

4:5 Following verse 4 are two proverbs (vv. 5-6) that grapple with an individual's attitude toward **toil**. The first proverb affirms **the fool folds his hands and ruins himself**. The phrase "folds his hands" is a common metaphor the sages used to describe the lazy person (cf. Prov 6:10; 24:33). The lazy person ruins himself. The phrase literally reads "eats his flesh." Qoheleth uses the hideous imagery of the cannibalism of one's own body to describe the self-destructive nature of indolence. The picture is of an individual

---

[18]The NIV appropriately translates the phrase כִּשְׁרוֹן הַמַּעֲשֶׂה (kišrôn hamma'ăśeh, "skillful of work") "achievement." The term kišrôn is used only in Ecclesiastes (2:11,21; 5:11).

sitting by himself, clasping his hands together and chewing on his knuckles (cf. 10:12). Verse 5 stands as the polar opposite of verse 4. If excessive work and competitiveness is not the answer, then neither is ceasing to work.

4:6 This leads to the second proverb in verse 6, a better-than proverb. The proverb announces, **better one handful with tranquillity**. "Tranquillity" is an appropriate way to translate the Hebrew word "rest" (נַחַת, *nāḥath*). The word does not mean inactivity or idleness, but rather peace, security (cf. 9:17). The phrase speaks of "one handful *with* tranquillity," not "of" tranquillity. The emphasis is not on the "full" but on the "hand." As a measurement, a handful indicated a very small amount (1 Kgs 17:12). The proverb declares a handful with tranquillity better **than two handfuls with toil and chasing after the wind**. The comparison is between a smaller amount with peace of mind and a larger amount with wearisome toil. The meaning of the proverb is quite similar to the statement made in Proverbs 15:16: "Better a little with the fear of the LORD, than great wealth with turmoil" (cf. Prov 16:8; 17:1).

Taken together, verses 4-6 create a tension. Both the lazy and the toiler destroy themselves. Too much as well as too little work is condemned. Instead it is better to work for just a small portion, the necessities of life, and possess tranquillity. These verses express a similar thought the sage prays in Proverbs 30:7-9, "give me neither wealth nor poverty."

⁷**Again I saw something meaningless under the sun:**
⁸**There was a man all alone;**
    he had neither son nor brother.
 There was no end to his toil,
    yet his eyes were not content with his wealth.
 "For whom am I toiling," he asked,
    "and why am I depriving myself of enjoyment?"
 This too is meaningless—
    a miserable business!

4:7-8 With these two verses, the number "two" comes into prominence in the rest of the chapter. The word occurs in six verses that follow (8,9,10,11,12,15). The number functions in three different situations: the lack of progeny (vv. 7-8), the need for companionship (vv. 9-12), and the successor to the king (vv. 13-16).

The first phrase in verse 7 repeats verbatim the phrase in verse 1: "Again I turned and I saw." Qoheleth makes another observation. He observes **a man all alone** (the Hebrew text reads "and there is not a second"). This man has no living relatives. Yet the loner is totally consumed in his toil. He can never experience satisfaction with the amount that he possesses. Finally the man comes to himself asking a sobering question, **"For whom am I toiling . . . and why am I depriving myself of enjoyment?"** This loner may be a miser who is so preoccupied with his work that he isolates himself from others (Prov 18:1).

Qoheleth concludes that what he does is *hebel* (**meaningless**). It is **a miserable business** (cf. the same phrase in 1:13; 5:13). It is noteworthy to compare this passage to an earlier observation made by Qoheleth in 2:18-21. There he concluded that it is senseless for a fool to inherit the results of the hard work for which one has toiled. Here he concludes that it is senseless for no one to inherit one's work. It makes little sense to toil only for personal gain. Humans require a cause bigger than themselves in order to experience meaning in work.

[9]**Two are better than one,**
      because they have a good return for their work:
[10]**If one falls down,**
      his friend can help him up.
 But pity the man who falls
      and has no one to help him up!
[11]**Also, if two lie down together, they will keep warm.**
      But how can one keep warm alone?
[12]**Though one may be overpowered,**
      two can defend themselves.
 A cord of three strands is not quickly broken.

4:9-12 The first phrase in verse 9 reads, "Better are the two than the one." The paragraph contrasts "the two" with "the one." "The two" **have a good return for their work**. Not that they make more money. Rather the two create a synergy in which they complement each other's talents and experiences. Verses 10-12 picture the two on a journey. The two are better than the one because **if one falls down, his friend can help him up** (v. 10). **But pity**[19] **the man who**

---

[19]The Hebrew text reads "but alas for him" (וְאִילוֹ, *wᵊ 'îlô*).

falls and has no one to help him up! If one falls into a pit or some kind of trap while traveling across country, he can receive immediate help from his friend. On a cold night when it is not possible to start a fire, the two can keep each other warm. And, finally, if they encounter robbers on their journey, **two can defend themselves**.

Qoheleth concludes his observations with a fitting proverb: **a cord of three strands is not quickly broken.** With the repetition of the number "two," the use of the number "three" in the saying heightens the effect at this juncture. The point: There is strength in numbers. The loner makes himself vulnerable. The one in community finds vigor. Only in community can one experience fulfillment in toil. In solitude, toil becomes nothing more than "pursuing the wind." Contrary to the grandiose expedition embarked upon in 1:1–2:23, Qoheleth acknowledges that peace resides in the ordinary, in companionship.

¹³**Better a poor but wise youth than an old but foolish king who no longer knows how to take warning. ¹⁴The youth may have come from prison to the kingship, or he may have been born in poverty within his kingdom. ¹⁵I saw that all who lived and walked under the sun followed the youth, the king's successor. ¹⁶There was no end to all the people who were before them. But those who came later were not pleased with the successor. This too is meaningless, a chasing after the wind.**

4:13-16 The final better-than saying in chapter 4 appears in these verses. Verse 13 states the principle at work in the form of a better-than proverb. Verses 14-16 contain an example story illuminating the proverb. The better-than proverbs generally reverse the typical expected scenario. In this case, an **old king** would normally be the exemplary person to honor. In contrast, a **poor youth**[20] possesses neither status nor experience. He is the undesirable. However, it is the youth who possesses wisdom and the king who exemplifies folly. With that additional quality thrown into the mix, the roles are reversed. In this case, **better a poor but wise youth than an old but foolish king.** The reason the king is foolish is because he **no longer**

---

[20]The word for "poor" (מִסְכֵּן, miskēn) is used only here and in 9:15-16. It describes someone who lacks social status, a commoner. The word for youth (יֶלֶד, yeled) describes a child, someone who has not reached full maturity.

knows how to take warning (see Prov 11:14; 15:22; 20:18; 24:6). The word for warning (זָהַר, *zāhar*) includes the idea of admonition and instruction (cf. 12:12). The king's problem is not age but openness to the advice of others (see Prov 9:7-9). This king, like "the one" described earlier (vv. 9-12), travels the journey of life alone.

The better-than saying is then supported by two example stories (vv. 14-16). The major question raised in these verses is how many youth are being described? Is there one or two?[21] The ambiguity arises because of the number of pronouns used in the text. It is difficult to know which pronoun refers to whom. The translation of the NIV assumes one youth.

However, I think it is more likely that two different youths are being depicted. The first youth is described in verse 14: **The youth may have come from prison to the kingship, or he may have been born in poverty within his kingdom**. The prison referred to was not a place where people were incarcerated in order to be reformed from their criminal ways. People were placed in prison for economic and political reasons. People who could not pay their debts were placed in prison. And prison became a source of forced labor until the debt was paid off. The youth who went from prison to the kingship was not a criminal but one who experienced poverty. This rags to riches story has spawned much speculation about a historical character lying behind the story. Many suggestions have been made regarding the identity of the two kings, including Joseph and Pharaoh, David and Saul, and Daniel and Nebuchadnezzar, but there is no way to know with any certainty.

Verse 15 appears to mention a second youth. A more literal translation of the Hebrew is, "I saw all the living who walked about under the sun follow (עִם, *'im*) the second youth (הַיֶּלֶד הַשֵּׁנִי, *hayyeled haššēnî*), the one who stood under him." "The one who stood under him" means the one who succeeded the king. Typically, when Qoheleth begins a verse with "I saw," he is shifting thought, which is what he appears to do in this verse. The youth/king in verse 14 is now succeeded by a second youth.

Verse 16 remains ambiguous but the idea is that the king who was once honored by the people will not maintain his popularity forever. As the NIV puts it, **those who came later were not pleased**

---

[21]Fox argues for three! (*A Time*, pp. 224ff).

with the successor. The king eventually falls out of favor with the people. It recalls the cycle described in the opening poem, "generations come and generations go" (1:4).

Regardless of how many youth the example story speaks of, the gist is that an inexperienced youth with no social status rises to the throne because of his wisdom. However, wisdom has limits. It can bring one to a position of leadership, but it cannot maintain a king's popularity in the eyes of the people.

Certain parallels exist between this example story and the one told in 9:13-15. Both describe a poor but wise person. Both stories compare the poor wise person to the king. Finally, neither wise person sees their wisdom come to fruition. Both fall out of favor with the people.

VI. THE INSATIABLE DESIRE FOR MORE (5:1-6:9)

The overarching theme of this block of material relates the insatiable cravings of humans to satisfy their appetites for wealth and material goods. Of the forty references to God in the book of Ecclesiastes, the greatest concentration is found in chapters 4 and 5. It is in chapter 5 that Qoheleth begins to offer ethical admonitions on life and worship. The ethical advice is rooted in a theology of God who is wholly different from humans and who reigns supreme (see Qoheleth's View of God in the Introduction). In the face of a world consumed by greed and which accepts the stark reality of the brevity of life, Qoheleth calls on humans to enjoy life by accepting the simple things that God gives.

^{5:1}**Guard your steps when you go to the house of God. Go near to listen rather than to offer the sacrifice of fools, who do not know that they do wrong.**

²**Do not be quick with your mouth,**
> **do not be hasty in your heart**
> **to utter anything before God.**
God is in heaven
> **and you are on earth,**
> **so let your words be few.**
³**As a dream comes when there are many cares,**
> **so the speech of a fool when there are many words.**

⁴When you make a vow to God, do not delay in fulfilling it. He has no pleasure in fools; fulfill your vow. ⁵It is better not to vow than to make a vow and not fulfill it. ⁶Do not let your mouth lead you into sin. And do not protest to the ˪temple˩ messenger, "My vow was a mistake." Why should God be angry at what you say and destroy the work of your hands? ⁷Much dreaming and many words are meaningless. Therefore stand in awe of God.

5:1-7 These verses describe the proper attitude individuals must have as they enter the temple to worship in the presence of God. Worshipers exercise restraint as they offer sacrifices (v. 1), extend prayers (vv. 2-3), and make vows (vv. 4-6) to God. The tone of reflection that dominated previous chapters changes here to one of admonition. Qoheleth advises caution, restraint, sincerity, and reverence. Qoheleth begins with the imperative, **guard your steps** (lit., "feet"). The metaphor of "watching your feet" describes a person's manner of moral conduct (Prov 1:15-16; 4:27). When a worshiper comes into the presence of God, he must take responsibility for his lifestyle. The worshiper draws **near to listen rather than to offer the sacrifice of fools.** Genuine listening to God (cf. Jas 1:19), which implies obedience, is better than trying to impress God with acts of piety. Qoheleth stands in agreement with the tradition, long taught by the prophets, that obedience is better than sacrifice (1 Sam 15:22; Amos 5:21-24). The last phrase in the verse describing fools remains ambiguous: **who do not know that they do wrong.**²² The NIV offers a viable translation. Through their life and worship practices, fools condition themselves to the point where they no longer recognize evil.

Qoheleth exhorts the worshiper to restrain his or her words when speaking to God (v. 2). For Israel's sages, any action done in haste is highly suspect (Eccl 7:9; cf. Prov 19:2; 20:25; 21:5; 28:20; 29:20). Those who are hasty with words demonstrate a lack of respect for others. Qoheleth admonishes the worshiper, **do not be hasty in your heart to utter anything before God.** The motive for exercising restraint is grounded in the nature of God himself: **God is in heaven and you are on earth so let your words be few.** Because such a disparity exists between God and human beings, mortals must constrain their speech. The constraint is exercised out of reverence for the

---

²²Literally, "for they do not know to do evil."

supremacy of God. In Ecclesiastes, God is described in terms of being wholly different from mortals (see Qoheleth's View of God in the Introduction). God resides in heaven. He does not dwell on earth. He does not simply reside in the human heart. This does not mean that Qoheleth's God is indifferent to humans. God demonstrates genuine concern. He gives them enjoyment and satisfaction and all the good gifts of life (2:24-26). God transcends human understanding and experience. Because he reigns supreme, humans limit their use of words in his presence.

It seems that Qoheleth quotes a proverb in verse 3 to emphasize his admonition. The proverb compares dreams and **the speech of a fool**. The proverb says **a dream comes when there are many cares**.[23] Dreams represent that which does not last, those brief moments in life (Job 20:8). Dreams and *hebel* ("vapor," "meaningless") are used almost synonymously in verse 7. A person's dreams and burdens are one and the same in that they do not last. They are insignificant. In the same way, the many words a fool utters are capricious. They contain nothing of substance.

In verses 4-6 Qoheleth turns his attention to uttering **a vow to God**. The admonition is based on the text in Deuteronomy 23:21-23, which gives directions in using a vow. Once again the problem is lack of restraint (cf. Prov 20:25). Vows were often made in order to manipulate God to do something for the worshiper. God became a kind of cosmic bellhop. Vows were easy to make. The worshiper made them without knowing whether they could actually be kept or without considering the cost (v. 6), but "God is in heaven" (v. 2). He cannot and will not be manipulated. In the end, **it is better not to vow than to make a vow and not fulfill it** (v. 5). As Supreme Being he holds mortals responsible for every word they utter. An unfulfilled vow incites God's anger (v. 6). Within the parameters God has set (3:1-15), humans have moral responsibilities.

The fundamental issue in this passage is one's attitude before God. The worshiper must take responsibility for a moral lifestyle ("watch your feet") and exercise restraint in uttering prayers and vows to God. Verse 7 expresses the attitude in a nutshell: **Therefore stand in awe of God** ("fear God"). He is Wholly Other.

---

[23]The word for "cares" (עִנְיָן, *'inyān*) is the same one Qoheleth used when he described human toil as a grievous "burden" (1:13; 4:8).

⁸If you see the poor oppressed in a district, and justice and rights denied, do not be surprised at such things; for one official is eyed by a higher one, and over them both are others higher still. ⁹The increase from the land is taken by all; the king himself profits from the fields.

5:8-9 It is difficult to see the immediate connection these verses have with the previous paragraph. Verses 8-9 seem to be related more to what follows than to what precedes. In the Hebrew text these two verses are unclear. We can, however, understand the thrust of their message. The concern is with oppression, namely economic oppression. Qoheleth already addressed the general subject earlier (3:16 and 4:1). The importance of practicing justice and righteousness cuts across all of Israel's professional institutions, including the prophetic office, the priesthood, and the monarchy. In the midst of his quest for meaning, Qoheleth never calls into question the obligation to practice justice. Yet Qoheleth warns the reader, **Do not be surprised** if justice and righteousness are absent.

Why does injustice abound? He explains, **for one official is eyed by a higher one, and over them both are others higher still.**[24] The word for "official" (גָּבֹהַּ, *gābōah*) literally means "haughty one." The picture is of bureaucrats clamoring to rise to the top, concerned only with self-promotion. They "watch out for" (NIV, "eye"), that is, they protect each other's interests. In the process, they trample on the needs of the poor. The picture is not of higher officials holding lower officials accountable in a kind of checks-and-balances system. Rather, this describes a dishonest bureaucracy, a whole network of corruption.[25] Corruption exists from the ground up. These ambitious officials are out to make sure they get their fair share. The system protects the officials but not the oppressed.

Verse 9 can be interpreted in either a negative or positive way. The NIV interprets the verse negatively. The corruption is so pervasive that it reaches to the very top, to the king himself: **The increase from the land is taken by all; the king himself profits from the fields.** The king, the very one who was to administer justice, participates in the corruption.

---

[24]The sentence in Hebrew is rendered, "For high one above high one is watching, and over them are higher ones."

[25]Brown, *Ecclesiastes*, p. 58.

However, because of the syntax of the text, I believe it is preferable to interpret the verse in a positive way. The mention of the king serves as a corrective to the corrupted officials. The last three words in the Hebrew text are ambiguous, but they can be either translated "a king for a cultivated field" or "a king serves (is subject to) a field." Either way, the idea is that a king takes responsibility to uphold the agricultural enterprise of the people, which was the basis for economic survival and community identity (negative, e.g., Naboth's vineyard; 1 Kgs 21:1-19). Qoheleth desires such a king to bring about justice and righteousness.

[10]**Whoever loves money never has money enough;**
> **whoever loves wealth is never satisfied with his income.**
> **This too is meaningless.**

[11]**As goods increase,**
> **so do those who consume them.**
And what benefit are they to the owner
> **except to feast his eyes on them?**

[12]**The sleep of a laborer is sweet,**
> **whether he eats little or much,**
but the abundance of a rich man
> **permits him no sleep.**

> [13]**I have seen a grievous evil under the sun:**

wealth hoarded to the harm of its owner,
[14]   **or wealth lost through some misfortune,**
so that when he has a son
> **there is nothing left for him.**

[15]**Naked a man comes from his mother's womb,**
> **and as he comes, so he departs.**
He takes nothing from his labor
> **that he can carry in his hand.**

> [16]**This too is a grievous evil:**

As a man comes, so he departs,
> **and what does he gain,**
> **since he toils for the wind?**
[17]**All his days he eats in darkness,**
> **with great frustration, affliction and anger.**

5:10-11 The subject of oppression in verses 8-9 leads Qoheleth into a discussion of ambition and avarice here. Human greed lies at the base of economic oppression. In these verses (10-17) Qoheleth mixes proverbs, example stories, and reflections in good wisdom style to describe the grievous evil (vv. 13,16) of the discontented person. Verse 10 sets the tone, **Whoever loves money never has money enough; whoever loves wealth is never satisfied with his income**. Money (lit., "silver") never satisfies human desire, and the love for it leads to further consumption.[26] Qoheleth quotes a proverb to support his contention, **As goods increase, so do those who consume them**. Qoheleth maintains that the only benefit received from wealth is that the owner can **feast his eyes on them**.[27] The phrase describes the immediate experience of possessing material goods. That is, the only good that comes from possessing wealth is to enjoy it in the present.[28]

5:12 Qoheleth contrasts **the sleep of a laborer** and the **sleep of a rich man**. The contrast is not between the worker and the lazy, but between a poor worker and a rich worker. The laborer's or servant's sleep is **sweet** (pleasant) regardless of the circumstances. The rich worker has insomnia. The sleeplessness may result from overconsumption, indigestion, anxiety, or all of the above. Whatever it is, the rich are never satisfied.

5:13-14 Then Qoheleth relates a little example story. He observed **a grievous evil** (lit., "an evil sickness"): the hoarding of wealth. This hoarded wealth was somehow lost through a disaster or a poor investment. Afterward the **owner** had **a son**. The father now has nothing to pass on to his son. What an irony! Qoheleth calls it "a sickening tragedy" ("grievous evil"). The issue of passing on wealth to a future generation is a frequent topic in Ecclesiastes. In 2:19, Qoheleth spoke of the tragedy of passing on one's hard-earned wealth to a fool. In 4:8, he spoke of the tragedy of having no heir to inherit possessions. And in this scenario, the heir now has nothing to receive!

5:15 This leads Qoheleth to cite another popular saying, **Naked a man comes from his mother's womb, and as he comes, so he departs. He takes nothing from his labor that he can carry in his**

---

[26]First Timothy 6:10 may be an allusion to this text.

[27]The Hebrew text reads, "sees them with his eyes."

[28]Seow, *Ecclesiastes*, p. 220.

hand. The implication is that only as long as one lives can one receive enjoyment from possessions. Both Job (1:21) and Paul (1 Tim 6:7) quote this proverb.

5:16-17 Qoheleth again describes the insatiable desire of humans as a gross sickness (**a grievous evil**). The conspicuous consumers never achieve contentment. Thus they live and eat **in darkness, with great frustration, affliction and anger**. In Ecclesiastes darkness is often associated with anguish and death (2:14; 6:4; 11:8; 12:2). Those who are never satisfied live as though they were dead. Their lives are filled with frustration (כַּעַס, *kā'as*, "irritation"), affliction (חֳלִי, *ḥŏlî*, "sickness"), and anger (קֶצֶף, *qāṣeph*, "wrath"). The term for "affliction" ("sickness") is from the same root as the word that Qoheleth uses to describe unquenchable desires as an "evil sickness."

> [18]**Then I realized that it is good and proper for a man to eat and drink, and to find satisfaction in his toilsome labor under the sun during the few days of life God has given him—for this is his lot.** [19]**Moreover, when God gives any man wealth and possessions, and enables him to enjoy them, to accept his lot and be happy in his work—this is a gift of God.** [20]**He seldom reflects on the days of his life, because God keeps him occupied with gladness of heart.**

5:18-20 For a fourth time the reader arrives at another "oasis" in the *hebel* desert and comes to Qoheleth's perspective on the enjoyment of life.[29] In his commentary, Seow observes a sequence in Qoheleth's thought.[30] There are two ways that people demonstrate discontentment. The first is in their constant effort to acquire more (5:8-12). The second is in their attempts to hoard what they acquire (5:13-17). In verses 18-20, Qoheleth now offers the counterpart of this "gross sickness." To those who do not spend their lives seeking, pursuing, devouring, and acquiring, God gives enjoyment. Those who accept God's gift serve as a counterculture to the dominant trend of humanity.

The language in these verses is quite similar to the vocabulary used in 3:11-13. Both speak of that which is **proper** or "beautiful"

---

[29]Murphy takes the enjoyment texts as Qoheleth's statements of resignation, a kind of throwing up of the hands in frustrated surrender. He refers to them as Qoheleth's "resigned conclusions" (*Ecclesiastes*, pp. 27, 35, 53, 87). See 2:24-26.

[30]Seow, *Ecclesiastes*, p. 222.

(יָפֶה, *yāpheh*, 3:11). Both use the term **enjoy** (3:12-13). And both speak of **gift** (3:11,13).

The gift of enjoyment consists of the simple affairs of life: **eat**ing, **drink**ing, and **satisfaction** in work (v. 18). The fact that humans have been given only a **few days of life** highlights the necessity to seize these opportunities when they arise. Even though God is Wholly Other, he demonstrates loving care for his people.

Verse 20 caps the message. The meaning of the verse is not certain. The idea that a human **seldom reflects on the days of his life** refers to the reflecting ("call to remember") or "brooding" (NRSV) over the miseries, the anxieties about material possessions, and over what might have been. In Ecclesiastes there are appropriate as well as inappropriate ways to remember. To reflect on the fact that life is brief is an appropriate way to remember because it motivates one to appreciate the present (11:7-10; 12:1-7). To brood over days of yesteryear and wallow in the miseries of life is an inappropriate way to remember. Verse 20a speaks of the latter. The one who accepts the gift of God does not brood over the past days of his life, **because God keeps him occupied with gladness of heart**. The major question in this last phrase gravitates around the meaning of the word "occupied" (מַעֲנֶה, *ma'ăneh*). The word is unclear. Does it mean that God "preoccupies" human thoughts with joy?[31] Or does it mean that God "answers" or gives the "revelation" of joy to humans? Since Qoheleth is not interested in God revealing himself to humans (God is Wholly Other), it is probably better to understand it in the former sense.

6:1I have seen another evil under the sun, and it weighs heavily on men: 2God gives a man wealth, possessions and honor, so that he lacks nothing his heart desires, but God does not enable him to enjoy them, and a stranger enjoys them instead. This is meaningless, a grievous evil.

3A man may have a hundred children and live many years; yet no matter how long he lives, if he cannot enjoy his prosperity and does not receive proper burial, I say that a stillborn child is better off than he. 4It comes without meaning, it departs in darkness, and

---

[31]Sometimes God preoccupies humans with difficult or terrible things (1:13; 3:10).

in darkness its name is shrouded. [5]Though it never saw the sun or knew anything, it has more rest than does that man— [6]even if he lives a thousand years twice over but fails to enjoy his prosperity. Do not all go to the same place?

[7]All man's efforts are for his mouth,
    yet his appetite is never satisfied.
[8]What advantage has a wise man over a fool?
  What does a poor man gain
    by knowing how to conduct himself before others?
[9]Better what the eye sees
    than the roving of the appetite.
  This too is meaningless,
    a chasing after the wind.

6:1-2 The introduction to this passage, **I have seen another evil under the sun**, indicates a shift in thought and thus a new unit. Even though Qoheleth makes a slight shift in focus, there is continuity with the previous line of thought.

At first glance, this text seems to negate altogether the previous section. **God gives a man wealth, possessions and honor, so that he lacks nothing his heart desires, but God does not enable him to enjoy them, and a stranger enjoys them instead. This is meaningless, a grievous evil**. The "sickening evil" here is that God gives material goods, but a man cannot enjoy them. Seow observes something that is helpful in understanding the relationship.[32] In the previous passage, Qoheleth generalizes about the enjoyment of life as a gift from God. In this text, he states a possible exception to the rule. The former describes all people. The latter describes a single person. The former describes what God has already done. The latter describes what could be. As Seow concludes, "God has given humanity the gift to enjoy life. However, there may be instances in the future in which such a gift is not evident."[33]

6:3-6 Verses 3-6 are quite similar to 5:13-17. Qoheleth sets up a scenario: Let us say a person has many children and lives a long life, both of which are perceived by wisdom as a blessing. If this person does not enjoy what he or she possesses, then **I say that a stillborn**

---

[32]Seow, *Ecclesiastes*, p. 225.
[33]Ibid.

child is better off than he. In a hyperbolic example, Qoheleth says that a person could have **a hundred** offspring and live twice as long as Methuselah (Gen 5:26-27), but if that person is discontented, then it is better never to have experienced or even had an awareness of life. The insatiable desire of humans that drives them to acquire more is a miserable sickness.

6:7 The image is made even more graphic in the verses that follow. **All man's efforts are for his mouth, yet his appetite is never satisfied**. The discontented person toils unceasingly to fulfill his needs, but "his appetite[34] is never satisfied." The phrase picks up on the common image used of Sheol (the place of the dead) never being satisfied (Prov 27:20; 30:16). Death is personified as a beast always seeking to devour more. Qoheleth takes this image to describe the cravings of the avaricious. Their hunger is never gratified.

6:8 How do the questions in verse 8 connect with the preceding proverb? It may be that in the same way that people are never satisfied with attaining material goods, so they are never satisfied with attaining knowledge or wisdom or relational skills. The point of the verse is that if the **wise** have no **advantage** over the **fool** (see 2:13-16), then increasing wisdom in knowing how to get along with others does not do the **poor** any good either. The phrase **to conduct himself before others** literally reads "to walk before the living."

6:9 Qoheleth caps his thought with a better-than proverb: **Better what the eye sees than the roving of the appetite**. In other words, it is better to remain content with what is before you in the present, than to be led by wandering desires that are never satisfied. Qoheleth distinguishes between "seeing good" and "devouring good."[35] One sees and receives "good" as a gift from God. To pursue good in order to satisfy insatiable desires is a sickness. Qoheleth concludes with his familiar refrain **this too is meaningless, a chasing after the wind**. The refrain also serves in the first half of Ecclesiastes to indicate the completion of a train of thought. This is the last time the phrase "chasing after the wind" is used in the book.

---

[34]The word for "appetite" is נֶפֶשׁ (*nephes*). The word is often translated "soul." But it is multivalent in meaning. It can mean "life," "throat," or as here "appetite." The term is used four times in 6:1-9 (vv. 2,3,7,9). In Ecclesiastes it is used primarily to refer to hunger, thirst, or appetite in general (see Prov 19:2).

[35]Brown, *Ecclesiastes*, p. 66.

ECCLESIASTES 6:10–12:14

VII. THE SEARCH TO FIND WHAT IS GOOD (6:10–8:17)

With 6:10, a natural transition seems to occur in the movement of the book. The refrain "chasing after the wind" appears for the last time in 6:9, having recurred repeatedly in the first half of the book. The Masoretes, the medieval scribes who copied the material, note in the margin of the Hebrew text that verse 10 marks the physical midpoint of the book. Addison G. Wright has argued that 6:10-12 introduces phrases that dominate the second half of the book ("not find out" and "do not know").[1] It appears that 6:10-12 transitions the reader to the second half of the book and introduces two dominant themes: the quest to find out what is good and the human perplexity of not knowing.

TRANSITION (6:10-12)

[10]Whatever exists has already been named,
    and what man is has been known;
no man can contend
    with one who is stronger than he.
[11]The more the words,
    the less the meaning,
    and how does that profit anyone?

[12]For who knows what is good for a man in life, during the few and meaningless days he passes through like a shadow? Who can tell him what will happen under the sun after he is gone?

---

[1]Addison G. Wright, "The Riddle of the Sphinx: The Structure of the Book of Qoheleth," *CBQ* 30 (1968): 313-334.

6:10-12 These verses serve as a summary statement for the writer, identifying for him what makes life so perplexing. The verses offer theological reflections on the nature of human existence and on the being of God.

Humans are constrained by the limitations of their fragile nature. Humans cannot **contend with one who is stronger**. The "one who is stronger" probably refers to God. Verses 10-11 call to mind Job's quarrel with God. Job wanted to meet God in court in order to right the wrongs that he had suffered. For Job, though, God is too strong; he is too powerful for a lowly human being to contend with (Job 9:17-19). Rather than raging against God as did Job, Qoheleth simply confirms that humans cannot argue with him. Qoheleth believes that **the more words** one hurls at God, **the less the meaning**. The Hebrew text reads, "The more words, the more *hebel*" (vapor). Such rhetoric is empty (recall the worshiper in the temple in 5:2-3). So accept the limitations. The limitations are connected with the very nature of humanity whose lives Qoheleth describes as **few and meaningless days**, which pass **through like a shadow**. In this context, *hebel* ("meaningless") is better translated "fleeting" because it is surrounded by terms that describe the brevity of life. The days of human life are few and fleeting; they pass like a shadow.

Along with their fragile existence, humans must also live in the face of uncertainty. **Who knows what is good for man in life** (v. 12)? Humans are basically ignorant about the best course of action for the future.

Against the limitations of human nature lives the sovereign God. The text of verse 10 reads, "What will be (happen), its name has already been called." The one who has already named everything and knows everything is God. He knows what has happened and what will happen. God has foreordained the patterns of life (see 3:1-15). He has set the course of human affairs in motion, and no mortal can change that fact. Humans cannot alter present or future events.

Verses 10-12 set the frailty of human life against the supremacy of God. The conclusion? **For who knows what is good for a man in life?** This leads Qoheleth to introduce a whole series of proverbs.

A. PROVISIONAL GOOD IN THE FACE OF UNCERTAINTY (7:1-14)

At the conclusion of his summary statement in 6:10-12, Qoheleth surmised that no one could know "what is good for a man in life" (v. 12). Ironically, in the proverbs that follow in 7:1-12, Qoheleth claims that certain experiences are "good" or "better" (טוֹב, *ṭôb*).[2] Debate exists over how the following series of proverbs fits into the flow of the book, especially following on the heels of the conclusion that humans cannot know what is good.

Seow argues that 7:1-12 must be interpreted in light of the theological introduction (6:10-12) and conclusion (7:13-14). Since God is sovereign and no human can know what is good, then the proverbs that follow are offered by Qoheleth as a parody on those who hand out advice.[3] The proverbs sarcastically imitate the traditional wisdom of the wise. They do this by setting up a series of proverbial contradictions, which include: death/birth; funerals/weddings; sorrow/joy; grief/levity; rebuke/flattery. The combined effect of all the contradictions is that each cancels out the other, thus in the end affirming what Qoheleth concluded in 6:12: "For who knows what is good for a man in life?"

The indications are far from certain that Qoheleth sets up these proverbs as a type of "straw man" or caricature of traditional wisdom in order to undermine it. If this is Qoheleth's strategy, he does it in an extremely subtle way. In order to interpret Ecclesiastes properly, the reader must constantly hold different perspectives in tension. On the one hand, all of life is *hebel*. On the other hand, in the face of the uncertainties, Qoheleth calls on all humans to act responsibly. After all, God will judge human actions. So Qoheleth counters his *hebel* judgments with the summons to enjoy the present (2:24-26; 3:12-13,22; 5:18-20). A similar tension exists in 6:10–7:14. After Qoheleth concludes that no one can know what is good (6:12), he counters it with a series of proverbs that qualify the statement. Such contrasting perspectives are typical of Qoheleth's investigative process (e.g., 4:1-3). Though humans cannot know "good" as God knows it, within their limitations there are certain activities that the

---

[2]Both English words translate from the same Hebrew term.
[3]Seow, *Ecclesiastes*, pp. 240ff.

wise should cultivate. Mortals cannot know absolute good as God knows it, but they can discover what is good in a provisional sense. Some things are "better" than others.

The proverbs in 7:1-12 are not a random collection but focus on exploring what is good. The word "good" or "better" (טוֹב, *ṭôb*) is used nine times in verses 1-12. In addition, a thematic thread links the proverbs together. Verses 1-4 are connected to the subject of death. Verses 5-7 contrast the wise and the fool. And verses 8-12 describe qualities of wise living in light of the end.

> **7:1A good name is better than fine perfume,**
> **and the day of death better than the day of birth.**
> **2It is better to go to a house of mourning**
> **than to go to a house of feasting,**
> **for death is the destiny of every man;**
> **the living should take this to heart.**
> **3Sorrow is better than laughter,**
> **because a sad face is good for the heart.**
> **4The heart of the wise is in the house of mourning,**
> **but the heart of fools is in the house of pleasure.**

7:1 Verse 1 sets the tone for the proverbs that follow. The first line is a traditional proverb,[4] which confirms that possessing a good reputation exceeds the value of luxury (cf. Prov 22:1). Alongside the conventional wisdom Qoheleth adds a twist, **and the day of death better than the day of birth**. Does Qoheleth advocate death over life? Qoheleth values life over death (9:4-5), even though in certain circumstances there are exceptions (e.g., 4:2). In addition, nowhere in the book does Qoheleth ever commend suicide. So in this proverb Qoheleth is not speaking morbidly. The two lines parallel one another. **The day of death** stands parallel to a **good name**. Thus "the day of death" refers to the end of life when one's reputation is ultimately confirmed. Sirach 11:28 contains a proverb conveying a similar meaning: "Call no one happy [good] before his death; by how he ends, a person becomes known." In the sense of possessing an established reputation, the day of death is better than the day of

---

[4]The proverb combines alliteration and word balance to convey its message: words of similar sound, "name" and "oil," and the word "good" (used at the beginning and end of the proverb). טוֹב שֵׁם מִשֶּׁמֶן טוֹב (*ṭôb šēm miššemen ṭôb*).

birth. Interestingly, Qoheleth reverses the conventional process of giving a name. One receives a name at death, not at birth.

7:2 The next three verses are interpreted in light of verse 1. Verse 2 is also a better-than proverb and sets up another contrast: **It is better to go to a house of mourning than to go to a house of feasting**. The general reference is to funerals and weddings. In what way are funerals better than weddings? When a person contemplates death, it gives new perspective. One learns more about life from a wake than from a wedding. The proverb calls to mind the admonition of the psalmist: "Teach us to number our days aright, that we may gain a heart of wisdom" (Ps 90:12).

7:3 With verse 3, Qoheleth again seems to undermine conventional wisdom for the sake of discovering that which is good. **Sorrow is better than laughter, because a sad face is good for the heart.**[5] Fox interprets the verse in light of verses 5-6a. Both proverbs speak of the value of reproof. "Sorrow" (כַּעַס, *ka'as*) refers to the "irritation" or constructive reproof of another person. Such irritation at another's irresponsibility leads to strengthening the heart.[6] Verse 3 communicates the same message as verse 5. It is, however, better to interpret the proverb in its immediate context linked to them by the theme of death and mourning. The sorrow or irritation is not that of another but of the self. In honestly facing one's own irritations or frustrations, a person learns more about the true nature of joy, because **a sad face is good for the heart**. Knowledge and sorrow (*ka'as*) often go hand in hand (1:18).

7:4 The fourth proverb echoes similar sentiments to those expressed in verse 2. The wise person will often be found in the funeral parlor. In contrast, the fool will spend his days in feasting and levity. Qoheleth subverts traditional wisdom in order to identify a provisional good. It was Woman Wisdom that invited youth to her festive banquet in order to learn about life (Prov 9:1-6). Here Qoheleth invites the wise to a wake in order to teach a lesson.

The proverbs in verses 1-4 bring the reader face to face with another contradiction in Ecclesiastes. On the one hand, Qoheleth commends eating and drinking and enjoyment of life. On the other

---

[5]The Hebrew text reads, "In badness of face is a good heart," meaning that sober reflection is the basis of true joy.

[6]Fox, *A Time*, p. 252.

hand, he advocates approaching life with solemnity. The two remain in tension with one another. It is in facing the reality of one's own mortality that a person can enjoy life in its truest sense.

**[5]It is better to heed a wise man's rebuke
       than to listen to the song of fools.
[6]Like the crackling of thorns under the pot,
       so is the laughter of fools.
       This too is meaningless.
[7]Extortion turns a wise man into a fool,
       and a bribe corrupts the heart.**

7:5-6 These proverbs contrast the wise and the fool. Verses 5 and 6 stand together as a proverb unit addressing an issue that lies close to the heart of Israel's sages. Wisdom places a high value on reproof (see Prov 1:20-33; 9:8; 27:5). In this proverb, Qoheleth contrasts the **wise man's rebuke** and the **song of fools**. A subtle contrast is made between the singular "wise man" and the plural "fools." For the sake of personal growth, it is much better to receive the constructive criticism of one wise person than the flattery of many fools. The song of fools is further described in verse 6. It is compared to **the crackling of thorns under the pot.**[7] Because they provided quick combustion, dry thorns were often used to start a fire. They do not give off much heat, but they do make a lot of noise. Such is the nature of the song of fools; it makes a lot of noise but imparts little substance. The *hebel* judgment made at the conclusion of verse 6 may refer to the ineffectiveness of many words as alluded to in 5:7 and 6:11.

7:7 Verse 7 describes a wise man who becomes a fool. The NIV says that it is **extortion** that **turns a wise man into a fool**. The word for "extortion" is "oppression." The idea is that in the midst of relentless oppression, even the wise can compromise their values in order to gain relief (see the prayer of the sage in Prov 30:7-9). The proverb warns the wise that maybe the reason more people do not heed their words (v. 5) is that they are vulnerable to bribery.

**[8]The end of a matter is better than its beginning,
       and patience is better than pride.**

---

[7]A striking alliteration exists in the two verses (5-6a) between song (שִׁיר, *šîr*), thorn (סִיר, *sîr*), and pot (סִיר, *sîr*).

⁹Do not be quickly provoked in your spirit,
>   for anger resides in the lap of fools.
¹⁰Do not say, "Why were the old days better than these?"
>   For it is not wise to ask such questions.
¹¹Wisdom, like an inheritance, is a good thing
>   and benefits those who see the sun.
¹²Wisdom is a shelter
>   as money is a shelter,
> but the advantage of knowledge is this:
>   that wisdom preserves the life of its possessor.

7:8 These verses round out the litany of proverbs strung together in this unit and speak of the way the wise should live in light of the end. Verse 8 recalls the proverb mentioned in the first verse and sets up another contrast. The reason **the end** is better than **the beginning** is because the end reveals the outcome. This is why patience becomes such an important quality. In the face of the uncertainties of life, **patience is better than pride**. Job learned this (42:12). It is the advice Ahab gave to the king of Syria: "One who puts on his armor should not boast like one who takes it off" (1 Kgs 20:11).

7:9-10 Verses 9-10 contain two warnings. One is that those who would find good will not allow anger[8] to seethe and grow within them. They will develop the quality of patience. Hastiness is one of the deadly sins the sages spoke against. The other warning is not to brood over the past (recall 5:20). Instead, look at life as it is and wait patiently for the end when one will see everything more clearly. Qoheleth does not claim that the present is better than the past. Rather the present is where one must live responsibly.

7:11-12 The final proverb pair (vv. 11-12) commends **wisdom**. An evaluation of wisdom is stated in the final line of verse 12: **the advantage of knowledge is this: that wisdom preserves the life of its possessor**. Taken together, verses 11 and 12 maintain that wisdom is more advantageous than wealth.

¹³Consider what God has done:

Who can straighten
>   what he has made crooked?

---

[8]The word translated "anger" is the same word translated "sorrow" in verse 3.

¹⁴**When times are good, be happy;**
　　but when times are bad, consider:
God has made the one
　　as well as the other.
Therefore, a man cannot discover
　　anything about his future.

7:13-14 These concluding verses take the reader back to the
beginning of the unit in 6:10-12. **Consider what God has done** states
succinctly what Qoheleth seeks to understand (3:11; 8:17; 11:5). The
ways of God remain mysterious and inscrutable. No one can change
the course of life that he has set in motion. The crooked cannot be
straightened. As James Crenshaw puts it, "The universe has wrin-
kles."[9] So accept the ebb and flow as it comes (cf. 3:1-8). Accept the
good as well as the bad. And **consider: God has made the one as
well as the other**.

B. NO HUMAN STANDS RIGHTEOUS BEFORE GOD (7:15-29)

¹⁵**In this meaningless life of mine I have seen both of these:**
a righteous man perishing in his righteousness,
　　and a wicked man living long in his wickedness.
¹⁶**Do not be overrighteous,**
　　neither be overwise—
　　why destroy yourself?
¹⁷**Do not be overwicked,**
　　and do not be a fool—
　　why die before your time?
¹⁸**It is good to grasp the one**
　　and not let go of the other.
　　The man who fears God will avoid all ⌐extremes⌐.[a]

ᵃ*18 Or will follow them both*

7:15-18 Qoheleth begins by making another observation about
life. **In this meaningless life of mine I have seen both of these**
(v. 15). In this context, it is better to render *hebel* ("meaningless") as

---

[9]James Crenshaw, *Ecclesiastes,* Old Testament Library (Philadelphia:
Westminster Press, 1987), p. 139.

"fleeting."[10] Here "meaningless" modifies the expression "days" ("life") and appears to be more of a time reference. The text reads, "I have seen all (or both) of these in my fleeting days." What he witnessed was a reversal of what traditional wisdom taught: the righteous die early and the wicked live a long life! In other words, life does not always turn out the way it is supposed to. Nevertheless, Qoheleth does not claim that this is a general principle. He is saying that he has observed many exceptions to wisdom's rule.

He extends his thought in quite an odd way in verses 16-17. He admonishes, "Do not be overly righteous or wise and do not be overly wicked." These are strange statements indeed. Does this mean that a little wickedness is acceptable? Qoheleth is not advocating moderation in moral conduct in these verses. This is not the "Golden Mean" philosophy of the Greeks. A moderate amount of **wickedness** is not the point. The point is that neither the **righteous** nor the **wicked** hold privileged positions in this life. A person profits from neither extreme. The individual who practices excessive righteousness is the one who seems to trust in his goodness to get him through life. His problem is overconfidence. Qoheleth says the excessively righteous person is the one who does not admit mistakes (v. 20). So do not practice that kind of righteousness.

On the other hand, do not come from the perspective of the wicked, thinking that your wickedness will get you anywhere. Verse 17 ties in with verse 15 where Qoheleth concedes that the wicked can live a long, healthy life. Qoheleth warns the reader to think twice before believing that wickedness gives an advantage. Both the **overrighteous** and the **overwicked** can experience an untimely death. Neither perspective gives humans the upper hand. Instead, the proper perspective is to acknowledge human limitations. Accept that within every person there is a measure of both good and bad. Such a person is one **who fears God** (v. 18). The confidence in righteousness or wickedness alluded to in verses 16-17 contrasts with the fear of God in verse 18. Fearing God is the perspective Qoheleth advocates. Neither excessive righteousness nor wickedness, neither virtue nor vice profits anyone. The only course to follow is reverence toward God.

---

[10]Most of the time the *New Jewish Publication Society* (the TANAKH) translates *hebel* as "futility." On this occasion it translates the word "brief span" (Philadelphia, 1988).

[19]Wisdom makes one wise man more powerful
> than ten rulers in a city.
[20]There is not a righteous man on earth
> who does what is right and never sins.
[21]Do not pay attention to every word people say,
> or you may hear your servant cursing you—
[22]for you know in your heart
> that many times you yourself have cursed others.

[23]All this I tested by wisdom and I said,

"I am determined to be wise"—
> but this was beyond me.
[24]Whatever wisdom may be,
> it is far off and most profound—
> who can discover it?

7:19-20 Verse 19 must be interpreted in light of the context and especially the verse following it. The statement that **wisdom makes one wise man more powerful than ten rulers in a city** expresses a traditional wisdom belief. In spite of his waffling back and forth, Qoheleth still counts wisdom superior to folly, wealth, and power (cf. 2:12-16). In this context, the affirmation is qualified by what has already been said about overconfidence in wisdom (v. 16). Verse 20 qualifies the statement even further: **There is not a righteous man on earth who does what is right and never sins.** Here, reflecting on his earlier statement in verse 16, Qoheleth speaks of overconfidence in righteousness. No one can claim the absence of sin (1 Kgs 8:46). Paul's affirmation in the New Testament that "all have sinned and fall short of the glory of God" (Rom 3:23) hearkens back to Ecclesiastes and to Old Testament theology.

7:21-22 Verses 21 and 22 offer a concrete example of the fact that no one is without sin. Do not take the harsh words you hear others say about you seriously. When you hear others speak derogatorily about you, take it as an opportunity to be honest about yourself. Recall the criticism that you have leveled against others. The admonition advises the reader to take criticism with a grain of salt and to remember your own imperfections. No one is without sin.

7:23-24 Verses 23 and 24 once more speak of Qoheleth's search for wisdom. He affirms that his method of investigation is wisdom (see 1:13). He has not deviated from wisdom's procedure (2:3,9).

The irony is that earlier Qoheleth claimed that he succeeded in attaining wisdom (1:16). Now he admits that **this was beyond me.** Qoheleth may be speaking of two different types of wisdom. He may be distinguishing between what is sometimes referred to as lower wisdom, the practical common sense kind necessary for daily living. More than likely, however, the unattainable wisdom that Qoheleth speaks of is that which seeks to know what will be. It is that wisdom which desires to lift humans above their limits allowing them to understand all the "contradictions" (e.g., v. 15) of life. It is the wisdom that desires to know the mysteries of God (1:9; 3:11,15; 6:10). This kind of wisdom **is far off and most profound**[11]—**who can discover it?** (v. 24). The word for "discover" ("find") is used eight times in verses 24-29, indicating the intensity of Qoheleth's search. Wisdom remains elusive. It remains far off and most profound.

[25]**So I turned my mind to understand,**
> **to investigate and to search out wisdom and the scheme of things**
and to understand the stupidity of wickedness
> **and the madness of folly.**
[26]**I find more bitter than death**
> **the woman who is a snare,**
whose heart is a trap
> **and whose hands are chains.**
The man who pleases God will escape her,
> **but the sinner she will ensnare.**

[27]**"Look," says the Teacher,**[a] **"this is what I have discovered:**

"Adding one thing to another to discover the scheme of things—
[28]   **while I was still searching**
> **but not finding—**
I found one ⌊upright⌋ man among a thousand,
> **but not one ⌊upright⌋ woman among them all.**
[29]**This only have I found:**
> **God made mankind upright,**
> **but men have gone in search of many schemes."**

[a]**27 Or** *leader of the assembly*

---

[11]The verse more literally reads, "That which is distant and deep, deep, who will find it?"

7:25-29 Qoheleth uses "qualitative research" to discover wisdom. That is, he uses observation, reflection, and his mental faculties to **investigate** (תּוּר, *tûr*). This is the same word used repeatedly in Numbers 13 and 14 to speak of the Israelites "spying out" the land. Qoheleth engages in intense mental exploration. His intention is **to search out wisdom and the scheme of things**. Three times in these verses he mentions the desire to discover the "scheme of things" (חֶשְׁבּוֹן, *ḥešbôn*; vv. 25,27,29). The word he uses is an accounting term, which involves the idea of taking inventory, of calculating or adding up the facts of life. Qoheleth's investigation led him to explore wisdom's counterpart **wickedness** and **folly**.[12] Sometimes the line between wisdom and folly becomes blurred. It becomes difficult to distinguish them.

What he discovers in exploring **the madness of folly** is the woman. **I find more bitter than death the woman who is a snare, whose heart is a trap and whose hands are chains.** Is Qoheleth attacking the character of women? Is this a classic example of misogyny?[13] The reader should keep in mind that this whole paragraph is Qoheleth's search for wisdom. The reference here is not to women in general nor is it to a particular woman, but to "the woman." The verse echoes the language of the temptress described in detail in Proverbs 1–9. The sage describes the temptress as "bitter as gall," "her feet go down to death" (Prov 5:4f). The one who follows her is "like a bird darting into a snare" (Prov 7:23). Verse 26 personifies folly as does the sage in the book of Proverbs. Thus for Qoheleth, while wisdom remains elusive, folly is quite accessible but also dangerous. While it is true that the sociological context of wisdom was male oriented, this passage does not degrade womanhood. Throughout the rest of Ecclesiastes, there is no attack on an individual woman. In one of the summary passages, Qoheleth speaks respect-

---

[12]The phrase in the Hebrew text reads, "To understand the wickedness of folly (כֶּסֶל, *kesel*) and the folly (סֶכֶל, *sākal*) of madness (הוֹלֵלָה, *hôlēlāh*). The writer stacks up the synonyms (three) for folly to indicate he had truly immersed himself in understanding this dimension of life.

[13]Longman says that it is. He argues that Qoheleth's words are not canonical, only the words of the editor in the prologue and epilogue are (*Ecclesiastes,* p. 207). He maintains that the teachings of "Qoheleth are not the teachings of the book of Ecclesiastes any more than the speeches of the three friends constitute the normative teaching of the book of Job" (p. 204).

fully of women, "Enjoy life with your wife, whom you love, all the days of this meaningless life that God has given you under the sun . . ." (9:9).

With verse 27 the editor makes a rare cameo appearance. Only here, in the introduction, and in the conclusion does the reader hear his voice. **"Look," says the Teacher, "this is what I have discovered: "Adding one thing to another to discover the scheme of things**. Using accounting language, Qoheleth says that he added literally "one to one to find" the scheme of things. Once again the writer uses the accounting term (*ḥešbôn*; "the scheme of things"), meaning that Qoheleth engages in making calculations and taking inventory.[14]

His searching and calculating activities turn up nothing. What he did find was **one upright man among a thousand, but not one upright woman among them all**. This verse eludes meaning. Overall the passage is about wisdom and folly, not women, so it is difficult to understand precisely how it fits in the flow of thought. Technically speaking, in his wisdom search, Qoheleth found only one thousandth of a percent of men righteous, almost immeasurable. He discovered no women. Looking at the text in the larger context, Qoheleth's observation reflects on all of humanity, not primarily women. It calls to mind his earlier statement that "there is not a righteous man on earth who does what is right and never sins" (v. 20). Basically Qoheleth found no one, neither male nor female, who is righteous. The distinction between the male and female is so minuscule that, except for the trained observer, it remains undetected to the naked eye. Still he does make a distinction. Commentators offer a variety of explanations.[15]

Out of all his investigations he concludes one thing: **God made mankind upright, but men have gone in search of many schemes**. God made humans "right" or "straight" (יָשָׁר, *yāšār*). He gave humans

---

[14]The description here of Qoheleth may indicate his occupation as one who assembles and inventories wisdom material.

[15]Fox maintains that Qoheleth's remark is clearly misogynistic, "Qoheleth is not defending the honor of women. Qoheleth is crabby" (*A Time*, p. 266). Seow claims that verse 28b does not fit into the thought of the passage and therefore concludes that it is a "marginal gloss" (*Ecclesiastes*, p. 274). A few commentators believe that 28b is a quote, a proverb that Qoheleth refutes in his conclusion in verse 29.

balance and order in life, but humans have devised many scheming things.[16] While God has made things straight, humans have sought out many schemes and calculations. Their investigation is misdirected. The irony in Ecclesiastes is that humans cannot straighten what God has twisted (1:15; 7:13); yet they twist what God has straightened out. With this conclusion, Qoheleth places the blame for the human predicament upon men and women, not God. Within a universe controlled by a sovereign God and in which God has made everything appropriate for its time (3:1-15), humans still take responsibility for their lives. Their searching is out of sync with God's work in the world.

C. GOOD IN THE PRESENCE OF POWER AND INJUSTICE (8:1-17)

Chapter 8 continues the development of the idea stated in 6:11-12, "who knows?" The question is asked three times in this chapter (vv. 1,7,17).

8:1Who is like the wise man?
Who knows the explanation of things?
Wisdom brightens a man's face
and changes its hard appearance.

2Obey the king's command, I say, because you took an oath before God. 3Do not be in a hurry to leave the king's presence. Do not stand up for a bad cause, for he will do whatever he pleases. 4Since a king's word is supreme, who can say to him, "What are you doing?"

5Whoever obeys his command will come to no harm,
and the wise heart will know the proper time and procedure.
6For there is a proper time and procedure for every matter,
though a man's misery weighs heavily upon him.
7Since no man knows the future,
who can tell him what is to come?

---

[16]This is the third time the writer uses the word חִשָּׁבוֹן (ḥiššābôn, see vv. 25,27). Here the word carries the meaning of inventions of the human mind (BDB, p. 364).

[8]No man has power over the wind to contain it[a];
    so no one has power over the day of his death.
As no one is discharged in time of war,
    so wickedness will not release those who practice it.

[9]All this I saw, as I applied my mind to everything done under the sun. There is a time when a man lords it over others to his own[b] hurt.

[a]8 Or *over his spirit to retain it*   [b]9 Or *to their*

The issue of power is the subject of the first nine verses. How does the wise person conduct himself in the presence of the absolute power of the king (vv. 2-6)? How do commoners use the power they possess (vv. 7-9)? Though the skills of the wise can equip one to maneuver the perilous waters of power, they do not guarantee certainty. No one knows or controls the outcome for certain.

8:1 Verse 1 contains two rhetorical questions. The first **who is like the wise man?** expects a response, "No one," even though it could be that those who follow the advice in the succeeding verses are the ones who will be like the wise. At any rate, the question demonstrates an exalted view of the sage. The very next question brings that exalted view into check, as so often happens in Ecclesiastes. **Who knows the explanation of things?** This question expects a similar response: "no one." Even the wisest of the wise cannot explain or understand everything.[17] The acknowledgment is similar to the confession Agur made in Proverbs 30:2-3.

Having said that, the writer goes on to reveal the kind of advice that wisdom can offer. **Wisdom brightens a man's face and changes its hard appearance** (v. 1b). Though earlier, Qoheleth claimed that with much wisdom came much sorrow (1:18), here he claims that on certain occasions it brightens or brings "light" to the face. How wisdom changes the face is not specified. The observation comes, however, in the context on advice about the king. In the presence of a king, a cheerful countenance can make a good first impression.

8:2-4 In verses 2-6 the sage imparts advice on how to deal wisely with the absolute power of the king. As elsewhere in the Old

---

[17]The word for "explanation" (פֵּשֶׁר, *pēšer*) occurs only here in the Old Testament. The term *pesher* later came to refer to the commentaries the Qumran community wrote to explain their Scriptures.

363

Testament, the language used here to describe the king's power is similar to the language used to describe the power of the LORD. Qoheleth does not question what the king does. His concern is exclusively with one's response to it. The reason that one must **obey the king's command** is because of one's responsibility to God. **You took an oath before God.** As God's representative, the king must be obeyed. One way obedience is demonstrated is by complying immediately with the king's wishes. So **do not be in a hurry to leave the king's presence** (v. 3). In addition, **do not stand up for a bad cause.**[18] In other words, do not go against the king's wishes. The mark of prudence in the presence of absolute power (**for he will do whatever he pleases**) is submissiveness. The **king's word is supreme** (v. 4).[19] Therefore, for anyone to have the audacity to say to the king, **"What are you doing?"** demonstrates the epitome of folly.[20]

8:5-7 Verse 5 reaffirms what the sage has already advised in responding wisely to the king. **Whoever obeys his command will come to no harm.**[21] The language once again reflects the close link between the authority of the king and divine authority. To obey the king is closely tied to honoring God. The sage calls for the community of faith to submit to those in authority.

The reason the wise have the ability to obey the king's commands is that they see the bigger picture; **the wise heart will know the proper time and procedure** (מִשְׁפָּט, *mišpāṭ*). Knowing that God has properly ordered the world gives the sage the patience to accept matters as they are. **For there is a proper time and procedure for every matter, though a man's misery weighs heavily upon him**

---

[18]The phrase "bad cause" literally reads "evil thing," and in this context seems to carry the idea of some kind of rebellion against the king. The NRSV understands the phrase to refer to that which is miserable or unpleasant and thus renders the verse: "Do not delay when the matter is unpleasant."

[19]The word for "supreme" (שִׁלְטוֹן, *šilṭôn*) is used three times in this chapter, here in this verse and in verses 8 and 9 where it refers to the power of the common person.

[20]The question recalls the image of the potter and the clay in Isaiah 45:9: "Woe to him who quarrels with his Maker, to him who is but a potsherd among the potsherds on the ground. Does the clay say to the potter, 'What are you making?' Does your work say, 'He has no hands'?"

[21]"Will come to no harm" translates the Hebrew text "will not know an evil cause." דְּבַר רָע (*dābār rāʿ*) is the same phrase used in verse 3 that the NIV translates "bad cause." Is this another reference to rebellion?

(v. 6). This verse harks back to 3:1 where similar language is used (namely, "time" and "matter"). The human misery[22] involves, as it does in Ecclesiastes, the inability to know God's timing and understand his ways. This is confirmed by the following verse (v. 7): **Since no man knows the future, who can tell him what is to come?** The wise have a feel for the proper sense of timing. In the mundane affairs of life, the sages can deal with the proper timing of things. When it comes to the universal scheme of things, it is a different matter. They know that God gives order and sequence to events in the world. But they do not know how it all fits together. Traditional wisdom acknowledged its own limits and the inability of the wise to know the future (Prov 27:1). Being trained in the theology and rhetoric of traditional wisdom, Qoheleth reveals his camaraderie with it, as he does all through the book. Qoheleth does not set himself against traditional wisdom. Rather his quarrel is with the dissonance he experiences between what he observes and what he believes. And it frustrates him!

8:8-9 At this point in his train of thought, the sage switches gears slightly and moves from speaking of the power of the king to the power of the common man and woman. There are certain things over which humans have no power (v. 8). At the same time, humans do have the power to hurt themselves and others (v. 9).

Verse 8 contains several examples of things over which humans exercise no control. For one, **no man has power over the wind to contain it**. In Hebrew the phrase reads, "There is no man who has power over the wind/spirit (רוּחַ, *rûaḥ*) to restrain the wind/spirit (*rûaḥ*)."[23] Alongside that the sage adds, **No one has power over the day of his death**. In the context of speaking of death in the second line, wind/spirit (*rûaḥ*) may refer to one's life-spirit, that is, that which God breathed into humans at birth (cf. 12:7). No person has the power to control either the ability to give life (i.e., the day of birth) or the day of his or her own death (3:2).

---

[22]The phrase "a man's misery (רָעַת הָאָדָם, *rā'ath hā'ādām*) weighs heavily upon him" is similar to earlier phrases used: "heavy burden" (1:13), "miserable business" (4:8), "grievous evil" (5:13,16).

[23]The phrase "restrain the wind" is quite similar to Qoheleth's repeated refrain in the first half of the book, "chasing the wind." If this is the association, then *rûaḥ* is to be interpreted as "wind" rather than "spirit."

The sage gives two other examples of that which is beyond human power. A soldier cannot be released from battle once he is engaged in fighting. No one can escape the consequences of **war** (v. 8c). Neither does **wickedness** save **those who practice it**. Wickedness does not share an escape route with its proprietor (v. 8d). In sum, Qoheleth gives concrete examples of the limits of human power. They exercise no control over the life-spirit, death, battle, or the results of wickedness.

Humans can use power to hurt (v. 9b). **There is a time when a man lords**[24] **it over others to his own hurt**. Humans may not have power over life and death, but they do have power to hurt. The question is who is the one hurt? The text leaves it intentionally ambiguous, **there is a time when a man lords it over others** "to harm him." People do have the power to hurt others, as well as themselves.

¹⁰**Then too, I saw the wicked buried—those who used to come and go from the holy place and receive praise**ᵃ **in the city where they did this. This too is meaningless.**

¹¹**When the sentence for a crime is not quickly carried out, the hearts of the people are filled with schemes to do wrong.** ¹²**Although a wicked man commits a hundred crimes and still lives a long time, I know that it will go better with God-fearing men, who are reverent before God.** ¹³**Yet because the wicked do not fear God, it will not go well with them, and their days will not lengthen like a shadow.**

¹⁴**There is something else meaningless that occurs on earth: righteous men who get what the wicked deserve, and wicked men who get what the righteous deserve. This too, I say, is meaningless.** ¹⁵**So I commend the enjoyment of life, because nothing is better for a man under the sun than to eat and drink and be glad. Then joy will accompany him in his work all the days of the life God has given him under the sun.**

¹⁶**When I applied my mind to know wisdom and to observe man's labor on earth—his eyes not seeing sleep day or night—** ¹⁷**then I saw all that God has done. No one can comprehend what goes on under the sun. Despite all his efforts to search it out, man**

---

[24]Once again as in verses 4 and 8, the word from the root שָׁלַט (*šālāṭ*, "power") is used.

cannot discover its meaning. Even if a wise man claims he knows, he cannot really comprehend it.

^a*10* **Some Hebrew manuscripts and Septuagint (Aquila); most Hebrew manuscripts** *and are forgotten*

These verses reveal an absurdity that the sage witnessed in his life. The absurdity relates to the reversal in the way in which the righteous and the wicked are treated. The wicked are living long, respected lives. It is absurd because it goes against his fundamental belief about how life is to operate.

8:10 What the sage saw in verse 10 introduces the absurdity: **I saw the wicked buried—those who used to come and go from the holy place and receive praise in the city where they did this**. Though there is ambiguity in the text,[25] the basic picture is that the wicked are not punished for their wickedness. They get a decent burial because they were respected in the community. The sage pictures a community that can no longer discern good from evil. It lives in moral turmoil. His conclusion is **this too is meaningless**. The *hebel* judgment on this occasion means absurdity.

8:11 The result of the wicked not being punished is that it serves as a bad example for the whole community. People are tempted to do wrong because it looks like there is a payoff for doing it (cf. 7:15): **When the sentence for a crime is not quickly carried out, the hearts of the people are filled with schemes to do wrong**.

8:12-13 Then the sage pauses and professes his fundamental belief. Some commentators believe that verses 12 and 13 are later additions intended to tone down the harshness of the text that precedes and follows. This does not have to be the case at all. Qoheleth is steeped in sapiential wisdom. He does not set himself against traditional wisdom. He lives within the tradition and accepts it, yet he

---

[25]The NIV interprets the entire verse to refer to the way the wicked are treated. Some commentators see a contrast between the wicked in the first half and the righteous in the second half. Murphy translates the verse: "Then I saw the wicked buried. They used to come and go from the holy place! But those were forgotten in the city who had acted justly" (*Ecclesiastes*, p. 79). There is dispute among commentators whether the word should be rendered "praise" or "forgotten." The Hebrew text reads "forgotten" (שָׁכַח, *šākaḥ*), but many ancient versions, including the LXX, read "praise." The NIV gives a plausible translation and one that makes a minimal alteration to the text.

cannot see how it squares with reality. He questions his own beliefs! In verses 12-13 the sage lays his theological cards on the table: **Although a wicked man commits a hundred crimes and still lives a long time, I know that it will go better with God-fearing men, who are reverent before God**. Regardless of the heinousness of the wicked, Qoheleth knows "that those who fear God will be better because they fear him."

Verses 12-13 use two better-than forms to communicate the fundamental belief. On the one hand, the sage affirms that it will go better with God-fearing men. On the other hand, **because the wicked do not fear God it will not go well** ("better") **with them** (v. 13). Reverence toward God remains a bedrock principle (3:14; 5:7; 7:18).

8:14 Just as quickly as he affirms his sapiential convictions, he falls back into relating what he has witnessed in the world. He just cannot get away from the dissonance between what he believes and what he sees: **There is something else meaningless that occurs on earth: righteous men who get what the wicked deserve, and wicked men who get what the righteous deserve**. He reverts to his struggle with the disparity between the righteous and the wicked. Once again he concludes that it is absurd.

8:15 In the midst of his struggle between what he believes and what he witnesses, he finds solid ground. Qoheleth not only exhorts reverence in the face of the inequities of life, he also counsels **enjoyment of life**. Verse 15 falls in line with the previous commendations to enjoy life (2:24-26; 3:12-13; 3:22; 5:17-20). It contains the same language of **eat**ing and **drink**ing and enjoying **work**. The enjoyment is not hedonistic. This enjoyment has firm theological roots: **God** gives it. This enjoyment is neither like the pleasure the king sought in chapter 2, which was for pleasure's sake, nor does this enjoyment ignore life's dark side. Instead, it reflects seriously about the reality of death and the incongruities of life. Out of this sober reflection, one is given the ability to enjoy the little things life offers along the way. No profit comes from this perspective on life, only satisfaction in the moment.

8:16-17 Verses 16 and 17 conclude where the chapter began. The upshot is that, regardless of the amount of effort put into "finding"[26]

---

[26]The word is used three times in verse 17, respectively translated "comprehend," "discover," "comprehend."

or understanding what God has done, no one, not even the wisest of the wise, can fathom his work. Even when one's **eyes** do not see **sleep day or night**, the results are the same. **No one can comprehend what goes on under the sun**. This brings the reader back to the verses that begin the second half of the book where Qoheleth claimed, "For who knows what is good for a man in life, during the few and meaningless days he passes through like a shadow? Who can tell him what will happen under the sun after he is gone" (6:12)?

VIII. THE COMMON DESTINY (9:1-12)

Verses 1-6 speak of the fate that awaits all humanity, religious and nonreligious alike, and that is death. In the face of the certainty of death, Qoheleth issues the most extended, as well as the strongest exhortation to enjoy life. (vv. 7-10). Then he reverts to his treatise on death, this time with a different dimension. Death is not only certain for all mortals, it is also unpredictable (vv. 11-12). The contrast is between the sovereignty of an inscrutable God and the vulnerability of mortals.

[9:1]**So I reflected on all this and concluded that the righteous and the wise and what they do are in God's hands, but no man knows whether love or hate awaits him. [2]All share a common destiny—the righteous and the wicked, the good and the bad,[a] the clean and the unclean, those who offer sacrifices and those who do not.**

As it is with the good man,
    so with the sinner;
as it is with those who take oaths,
    so with those who are afraid to take them.

[3]**This is the evil in everything that happens under the sun: The same destiny overtakes all. The hearts of men, moreover, are full of evil and there is madness in their hearts while they live, and afterward they join the dead. [4]Anyone who is among the living has hope[b]—even a live dog is better off than a dead lion!**
[5]**For the living know that they will die,**
    but the dead know nothing;
they have no further reward,
    and even the memory of them is forgotten.

⁶**Their love, their hate**
    and their jealousy have long since vanished;
never again will they have a part
    in anything that happens under the sun.

ᵃ2 Septuagint (Aquila), Vulgate and Syriac; Hebrew does not have *and the bad*   ᵇ4 Or *What then is to be chosen? With all who live, there is hope*

9:1 A new unit begins as Qoheleth once again reminds the reader of the seriousness of his investigation, **so I reflected on all this** (more literal, "I devoted my mind to making it all clear"). The phrase **but no man knows whether love or hate awaits him** is uncertain in regard to whom the love and the hate belong. The sage sometimes uses the polar opposites of love and hate as a way of expressing in general terms favor or disfavor (3:8). Is it God's or humans'? If it refers to humans, then love and hate are inclusive of human action, and the result of their action is perplexing. It remains **in God's hands**. If it refers to God, then it represents God's favor or disfavor toward mortals. In other words, because God's ways are inscrutable no one can know whether the future will be favorable or unfavorable toward humans. Regardless of whose love or hate it is, these attitudes are in God's hands. He determines the outcome.

9:2-3 Qoheleth carries it further. **All share a common destiny**, literally "one fate" (מִקְרֶה, *miqreh*; v. 2). The fate referred to here is death. This fate does not have anything to do with chance or luck. Qoheleth mentioned this fate earlier in 2:14-15; 3:9. There he spoke of the same fate coming to the wise and the foolish, to humans as well as animals. That fate was death. To emphasize that no one escapes this destiny, Qoheleth lists a series of six opposing pairs. Within the list, references to liturgical practices are mentioned: **clean** and **unclean**, **those who offer sacrifices** and not offering sacrifices. Ethical qualities are also highlighted: **righteous** and **wicked**, the **good man** and **the sinner**. Regardless of one's moral character or the degree of religious devotion, a common destiny awaits all. One's preference in lifestyle does not make him or her immune from death. **This is the evil in everything that happens under the sun: The same destiny overtakes all** (v. 3). The evil referred to is death. "Evil" is not used here in the sense of that which is morally corrupt but in the sense of tragedy or calamity. The ubiquitous nature of death leads humans to **evil** (misery) and

madness (v. 3b).[27] The reference then to **the hearts of men** being **full of evil** is not a reference to original sin. It lies closer to the temptation of humans to live a life of folly in the face of the imminence of death.

9:4 Verses 4-6 continue the focus on death. The NIV includes a footnote with the first part of verse 4. Considering both the Hebrew text and the context of these verses, the footnote is the better reading. The footnote reads, "What then is to be chosen? With all who live, there is hope." This is the closer reading of the Hebrew text.[28] That is, what person is exempt from death? The answer is no one, which is the point he has been hammering home all along. What kinds of hope do the living have? The irony is that the living have hope or certainty about death![29] This is not as bizarre as it may initially appear. What Qoheleth appears to mean is that certainty of death drives people to live in the present.

This is where the sage interjects his familiar proverb, **Even a live dog is better off than a dead lion!** The better-than saying contrasts two creatures to illustrate the extreme in reputations. On the one hand, a dog in Hebrew culture was despised (1 Sam 17:43; Prov 26:11). The dog represents a contemptible reputation. On the other hand, the lion stood for that which is noble, an honorable reputation. Aligning these two animals with life and death respectively sets up a tension: a living contemptible dog and a dead noble lion. With the proverb, Qoheleth highlights his point that life is a mixed bag. Life in the face of death is contemptible. It is still better to be alive than dead, even though one may have an esteemed reputation. Where Proverbs claims that the fear of the LORD is the beginning of wisdom, Qoheleth claims that the awareness of death's certainty is the beginning of wisdom.[30]

9:5-6 Qoheleth lays out the advantages of the living over the dead in verse 5. The dead have no hope, they possess no knowledge, they no longer have a **reward**, and their **memory is forgotten**. In the

---

[27]"Madness" (הֹלֵלוֹת, *hôlēlôth*) is another synonym for "folly."

[28]The *Qere* (the Masorite marginal notes) reads "whoever is associated with."

[29]The hope may also relate to the "portion" of enjoyment that God gives humans while they are living (vv. 7-10).

[30]Brown, *Ecclesiastes*, p. 93.

next verse, Qoheleth specifies what it is that has been forgotten: **their love, their hate and their jealousy**. The memory that the living have of the deceased's experience with love and hate and jealousy is short-lived.[31] The joys and the sorrows, the fortunes and misfortunes of the dead are soon forgotten.

[7]Go, eat your food with gladness, and drink your wine with a joyful heart, for it is now that God favors what you do. [8]Always be clothed in white, and always anoint your head with oil. [9]Enjoy life with your wife, whom you love, all the days of this meaningless life that God has given you under the sun— all your meaningless days. For this is your lot in life and in your toilsome labor under the sun. [10]Whatever your hand finds to do, do it with all your might, for in the grave,[a] where you are going, there is neither working nor planning nor knowledge nor wisdom.

[11]I have seen something else under the sun:

The race is not to the swift
> **or the battle to the strong,**
nor does food come to the wise
> **or wealth to the brilliant**
> **or favor to the learned;**
but time and chance happen to them all.

[12]Moreover, no man knows when his hour will come:

As fish are caught in a cruel net,
> **or birds are taken in a snare,**
so men are trapped by evil times
> **that fall unexpectedly upon them.**

[a]*10* Hebrew *Sheol*

9:7-9 In verses 1-6, Qoheleth firmly established that death is no respecter of persons. The destiny of all is the same. In light of that fact of life, Qoheleth turns to admonish the living about what they are to do. He admonishes them to enjoy life (vv. 7-10). This passage is quite similar to the earlier passages that reflect on this (2:24-26; 3:12-13; 3:22; 5:18-20; 8:15), except this time there is a difference in

---

[31]Some take this to refer to the feelings the living have for the deceased. The living no longer have feelings of love or hate or jealousy for the ones who have died.

intensity. This is the longest of the enjoyment passages. In addition, Qoheleth does not simply make an observation about enjoying life, he issues a series of imperatives: **go**, **eat**, **drink**, **be clothed in white**, **enjoy life with your wife**. He has just stepped up the passion of his admonition. Here is the appropriate response to the certitude of death: enjoy the present moments of life.

What does the sage mean when he announces **for it is now that God favors**[32] **what you do** ("God already favors what you do," v. 7)? This is not a divine sanction levied on whatever whim humans decide to act upon. The idea is that within the gifts that God has already bestowed on humans, God already favors what you do. These verses affirm that God does not simply *allow* humans to experience enjoyment, he *desires* them to experience it.

The image in verse 8 of being **clothed in white** portrays a festive atmosphere. **Anoint**ing the **head with oil** is an image also used in the Old Testament to refer to feasting and celebration (Ps 23:5; 133:2). Verse 8 simply extends the portrait of the previous verse: enjoy the simple pleasures of life. Earlier in 7:2,4, Qoheleth maintained that it was better to go to the house of mourning than to the house of feasting and enjoyment. The admonition here does not contradict that piece of advice. Qoheleth's earlier point was that, out of serious reflection on sorrow and death, one learns to truly enjoy life.

To the previous imperatives, Qoheleth adds another command, **Enjoy life with your wife** (v. 9; lit., "see life with a wife which you love"). This admonition closely parallels Proverbs 5:18-19. Enjoy your spouse **all the days of this meaningless life**. Here the *hebel* judgment means brief, or the "fleeting days of your life." (The TANAKH translates the verse "enjoy happiness with a woman you love all the fleeting days of life that have been granted to you under the sun—all your fleeting days."[33])

9:10 The final admonition appears in verse 10. Qoheleth exhorts the reader, **whatever your hand finds to do, do it with all your might**. This is not an exhortation simply to flail around with your

---

[32]Note, in contrast, Amos 5:22 where God did not favor Israel's sacrifice. The term "favor" or "delight" (רָצָה, *rāṣāh*) is the word frequently used in Proverbs in contrast to what the LORD detests or abhors (11:1,20; 12:22; 15:8).

[33]See comments on *hebel* in 7:15-18.

hands, and whatever they grasp, work hard at it. Rather whatever fits
your hand, that is, what you have the ability to do, put every ounce
of effort you have into seeing the task to completion. The reason is
that death is coming, and when it arrives, there is nothing left to do.
Qoheleth lists the activities of **working, planning,**[34] **knowledge,** and
wisdom. These cannot be done **in the grave** (i.e., Sheol). These activities further define what the sage means by enjoyment. Planning,
knowledge, and wisdom are all intellectual activities that humans are
to engage in and enjoy.

9:11-12 This series of imperatives that admonish one to enjoy life
are bracketed between Qoheleth's reflections on the sobering reality that no one escapes death. When one looks death squarely in the
face, one better understands life and the call to enjoy it. With verses 11-12, Qoheleth once again takes up the thought of death.

The words, **I have seen something else under the sun** (lit., "I
turned and saw") frequently mark a transition in thought for
Qoheleth. Once again the sage reflects on the fate that every mortal
faces. This time, however, he wrestles with the reality that this fate
often comes quite unexpectedly. He begins by stating that no one
can predict the outcome of events. What should be the expected
consequences often are not.

Qoheleth gives five examples of the unexpected: **The race is not to
the swift or the battle to the strong, nor does food come to the wise
or wealth to the brilliant or favor to the learned**. The list contains two
general categories: that which relates to the physical world (running
and fighting) and that which pertains to the mental (wisdom and learning). In spite of their talents and preparation, neither the swift nor the
strong always win. In spite of their mental abilities and training, the
wise do not always succeed. The last three terms are synonyms ("wise,"
"brilliant,"[35] "learned"), all pertaining to the activity of the sage.
Sometimes events in life occur randomly. Therefore, one cannot
always predict the outcome. The implication, as Qoheleth has stated
before (e.g., 4:13-16), is that the wise do not always have the necessities
of life (namely, food) nor are they always identified by the possession
of wealth. Other factors beyond human control come into play.

---

[34]The same word (חֶשְׁבּוֹן, ḥešbôn) used in 7:25,27,29 is translated "schemes."
[35]The term for "brilliant" is the same used in Proverbs to identify "the
understanding one" (Prov 1:5; 10:13; 14:6,33; 15:14, etc.).

The reason humans cannot control the outcome is that **time and chance**[36] **happen to them all**. In this phrase, the two words "time" and "chance" are nouns expressing the same idea. Qoheleth is not expressing a belief in luck or a *Que será será* philosophy of life. In Qoheleth's theology, God controls time and chance (recall 3:1-15). The problem is that humans neither know God's time nor understand the bigger picture of God's purpose in the world, so things do not necessarily come out the way humans expect them to.

The text moves from the random misfortunes that humans experience to the fate of all: death. **Moreover, no man knows when his hour will come** (v. 12). No person knows his or her "time" (עֵת, *'ēth*). This verse recalls the thought of the poem in 3:1-8, only here the specific focus of the "time" is death. Qoheleth follows this affirmation with two examples from the natural world of the unexpected nature of death. A fisherman's **net** cast into the water does not distinguish between the type or age or value of the **fish**. All that the net catches, it kills. Death comes suddenly and without warning. The same is true with a bird **taken in a snare**. The snare does not respect the species of bird. It catches all by surprise. Humans experience the same phenomenon: **men are trapped by evil times that fall unexpectedly upon them**. The purpose of the observation is to exhort the reader to enjoy the life that God gives in the present moment (9:7-10).

IX. THE LIMITATIONS AND VALUES OF WISDOM (9:13–11:6)

A. THE POOR WISE MAN AND THE VALUE OF WISDOM (9:13–10:4)

[13]**I also saw under the sun this example of wisdom that greatly impressed me:** [14]**There was once a small city with only a few people in it. And a powerful king came against it, surrounded it and built huge siegeworks against it.** [15]**Now there lived in that city a**

---

[36]The word for "chance" (פֶּגַע, *pega'*) is different from the word used earlier for "fate" (מִקְרֶה, *miqreh*). But the word "happen" that follows in this text is from the same root word for "fate" (קָרָה, *qārāh*). The word "chance" can carry the negative connotation here of "misfortune" or "disaster" and may be synonymous with "evil times" in verse 12.

man poor but wise, and he saved the city by his wisdom. But nobody remembered that poor man. ¹⁶So I said, "Wisdom is better than strength." But the poor man's wisdom is despised, and his words are no longer heeded.

9:13-16 These verses contain an example story. It is like a parable in that it is a story that could have actually happened but did not necessarily occur. The story contrasts a **powerful king** with a **poor wise man**. The contrast is highlighted by the repeated use of the word "great." The story **greatly impressed** the sage (v. 13). The "powerful" ("great") king laid **huge** ("great") **siegeworks** against the city. The great king came up against a **small city** that had just **a few people in it**. The great king discovered that in that little city lived **a man poor but wise**. Once again wisdom is associated with poverty. The poor wise man **saved the city by his wisdom**. Qoheleth does not detail how the wise man saved the city. Given the nature of wisdom and the ability of the sages to use words, it seems likely that he used some kind of diplomacy to persuade the great king to cease from destroying this little town (see Prov 25:15).

One question commentaries raise with this story is whether the wise man actually saved the town. The text supports the argument that the wise man did save the city: "and he saved the city by his wisdom" (v. 15). However, some interpret the phrase to mean "and he could have saved the city" because the following statement reads, **but nobody remembered that poor man** (v. 15). In other words, the city was destroyed because the town's people did not remember the potential resources available to them. However, the term "remembered" works better with an actual past event than with a potential event. Ultimately, the question of whether the sage actually saved the town is a moot point because the story is a parable.

The point is that wisdom is stronger than brute force. Yet wisdom does not necessarily result in one getting ahead in this life. To paraphrase the thought of verse 11, the wise do not always receive favor or honor. In times of desperation, the wisdom of a commoner is sought. After the crisis has passed, the commoner is soon ignored or forgotten. **The poor man's wisdom is despised, and his words are no longer heeded** (v. 16b).[37]

---

[37]Seow, *Ecclesiastes*, pp. 306, 322.

Verse 16b does not appear to restate what happened in verses 13-15. Rather it describes the response of the delivered city: ingratitude. **Wisdom** may be **better than strength**, but in the human community wisdom is also despised. The community fails to appreciate the commoner's wisdom, only Qoheleth remembers it. Qoheleth's conclusion is that wisdom remains a reliable tool in the face of the uncertainties and misfortunes of life. Do not give up on wisdom.

¹⁷**The quiet words of the wise are more to be heeded**
    than the shouts of a ruler of fools.
¹⁸**Wisdom is better than weapons of war,**
    but one sinner destroys much good.

9:17-18 Following the example story, two proverbs affirm the principle taught. **The quiet words of the wise are more to be heeded than the shouts of a ruler of fools** (v. 17). Verse 17 contrasts starkly with verse 16. There is a contrast between "words no longer heeded" and "words" that are "to be heeded." The community does not honor the wise man's words. The proverb rebukes those who do not listen or obey the quiet words of the wise. Quiet words of the wise have more influence than the shouts of a ruler of fools. The emphasis is on the way words are spoken, either with restraint or with a lack of restraint. The principle in verse 17 is related to the thought in Proverbs 25:15: "Through patience a ruler can be persuaded, and a gentle tongue can break a bone."

Qoheleth in verse 18 restates the point made in verse 16: **Wisdom is better than weapons of war**. The benefits wisdom offers can be easily wiped out: **but one sinner destroys much good**. The term for "sinner" here should not be understood to involve a moral judgment. Rather in the context of speaking of wisdom, the term carries the idea of incompetence and is better associated with the character of the fool (see 10:1). One fool, or for that matter one foolish act, can negate all the good that the wise do.

^{10:1}**As dead flies give perfume a bad smell,**
    so a little folly outweighs wisdom and honor.
²**The heart of the wise inclines to the right,**
    but the heart of the fool to the left.
³**Even as he walks along the road,**
    the fool lacks sense
    and shows everyone how stupid he is.

⁴If a ruler's anger rises against you,
   do not leave your post;
   calmness can lay great errors to rest.

10:1 Chapter 10:1 drives the point home. **As dead flies give perfume a bad smell, so a little folly outweighs wisdom and honor.** Costly goods such as perfume are quite susceptible to contamination. One little insect can taint the whole bottle. We might say, "One bad apple spoils the whole barrel." Similarly, as influential as wisdom is, it remains vulnerable to the forces of folly. Earlier Qoheleth claimed that "a good name is better than fine perfume" (7:1). While that remains true, 10:1 maintains that the reputation of the wise can easily be destroyed by one careless act of folly (Prov 25:26 says something similar about the righteous). Wisdom's vulnerability may be related to the nature of humanity that seeks to acquire it. By nature, humans tend to follow folly's path of least resistance. This makes wisdom, and all that is good, easily exposed to attack.

10:2-3 If fools contaminate the benefits of wisdom, they also hurt themselves (vv. 2-3). To speak of the wise **heart** inclining **to the right** and the foolish **heart to the left** is a metaphor contrasting the lifestyle of the wise and the foolish (v. 2; cf. "light" and "dark" in 2:13). "The right" represents strength, power, and justice. "The left" represents perversion, incompetence, and weakness. Wisdom and folly are poles apart. A **fool** is easily distinguished from a **wise** person, even in the mundane activity of walking (v. 3). In 9:16–10:3, Qoheleth expresses his continuous struggle with the value of wisdom, a kind of love/hate relationship (2:12-17). Yet in spite of its limitations and the lack of respect wisdom receives, Qoheleth never advises the reader to pursue folly.

10:4 Verse 4 echoes the advice the Teacher gave earlier in 8:2-4 regarding the king, only here it is an official of lesser status, perhaps a local government official (**ruler**) that is involved. **When a ruler's anger**[38] **rises against you, do not leave your post.** The courtier is admonished to keep his composure in such a volatile situation. Instead of reacting in kind to the emotion, one must do the opposite and practice restraint. **Calmness can lay great errors to rest.**

---

[38]The word "wind/spirit" (רוּחַ, *rûaḥ*) is used here to describe anger. On occasion this word refers to a person's temper (cf. Prov 16:32).

What the NIV translates as "calmness" is the word for "healing" (Prov 14:30; 15:4). Here the word carries the idea of that which soothes, which is all that medications of that day could do anyway. In the presence of an irate official, the sage soothes or calms troubled waters. He must not flee from the situation but must directly confront the anger with a controlled response that defuses the tense situation. The advice given in verse 4 may serve as an illustration of the proverb in 9:17. There the "quiet words of the wise" are contrasted with the ranting and railing of a "ruler."[39] The calm words of the wise have more influence than the tirades of a person in a position of power (Prov 16:14; 25:15).

B. PROVERBIAL ADVICE REGARDING
THE VALUE OF WISDOM (10:5-15)

In chapter 10, Qoheleth resorts to proverbial material to communicate his message. Certain thematic and verbal connections exist between the proverbs collected here, but it remains a loose connection. Chapter 10, along with chapter 7, may be an example of what the editor claims occupies much of Qoheleth's time. At the conclusion of Ecclesiastes, the editor says that the Teacher "searched out and set in order many proverbs" (12:9).

The proverbs in chapter 10 primarily profess a traditional wisdom mentality; certain types of actions produce certain consequences. Qoheleth does not set himself against traditional wisdom as it is sometimes thought. It appears that he accepted the wisdom he was taught. Rather, Qoheleth tries desperately to square what he believes with the discrepancies he sees in the world. Chapter 10 immerses the reader in the traditional world of wisdom as it is found in some of the collections of proverbs in the book of Proverbs. In spite of the continual quarrel he has with what he believes, he never gives up on traditional wisdom.

⁵**There is an evil I have seen under the sun,**
      the sort of error that arises from a ruler:
⁶**Fools are put in many high positions,**
      while the rich occupy the low ones.

---

[39]The same word is used for "ruler" (מוֹשֵׁל, *môšēl*).

⁷I have seen slaves on horseback,
    while princes go on foot like slaves.

10:5-7 These verses cluster around the inversion of the normal
social order of things. The Teacher begins with the frequent statement of observation, **There is an evil I have seen under the sun.**
What he observed was an **error that arises from a ruler.** The error
described stems not from an accident or oversight but from a
thoughtless mistake. Those in positions of power are by no means
immune to making major blunders in their decisions. The error
made in this instance was in putting the wrong people in positions
of authority, which basically turns the whole social order upside
down (cf. Prov 30:21-23).

Verses 6-7 give an example of this kind of mistake. **Fools** and
slaves are placed in positions of power. The word used for "fools"
(סֶכֶל, *sekel*) appears only here in the Old Testament and refers to the
half-wit (the one we might call a "moron").[40] Such individuals make
the decisions and run the political system. On the other hand, **the
rich** and **princes** are displaced. These verses picture a society in
chaos, displaying no sense of order. Qoheleth's point seems to be
that no one can guarantee that the present social order will remain
stable. It is quite possible to overthrow the current system. Life
remains unpredictable (v. 14b). In the end, wisdom does not always
win. The officials, and even the people, may reject wisdom's order.

⁸Whoever digs a pit may fall into it;
    whoever breaks through a wall may be bitten by a snake.
⁹Whoever quarries stones may be injured by them;
    whoever splits logs may be endangered by them.
¹⁰If the ax is dull
    and its edge unsharpened,
  more strength is needed
    but skill will bring success.
¹¹If a snake bites before it is charmed,
    there is no profit for the charmer.

10:8-11 Verses 8-9 describe the occupational hazards of daily life.
Verses 10-11 speak of the necessity of using wisdom in the activities

---

[40]Other forms of the noun are used in Ecclesiastes 2:13,19; 10:13-14.

one undertakes. Verses 8 and 9 give four examples of everyday activities: digging a pit, breaking down a rock wall, quarrying stones, and splitting logs. All of these activities involve the use of a metal instrument to accomplish the work. The verb tense used with all four of the activities indicates the existence of an ever-present danger. So **whoever digs a pit may fall into it**. This image occurs on several occasions in the Old Testament (Prov 26:27; Ps 7:15; 9:15; 35:7-8; 57:6). One always remains at risk of falling into a hole one has dug at an earlier point. The very nature of life carries with it uncertainties.

Whoever breaks through a wall may be bitten by a snake (v. 8b). The wall referred to here may be a stone fence built along a roadway. Or it may be a stone wall around a vineyard or orchard of some kind. Whichever it is, walls typically were made from uncut rocks that were stacked on top of each other without the use of mortar. Snakes found the crevices in such walls ideal places for nesting. When a landowner decided to remove the wall for whatever reason, he made himself vulnerable to a poisonous snake (see Amos 5:19). In the simple routines of living, accidents occur.

The ordinary tasks of quarrying **stone** or splitting **logs** also put one at risk. Digging stones, which were quite plentiful in that region, carried with it the potential for injury (1 Kgs 5:17). The one who **splits** logs is no less immune from danger. Occupational hazards remain a part of modern culture. Industrial accidents and farm accidents continue to happen with unnerving regularity. A moment's loss of concentration can undo much good (9:18). Practical wisdom is a necessary part of everyday living, even though wisdom cannot ensure safety.

No one remains exempt from the uncertainties of life. The commoner exposes himself daily to ever-present occupational hazards. Even the rich and powerful can unexpectedly lose their positions (vv. 6-7). The proverbs in verses 5-11 depict a whole series of reversals. The message once again is summed up in verse 14b: "No one knows what is coming—who can tell him what will happen after him?"

Show wisdom in whatever activities one undertakes. Wisdom can make the ordinary activities of life go smoother: **if the ax is dull and its edge unsharpened, more strength is needed but skill will bring success** (v. 10). In chopping wood, a worker must exert more energy and take more time if the ax blade is dull. If wisdom is appropriately employed,[41] however, one can easily increase the efficiency and productivity of one's work.

Verse 11 seems to create a contrast with verse 10. Both verses use the catchword "advantage" (יִתְרוֹן, *yithrôn*, **profit**), a keyword in Ecclesiastes. In verse 10, the NIV translates it "success." In verse 11, it is translated "profit." Wisdom can resolve some problems (v. 10), but not others because there is no profit (v. 11).[42] In the case of the snake **charmer**,[43] wisdom cannot undo the damage.

Overall, verses 8-11 speak of conventional wisdom with its belief in the act- or character-consequence scenario. Certain actions will produce certain consequences. Accidents happen, and sometimes humans bring those accidents on themselves. What the Teacher affirms is that humans must take responsibility for their own behavior. So while the Teacher holds firmly to an all-sovereign, inscrutable God who controls the whole order of life, he also holds to the belief in human freedom. Sibley Towner puts it this way: "God may have the whole world in the divine hands, but there is a sphere within that sphere in which human beings are fully responsible."[44]

[12]**Words from a wise man's mouth are gracious,**
  but a fool is consumed by his own lips.
[13]**At the beginning his words are folly;**
  at the end they are wicked madness—
[14] **and the fool multiplies words.**

 No one knows what is coming—
  who can tell him what will happen after him?
[15]**A fool's work wearies him;**
  he does not know the way to town.

10:12-15 In the larger context, this unit of proverbial material continues to deal with the value of wisdom. The proverbs focus primarily on the character of the fool, particularly the words he speaks. His speech is self-destructive (v. 12b), completely inane (v. 13), and verbose (v. 14a). The picture of the fool in verse 12b is that he **is**

---

[41]The phrase literally reads, "an advantage is to make wisdom suitable." The NIV appropriately translates the text.

[42]See Seow, *Ecclesiastes*, p. 326.

[43]Snake "charmer" is literally "master of the tongue."

[44]Sibley Towner, "Ecclesiastes," *New Interpreter's Bible* (Nashville: Abingdon, 1997), p. 350.

consumed by his own speech. He devours himself (recall 4:5 where the fool chews on his own knuckles). The **words from a wise man's mouth are gracious**. This verse seems to be close in thought to the proverbs in 9:18 and 10:4, where the calmness of the sage's speech stands against the harangue of the ruler.

From **beginning** to **end**, a fool's **words** are completely worthless (v. 13). They start out as **folly**, and they go down hill from there to **wicked madness**. The sentence at the end of verse 14 may refer to the fool, or it may be an overall conclusion Qoheleth makes regarding life. Or these two may be closely related. The many words the fool multiplies may be connected to the fool spouting off claims about knowing what is in store for the future. Qoheleth counters that **no one knows what is coming** (Prov 27:1).

The Teacher observes **that a fool's work wearies him** (v. 15). The work of the fool in this context may refer to his many words. He wears himself out from the redundancy of his words. The fool is totally disoriented when it comes to knowing about life: **he does not know the way to town**. The phrase may be some popular idiom used by the sages to describe a fool. How can such a person who stumbles around in his own backyard have anything to say about the future? For Qoheleth the fool serves as a foil against which to reflect on the real value of wisdom and the graciousness of wisdom's language.

C. PROVERBIAL ADVICE ABOUT ACTING WISELY IN THE KING'S PRESENCE (10:16-20)

[16]**Woe to you, O land whose king was a servant**[a]
    and whose princes feast in the morning.
[17]**Blessed are you, O land whose king is of noble birth**
    and whose princes eat at a proper time—
    for strength and not for drunkenness.
[18]**If a man is lazy, the rafters sag;**
    if his hands are idle, the house leaks.
[19]**A feast is made for laughter,**
    and wine makes life merry,
    but money is the answer for everything.
[20]**Do not revile the king even in your thoughts,**
    or curse the rich in your bedroom,

> **because a bird of the air may carry your words,**
> **and a bird on the wing may report what you say.**

^a*16* Or *king is a child*

10:16-17 These verses (16-20) consist of a series of loosely related sayings. Verses 16 and 17 speak about the **king** and stand in antithesis to one another. Using the form of a **woe**, verse 16 pronounces a judgment on incompetent rulers of the land. The king **was a servant** (lit., "child," see NIV footnote). To describe the king as a child is to proclaim the king unqualified to rule. He is too inexperienced and immature to provide leadership. The indication of this is seen in the next line, **and whose princes feast in the morning**. Drinking and feasting in the morning indicate irresponsibility and a king who exercises no control over his court. The "king" who "was a servant" recalls the upside-down world described in 10:6 where, "Fools are put in many high positions, while the rich occupy the low ones." In contrast to the unqualified king is the **king** who **is of noble birth** (v. 17). This king runs a disciplined court **whose princes eat at a proper time**. These princes have the discipline to know when it is appropriate to eat — an important quality of wisdom. They also display the **strength** or self-control not to get drunk. This is the advice king Lemuel received from his mother (Prov 31:4-5). Two contrasting styles of leadership are displayed in these two verses: one immature and self-indulgent, the other disciplined and sensitive to what is appropriate.

10:18 Verse 18 takes up a common theme in wisdom: laziness (see Prov 24:30-34; 26:13-16). The verse contrasts the "low" (מְמָךְ, *māmāk*, **sag**) **rafters** with the lazy person's hands "sinking" (שִׁפְלוּת, *šiphlôth*, "being **idle**"). The houses in Palestine had flat roofs. The walls were built of stone, and they used wooden beams as rafters for the roof. Without constant maintenance, the roofs were susceptible to leaking (see Prov 27:15). A lazy person could bring about the demise of his whole house.

10:19 The text of verse 19 can be interpreted either positively or negatively. When one thinks of the exhortations to enjoy life sprinkled in the book, this proverb could be interpreted positively to refer to such a lifestyle. Then, in order to feast and drink good wine, one must have money. So **money is the answer for everything**. The proverb could also serve as a criticism of those who do not control their desire for pleasure. All they do is **feast** and drink **wine**. The text may illustrate the point made in verse 16. If a negative bent is intended, then the word for "answer" is better translated "preoccupy."[45] Money becomes the preoccupation of these rulers.

It is difficult to know whether verses 18 and 19 are isolated proverbs or whether the writer intends to connect them with the previous sayings regarding the kings of the land. Seow argues for interpreting them in connection with the previous verses.[46] The indolent leader's royal house stands in disrepair because he and his court engage in merrymaking at all hours of the day. Therefore, the two proverbs serve as a criticism of those in power. The difficulty in knowing whether to interpret the proverbs independently or in context also plays a role in whether they will be interpreted positively or negatively. This is the nature of proverbs. Their multivalent quality enables them to be understood in different ways.

10:20 Verse 20 admonishes the reader, **do not revile the king even in your thoughts, or curse the rich in your bedroom**. This proverb seems to stand in stark contrast to verse 16 where an immature king is criticized. Not knowing the background out of which the proverb arose makes it next to impossible to reconcile the two. However, reconciliation is not necessarily the goal of interpreting proverbs (recall Prov 26:4-5). One can at least say that in some contexts Qoheleth criticizes the governing class. On other occasions, he admonishes individuals not even to think derogatory thoughts **because a bird of the air may carry your words**. Informants of the king could easily disclose your feelings to the king or to those in power. From this saying comes the English phrase, "A little bird told me."

D. WISDOM IN THE MIDST OF THE UNKNOWN (11:1-6)

[1]**Cast your bread upon the waters,**
    for after many days you will find it again.
[2]**Give portions to seven, yes to eight,**
    for you do not know what disaster may come upon the
        land.

---

[45]Seow, *Ecclesiastes*, pp. 332-333. Seow translates the phrase, "And money preoccupies everyone" (p. 328).
[46]Ibid., p. 340.

³**If clouds are full of water,**
> **they pour rain upon the earth.**
Whether a tree falls to the south or to the north,
> **in the place where it falls, there will it lie.**
⁴**Whoever watches the wind will not plant;**
> **whoever looks at the clouds will not reap.**
⁵**As you do not know the path of the wind,**
> **or how the body is formed^a in a mother's womb,**
so you cannot understand the work of God,
> **the Maker of all things.**
⁶**Sow your seed in the morning,**
> **and at evening let not your hands be idle,**
for you do not know which will succeed,
> **whether this or that,**
> **or whether both will do equally well.**

^a5 Or *know how life* (or *the spirit*) / *enters the body being formed*

11:1-2 Once again the passage consists of a series of proverbs strung together. However, in this text there appears to be a stronger connection between the individual sayings. It is important to take note of the repeated phrase **you do not know/understand** (four times). All through chapters 9 and 10, the writer emphasizes the theme of "not knowing." Overall the passage moves from the uncertainty of disasters to the uncertainty of the weather, from the mystery of life to the ultimate mystery of God's work.

The first two verses are usually understood as closely linked together, but their meaning is debated. Once again the existence of diverse meanings of proverbs is evident. Two dominant interpretations exist.

The long-standing interpretation of the verses understands them to refer to doing good deeds.[47] Verse 1 describes a spontaneous act of kindness done without thought of compensation. The image used is of a flat piece of hard bread that one releases or "sends" out on the surface of the water.[48] Releasing bread on the water symbolizes one who willingly takes risks in doing good to others. If reward

---

[47]Fox, *A Time*, p. 312. Seow, *Ecclesiastes*, pp. 342-344.

[48]The word the NIV translates "cast" (שָׁלַח, *šālaḥ*) does not mean to throw out or scatter but to "send," to "let go."

comes, it comes as a surprise. The phrase **you will find it again** does not necessarily envision someone who diligently seeks out a treasure but one who unexpectedly comes upon a gift. The admonition calls on readers to send forth spontaneous deeds of kindness without expecting something in return.[49] A proverb in Ankhsheshonqy 19:10 makes a similar point, "Do a good deed and throw it in the water; when it dries you will find it."[50]

The proverb in verse 2 affirms the principle but from a different angle. Whereas verse 1 claims that the giver may possibly find compensation for acts of benevolence, verse 2 claims that one must practice generosity even in the face of not knowing what the future holds. The proverb admonishes the reader to **give portions to seven, yes to eight**. The numerical sequence of seven and eight is a common figure of speech used in the Old Testament referring to that which is numerous or many (cf. Amos 1–2; Prov 30:15-30). In other words, the proverb exhorts individuals to share their possessions in as many different ways as possible. As Brown puts it, the reader is called on to diversify not financial investments but benevolent acts.[51] Spread your generosity abroad in spite of the fact that **you do not know what disaster may come upon the land**. Do not hold back from generosity because you anticipate misfortune or economic or political collapse. Take risks in practicing liberality.

More recently commentators have favored the interpretation that understands verses 1 and 2 to refer to some type of commercial trade.[52] The admonition calls on the investor to take calculated risks in investing in overseas trade (v. 1) and to diversify one's investments to decrease the likelihood of a disaster wiping out all of one's financial resources (v. 2). We would say today, "Don't put all your eggs in one basket." Reference is usually made to Proverbs 31:14, which pictures the capable woman as being "like the merchant ships, bringing her food from afar" (cf. also Isa 18:2). The *New English Bible*

---

[49]Seow, *Ecclesiastes*, p. 343.

[50]See James Crenshaw, *Education in Ancient Israel: Across the Deadening Silence* (New York: Doubleday, 1998), p. 79. Note also the saying in *Sirach*: "Lose your silver for the sake of a brother or a friend, and do not let it rust under a stone and be lost" (29:10).

[51]Brown, *Ecclesiastes*, p. 103.

[52]Crenshaw, *Ecclesiastes*, p. 178. Towner, "Ecclesiastes," p. 349. Murphy says that the text says nothing about "alms-giving" (*Ecclesiastes*, p. 106).

interprets the verses, "Send your grain across the seas, and in time you will get a return. Divide your merchandise among seven ventures, eight maybe, since you do not know what disasters may occur on earth."[53]

Of these two interpretations, the former, practicing deeds of kindness, carries more weight. The problem with viewing the verses as describing commercial investments is that, according to verse 1, no gain is made in this venture. One only finds, unexpectedly, what was sent out earlier. Simply to **find** the investment that one had made earlier does not seem like much of an incentive for investing. Having said that, however, because verses 1 and 2 are proverbs, they may have more than one meaning.

11:3-4 Verses 1 and 2 admonish the reader to take risks even in the face of an uncertain future. Verses 3 and 4 describe the uncertainty of the weather that a farmer must live with. In Wisdom Literature, weather is symbolic of that which is unpredictable. A farmer can know that clouds bring rain and trees do fall. But he cannot always know the precise time of such events. Nature is beyond human control. The sage says, **if clouds are full of water, they pour rain upon the earth**. True, one knows that when clouds become weighted with moisture they will eventually release it in the form of rain. When and where that occurs, no one knows for certain. Then Qoheleth makes an observation about trees that seems so obvious it is ridiculous even to say: **whether a tree falls to the south or to the north, in the place where it falls, there will it lie**. The point of the saying is that when the wind blows over a tree, humans have absolutely no control over where that tree will fall. Humans know that trees fall. What we do not know is when or where. Humans cannot predict future events.

This observation about weather is now given a specific context in verse 4. Qoheleth has already affirmed that God has set forth general times for events to occur. There is "a time to be born and a time to die, a time to plant and a time to uproot" (3:2). Even though farmers

[53]*The New English Bible* (New York: Cambridge University Press, 1972). Compare also the *Today's English Version*: "Invest your money in foreign trade, and one of these days you will make a profit. Put your investments in several places—many places even—because you never know what kind of bad luck you are going to have in this world" (New York: American Bible Society, 1981).

know the general times and seasons, they do not know precise times. The right time is always uncertain. If you are looking for just the right time, you will seldom get it correct. So the sage, using the farmer as an example, exhorts the reader, **whoever watches the wind will not plant; whoever looks at the clouds will not reap**. The image is of a farmer who constantly broods about the weather; such brooding results in paralysis. He is so fearful about planting and harvesting at the precise time that he never acts. The point is that there is a time to plant and a time to reap. However, do not be too meticulous in calculating the right time. Farming involves taking risks. A farmer can be too cautious. So, go ahead, "Cast your bread upon the waters."

11:5 Verse 5 now uses a different example of the mysteries of life. The main question in this verse revolves around how to translate the word רוּחַ (*rûaḥ*), what the NIV renders **wind**. The translation of the word varies depending on the context. Sometimes it is rendered "spirit," sometimes "wind," sometimes "breath" or "life-spirit" (i.e., the giving of life). In verse 4, the same word is translated "wind," so it is possible that this is the same way to translate it here. However, in verse 5, the image of the verse centers around the new life in a **mother's womb**.[54] Since the word רוּחַ (*rûaḥ*) appears in a sentence which speaks of the fetus in the womb, it is best translated "breath" or "life-breath." The verse then conveys a single image (life in the womb) as opposed to two images (wind and life in the womb), assumed by the NIV. The NRSV understands the verse as communicating a single image and translates it, "Just as you do not know how the breath comes to the bones in the mother's womb, so you do not know the work of God, who makes everything." That is, humans have no capacity to understand the giving of life in the womb. It remains a complete mystery (cf. Ps 139:14-16).

The sage uses mystery of life in the womb as an analogy for the point he really wants to make, and that is the mysterious activity of God: **so you cannot understand the work of God, the Maker of all things** (5b). Just as **you do not know** how life is given in the womb, so you do not understand or "know" (same phrase is used) the work of God. The proverb highlights human ignorance.

---

[54]The phrase "mother's womb" in the Hebrew text is "the full one" and serves to parallel the image in verse 3 which depicts clouds that are full of water.

11:6 Verse 6 summarizes the thought developed in this unit. **Sow your seed in the morning, and at evening let not your hands be idle**. That is, sow whenever the opportunity arises. Take risks and be responsive to the appropriate moments. Do not allow uncertainty to lead to idleness.[55] Be diligent and responsible. **For you do not know which will succeed, whether this or that, or whether both will do equally well**. Take every opportunity possible to work and to plant, since "you do not know" which sowing will succeed. In spite of uncertainties about the future, paralysis is not an option. The verse calls on developing a balance between spontaneity and responsibility.[56] Verse 6 is similar in thought to verses 1 and 4. In light of the best human calculations, do not be afraid to take risks in life when it comes to fulfilling your responsibilities and especially when it comes to performing deeds of kindness.

In the presence of uncertainty, the wise person learns to adjust to the curves that life throws. He or she does not fear taking risks. The wise are prodigal in their generosity, even though they do not know what the future holds.

X. A POEM ON AGING AND DEATH (11:7–12:8)

This is the concluding admonition made by Qoheleth. It also contains the last of the "joy" passages in the book. Even though so much of life is a mystery and is lived in the shadow of death, one must seek joy in the present moment because it is a gift from God. The language of "light" and "darkness" and "remember" (vv. 7-8) links verses 7-10 with 12:1-8 (vv. 1-3). The admonitions to "enjoy" and to "remember" express two dominant themes in these verses.

[7]**Light is sweet,**
  and it pleases the eyes to see the sun.
[8]**However many years a man may live,**
  let him enjoy them all.
But let him remember the days of darkness,

---

[55]The Hebrew text reads, "Do not let your hand rest." The phrase calls to mind Qoheleth's earlier exhortation in 9:10: "Whatever your hand finds to do, do it with all your might."

[56]Seow, *Ecclesiastes*, p. 346.

for they will be many.
Everything to come is meaningless.
⁹Be happy, young man, while you are young,
        and let your heart give you joy in the days of your youth.
  Follow the ways of your heart
        and whatever your eyes see,
  but know that for all these things
        God will bring you to judgment.
¹⁰So then, banish anxiety from your heart
        and cast off the troubles of your body,
        for youth and vigor are meaningless.

11:7-8 In verse 7, **light** and **sun** are metaphors for life (Job 3:16; 33:28,30). The phrase **light is sweet** is an affirmation of life and expresses the joy of being alive. Regardless of the incongruities and mysteries of life, Qoheleth can still affirm the pleasure of life, which he states more explicitly in verse 8: **let him enjoy** all the years that he lives. A person is to enjoy life in the present because **the days of darkness** are coming. "Darkness" represents death. Qoheleth exhorts the reader to **remember** the days of darkness. This remembering is for the sake of enjoying the present. Thinking about the end (cf. 7:1), death, enables one to live more fully in the present. One no longer lives life recklessly but makes every moment count. The verse concludes by affirming that **everything to come is meaningless**. "Everything to come" probably refers to people or generations coming and going (cf. 5:15-16). The idea is that nothing in this life is permanent. That which is to come is ephemeral (הֶבֶל, *hebel*). In this context, it is better to translate *hebel* as "fleeting" rather than "meaningless."

11:9 In verse 9, Qoheleth issues an imperative: **be happy, young man, while you are young and let your heart give you joy in the days of your youth.** The word for "happy" (שָׂמַח, *śāmaḥ*) is the same word used for "enjoy" in verse 8. The admonition is addressed to a young man. Youth refers not only to a certain time of life, but it also represents making the most of the moment. Seizing the joy of the moment is not the sole possession of youth.[57] For Qoheleth, to enjoy life is a divine imperative. The admonition to **follow the ways of**

---

[57]Brown, *Ecclesiastes*, p. 107.

your heart is another way to describe the call to enjoy life. That is, do not allow the stresses and anxieties of life to weigh you down (v. 10). And **know that for all these things God will bring you to judgment.** On whom will God bring judgment? He will bring it on those who refuse to enjoy life. God holds individuals accountable for failing to enjoy life because God has given enjoyment as a gift to those who fear him (2:24-26; 9:7-9). In this verse, divine judgment is "not a corrective but an incentive" for making the most of life.[58]

11:10 Verse 10 complements the previous verses. In order to experience the enjoyment of life, you must eliminate **anxiety from your heart and cast off the troubles of your body.** Anxiety and trouble are the antitheses of joy (cf. Matt 6:27-34). According to the NIV, **youth and vigor are meaningless** (הֶבֶל, *hebel*). It is not that the time of youth is meaningless. Qoheleth has just admonished youth to "be happy while you are young" (v. 9). Rather *hebel* should be translated "fleeting." The time of youth lasts only momentarily when one looks at how quickly death approaches.

Verses 7-10 do not call for reckless living or self-abandonment. Rather these verses should be understood in light of the other joy passages in the book (2:24-26; 9:7-9). Two reasons are given as to why one should enjoy life. For one, life is transient (*hebel*; vv. 8b,10b). For another, God desires that those who fear him enjoy life (v. 9b). As Brown observes, this is Qoheleth's sapiential *shema* (i.e., the greatest command): enjoy life.[59]

This next unit is closely tied with the previous verses by a similar vocabulary and theme. While 11:7-10 emphasizes the value of enjoying the present, 12:1-8 emphasizes the future time when one can no longer enjoy life.

The NIV (in contrast to the NRSV) appropriately prints this passage in poetic form. Many different suggestions have been given for understanding the images in this poem. They include an aging body, death, a thunderstorm, a decaying house, a funeral, and eschatological destruction. Parts of the text are open to allegorical interpretation

---

[58]Ibid., p. 105. Richard Clifford remarks, "God will judge you for not enjoying the present" (*The Wisdom Literature*, Interpreting Biblical Texts [Nashville: Abingdon, 1998], p. 110).

[59]Brown, *Ecclesiastes*, p. 107.

(v. 3), but other parts are not (v. 5a). The poem mixes these elements. Overall, the variety of images (decaying house, thunderstorm, funeral, etc.) and literary forms (metaphor, allegory, literal language) used, work together to highlight death's imminence.

The poem describes the end of life. Qoheleth prefers the end of matters over the beginning because at that point one has a better perspective on life (7:1). Chapter 12:1-8 brings an end to the perpetual motion described in the beginning poem in 1:2-11, where the world was in constant motion. Generations, seasons, and weather come and go. Now in the final poem, it all grinds to a halt: doors are closed, daily activities cease, and the human body returns to the dust. The poem emphasizes that humans must enjoy life before it is too late.

> [1]Remember your Creator
>> in the days of your youth,
> before the days of trouble come
>> and the years approach when you will say,
>> "I find no pleasure in them"—
> [2]before the sun and the light
>> and the moon and the stars grow dark,
>> and the clouds return after the rain;
> [3]when the keepers of the house tremble,
>> and the strong men stoop,
> when the grinders cease because they are few,
>> and those looking through the windows grow dim;
> [4]when the doors to the street are closed
>> and the sound of grinding fades;
> when men rise up at the sound of birds,
>> but all their songs grow faint;
> [5]when men are afraid of heights
>> and of dangers in the streets;
> when the almond tree blossoms
>> and the grasshopper drags himself along
>> and desire no longer is stirred.
> Then man goes to his eternal home
>> and mourners go about the streets.
> [6]Remember him—before the silver cord is severed,
>> or the golden bowl is broken;
> before the pitcher is shattered at the spring,
>> or the wheel broken at the well,

⁷**and the dust returns to the ground it came from,**
    and the spirit returns to God who gave it.
⁸**"Meaningless! Meaningless!" says the Teacher.**ᵃ
    "Everything is meaningless!"

ᵃ**8 Or** *the leader of the assembly*; **also in verses 9 and 10**

12:1 The poem begins, **Remember your Creator in the days of your youth** (12:1). The Teacher continues the admonition begun in 11:7-10. To remember the Creator is to experience the ultimate joy of life. One must remember, however, **before the days of trouble come**. The threefold repetition of the "before . . ." phrase (vv. 1,2,6) serves to call the reader back each time to this beginning admonition, "remember your creator." The admonition is closely related to the exhortation to fear God (3:14; 5:7; 7:18; 8:12; 12:13).

12:2 The description begins in verse 2. Overall the poem is about the imminence of death. The descriptions, however, are mixed along the way between literal and metaphorical. The reader could take verse 2 more literally and see it describing the coming of a storm. The storm serves as an image for the onslaught of health problems that often accompany old age. Realizing this, individuals are to seize the moment **before** that time comes.

12:3 The description continues in the following verses where the writer mixes the allegory and the literal. Verse 3 could refer to the demise of home or an estate (i.e., a more literal interpretation): the **keepers** or guardians, **strong men**, servants at the mill, women **looking through the windows**. Decay sets in; activity slows until it finally ceases. The description could also be an allegory for different parts of the body. The **keepers of the house** are arms or trembling hands. The "strong men" are an allegory for legs. **Grinders** represent teeth. And **those looking through the windows** refers to the eyes. Either way, Qoheleth paints a bleak picture of old age as a means of exhorting readers to remember their Creator in the days of their youth.

12:4 The initial images in verse 4 appear to be more literal and refer to the cessation of commerce and social activity: **when the doors to the street are closed and the sound of grinding fades**. The images speak about the demise of village life, possibly because of the coming storm (v. 2). It is possible, however, to understand verse 4 allegorically and continuing the description of the body parts. If so, verse 4a refers to the loss of hearing. Verse 4b describes the loss of sleep experienced by the aged: **when men rise up at the sound of birds**. Thus the poem depicts a cruel paradox in old age. One's hearing declines. At the same time one wakes up at the slightest sound of a bird. In addition, the voice loses its strength and clarity: **but all their songs grow faint**.

12:5 Verse 5a refers to the elderly's fear of heights and their insecurity in venturing out in public places (the image seems more literal here). With the remainder of verse 5, one could more naturally interpret it as an allegory of the aging process. The **almond tree** blossoming signifies the hair graying. **The grasshopper drags himself along** may indicate the loss of energy. And the loss of **desire** (אֲבִיּוֹנָה, *'ăbîyônāh*)[60] indicates a loss of health or vibrancy. The result is that **man goes to his eternal home and mourners go about the streets**.

12:6-7 Verse 6 once again (cf. vv. 1 and 2) reminds the reader of the fundamental admonition of the poem: to **remember him— before** it is too late. Here a series of metaphors are used to describe the finality of death. **The silver cord is severed, or the golden bowl is broken**. The golden bowl may be the container of oil on a lamp stand. Because the silver cord and the golden bowl appear in close proximity, the silver cord may also refer to part of a lamp stand. Whatever their specific use, the emphasis is on valuable objects being broken. The shattering of the objects symbolizes the finality of death. As Seow observes, the human body is compared to an earthen vessel (cf. 2 Cor 4:7) which returns to the dust from which it came.[61] The second half of the verse also describes valuable objects that are shattered and rendered useless: **before the pitcher is shattered at the spring, or the wheel broken at the well**. All four images depict the end of that which once was precious and useful. So, too, is it with human life. The human life-force, **returns to God who gave it** (v. 7), and the body remains as dust.

12:8 Verse 8 concludes the poem and ties into the earlier observation in 11:8 and 10 that the generations to come as well as the time of youth are fleeting moments; they are *hebel*. The verse also echoes 1:2. Thus the book ends the way it began, advocating that all

---

[60]This is the only time the word appears in the Old Testament. The term refers to the caper berry, a fruit of the caper bush. The berry had medicinal value. Some think the berry helped to stir sexual appetite. For more detailed analysis see Seow, *Ecclesiastes*, p. 363.

[61]Seow, *Ecclesiastes*, pp. 282-283.

of life is ephemeral and beyond human control. All that comes into existence quickly passes away. Nothing lasts and in the end, life remains a mystery. The NIV's insistence on consistently translating *hebel* as **meaningless** misses the richness and variety of meaning the word carries (see Introduction).

XI. EPILOGUE (12:9-14)

This material is written by an author other than Qoheleth. These verses refer to Qoheleth in the third person, while the writer speaks in the first person in the rest of the book (except in 1:2 and 7:27). However, Fox offers a persuasive argument for the idea that the voice in the epilogue is the same voice that speaks all through the book. In the main body of the book, the writer assumes the persona of Qoheleth, a wise man passing on his experiences to his son. In the epilogue, he steps out of his persona and makes some concluding observations.[62] Fox's position has the advantage of understanding the epilogue as an integral part of the whole and not a later addition tacked onto the book to make it more "orthodox." The epilogue, while using different language, affirms the work of Qoheleth.

[9]Not only was the Teacher wise, but also he imparted knowledge to the people. He pondered and searched out and set in order many proverbs. [10]The Teacher searched to find just the right words, and what he wrote was upright and true.

[11]The words of the wise are like goads, their collected sayings like firmly embedded nails—given by one Shepherd. [12]Be warned, my son, of anything in addition to them.

Of making many books there is no end, and much study wearies the body.

[13]Now all has been heard;
here is the conclusion of the matter:
Fear God and keep his commandments,
for this is the whole ⌊duty⌋ of man.
[14]For God will bring every deed into judgment,
including every hidden thing,
whether it is good or evil.

---

[62]Fox, *A Time*, pp. 365-366.

12:9-10 Verses 9-10 speak of a particular sage, Qoheleth. Verse 11 speaks of sages in general, which includes Qoheleth. In verse 9, the **Teacher** imparts his **knowledge to the people**. Qoheleth, the Teacher, directs his advice not only to royalty in the court but also to the commoners. Wisdom is not the exclusive domain of any specific social class. Rather it is the possession of all who seek it.

The Teacher is engaged in a rigorous process in which **he pondered and searched out and set in order many proverbs** (v. 9). In order to impart wisdom to the people, the Teacher listens to, examines, and arranges proverbial wisdom. In other words, he engages all his study resources. In the tradition of the sages, the Teacher places a priority on finding the appropriate word for the occasion (v. 10). One of the important characteristics of the sage was to speak the right word for the occasion (Prov 15:23; 16:24). Qoheleth speaks both words of "delight" (חֵפֶץ, *ḥēpheṣ*, **upright**) and words of "truth" (אֱמֶת, *'ĕmeth*, **true**).

12:11 With verse 11 the writer broadens the scope to include not just Qoheleth but **the words of the wise**. Their words are described as **goads**, a staff with nails embedded in the end used by shepherds to prod sheep or oxen along the right path. Though the speech of the wise is delightful and truthful, it is also at times painful (cf. Prov 27:5-6).

The term **Shepherd** in this passage does not refer to the LORD (even though the NIV leaves that indication). If "Shepherd" is a reference to God, then the emphasis in this passage shifts from the words of the wise to the one Shepherd and becomes a way of affirming monotheism. The emphasis in the passage, however, is on the words of the wise and a comparison with what a shepherd does for his sheep. As shepherds use goads to keep sheep on the right way, the wise use words in the same manner.

12:12 When the writer says, **Be warned, my son, of anything in addition to them**, he is making a statement similar to that found in Deuteronomy 12:32 and Revelation 22:18-19. It serves as a warning to those who would be tempted to add any more words to what Qoheleth has already said. It is an affirmation that the text of Ecclesiastes is reliable.[63]

---

[63]Seow, *Ecclesiastes*, p. 394.

The second half of verse 12 is one of the most familiar verses in all of Ecclesiastes: **Of making many books there is no end, and much study wearies the body**. The idea is similar in thought to the ceaseless activity described in the opening poem (1:3-8). The emphasis is on excessive writing being wearisome. Qoheleth himself is engaged in rigorous study as he ponders and seeks out and arranges proverbs (v. 9). Earlier Qoheleth admonished the reader to work hard: "Whatever your hand finds to do, do it with all your might" (9:10), but it seems that one can overdo it.

12:13-14 The writer comes to the point where he sums it all up in one sentence: **Fear God and keep his commandments, for this is the whole duty of man**. This statement does not contradict what Qoheleth has taught continually, as some would argue. All along, Qoheleth advises the reader to "fear God" (3:14; 5:7; 7:18; 8:12-13) and to "remember your Creator" (12:1). This statement also echoes the "joy passages" dispersed through the book (cf. 2:24-26; 3:12-13; 3:22; 5:18-20; 8:15; 9:7-10; 11:7-10).

The one new dimension the editor adds at this point is the exhortation to keep his commandments. Wisdom Literature (Job, Proverbs, and Ecclesiastes) does not usually speak of divine commands. Wisdom does not speak contrary to the law; its teachings affirm the instruction of the law. However, law is simply not in the provenance of wisdom's work. Combining fear of God with the law is most fully developed in Sirach (e.g., Sirach 1:26-30).

To fear God and keep his commandments is the whole duty of man. The last phrase literally reads "for this is the entirety of man." The word "duty" is not in the Hebrew text. The idea is that fearing God and keeping his commands is the essence or substance of what humans are about. For the writer to exhort the reader to "fear God . . . for this is the essence of humanity" fits with the summary statements in Ecclesiastes (2:24-26; 3:12-13; 3:22; 5:18-20; 8:15; 9:7-10; 11:7-10). **God** will ultimately hold accountable those who do not fear him (v. 14). Whether **good or evil**, God will expose and judge every action, even that which is **hidden** (cf. 11:9).

SONG OF SONGS

INTRODUCTION

The Song of Songs holds a special place in the history of the church and synagogue. By A.D. 1200 over 100 commentaries had been written on the book. The Song has generated more exposition than any other biblical book, except for Genesis and Psalms.[1] Origen alone wrote ten volumes of commentaries on the Song.[2] Bernard of Clairvaux (1090–1153) preached eighty-six sermons and only got to the beginning of chapter 3! Especially during the early and medieval periods, this book played an important role in the life of the church. However, since the middle of the nineteenth century, when scholars turned away from an allegorical interpretation (focusing on divine love) to a more literal interpretation (focusing on human love), not as much has been written and even less has been preached from the Song.

BRIEF HISTORY OF INTERPRETATION

ALLEGORICAL INTERPRETATION

The Song of Songs contains dialogue between a man and a woman deeply in love with each other who express their love in the most intimate language. However, for centuries Jewish and Christian interpreters interpreted this dialogue allegorically. Until the middle of the nineteenth century, the allegorical interpretation of the Song remained dominant. It is likely that early interpretation adopted the allegorical approach because of the dominant view that the physical side of humanity was inherently evil.

[1] Ellen F. Davis, *Proverbs, Ecclesiastes, and the Song of Songs* (Louisville: Westminster John Knox Press, 2000), p. 231.
[2] J.P. Tanner, "The History of the Interpretation of the Song of Songs," *Bibliotheca Sacra* 154 (1997): 27-28.

The fundamental allegory of Jewish interpretation was that the man in the poems represents God and the woman represents Israel.[3] The Song became then an allegory of the history of God and his people Israel. Early Christian interpreters followed suit. The first Christian known to open the door to allegorical interpretation was Hippolytus (d. 235).[4]

Among Christian interpreters, Origen (c. 185–c. 254) was the dominant voice in promoting the allegorical interpretation. For Christians, the Song was a love poem about Jesus (the man) and the church (the woman). These early interpreters did not accept these songs at face value; they are not about human love but divine love.

Some of the early church fathers felt that the Song of Songs could easily be misinterpreted, which is more than likely one of the reasons why they produced so many commentaries. The book was suitable only for the mature student. Jerome gives the following advice to a mother about educating her daughter in the Scriptures:

Let her treasures be not silks or gems but manuscripts of the holy scriptures . . . . Let her begin by learning the psalter, and then let her gather rules of life out of the proverbs of Solomon. From the Preacher [Ecclesiastes] let her gain the habit of despising the world and its vanities. Let her follow the example set in Job of virtue and of patience. Then let her pass on to the gospels never to be laid aside once they have been taken in hand. Let her also drink in with a willing heart the Acts of the Apostles and the Epistles. As soon as she has enriched the storehouse of her mind with these treasures, let her commit to memory the prophets, the heptateuch [Genesis–Judges], the books of Kings and of Chronicles, the rolls also of Ezra and Esther. When she has done all these she may safely read the Song of Songs but not before: for, were she to read it at the beginning, she would fail to perceive that, though it is written in fleshly words, it is a marriage song of a spiritual bridal. And not understanding this she would suffer from it.[5]

---

[3]Weston W. Fields, "Early and Medieval Jewish Interpretation of the Song of Songs," *Grace Theological Journal* 1 (Fall, 1980): 221-231.
[4]Roland E. Murphy, *The Song of Songs*, Hermenia (Minneapolis: Fortress Press, 1990), pp. 14-15. Murphy offers an appreciative summary of various allegorical interpretations (pp. 11-41).
[5]Philip Schaff and Henry Wace, eds., "St. Jerome: Letters and Select Works," 2nd series, vol. VI, Letter CVII, *Nicene and Post-Nicene Fathers* (Grand Rapids: Eerdmans, 1979), p. 194.

The Song was to be read after all the other books of the Bible. If the daughter was to memorize the first seven books of the Bible plus Kings and Chronicles, it seems that Jerome is actually saying she should *not* read the Song at all! At any rate, the belief was that the Song is not meant for the immature.

Between 1135 and 1153 Bernard of Clairvaux preached eighty-six sermons on only the first two chapters of the Song of Songs. The allegorical interpretation enabled early church fathers and preachers to generate volumes of commentaries, lectures, and sermons from the book.

LITERAL OR NATURAL INTERPRETATION

Toward the middle of the nineteenth century and the coming of the Enlightenment, the allegorical interpretation was rejected. From that point on the more literal or natural interpretation of the book held sway. Most commentators today understand the Song to be not about divine love but human love.

Walter Kaiser compares the Song of Songs to the instruction poem used in Proverbs 5:15-23 and maintains that the Proverbs passage is closely related in language and thought to the Song. As a result of his comparison, he concludes that Proverbs 5:15-23 is the interpretive key to the Song of Songs. The overlap between the two texts argues in favor of reading the Song as love poems between a man and a woman rather than an allegory of Christ and the church. The purpose of both is to teach the exclusivity of marriage and the joys of marital fidelity. As a result, Kaiser concludes, "this is the best way to understand the Song."[6]

The Song is obviously not allegorical in the sense of John Bunyan's *Pilgrim's Progress*. No signs or clues within the book indicate that it should be interpreted in this way. Still, there are various proposals for interpreting it from the literal perspective. They can be divided into two primary camps. On the one hand, some inter-

---

[6]Walter C. Kaiser Jr., "True Marital Love in Proverbs 5:15-23 and the Interpretation of Song of Songs," *The Way of Wisdom: Essays in Honor of Bruce K. Waltke*, ed. by J.I. Packer and Sven K. Soderlund (Grand Rapids: Zondervan, 2000), p. 113.

pret the book as a narrative or drama that unfolds between two or possibly three characters. On the other hand, others view the book as a collection of love poems, an anthology.

Dramatic Interpretation

Toward the end of the eighteenth century, Friedrich Jacobi (1772) offered a dramatic interpretation of the Song that inaugurated the search for uncovering an overall plot to the love poems.[7] He argued that the basic plot of the poems centered on Solomon's quest to win the love of a Shulammite woman. Solomon must, however, compete with a poor shepherd boy for her love. In the end, the woman rejects the advances of Solomon and expresses her exclusive devotion to the shepherd boy. The Song as a type of morality play affirms that true love cannot be bought, even by the wealth of a great king. Some scholars continue to hold this view.[8]

Those who propose a narrative plot to the book often disagree over who the characters are and how the plot unfolds. Some have proposed two characters, Solomon and the Shulammite, with whom he is in love. Others propose a triangulation between Solomon, the Shulammite, and a shepherd boy. Iain Provan accepts the latter perspective, but with the view that the woman is already married to Solomon.[9]

Some major problems, however, exist with the dramatic interpretation. First, if one views the love poems as expressions of Solomon's love for the Shulammite who is not yet a part of his harem, then the poems become Solomon's attempt to seduce her, which destroys their aesthetic beauty.[10] Second, in order for the poems to unite around a sequential plot, the interpreter must read between the lines to fill in the gaps. The interpreter must impose almost as much detail on the text as one who reads the poems allegorically. For example, it is not easy always to know who the

---

[7]Murphy, *Song*, p. 38.

[8]Kaiser, "True Marital Love," pp. 112-114. C.H. Bullock, *An Introduction to the Old Testament Poetic Books* (Chicago: Moody, 1979), pp. 232-254.

[9]Iain Provan, *Ecclesiastes, Song of Songs*, The NIV Application Commentary (Grand Rapids: Zondervan, 2001), pp. 245-246.

[10]Duane A. Garrett, *Proverbs, Ecclesiastes, Song of Songs*, The New American Commentary (Nashville: Broadman Press, 1993), p. 359.

speaker is in a particular instance. It is hard to know when the woman is addressing Solomon and when she is addressing the shepherd boy. Finally, the text gives no signs within it to indicate that an unfolding plot is the way the poems should be interpreted.

An Anthology of Love Poems

Another way to interpret the Song from a literal or natural perspective is to understand it as a collection of love poems, similar to what is found in the book of Psalms. The songs are collected in a way that basically sets up an ongoing dialogue between two intimate lovers. The songs do not contain an unfolding plot. Yet neither are they completely random.

Continuity exists with the characters, common metaphors, recurring refrains, and theology of the Song. The consistency in the character description of the man and woman indicates a basic unity of the material (e.g., the woman is referred to as "my friend/darling"; 1:9,15; 2:2,10,13; 4:1,6; 5:2; 6:4). A number of images and metaphors are repeated in the book (images of gardens, water, fountain, etc.). There is also the repetition of certain refrains and themes. For example, the "description" poems utilize common images and repeat certain refrains (4:1-7; 6:4-9; 7:1-6). Also the refrain "my love is mine and I am his" is repeated in the book (2:16; 6:3; 7:10).[11] Further, several poems conclude with the following refrain: "Do not arouse or awaken love until it so desires" (2:7; 3:5; 8:4). All of this repetition creates a unity among the poems, even though the material does not develop a sustained plot.

I take the position in this commentary that the Song is a single poem that is artistically arranged. After all, it is called the *Song* (singular) of Songs. Though it is not a tightly knit piece of work in the form of a drama or plot, it does contain continuity.

André LaCocque aptly describes the movement of the Song not as a narrative but as cyclical: "And thus the Canticle is an endless song," "a round."[12] LaCocque says that the cyclical movement is

---

[11]Compare also the refrain in 2:9a, 2:17c and 8:14. Compare 6:11 with 7:12. Compare 3:1-2 with 5:6 and 3:3 with 5:7.

[12]André LaCocque, *Romance, She Wrote: A Hermeneutical Essay on Song of Songs* (Harrisburg, PA: Trinity Press, 1998), p. 190.

most dramatically displayed when the poem comes to the final chapter. Chapter 8 echoes much of the language of chapter 1. For example, 8:1 recalls 1:2 and the young woman's desire for the lovers to kiss. Chapter 8, verse 6 uses the word "love" (אַהֲבָה, 'ahăbāh) which recalls the term from 1:3-4. Verse 12 returns to the image of the woman as "vineyard" (כֶּרֶם, kerem) where it was first introduced in 1:6. Verse 14 uses the language of 1:4.[13]

In addition, the only two times the woman's brothers are mentioned in the Song are at the beginning in 1:6 and at the conclusion in 8:8-9. All of these connections are strong evidence for understanding the Song as a unified whole.

OTHER INTERPRETIVE APPROACHES

Marvin Pope, in his massive volume on the Song, maintains that one should interpret the book from the background of a funeral celebration. After a lengthy argument, Pope concludes, "Certain features of the Song of Songs may be understood in the light of the considerable and growing evidences that funeral feasts in the ancient Near East were love feasts celebrated with wine, women, and song."[14] Pope connects the Song with the funeral celebration, the marzeah (or as he translates it, the "sprawlers' banquet") in Amos 6:7.[15] The key text for him is a statement made in 8:6: "for love is as strong as death, its jealousy unyielding as the grave." But outside this reference to death, little else in the book suggests a funeral rite.

Some scholars have interpreted the Song as songs and poetry for a seven-day wedding ceremony.[16] However, it appears that few of the poems collected in the book are wedding songs.[17] So the question remains, what does one do with the rest of the material in the book?

---

[13]See ibid., p. 191.

[14]Marvin Pope, *Song of Songs*, The Anchor Bible (Garden City: Doubleday, 1977), p. 228.

[15]Ibid., pp. 214, 216.

[16]Murphy, *Song*, p. 39. Pope in his commentary also rehearses the views that favor this interpretation, pp. 141-145.

[17]The descriptive wedding poems are sometimes understood to be from the same genre of poems found in the ancient Arabic culture, often referred to as *wasf* (e.g., 4:1-7; 5:10-16; 6:5-7; 7:1-8).

One of the popular ways to approach Song of Songs today is to see it as a sex manual for Christians. Joseph C. Dillow takes this approach in his book *Solomon on Sex*.[18] Tom Nelson of Denton Bible Church in Denton, Texas, holds seminars across the country for churches, young married couples, and singles using the Song as a "how to" book for healthy sexual fulfillment. One of his sermon series is entitled "Love Song: From Attraction to Faithfulness." Claiming never to have read a commentary on the Song of Songs, his reading of the book over a period of years has led him to the following plot or scheme in the Song: The Art of Attraction (introduction), The Art of Dating (2:8–3:5), The Art of Intimacy (3:6–5:1), The Art of Conflict (5:2–6:13), The Art of Deepening (7:1–8:4), The Art of Faithfulness (conclusion).[19]

The Song, however, is not a sex *manual*. It does not offer advice about dating or dealing with conflict. It is *poetry* intended to evoke a mood in which love is celebrated in the appropriate context. It is *poetry* that creates an atmosphere of mutual respect, intimacy, and exclusivity.

CHARACTERS

Even though the Song has no overarching narrative, the characters depicted in the poems have a consistent persona. The most dominant voice heard is the woman's. She speaks more often than the man. She often initiates the dialogue. The man describes her as beautiful (e.g., 4:1-7). To him she is the "most beautiful of women" (1:8). He calls her by various terms of endearment including "my sister, my darling, my dove" (5:2). The one most commonly preferred by the young man is "my darling." The young woman in contrast describes herself with modesty (e.g., 1:5-6).

---

[18]Joseph C. Dillow, *Solomon on Sex* (Nashville: Thomas Nelson, 1977). Speaking of the Song of Songs Dillow says, "Amid the current deluge of marriage manuals and sensational guides to liberated lovemaking, one small, beautiful book deserves all the attention the others are clamoring for. . ." (p. 7).

[19]Tom Nelson, *Love Song: From Attraction to Faithfulness*, Denton Bible Church, Denton, TX. Six sermons delivered from 9-1-1991 to 10-6-1991, audiocassette series.

The next most prominent person in the poems is the young man. The most common term the young woman uses to describe him is "lover" (e.g., 1:13-14). He is, in her eyes, handsome and charming (1:16). He is to her a "king" (1:4,12; 7:5) and a "shepherd" (1:7). Sometimes the man pursues the woman (e.g., 2:8-14; 5:2-4).

A group of women also play a role in the Song. They are variously referred to as the maidens (1:3), the daughters of Jerusalem (1:5), and the daughters of Zion (3:11). These women appear to be city girls who are young and naïve about matters of love. Sometimes the young woman must instruct them in the ways of love and intimacy (e.g., 2:7; 3:5; 8:4). Sometimes they serve as a sounding board for the young woman to launch into a description of her lover (5:9-16). Sometimes they serve as a foil, a contrast between the young woman who is country (depicted as a vineyard) and the women who are city (from Jerusalem).

Family members of the young woman, as well, play a minor role in the poems. Mention is made of her brothers (1:5-6; 8:8-9) who "guard" her (overprotect her) in the absence of her father. The mother is usually mentioned in contexts dealing with sexuality (3:4; 6:9; 8:1).

AUTHORSHIP

Christian tradition has typically considered Solomon as the author of the book. The superscription in the NIV reads, "Solomon's Song of Songs" (v. 1). The Hebrew text literally reads, "Song of Songs which is to/for Solomon." The preposition ל can either be translated "to" or "for." In this context, it is almost certain that the preposition refers to the one to whom the book is *dedicated* rather than to the *author* of the book.

Solomon's name occurs in 1:1,5; 3:7,9,11; and 8:11-12. His name appears in the book only in third person references, never in the first person. As such the poems do not naturally read as poems composed by Solomon. The two primary texts where Solomon is mentioned are 3:6-11 and 8:11-12. In the first text, the passage imagines the grandeur of the young couple's wedding as being as impressive as Solomon's wedding. Theirs is a wedding fit for royalty.[20] In the

---

[20]Tremper Longman III, *Song of Songs* (Grand Rapids: Eerdmans, 2001), p. 6.

second text (8:11-12), Solomon is depicted in a negative way. He is the one who tries to buy love but is rebuked for doing so. Obviously, Solomon composed neither text.

Solomon's reputation for having many wives and concubines (1 Kgs 11:1-6) stands against the mutually exclusive devotion the lovers possess for each other found in the dialogues of the poems. In many ways, Solomon represents the foil the author uses to highlight the undivided devotion between a man and a woman. Solomon's relationships are in antithesis to the relationship described in Song of Songs. In 8:11-12, Solomon is viewed as a womanizer. Thus it is unlikely that he is the author of these poems, at least those that speak of the exclusivity of love and intimacy.

Solomon, however, was known for composing over a thousand songs (1 Kgs 4:32). It is possible, therefore, that some of the poems in the Song could have been written or inspired by him, but not the whole collection. In the final analysis, the human author of the book remains anonymous. Its divine authority is confirmed by its inclusion in the Christian canon.

THEOLOGICAL MESSAGE

Modern biblical theology has neglected the Song of Songs. One reason is that it is hard to understand how language about sexual love can be a part of God's redemptive purpose for humanity. Redemption, though, is not about leaving the physical body behind and retreating into asceticism. No dichotomy exists in Scripture between the physical and the spiritual. In its proper context, humans express and celebrate human sexuality as a part of their spirituality.

In celebrating sexuality, the Song expresses a theology of human intimacy. The lyrics are erotic but not pornographic.[21] The material is not pornographic because the lovers express deep respect for one another in a mutually exclusive relationship. Each extols the other's beauty as an expression of admiration. Neither the woman (1:2,4) nor the man (7:8-9) is embarrassed about the desire for sexual expression with the other. Open dialogue about lovemaking is nothing to be ashamed of.

---

[21]Murphy, *Song,* p. 102.

Contemporary secular culture perverts the sexual relationship by taking it out of its proper context of marital commitment. In such a culture, males and females often use sex as a way to manipulate, control, and express power, thus distorting its purpose. It is bought and sold as a commodity. Contemporary culture does not know how to talk about sexual expression other than in a perverted sense. As a result, some Christians swing to the other extreme and view sex as unclean. They react by repressing sexual feelings and desires.

To those who repress sexuality, Iain Provan reminds Christians that there is *one* biblical book devoted to love and sex. To those who view sexual expression as an open license, he reminds the reader that there is *only one* book in the Bible devoted to love and sex.[22] Christians do not allow culture's perversion to determine their response. Instead, the church is not embarrassed about sexuality but celebrates it in its proper context. The reciprocal love between a man and a woman models an important dimension of humanity that is God-given. The differentiation between the sexes (Gen 1:26-31) is a part of the God-given design of human fulfillment. Therefore, the gift of human sexuality is not deified; rather it is a gift for God's people to enjoy.

The sex appeal experienced between the two lovers, however, is not ultimately based on the physical attraction but on the exclusive commitment they make to one another. Because their "love is as strong as death" (8:6), they are physically attracted to one another. Their physical attraction is the *result* of the deep commitment they express to one another (8:6-8). The stronger their commitment, the greater their attraction to each other.[23]

The Song of Songs presents a view of human relationships that is neither hierarchical nor exploitative. The Song recalls the partnership between males and females that God intended from the beginning (Gen 1:26-28). The man (אִישׁ, *'îš*) and the woman (אִשָּׁה, *'iššāh*) complement one another (Gen 2:23). In the Song, the relationship between the woman and the man is equal and reciprocal. Both consider the other to be superior to anyone else (2:1-3). There is no masculine dominance and no submissive stance. They enter

[22]Provan, *Ecclesiastes, Song*, p. 253.
[23]I'm indebted to Rick Marrs for this thought. Marrs, *Preaching from Song of Songs* (Austin, TX: Institute for Christian Studies, May 18-21, 1998), audiotape.

into the relationship as partners, each freely giving themselves to one another physically and emotionally. In the Song, the curse of the Fall (Gen 3:16) is reversed. No more dominion of one gender over the other.

This egalitarian relationship, however, is still in process. The couple does not achieve a full redemptive state. They are in the now but not-yet times (to impose a Pauline template on them; Romans 5–8). Lurking in the background of this reciprocal relationship is the threat of male domination over the female. The watchmen physically abuse the woman (5:7). As their sister, her brothers understand her to be their possession (1:5-6; 8:8-9). King Solomon continues to buy and accumulate women for his harem (8:11-12). The woman must continue to battle male domination.

The NIV labels the man the "lover" and the woman the "beloved." The problem with these labels is that it makes the man more active and the woman passive. In the Song, however, the woman is not passive. In fact, the woman initiates the communication between the two (1:2-7). All through the poems, hers is the dominant voice. The Song concludes with the woman offering the final invitation to the man (8:14).

The emphasis in the book rests on fidelity, commitment, and exclusivity (2:16; 6:3; 7:10). Some have noted that the poem does not explicitly connect intimacy with marriage.[24] But the Song does *not* advocate "open relationships." The two lovers regard themselves in a covenant relationship, even though it appears that others do not (8:1b). In chapters 4:1–5:1, the man calls the woman his "bride" and "sister." And the book places emphasis on the exclusivity of their relationship. The relationship portrayed is reminiscent of the Genesis 1–2 story.

In addition, since the Song is a collection of poems, it seems reasonable to conclude that the relationship this couple shares may not be the same throughout. In some cases the actions and intimacy of the couple imply a married state (1:4). In other cases they are not married (8:8-10).

In the Old Testament, sexual intercourse was strictly forbidden outside the context of marriage (Leviticus 18–19; Deut 5:18). The

---

[24]Elizabeth Huwiler, *Proverbs, Ecclesiastes, Song of Songs*, New International Biblical Commentary (Peabody, MA: Hendrickson Publishers, 1999), p. 243.

social background of the Old Testament demanded adherence to moral standards when it came to the practice of sexual intercourse (read Deut 22:13-29). The Song of Songs is deeply embedded within this theological and social context.

Let me make one final observation regarding the theology of the Song of Songs. As I stated earlier, I do not believe that the Song is an allegory of God and Israel or of Christ and the church. However, Scripture consistently describes God's love for humans in terms of human relationships (e.g., Hosea 1–3; Ezekiel 16; Eph 5:21ff). God related to Adam and Eve in the garden in terms of human intimacy. God walks in the garden and converses with the man and the woman.

By exploring this connection between human and divine love in Scripture, André LaCocque surfaces a deeper level of theology at work in the Song of Songs. He investigates the possibility that the writer of the Song mines the similes and metaphors found in other parts of Scripture, especially the prophets, which describe God's relationship to his people and then recasts those images in language that describes the love between a man and a woman.[25] In other words, the poet relies heavily on the sacred language of other biblical texts to depict the intimate relationship between the young lovers in the Song. This "intertextual" reading makes the Song a profoundly theological text.[26] Ultimately, where there is the presence of mutually exclusive and committed love between two people, God is present.

This is not an allegorical reading of the Song. Allegory claims that a text means something completely different from its natural sense. In contrast, an intertextual reading interprets the love poems in terms of their natural sense. Such a reading also reveals that the language has been co-opted from other biblical texts about God and his people and "reincarnated" by the writer of the Song to portray the love between two human beings.

Let me offer a few samples of intertextuality at work that LaCocque identifies. In the Song 2:16 the refrain "My lover is mine and I am his" (cf. 6:3; 7:10) echoes the oft-repeated statement in the Old Testament: "I am your God and you are my people" (Lev 26:12; Jer 7:23; 11:4; 24:7; 31:33; Ezek 34:30-31; Deut 26:17-18; 29:12). The motif of quest in 3:1 and 5:6 recalls the religious search for God (Isa

---

[25]LaCocque, *Romance,* p. 56.
[26]Ibid., p. 67.

26:9). The theme of searching and finding or not finding Yahweh is a common theme in the prophets (Isa 51:1; 65:1; Jer 29:13). The description of the woman in 4:11-12 (e.g., 11b "The fragrance of your garments is like that of Lebanon") comes from the oracle in Hosea 14:4-8 which depicts the restoration of Israel to God. The poet uses theological language to speak of human relationships.

The interpretation of the Song should begin with the level of human love. On a secondary level there is a place for reading the Song, in quite general terms, from the perspective of the human and divine relationship. This does not mean that the reader has liberty to allegorize the poems as descriptions of the spiritual relationship between God and humanity. But it does acknowledge that the writer of the Song seems to have taken prophetic language used to describe God's relationship to humans and infused that language into poems describing human love.

From an intertextual reading one can conclude that loving God is inseparable from loving one's neighbor. The more one understands and lives out the covenant relationship of marriage, the better one understands the human and divine relationship.

LITERARY STRUCTURE

The following offers a brief overview of how the Song unfolds structurally. The Song opens abruptly, "Let him kiss me with the kisses of his mouth" (1:2). The poem thrusts the readers into a relationship already in full stride. In 1:2-7 the woman initiates the encounter by longing for her lover and by describing herself with modesty (vv. 5-6). In the next section (1:8–2:7), the man arrives on the scene and a dialogue ensues between the two lovers. It is a dialogue of mutual admiration (1:15-17; 2:1-4). The woman then reminisces about her lover (2:8-17). She reflects on his arrival, invitation, request, and their mutual love. Once again in 3:1-5, the woman seeks out her lover. The woman desires a royal wedding for her lover and herself (3:6-11).

In the next section (4:1–5:1), the man's voice dominates. He begins with a physical description of the woman (4:1-6; called a *wasf*, an Arabic word meaning "description"). The man invites his lover to leave Lebanon (v. 8) and become accessible to him. This is followed by a poem of admiration (4:9-16). The woman responds by inviting the man (v. 16), and the lovers are encouraged to enjoy themselves.

Chapter 5:2–6:12 contains a sequence of dialogues between the woman and the daughters of Jerusalem. The dialogues embody a theme of finding and not finding (5:2-8). The daughters of Jerusalem ask for a description of the lost lover (v. 9). In 5:10-16, the woman gives a physical description reminiscent of royalty. Ultimately the reader discovers that the lost lover is already in her garden and in her presence (6:2-3). Her lover is always with her. The man speaks, expresses admiration, and describes her beauty (6:4-12).

Chapter 7:1–8:4 begins with a physical description (*wasf*) of the woman (vv. 1-7). The man expresses his yearning for her (vv. 8-9). She speaks in verses 10-13 offering an invitation. The book concludes with a series of love poems (8:5-14) that reflect back to the beginning and leave the impression that the cycle is about to start all over again (vv. 13-14). Just as the Song began with the relationship already in process, so it concludes with the lovers continuing to seek out and invite one another.

OUTLINE

BIBLIOGRAPHY

Bergant, Dianne. *The Song of Songs*. Collegeville, MN: The Liturgical Press, 2001.

Bullock, C.H. *An Introduction to the Old Testament Poetic Books*. Chicago: Moody, 1979.

Davis, Ellen F. *Proverbs, Ecclesiastes, and the Song of Songs*. Louisville, KY: Westminster John Knox Press, 2000.

Dillow, Joseph C. *Solomon on Sex*. Nashville: Thomas Nelson, 1977.

Fields, Weston W. "Early and Medieval Jewish Interpretation of the Song of Songs." *Grace Theological Journal* 1 (Fall, 1980): 221-231.

Garrett, Duane A. *Proverbs, Ecclesiastes, Song of Songs*. The New American Commentary. Nashville: Broadman Press, 1993.

Goulder, Michael D. *The Song of Fourteen Songs*. JSOTSupp. 36. Sheffield: JSOT Press, 1986.

Haldar, A. "Lebanon." In *The Interpreter's Dictionary of the Bible*, vol. 3. Ed. by George Arthur Buttrick. Nashville: Abingdon Press, 1962.

Hamilton, Mark W. "The Body Royal: The Social Poetics of Kingship in Ancient Israel." Ph.D. diss., Harvard University, 2000.

Huwiler, Elizabeth. *Proverbs, Ecclesiastes, Song of Songs*. New International Biblical Commentary. Peabody, MA: Hendrickson Publishers, 1999.

Kaiser, Walter C., Jr. "True Marital Love in Proverbs 5:15-23 and the Interpretation of Song of Songs." *The Way of Wisdom: Essays in Honor of Bruce K. Waltke*. Ed. by J.I. Packer and Sven K. Soderlund. Grand Rapids: Zondervan, 2000.

LaCocque, André. *Romance She Wrote: A Hermeneutical Essay on Song of Songs*. Harrisburg: Trinity Press, 1998.

Longman, Tremper, III. *Song of Songs*. The New International Commentary. Grand Rapids: Eerdmans, 2001.

Marrs, Rick. *Preaching from Song of Songs*. Austin, TX: Institute for Christian Studies, May 18-21, 1998. Audiotape.

Meyers, Carol. *Discovering Eve: Ancient Israelite Women in Context.* New York: Oxford University Press, 1988.

Murphy, Roland E. *The Song of Songs*. Hermenia. Minneapolis: Fortress Press, 1990.

Nelson, Tom. *Love Song: From Attraction to Faithfulness.* Denton Bible Church, Denton, TX. Six sermons delivered from 9-1-1991 to 10-6-1991. Videocassette series.

Pope, Marvin H. *Song of Songs*. The Anchor Bible. Garden City: Doubleday, 1977.

Provan, Iain. *Ecclesiastes, Song of Songs*. The NIV Application Commentary. Grand Rapids: Zondervan, 2001.

_____ . "The Terrors of the Night: Love, Sex, and Power in Song of Songs 3." In *The Way of Wisdom: Essays in Honor of Bruce K. Waltke*. Ed. by J.I. Packer and Sven K. Soderlund. Grand Rapids: Zondervan, 2000.

Schaff, Philip, and Henry Wace, eds. "St. Jerome: Letters and Select Works." In 2nd series, vol. VI, Letter CVII. *Nicene and Post-Nicene Fathers*. Grand Rapids: Eerdmans, 1979.

Snaith, John. *Song of Songs*. The New Century Bible Commentary. Grand Rapids: Eerdmans, 1993.

Tanner, J.P. "The History of the Interpretation of the Song of Songs." *Bibliotheca Sacra* 154 (1997): 27-28.

Trever, J.C. "Mandrake." In *Interpreter's Dictionary of the Bible*, vol. 3. Ed. by George Arthur Buttrick. Nashville: Abingdon Press, 1962.

Walsh, Carey. *Exquisite Desire: Religion, the Erotic, and the Song of Songs*. Minneapolis: Fortress, 2000.

Weems, Reneta. "Song of Songs," *New Interpreters Bible* (Nashville: Abingdon, 1997).

Zohary, M. "Flora." In *Interpreter's Dictionary of the Bible*, vol. 2. Ed. by George Arthur Buttrick. Nashville: Abingdon Press, 1962.

SONG OF SONGS

I. HEADING (1:1)

[1]Solomon's Song of Songs.

1:1 The writer who compiled this song believed that this was the greatest of all songs; it was the **Song of Songs**. The phrase is a superlative similar to others found in the Old Testament, such as "holy of holies" (Exod 26:33-34) or "vanity of vanities" (Eccl 1:1) or "king of kings" (Dan 2:37).

The name of **Solomon** is mentioned seven times in the book including this heading (1:1,5; 3:7,9,11; and 8:11-12). Questions arise regarding his connection with the Song (see Authorship in Introduction). Is this Song related to one of Solomon's love affairs (e.g., his relationship with Abishag the Shunammite; 1 Kgs 1:3,15; 2:17-22)? It seems unlikely. The Shulammite mentioned in 6:13 is similar but only in sound. No solid evidence exists for understanding the two as synonymous (see comments on 6:13).

Solomon does not stand as a model of fidelity to one woman as the Song of Songs portrays (1 Kgs 11:1-6). Solomon with his wealth, splendor, and many women stands as the negative counterpart to the exclusive commitment that is expressed between the two lovers portrayed in this Song. It seems unlikely, therefore, that he is the author of this material.

So what is his connection with this book? Solomon's name is often connected with the larger wisdom corpus (e.g., Proverbs and Ecclesiastes). The writer of 1 Kings also says that Solomon wrote 1,005 songs (1 Kgs 4:29-34). More than likely, Solomon's name is attached to this book because of his reputation as a poet. Because of his splendid poetic ability, this Song is *dedicated* to Solomon: "The Song of Songs which is *for* Solomon."

II. THE LOVERS' INITIAL PRESENTATION (1:2-17)

[2]Let him kiss me with the kisses of his mouth—
  for your love is more delightful than wine.
[3]Pleasing is the fragrance of your perfumes;
  your name is like perfume poured out.
  No wonder the maidens love you!
[4]Take me away with you—let us hurry!
  Let the king bring me into his chambers.
We rejoice and delight in you[b];
  we will praise your love more than wine.
How right they are to adore you!

[b]*4 The Hebrew is masculine singular.*

1:2-4 The woman opens the dialogue with a poem of yearning for her lover. That the woman initiates the dialogue is especially remarkable in a patriarchal culture. The book begins and ends with the words of the woman (see 8:14).

The reader is introduced to a relationship that is already in full stride. The woman wastes no words but gets right to the point: **Let him kiss me with the kisses of his mouth**. She is confident and assertive in her approach. She longs for his kisses, which are **more delightful than wine** (cf. 4:10). Because of her lover's uniqueness, other women are infatuated with him as well. So the woman proclaims, it is **no wonder the maidens love you** (v. 3b). The woman yearns for her lover's presence and for him to whisk her away.

Then she proclaims, **let the king bring me into his chambers** (v. 4b). Some argue that the king is Solomon and that this verse indicates that the young woman is a part of his harem. She has been taken against her will to be one of the many women in the royal harem.[1] The woman desires to be released from the harem by pleading with the lover to **take me away with you!** This interpretation understands the lover and the king as two different people. However, the interpreter must read too much into the text to come up with this "plot" (see Dramatic Interpretation in Introduction).

It is better to understand the term "king" as a term of endearment for the woman's lover. The woman uses royal imagery to

---

[1]Provan, *Ecclesiastes, Song,* p. 266.

describe her lover (see 1:12; 7:5).[2] The lover is a king who brings her into his presence. We might say that he is her "Prince Charming." Such love makes the couple feel like royalty.[3] All through the Song the love poems use royal language to describe the lovers' relationship. The woman uses it to describe their wedding (see 3:6-11). She also uses royal imagery to describe the physical features of her lover (see 5:10-16).

For the king to bring her into his chambers assumes marriage and sexual intimacy (cf. Judg 15:1; Joel 2:16). Since the Song of Songs is not a narrative sequence, some poems assume a covenant relationship between the lovers while others do not (cf. 8:8-9).

[5]**Dark am I, yet lovely,**

    O daughters of Jerusalem,

    dark like the tents of Kedar,

    like the tent curtains of Solomon.[a]

[6]**Do not stare at me because I am dark,**

    because I am darkened by the sun.

My mother's sons were angry with me

    and made me take care of the vineyards;

    my own vineyard I have neglected.

[a]5 Or *Salma*

1:5-6 These verses contain a self-description of the woman and her relationship to her brothers. The woman describes herself as **dark am I, yet lovely.** "Dark" is not a reference to her being black in the sense of race, as some have argued.[4] As the Song discloses, her darkness is due to overexposure to the sun as she worked in the **vineyards** (v. 6; cf. Job 30:30). She is dark, yet she is still able to say that she is lovely. That is, she is able to accept her physical appearance.

---

[2]Murphy, *Song,* pp. 83, 127. A good treatment of the meaning of "king" is found in Mark W. Hamilton, "The Body Royal: The Social Poetics of Kingship in Ancient Israel" (Ph.D. diss., Harvard University, 2000), pp. 303-322.

[3]John Snaith, *Song of Songs,* The New Century Bible Commentary (Grand Rapids: Eerdmans, 1993), p. 16.

[4]Reneta J. Weems argues at length for translating שָׁחַר (*šāḥar*) literally as "black." Weems, "Song of Songs," *New Interpreters Bible* (Nashville: Abingdon, 1997), pp. 382-383. Though the word means "black" (BDB, p. 1007), it does not mean it in the racial sense of the word. Modern racial problems should not be imposed on this verse. The NRSV does a disservice by translating the phrase "I am black and beautiful."

In verse 6 the readers learn why the woman's skin is dark. It is because she has been punished by her brothers (**my mother's sons**). Because they were angry with her, they forced her to work in the vineyards. As a result, she was not able to take care of her own **vineyard**.

The word "vineyard" is often used in the Song as a reference to the woman (7:12; 8:12).[5] The woman uses the term to refer to herself. Because of the hard work in the vineyards, she was not able to care for her own complexion. Thus her skin became dark. Dark, tanned skin was not admired. Light, fair skin was a sign of beauty (however, in 6:10 the woman is described as being "fair as the moon"). In the eyes of others around her, such as the **daughters of Jerusalem**, her appearance leaves much to be desired.[6] In the eyes of her lover, however, the woman's beauty is beyond comparison (e.g., 2:2; 4:1-5). The woman is made beautiful through love.

The brothers are one group of males that appear to abuse and mistreat the woman. They represent the male-dominated society of the day (cf. 8:8-10). It is against this male domination and abuse that the woman enters into a relationship of mutuality with her lover.

Verse 5 introduces the reader to the daughters of Jerusalem. Who are these women? Are they rivals, a bridal party, a part of the king's harem? The daughters do not appear in an adversarial role in the song. Neither are they fully interactive partners with the woman. Rather sometimes they serve as a foil with which the woman is contrasted (a country girl in contrast to city girls). Sometimes they are viewed as naïve women whom the woman must instruct in the ways of love (cf. 2:7; 3:5; 8:4). Sometimes they serve as a sounding board for the woman in order to enable the dialogue to continue (cf. 5:8-9; 6:1).

[7]Tell me, you whom I love, where you graze your flock
    and where you rest your sheep at midday.
Why should I be like a veiled woman
    beside the flocks of your friends?
[8]If you do not know, most beautiful of women,
    follow the tracks of the sheep

---

[5]For the sexual symbolism of "vineyard," see Pope, *Song,* pp. 323-325.

[6]The poems appear to set up a contrast between the country girl who is a common laborer and the city girls (daughters of Jerusalem) who are supposedly more sophisticated.

and graze your young goats
>> by the tents of the shepherds.
⁹I liken you, my darling, to a mare
>> harnessed to one of the chariots of Pharaoh.
¹⁰Your cheeks are beautiful with earrings,
>> your neck with strings of jewels.
¹¹We will make you earrings of gold,
>> studded with silver.

1:7 The woman describes her beau as a shepherd tending **sheep** (v. 7). She wants to know where she can find him: where do **you rest your sheep at midday?** That is, where does he pause to rest and relax in the heat of the day? She longs to meet him there.

Why should I be like a veiled woman beside the flocks of your friends? (v. 7b). The meaning of the phrase is uncertain. She may be saying that if she does not know a specific location where they can rendezvous, she will be forced to cover herself and go in search of him. Why she must cover herself is uncertain. Maybe she must hide her identity in order to keep their love secret since others do not accept their love as legitimate (cf. 8:1). The danger is that in covering herself she might be mistaken for a prostitute (cf. Gen 38:14-15).[7]

1:8 Verses 8-11 appear to be a response to the question in verse 7, so it seems natural to assume that a change in speakers occurs. The man enters into the dialogue and replies to the young woman. The dialogue takes on the appearance of a friendly tease, a sensual game of hide-and-seek between the two lovers.

The imagery of shepherd and shepherdess are used to describe the lovers. This is the only time the man is depicted by the woman as a shepherd. Like "king" (see v. 4), "shepherd" is a term of endearment. On other occasions in the Song, the term "browse" (רָעָה, rā'āh) is used to describe the man as "browsing" among the lilies (i.e., to "feed" or "pasture" 2:16; 6:2,3). Picturing the man as browsing, however, is not the image of a shepherd.

The presence and absence of either one or the other of the lovers is a frequent theme in the Song. One seeks out the other while the other plays hard to get. The hide-and-seek game is an expression of affection and romance. The motif is a playful one for the lovers.

---

[7]See Murphy, *Songs,* p. 131.

1:9 Verses 8-11 contain the first words of admiration from the man. The man refers to the woman as **my darling** (רַעְיָה, *raᵃyāh*) or "my friend/companion" (v. 9a). This is the most frequent term used to describe the female lover (1:9,15; 2:2,10,13; 4:1,7; 5:2; 6:4).[8] It is a term of endearment. She is his belle.

The male lover likens the woman **to a mare harnessed to one of the chariots of Pharaoh** (v. 9a). Marvin Pope suggests that the meaning of this phrase becomes clearer when one understands that pairs of *stallions* pulled Pharaoh's chariots.[9] The Hebrew does not contain the word "harness" but simply says "a mare among the chariots of Pharaoh." Sometimes armies used the defensive strategy of letting loose a mare in heat among the stallions pulling chariots, distracting the stallions so they could not continue the attack. As Carey Walsh puts it, a "woman's sexuality had the power to throw a powerful army into confusion."[10]

1:10-11 The words of admiration continue in verses 10-11. The first person plural is used in verse 11, **we**. It appears that other men admire her beauty just as other women admired the man (vv. 3-4). The focus is on the ornaments that enhance the woman's attractiveness.

[12]**While the king was at his table,**
    my perfume spread its fragrance.
[13]**My lover is to me a sachet of myrrh**
    resting between my breasts.
[14]**My lover is to me a cluster of henna blossoms**
    from the vineyards of En Gedi.

1:12-13 The woman appears to be the speaker in these verses. One question raised in these verses is, is there a contrast between verse 12 and verses 13-14? That is, is there a contrast between the **king** (i.e. Solomon) and the **lover**? Those advocating a narrative plot to the book say "yes," arguing that there is no intimacy between the

---

[8]The female lover quotes her beloved in 5:2 using four terms of endearment to describe her, one of them being my darling; "my sister, my darling, my dove, my flawless one." The woman uses the term (*raᵃyāh*) once to refer to the man (5:16).

[9]Pope, *Song,* pp. 338-339.

[10]Carey Walsh, *Exquisite Desire: Religion, the Erotic, and the Song of Songs* (Minneapolis: Fortress, 2000), p. 135.

woman and the king in verse 12, while there is between the woman and her lover in verses 13-14 (see Brief History of Interpretation in the Introduction).

The tone of verse 12, however, does not seem negative but affirmative. It is better to understand "king" as a metaphor for "lover," as was the case in verse 4. "King" is a term of adoration. The focus of both verses 12 and 13 appears to be on the aromatic odor given off by the two lovers, serving as an invitation for both to share in physical intimacy. **Myrrh** is an aromatic resin extracted from certain trees that is associated with lovemaking (cf. Prov 7:14-20). Walsh says it has a "rich, woody, sweet scent, and is available as incense still today."[11] The lover lying between the woman's **breasts** like a pouch of myrrh, depicts an erotic scene. The woman's breasts are mentioned eight times in the Song (1:13; 4:5; 7:3,7,8; 8:1,8,10).

1:14 Henna was a shrub or tree. The leaves from this plant were crushed and mixed with water to form a paste that made a yellow, orange, or red dye. Arab women used the dye mainly for coloring the nails of fingers and toes.[12] The **cluster of henna blossoms** also produces a pleasing aroma. However, some suggest the emphasis is not so much on the aroma as on the shape of the henna plant. It is a plant that takes the shape of a male sex organ.[13] **En Gedi** (v. 14) was an oasis on the western shore of the Dead Sea. It was the place to which David fled to escape from Saul (1 Sam 24:1). En Gedi, as a place of privacy for the lovers, stands in contrast to the city as a place of alienation (5:6-7).

For the first time in verses 13 and 14, the woman refers to the man as **my lover** or "my love" (דּוֹדִי, *dôdî*). This is the most common term she uses to describe her beau.[14] The use of the term **vineyards** may be an indirect reference to the woman herself (cf. v. 6).

15How beautiful you are, my darling!
Oh, how beautiful!
Your eyes are doves.

---

[11]Walsh, *Desire,* p. 226 (fn).

[12]M. Zohary, "Flora," *IDB,* vol. 2 (Nashville: Abingdon Press, 1962), p. 290.

[13]Snaith, *Song,* p. 24.

[14]דּוֹד (*dôd,* "beloved, lover") is used 31 times in the book: 1:13,14,16; 2:3,8,9,10,16,17; 4:16; 5:2,4,5,6[2×],8,9[2×],10,16; 6:1[2×],2,3[2×]; 7:10,11, 12,14; 8:5,14 (BDB, p. 187).

¹⁶**How handsome you are, my lover!**
    Oh, how charming!
    And our bed is verdant.
¹⁷**The beams of our house are cedars;**
    our rafters are firs.

1:15-17 The lovers make a quick exchange of mutual admiration for one another. All through the love song, the lovers can never express enough admiration for one another. The man speaks in verse 15 using his typical designation for the woman, **my darling**. And the woman replies in verses 16 by using her favorite description, **my lover**. Both exclaim each other's beauty using the same word in Hebrew, **how beautiful** (יָפֶה, *yāpheh*). The man focuses on the beauty of the eyes of his darling, describing them as **doves** (cf. 4:1).[15] The woman speaks of the bed they share: **our bed is verdant**. It is green because it is covered with the flora and fauna of the forest. **The beams** of their **house** are made of **cedar** and its **rafters are firs**. The image of royalty appears once again as the woman describes their meeting place as a royal palace (cf. vv. 4,12). Cedar and fir signify royal luxury.

III. THE EXCLUSIVITY OF LOVE (2:1-17)

¹**I am a rose^a of Sharon,**
    a lily of the valleys.
²**Like a lily among thorns**
    is my darling among the maidens.
³**Like an apple tree among the trees of the forest**
    is my lover among the young men.
 I delight to sit in his shade,
    and his fruit is sweet to my taste.
⁴**He has taken me to the banquet hall,**
    and his banner over me is love.
⁵**Strengthen me with raisins,**
    refresh me with apples,
    for I am faint with love.

---

[15]Once the woman describes the man's eyes as being "like doves beside springs of water" (5:12).

⁶**His left arm is under my head,**
    and his right arm embraces me.
⁷**Daughters of Jerusalem, I charge you**
    by the gazelles and by the does of the field:
 Do not arouse or awaken love
    until it so desires.

ª*1 Possibly a member of the crocus family*

2:1 The dialogue continues with the woman comparing herself to a flower: **I am a rose of Sharon, a lily of the valleys**. Debate ensues over whether this is a modest statement on the part of the woman or an extravagant claim regarding her own unique beauty. Uncertainty exists about the kinds of flowers to which she is referring. Is the "rose" the same kind of flower we call a rose in North America? If so, then this flower was extremely rare in Palestine at that time. As such it may refer to the rarity of the woman's beauty. Pope asserts that the rose was not native to Palestine and was brought in later from Persia and Armenia.[16] Or is the rose mentioned here a common wild flower? The LXX translates it in this latter sense using the common word for flower (ἄνθος).

It seems better to translate the word as a common flower or crocus[17] and understand the woman expressing a level of modesty in her comparison. The Good News Bible appropriately translates the phrase in the following way: "I am only a wild flower." This fits better with the woman's self-description made in 1:6: "Do not gaze at me because I am dark."

The **lily**, referred to in the second line, also serves to reinforce the interpretation of the rose as a common flower. The lily is mentioned eight times in the Song (2:1,2,16; 4:5; 5:13; 6:2,3; 7:2). "Lily" may be a generic term for springtime flowers in the valleys of Palestine. Animals are described as feeding among the lilies (4:5; 6:2). Both of these flowers emphasize that the woman does not see herself as anything out of the ordinary.

2:2 In verse 2 the man picks up on the lily imagery and turns the modesty of the woman into the highest expression of admiration: **Like**

---

[16]Pope, *Song,* p. 367.

[17]The Hebrew term for "rose" is חֲבַצֶּלֶת (*ḥăbaṣṣeleth*) which BDB translates "meadow-saffron or crocus," p. 287. The only other occurrence of this word is found in Isa 35:1.

a lily among thorns is my darling among the maidens. He paints a stark contrast between his darling and other women. In comparison she is like a lily among thorns. Her beauty far surpasses anyone else.

2:3 After the brief expression of adoration on the part of the man, the woman launches into a song of adoration regarding her lover. She begins by returning the compliment: **Like an apple tree among the trees of the forest is my lover among the young men** (v. 3). He too is unique among men. He stands out as a special tree, a fruit tree, among other ordinary trees of the forest. The apple tree was a symbolic place of romance and love. As a tree, the lover protects and provides pleasure for his darling. He protects her from the sun and provides refreshment.

2:4 He has taken me to the banquet hall is literally "he has brought me to the house of wine" which conveys more of a rural than an urban setting. It is in keeping with the image of the woman as vineyard. The meaning of the phrase, **his banner over me is love**, is unclear (v. 4b). The word "banner" (דֶּגֶל, *degel*) may refer to some kind of military image (Ps 20:1-5).[18] The man serves as a royal bodyguard looking after the queen he deeply admires.[19] In this context, the protection he offers is **love** (אַהֲבָה, *'ăhăbāh*). The image of "banner" also implies commitment.

2:5-6 Because the woman is **faint with love** for her lover, she needs to receive the refreshment of **raisins** and **apples** (v. 5). The implication is that her lover will provide her with this nourishment. The description in verse 6, in this context, is a description of intimacy. Another poem uses the refrain again in 8:3.

2:7 The woman concludes this part of her dialogue with an admonition to the **daughters of Jerusalem**. The admonition comes in the form of a refrain that occurs elsewhere in the Song (3:5; 8:4): **Do not arouse or awaken love until it so desires.** Snaith takes this to mean that the woman exhorts the daughters not to disturb the lovemaking of the two until they have been satisfied.[20] In other

---

[18]The word (*degel*) is used repeatedly in Numbers to describe the military units of different tribes. Each person is described as camping or breaking camp according to his "banner" (Num. 1:52; 2:2-3,10,17-18; 10:18). *Degel* is used on several other occasions in the Song (5:10; 6:4,10). In 5:10 the NIV translates the word "outstanding."

[19]Provan, *Ecclesiastes, Song*, p. 285.

[20]Snaith, *Song*, p. 33.

words, the admonition serves as a "Do Not Disturb" sign. LaCocque interprets the refrain as a criticism of the custom of parents requiring young teenagers to marry without their consent and without feelings of mutual love for one another.[21]

The NIV, as well as the NRSV, translates the refrain in the sense of not arousing love until the time is right. Given the emphasis in the Song on the mutually exclusive commitment made between the two lovers (e.g., 8:6-7), this interpretation better fits the context. The refrain warns against activating the powers of love outside the confines of a committed relationship. Outside the confines of the mutual commitment between two individuals who deeply respect each other, love is destructive. Within the confines of such a relationship, love's power brings healing and results in celebration. As the writer of Ecclesiastes implies, there is a proper and improper time for love (Eccl 3:1-8).

In light of the seeking and finding motif developed in the Song, the refrain also highlights the theme of delayed gratification. Just at those times when the lovers find one another, one once again eludes the other. The refrain, "do not arouse or awaken love until it so desires," serves as a literary device to help sustain the suspense in the poems.

[8]**Listen! My lover!**
    Look! Here he comes,
  leaping across the mountains,
    bounding over the hills.
[9]**My lover is like a gazelle or a young stag.**
    Look! There he stands behind our wall,
  gazing through the windows,
    peering through the lattice.
[10]**My lover spoke and said to me,**
    "Arise, my darling,
    my beautiful one, and come with me.
[11]**See! The winter is past;**
    the rains are over and gone.
[12]**Flowers appear on the earth;**
    the season of singing has come,

---

[21]LaCocque, *Romance,* p. 86.

the cooing of doves
>   is heard in our land.
[13]The fig tree forms its early fruit;
>   the blossoming vines spread their fragrance.
Arise, come, my darling;
>   my beautiful one, come with me."

[14]My dove in the clefts of the rock,
>   in the hiding places on the mountainside,
show me your face,
>   let me hear your voice;
for your voice is sweet,
>   and your face is lovely.
[15]Catch for us the foxes,
>   the little foxes
that ruin the vineyards,
>   our vineyards that are in bloom.

[16]My lover is mine and I am his;
>   he browses among the lilies.
[17]Until the day breaks
>   and the shadows flee,
turn, my lover,
>   and be like a gazelle
or like a young stag
>   on the rugged hills.[a]

[a]*17 Or the hills of Bether*

2:8-17 This unit is marked off by an inclusion. It begins with the image of **hills**, a **gazelle**, and a **stag** and concludes in verse 17 with the same images. It is also marked off at the conclusion by a refrain (v. 16) that is repeated later in the book (6:3; 7:10).

The woman envisions her lover bounding toward her, arriving at her home, and then attempting to woo her into a relationship with him. She sees him standing outside gazing through the windows, waiting for the right moment to extend his appeal. In verse 10b, the woman imagines the appeal her lover makes to her, enticing her to come with him.

The tone of the passage is one of urgency with the repetition of the word **Look!** (or "pay attention!"; vv. 8,9,11; Hebrew הִנֵּה, *hinnēh*). The man seeks to entice the woman out of her house where she remains hidden and inaccessible. But the outside world is a danger-ous place for a woman (cf. v. 15 and also 1:6; 5:7). He persuades her to come out by singing a beautiful song of praise to spring.

Verses 11-13 describe the passing of **winter** and the coming of springtime. Winter was the rainy season of the year. The man invites the woman to experience the delights of a garden with him. The imagery depicts newness, freshness, and anticipation. Romance and springtime have always gone together.

Once again this poem highlights the presence and absence theme, a teasing game that the lovers play. The lovers experience the ebb and flow of the relationship in terms of separation and togetherness (unity) with one another. It is a part of their relation-ship. They cannot always be together. And when separated, they must work to come back together again. On one level, it is a playful teasing in which they engage. On another level, it expresses the real-ity of a relationship that involves both oneness and separation and results in contentment as well as pain.

In the context of the passage, it is best to understand verse 15 as the voice of the woman. One of the obstacles that keeps the lovers sep-arated is **the little foxes that ruin the vineyards**. "Vineyards" is a metaphor for young women (cf. 1:6). Foxes were notorious for destroying vineyards. Who the foxes represent is uncertain. They could represent young men out to violate young women. Neverthe-less whomever the foxes represent, they ultimately symbolize obsta-cles that stand in the way of the two lovers. The woman calls on her lover to protect her from these little foxes.

The poem concludes with the woman once again in the arms of her lover after the encounter with the foxes. She expresses the mutual and reciprocal love she shares with him through the words of a refrain: **My lover is mine and I am his**. This "mutual posses-sion" refrain, which appears again in 6:3 and 7:10, highlights an important motif in the Song: the exclusive love and respect that the two share for one another. Neither partner uses force or coercion to get their way. Rather, the two share love in a give-and-take relation-ship. Such a relationship is amazing when one considers the male-dominated culture of the day (read, e.g., the story of Xerxes and Vashti in Esther 1). Women were the property of the male members of their family. The Song of Songs offers a counterculture view-

point. By choice, the woman can extend or withhold herself from
the man. The man and woman deeply respect one another.

One way they show respect for each other is in the give-and-take
of conversation. Chapters 1–2 describe an ongoing dialogue
between the two lovers. The Song does celebrate the physical body
in the relationship (e.g., 4:1-7; 5:10-16), but it views the relationship
between a man and a woman holistically. Continual and intimate
conversation occurs before they experience physical contact and
sexual satisfaction.

IV. THE WOMAN YEARNS FOR HER LOVER AND THEIR WEDDING DAY (3:1-11)

Chapter 3 contains two poems. The first includes verses 1-5 and
the second verses 6-11. The two poems have certain linguistic ties
with each other. In both, the mother plays a role (vv. 4,11). And both
speak of events that take place during the nighttime (vv. 1,8).
However, the two poems remain distinct in thought and imagery.

¹All night long on my bed
       I looked for the one my heart loves;
       I looked for him but did not find him.
²I will get up now and go about the city,
       through its streets and squares;
   I will search for the one my heart loves.
       So I looked for him but did not find him.
³The watchmen found me
       as they made their rounds in the city.
       "Have you seen the one my heart loves?"
⁴Scarcely had I passed them
       when I found the one my heart loves.
   I held him and would not let him go
       till I had brought him to my mother's house,
       to the room of the one who conceived me.
⁵Daughters of Jerusalem, I charge you
       by the gazelles and by the does of the field:
   Do not arouse or awaken love
       until it so desires.

3:1-5 This poem envisions a dreamlike experience of the woman (v. 1a). The poem in 5:2-7 also recounts a corresponding dreamlike state. Unlike the first two chapters of the book, which have their setting in a rural context, this one takes place in the city (vv. 2-3).

In her dreamlike state, the woman finds herself once again separated from her lover. She aggressively launches a seek-and-find mission. She encounters **the watchmen** but they seem neither to help nor hinder her in her search (cf. 5:7).[22] Or perhaps because the incident is surreal she experiences only a partial encounter with the watchmen. When she finally finds her lover, she takes him to her **mother's house**[23] where they are reunited in the room where she was conceived (v. 4).[24] The lovers overcome the obstacle of separation. But can they remain together? All through the book they continually experience the frustrations of separation and togetherness. Their relationship does not experience immediate or spontaneous consummation; it is defined more by delayed gratification.

The mother's house appears to stand for a place of intimacy. Isaac and Rebekah, for example, consummate their marriage in their mother's tent (Gen 24:67). In the Song, the woman leads the man into the private world of her mother's house where they can express their exclusive and intimate love for one another (cf. 8:1-3). An additional observation worthy of note is that mothers seemed to play an important role in arranging the marriage of their daughters (cf. Ruth 1:8-9).

The poem ends once again with an admonition to the **daughters of Jerusalem**: **Do not arouse or awaken love until it so desires** (v. 5). The admonition reminds the daughters that love is not to be trifled with. It is dangerous when activated outside a mutually exclusive relationship of two people expressing a deep commitment to one another.

⁶Who is this coming up from the desert
    like a column of smoke,

---

[22]For other references to city watchmen see Ps 127:1; 130:6; Isa 21:11f.

[23]Compare Gen 24:28; Ruth 1:8. For a discussion of the term "mother's house" in contrast to the more familiar "father's house," see Carol Meyers, *Discovering Eve: Ancient Israelite Women in Context* (New York: Oxford University Press, 1988), pp. 177-181.

[24]A number of references are made in the Song to the mother: 1:6; 3:4,11; 6:9; 8:2,5.

perfumed with myrrh and incense
>   made from all the spices of the merchant?
[7]Look! It is Solomon's carriage,
>   escorted by sixty warriors,
>   the noblest of Israel,
[8]all of them wearing the sword,
>   all experienced in battle,
>   each with his sword at his side,
>   prepared for the terrors of the night.
[9]King Solomon made for himself the carriage;
>   he made it of wood from Lebanon.
[10]Its posts he made of silver,
>   its base of gold.
>   Its seat was upholstered with purple,
>   its interior lovingly inlaid
>   by[a] the daughters of Jerusalem.
[11]Come out, you daughters of Zion,
>   and look at King Solomon wearing the crown,
>   the crown with which his mother crowned him
>   on the day of his wedding,
>   the day his heart rejoiced.

[a]10 Or *its inlaid interior a gift of love / from*

3:6-11 Scholars offer a variety of interpretations for understanding this poem. I briefly mention three of the more prominent ones. First, some argue that to properly understand the poem, one must interpret it from a mythological context. The poem portrays the wedding of a god and goddess. Second, some maintain that the poem describes an actual historical event, a wedding processional associated with **King Solomon**. Third, Solomon and his wealth serve as a metaphor to describe the "royal love" of the two lovers. That is, the poem demonstrates yet another way the Song uses regal imagery to depict the relationship between the man and the woman. Royal experiences are appropriated to nonroyal figures.[25]

Of the variety of interpretive approaches that have been offered to explain the poem, one of the issues boils down to whether the

---

[25]Mark Hamilton in his dissertation concludes that the poem creates "a royal character who, fictitiously, bears the name of the great Israelite monarch." See Hamilton, "The Body Royal," p. 321.

poem recounts an actual historical event or whether it uses royal imagery to describe the wedding of the two lovers.

As an historical event, some scholars choose to interpret the poem as a counterimage to the relationship described between the two lovers. For example, Iain Provan argues that this poem stands in intentional contrast to the previous one in 3:1-5.[26] In the previous poem, one man and one woman give themselves freely in commitment to one another. In this poem, the character of Solomon seeks sexual gratification with many women. He knows no intimacy or fulfillment. Provan interprets the **carriage** in verse 7 (מִטָּה, *miṭṭah*)[27] and verse 9 (אַפִּרְיוֹן, *'appiryôn*)[28] as Solomon's bed (carriage-bed). The overall image described is of a large stationary structure (v. 10), not a movable object.[29] Solomon "drives" around in his chariot-bed, forcing himself on the **daughters of Jerusalem**. Verse 6 is an allusion to the sacrifice of the female victim lying on the altar of Solomon's bed. The desert is a metaphor for bed, a harsh and dangerous place to be. The **warriors** (v. 7) are elite guards whom Solomon stations around his bed as much to keep women in as to keep intruders out.[30] Provan understands 3:6-11 as a bitter satire about Solomon's "sacrificial female victims."[31] The poem exposes the perversity of Solomon's lifestyle. Though intriguing, Provan's interpretation requires too much speculation in imposing his details on the poem.

In contrast to interpreting the poem as depicting an historical event in the life of Solomon, it is better to take the text seriously as poetry. As poetry, it uses the language of royalty and of Solomon's wealth to describe the wedding of the two lovers. Other poems in the Song use regal imagery to flatter the beau (e.g., 1:4,12; 5:10-16). From this perspective, the royal fiction depicts the woman's fantasy about her approaching wedding day. This is her wedding procession. The imagery of desert, smoke, and burning incense highlight

---

[26]Provan, *Ecclesiastes, Song,* p. 304. See also Provan, "The Terrors of the Night: Love, Sex, and Power in Song of Songs 3," in *The Way of Wisdom: Essays in Honor of Bruce K. Waltke*, ed. by J.I. Packer and Sven K. Soderlund (Grand Rapids: Zondervan, 2000), pp. 150-167.

[27]BDB define *miṭṭah* as "couch" or "bed," p. 641.

[28]BDB define *'appiryôn* as "sedan, litter, palanquin," p. 68.

[29]Provan, *Ecclesiastes, Song,* pp. 300-301.

[30]Ibid., p. 303.

[31]Ibid., p. 304.

the opulence of the wedding procession. This interpretation is more consistent with the nature of the Song as poetry and with the frequent use of imperial language in the book.

The **carriage** mentioned in verse 7 and described in verses 9-10 is a litter or palanquin, which is like a portable recliner. The litter symbolizes wealth, luxury, and power. So valuable is the one who rides in the palanquin that it is escorted by sixty of the finest battle-experienced soldiers in Israel who are on constant guard (vv. 7-8). The word for **seat** (מֶרְכָּב, *merkāb*) in verse 10 is the masculine form of the same word in 6:12 for "chariot" (מֶרְכָּבָה, *merkābāh*).

The carriage is described in some detail in verses 9-10. It is made out of **gold** and **silver** and **upholstered** with the royal color of **purple**. The **interior** is **lovingly inlaid by the daughters of Jerusalem**. Pope thinks this means that "love scenes" were painted on the interior of the litter.[32] However, it may mean that the women who made the material for the litter did so with tender loving care. The ultimate purpose in describing the wealth and grandeur of **Solomon's** wedding is to appropriate it to the magnificence of the wedding of the two lovers.[33]

V. THE MAN LONGS FOR HIS BRIDE (4:1–5:1)

Chapter 4:1–5:1 is the only unit of material in the Song of Songs in which the man's voice is more prominent than the woman's. The woman speaks only in 4:16. The poem in verses 1-7 is the first of four songs describing the physical beauty of the two lovers. These descriptive poems are often referred to as *wasfs* (an Arabic word meaning "description"). Three of the poems praise the woman's body (4:1-7; 6:4-10; 7:1-9) and one praises the man's (5:10-16). Verses 1 and 7 serve as an inclusion marking this poem off as a single unit.

Scripture rarely describes the physical features of a person. No physical description of Jesus exists. Characters in Scripture are described in only the most general way. David is handsome (1 Sam 16:12). Tamar is beautiful (2 Sam 13:1). Absalom is described as handsome with long hair (2 Sam 14:25-26). Physical beauty was not

---

[32]Pope, *Song,* p. 445.
[33]Longman, *Song,* p. 136.

a significant matter (1 Sam 16:7). So when it comes to the Song of Songs, these physical descriptions stand out.

In 1:5-6 the woman is unveiled and exposed to the sun; her complexion ravaged by the elements. In contrast, in this descriptive poem the woman is veiled; she appears more refined. The poet unfolds a sophisticated description of the woman's body. But it is the same woman.[34] The description in chapter 1 is self-description. Even though in her own eyes her complexion may not be beautiful, she still can accept herself as "lovely." The modesty of her self-description also comes out in 2:1 where she describes herself as a common flower. In this descriptive poem, however, the perspective comes from the lover who perceives her differently than she perceives herself (cf. 2:1 and 2). It is the same woman but a different viewpoint. The lover is not engaged in an attempt at seduction but an expression of appreciation, which is mutually shared by the woman (see her description of the man 5:10-16).

[1]**How beautiful you are, my darling!**
> **Oh, how beautiful!**
> **Your eyes behind your veil are doves.**
Your hair is like a flock of goats
> **descending from Mount Gilead.**
[2]**Your teeth are like a flock of sheep just shorn,**
> **coming up from the washing.**
Each has its twin;
> **not one of them is alone.**
[3]**Your lips are like a scarlet ribbon;**
> **your mouth is lovely.**
Your temples behind your veil
> **are like the halves of a pomegranate.**
[4]**Your neck is like the tower of David,**
> **built with elegance[a];**
> **on it hang a thousand shields,**
> **all of them shields of warriors.**
[5]**Your two breasts are like two fawns,**
> **like twin fawns of a gazelle**
> **that browse among the lilies.**

---

[34]Snaith argues that this is a different woman than the one in chapter 1 (*Song*, p. 58).

[6]**Until the day breaks**
          and the shadows flee,
I will go to the mountain of myrrh
          and to the hill of incense.
[7]**All beautiful you are, my darling;**
          there is no flaw in you.

[a]*4 The meaning of the Hebrew for this word is uncertain.*

4:1-2 The *wasf* proceeds downward from the **eyes** to the breasts. The description is evocative and representational. Verse 1 is identical to 1:15. The woman's **eyes are doves**, meaning that her eyes are *like* doves just as her **hair is** *like* **a flock of goats** and her **teeth are** *like* **a flock of sheep.** How her eyes compare to doves is not certain. It could be that they are like a dove's shimmering color. Or her eyes flutter in a romantic way like the fluttering of a dove.

Her hair is compared to a flock of goats **descending from Mount Gilead** (v. 1b). That is, her long hair flows loosely down her back like a heard of goats gracefully moving down a mountainside. Her teeth are like a flock of sheep **just shorn, coming up from the washing** (v. 2a). Her teeth remind the poet of the whiteness of newly sheared sheep. **Each has its twin; not one of them is alone** (v. 2b). In other words, her upper teeth evenly match her lower teeth with none missing. Though beauty may be defined differently by different cultures, one universal sign of beauty may be the whiteness and uniformity of a woman's teeth. The description is especially amazing in light of the absence of dental hygiene in ancient culture.

4:3 The man continues the detailed description of the woman's face as he speaks of her **lips** and **mouth**. The **pomegranate** was a pleasingly red color, round, and sweet to the taste. The woman's **temples** or cheeks are compared to this fruit (v. 3b). Not only do her cheeks have color, but they are also round, not sunken, like pomegranate. In other words, she is well fed and in good health.

4:4 From her face, the lover moves down to her **neck**, which he describes as being **like the tower of David, built with elegance.** The emphasis is not so much on the *physical appearance*, for example a long thick neck like an athlete, as it is on the *value* of her neck. She is strong and dignified.[35] As a whole, verse 4 employs military images to portray

---

[35]Longman, *Song,* p. 146.

the woman's beauty. On her neck **hang a thousand shields, all of them shields of warriors**. These weapons hanging on the tower are used for protection; this is a fortified city. The man may be implying that the overwhelming beauty of the woman intimidates him. How could he or anyone else for that matter approach her?[36]

The poet frequently uses military images to describe the belle and her surroundings. For example, the pools and reservoirs in 7:4 are for military purposes. The "wall" and the "door" in 8:9 are used in military operations related to the siege of a city. The reference to the "banner" appears to be a military term (2:4; 6:4,10). The description of her neck being like the tower of David fits into this motif of military imagery used in the Song.

4:5 Reference to the woman's breasts indicates intimacy. Her breasts are compared to **twin fawns of a gazelle that browse among the lilies** (v. 5). Gazelles were known for their beauty and gracefulness. The use of "twin" denotes the symmetry of the breasts. That the breasts are compared to fawns may indicate smallness and youthful vigor. Her breasts are petite and equal in size (cf. 7:3). Pope observes that, according to Arabic custom, the ideal attribute for a woman was to have small breasts.[37] Smallness of breasts may also indicate virginity because the woman has not yet nursed.

4:6-7 Verses 6 and 7 conclude the descriptive poem and recall the reader back to the beginning line. **The mountain of myrrh** and **the hill of incense** may refer to the body of the woman. The images contain sensual overtones. Myrrh was a type of aphrodisiac, giving off a sexually stimulating aroma (see also Ps 45:8). The man cannot heap enough praise on his lover: **All beautiful you are, my darling; there is no flaw in you.** Carey Walsh appropriately observes that the poetry of this song requires that the lover take time to appreciate the beauty of the one he loves. Love is not something that two lovers can rush. There is no place for impatience or immediate gratification.[38]

[8]Come with me from Lebanon, my bride,
    come with me from Lebanon.

---

[36]LaCocque refers to one commentator who sees the image in verse 4 as meaning that the woman is so beautiful that a thousand soldiers would lay down their implements of war at her feet in surrender (*Romance*, p. 105).

[37]Pope, *Song*, p. 470.

[38]Walsh, *Desire*, p. 65.

Descend from the crest of Amana,
    from the top of Senir, the summit of Hermon,
from the lions' dens
    and the mountain haunts of the leopards.
⁹You have stolen my heart, my sister, my bride;
    you have stolen my heart
with one glance of your eyes,
    with one jewel of your necklace.
¹⁰How delightful is your love, my sister, my bride!
    How much more pleasing is your love than wine,
    and the fragrance of your perfume than any spice!
¹¹Your lips drop sweetness as the honeycomb, my bride;
    milk and honey are under your tongue.
    The fragrance of your garments is like that of Lebanon.
¹²You are a garden locked up, my sister, my bride;
    you are a spring enclosed, a sealed fountain.
¹³Your plants are an orchard of pomegranates
    with choice fruits,
    with henna and nard,
¹⁴   nard and saffron,
    calamus and cinnamon,
    with every kind of incense tree,
    with myrrh and aloes
    and all the finest spices.
¹⁵You are[a] a garden fountain,
    a well of flowing water
    streaming down from Lebanon.

¹⁶Awake, north wind,
    and come, south wind!
Blow on my garden,
    that its fragrance may spread abroad.
Let my lover come into his garden
    and taste its choice fruits.

⁵:¹I have come into my garden, my sister, my bride;
    I have gathered my myrrh with my spice.
I have eaten my honeycomb and my honey;
    I have drunk my wine and my milk.

Eat, O friends, and drink;
    drink your fill, O lovers.

ᵃ15 Or *I am* (spoken by the *Beloved*) *gone out to him when he spoke*

440

4:8 A dialogue ensues among the lovers with the man speaking most of the time. The woman responds only in verse 16. The man opens the conversation by referring to the woman as **my bride** (כַּלָּה אִתִּי, *kallāh 'ittî*; "a bride with me"). Six times in this section, and only here in the Song, the paramour uses this term of endearment to refer to his "friend" or "darling" (4:8,9,10,11,12; 5:1).[39] The word assumes the two are in a committed relationship with one another. Lebanon is the generic name for the mountain range that runs along the coast of North Israel. Some of the mountain summits tower 11,000 feet high.[40] **Amana, Senir** and **Hermon** are other mountains in this range. The mountains signify the distance and inaccessibility of the woman (2:14). Describing the wild animals that inhabit the region further highlights her remoteness: **the lions' dens and the mountain haunts of the leopards.** The uniqueness and elusiveness of the woman intimidates the man. The man cannot force himself upon her. He can only enter into relationship with her at her invitation. The relationship they strive for is not easy to attain; this is not an easy-come, easy-go association. It involves work, respect, commitment, and mutual consent.

4:9-11 Verses 9-11 contain a song of admiration the man speaks to the woman. He not only calls his lover **my bride,** he also refers to her for the first time as **my sister** (cf. 4:10,12; 5:1,2). "My sister" does not indicate a sibling connection but an intimate relationship. The man exclaims, **with one glance of your eyes you have stolen my heart.** The woman's dazzling eyes have an enchanting effect on the man. A young man in love today might say, "She drives me crazy!" Verses 10-11 recall the praise the woman gives to the man in 1:2-3.

4:12-15 Verses 12-15 depict the woman as a **garden** (גַּן, *gan*) which is in keeping with the vineyard metaphor the woman uses to describe herself (1:6; 8:12). She is not just an open garden anyone can come to and enjoy, she **is a garden locked up** (v. 12). The images of **locked up** and **sealed** imply virginity. She is inaccessible except to the one person she chooses to allow in. It appears that she has allowed her lover into the garden because he knows the **choice fruits** and **spices** that grow there: **Pomegranates, nard and saffron,**

---

[39]Sometimes, as in the book of Ruth, the word can refer to a daughter-in-law.

[40]A. Haldar, "Lebanon," *IDB,* 3:105.

calamus and cinnamon, with every kind of incense tree, with myrrh and aloes and all the finest spices (vv. 13-14). These verses mention over a half dozen different spices. Very few of these spices grow in the region of Palestine. The description appears to be that of a royal garden in Palestine where gardeners grew exotic plants imported from other countries.

4:16–5:1 In verse 16 the woman responds allowing the **fragrance** of her **garden** to reach the **lover**. The **north** and **south winds** stir up the aroma of the garden for her lover. The emphasis is *not* on the fact that the fragrance is **spread abroad**. The fragrance is intended only for the lover. It is better to translate the phrase, "Blow upon my garden that its spices will flow" (הָפִיחִי גַנִּי יִזְלוּ בְשָׂמָיו, *hāphîḥî gannî yizlû bᵉśāmāyw*). She opens her garden and permits only him to smell and **taste its choice fruits**. Taste, not smell or touch, is the dominant sense in the Song.[41] The locked garden (v. 12) is now open. And **my** garden becomes **his garden**. The lover responds to the invitation and enters the **garden** (v. 5:1). A group of friends, associated with either the man or the woman, encourage the lovers to **eat and drink your fill** (v. 5:1b).[42] Eating and drinking are often associated with lovemaking.

Significant parallels exist between this garden song (4:12–5:1) and the poem used in Proverbs 5:15-23.[43] In both, **water** images are used as metaphors for the joys of intimacy with one's wife: springs, fountains, wells of flowing water, and streams. Water provides life and joy. In the Song the woman is described as a garden with all kinds of vegetation, flora and fauna, and an abundance of water. "Garden" and "fountain" are metaphors the poem uses in tandem (vv. 12,15). In addition, both poems emphasize the exclusivity of the relationship. Proverbs 5:16-17 makes this admonition: "Should your springs overflow in the streets, your streams of water in the public squares? Let them be yours alone, never to be shared with strangers." In a similar vein, the Song describes the woman as a garden locked up, **a spring enclosed, a sealed fountain** (v. 12).

---

[41]Walsh, *Desire,* p. 116.

[42]Walsh misinterprets this verse, arguing that it expresses a nonmonogamous spirit (ibid., p. 125). She says the invitation in 5:1 is an invitation for others to share in the sexual pleasure.

[43]See Walter Kaiser Jr., "True Marital Love," pp. 106-116.

Proverbs 5:15-23 uses the image of the woman as a deer: "A loving doe, a graceful deer — may her breasts satisfy you always, may you ever be captivated by her love." The Song also describes the woman in this way (2:9,17; 4:5; 7:3).

The significance of the overlap in the use of metaphors is that it is clear that the instruction poem in Proverbs 5:15-23 describes the relationship between a husband and wife, as verse 18 specifies: "May your fountain be blessed, and may you rejoice in the wife of your youth." It is natural to assume that the Song portrays a similar kind of relationship. Kaiser concludes that, "there is every confidence that this is the best way to understand the Song."[44]

While I am deeply sympathetic to Kaiser's position, a number of elements in the Song indicate that the relationship between the two lovers is not completely consummated. It does not appear that their relationship has received the approval of the community (1:7; 8:1). The image of the woman as "bride" indicates a commitment, but does it mean they are married? In addition, the reader must keep in mind that the Song is an anthology of love poems and not an unfolding narrative plot. In some poems one can assume the lovers are married. In others one assumes they are not (e.g., 8:8-9).

VI. THE WOMAN LONGS FOR HER LOVER (5:2–6:12)

In chapter 5:2-6:12 the woman dominates the conversation. In 5:2-7, she describes another dreamlike experience (cf. 3:1-5). In verses 8-9, the woman and the daughters engage in a brief dialogue. In verses 10-16, the woman describes the physical beauty of the man. Chapter 6:1-3 contains a search motif in which a dialogue once again takes place between the woman and the daughters. In chapter 6:4-10 the man describes the physical beauty of the woman. The unit concludes with a tryst between the two lovers (vv. 11-12). These verses once again expose the reader to the intense emotional rollercoaster ride of an intimate relationship that moves from joy and hope (5:4b) to grief and despair (5:6).

---

[44]Ibid, p. 113.

²I slept but my heart was awake.
            Listen! My lover is knocking:
    "Open to me, my sister, my darling,
            my dove, my flawless one.
    My head is drenched with dew,
            my hair with the dampness of the night."
³I have taken off my robe—
            must I put it on again?
    I have washed my feet—
            must I soil them again?
⁴My lover thrust his hand through the latch-opening;
            my heart began to pound for him.
⁵I arose to open for my lover,
            and my hands dripped with myrrh,
    my fingers with flowing myrrh,
            on the handles of the lock.
⁶I opened for my lover,
            but my lover had left; he was gone.
            My heart sank at his departure.ᵃ
    I looked for him but did not find him.
            I called him but he did not answer.
⁷The watchmen found me
            as they made their rounds in the city.
    They beat me, they bruised me;
            they took away my cloak,
            those watchmen of the walls!
⁸O daughters of Jerusalem, I charge you—
            if you find my lover,
    what will you tell him?
            Tell him I am faint with love.

ᵃ6 Or *heart had gone out to him when he spoke*

5:2 These verses appear to contain a second dreamlike report by the woman (cf. 3:1-5).⁴⁵ Since the text is poetry, whether or not she is actually dreaming is not an issue. The poem opens by observing

---

⁴⁵Michael D. Goulder understands the poem to describe actual events that occur on the night after the wedding ceremony. Goulder, *The Song of Fourteen Songs*, JSOTSupp. 36 (Sheffield: JSOT Press, 1986), pp. 40-43.

the woman's surreal state: **I slept but my heart was awake**. While she sleeps her heart (or "mind") remains active. She hears her **lover knocking** and then recalls the appeal he makes to her: **"Open to me, my sister, my darling, my dove, my flawless one. My head is drenched with dew, my hair with the dampness of the night."** As the lover pleads with her to open, he uses four terms to describe her. The first three he has used before (my sister, 4:9; my darling, 1:9; my dove, 2:14). The fourth one, "my flawless one" (תַמָּתִי, *tam-māthî*), he uses also to characterize her beauty (cf. 6:9, where the same word is used by the lover).

5:3-4 In her dreamlike condition, she is already in bed and appears somewhat agitated by having to rise again to answer the door (v. 3). There may be some playful teasing that is taking place between the lovers. She pretends to be disinterested, playing hard to get. This teasing serves the poet's purpose of delaying gratification until the proper time. She then becomes excited about his presence: **My heart began to pound for him** (v. 4b). The word for "heart" (מֵעֶה, *mē'eh*) in Hebrew is "belly" or "internal organs."[46] In this case, the word refers to a deep-seated passion.

5:5-6 Because his presence stirs her emotionally, she arises to receive her lover but arrives too late; he is gone. She grieves. The NIV says **my heart sank at his departure**. She is lovesick. The Hebrew text reads, "my soul went out" (we might say, "a part of me died").

The woman immediately initiates a new search (v. 6b). The two lovers experience the common frustration all too familiar to them by now of seeming never quite to catch up with each other. It is the motif of presence and absence, together and apart, united and separated.

5:7 Her search turns up no trace of him (v. 6b). The **watchmen** find her (v. 7). Unlike the benign encounter previously (3:3), this time they physically abuse the woman: **They beat me, they bruised me; they took away my cloak, those watchmen of the walls!** For this woman the "dream" turns into a nightmare. After the beating, the search seems to cease. However, since what she is recounting is surreal, the dreamlike condition may only reveal partial images and incomplete encounters.

---

[46]BDB, p. 588. The KJV takes the literal meaning and comes up with a translation that is now out of date and amusing, ". . . my bowels were moved for him."

The poetic language of the text is filled with sexual innuendoes and double entendres. "Feet" (v. 3b) is sometimes used as a euphemism for genitals (cf. Ruth 3:3-9; 2 Sam 11:8; Deut 28:57). "Hand" (v. 5) on occasion may allude to the penis.[47] The lover thrusts **his hand through the latch-opening**[48] could be a phrase referring to the act of intercourse. The language is left intentionally ambiguous. In the context of their commitment to one another, these lovers are not embarrassed but celebrate their sexuality.

[9]How is your beloved better than others,
    most beautiful of women?
 How is your beloved better than others,
    that you charge us so?

[10]My lover is radiant and ruddy,
    outstanding among ten thousand.
[11]His head is purest gold;
    his hair is wavy
    and black as a raven.
[12]His eyes are like doves
    by the water streams,
 washed in milk,
    mounted like jewels.
[13]His cheeks are like beds of spice
    yielding perfume.
 His lips are like lilies
    dripping with myrrh.
[14]His arms are rods of gold
    set with chrysolite.
 His body is like polished ivory
    decorated with sapphires.[a]

---

[47]In Isaiah 57:8 a reference is made to cult prostitution in which the Israelite participants have "made a pact with those whose beds you love, and you looked on their nakedness." The word for "nakedness" is hand (יָד, yād). In Song of Songs 5:14, reference is made to the "arms" (lit., hand), which stands parallel to a term in the second line that may refer to the penis (see 5:14).

[48]Literally, "my lover sent/put his hand into/from the hole." The Hebrew does not contain the word "latch." Murphy contends that "hole" does not carry enough evidence to indicate sexual activity. The man always remains on the outside (*Song*, p. 171).

> ¹⁵**His legs are pillars of marble**
> **set on bases of pure gold.**
> **His appearance is like Lebanon,**
> **choice as its cedars.**
> ¹⁶**His mouth is sweetness itself;**
> **he is altogether lovely.**
> **This is my lover, this my friend,**
> **O daughters of Jerusalem.**

^a*14 Or lapis lazuli*

5:9 In verses 8 and 9 a dialogue ensues between the woman and the **daughters of Jerusalem**. The woman pleads with the daughters to help her find her lover. The daughters ask why the woman should be so intense in her search for this particular man. They knew there were other suitors she could find. So they inquire of the woman: **How is your beloved better than others, that you charge us so?** This gives the woman the opportunity she wants to describe her lover's unique and handsome qualities. At the conclusion of the descriptive poem (*waṣf*), she once again turns to her women friends and exclaims, "This is my lover, this my friend, O daughters of Jerusalem."

5:10-16 What follows in verses 10-16 is the only physical portrait of the man in the Song. For that matter, this is the only description of a male body in all of Scripture. Because of the material elements used to describe his features (**gold, polished ivory, pillars of marble, cedars**), the portrayal is reminiscent of a royal statue.[49] The description moves from the head downward to the legs.

The woman begins by emphasizing his uniqueness: **My lover is radiant and ruddy, outstanding among ten thousand** (v. 10). The reference to radiance may mean that in light of the precious metals used to depict the man, he may give off a healthy glow. Related to that is his ruddy or red complexion, indicating that he is attractive and in good health. David was described in a similar manner (cf. 1 Sam 16:12; 17:42). The word for "outstanding" is the Hebrew word דָּגַל (*dāgal*) and was earlier used in 2:4 as a noun translated

---

[49]Based on comparisons with Mesopotamian *waṣfs* of male deities, Mark Hamilton argues that this *waṣf* is similar in kind. The poem uses analogous language to describe the body of a king, who is the male lover in the Song. See Hamilton, "The Body Royal," pp. 315-320.

"banner." Its meaning here is uncertain, but in this context, because of his physical beauty, it seems to refer to his conspicuousness. The NIV offers a viable translation.

The man is portrayed in royal appearance (reminiscent of Dan 2:31-33; 3:1) in keeping with other royal imagery used in the poems. His **head is purest gold** (v. 11a). Not only that, at the conclusion of the poem it is said that **his legs are pillars of marble set on bases of pure gold** (v. 15). So from head to toe this "king" is made of pure gold.

His hair is wavy and black as a raven (v. 11b). The word for "black" (שָׁחֹר, šāḥōr) is the same word the woman uses to describe her complexion in 1:5,6. "Black" is often associated with youth and good health. In Ecclesiastes 11:10 the writer says "youth and black hair (הַשַּׁחֲרוּת, hašaḥărôth) are fleeting."

His eyes are like doves by the water streams, washed in milk, mounted like jewels (v. 12). Her eyes were also compared to doves (4:1). "Washed in milk" may be a reference to the whites of the eyes. If so, his dark shimmering eyes are said to glisten against the whites of his eyes, which appear to be washed in milk. The reference to **cheeks** may be to the man's beard (v. 13). Most men wore beards at this time.[50] If so, then his beard is **like beds of spice** (cf. Ps 133:2). Whether cheeks or beard, the emphasis is on smell rather than appearance.

In the second line of verse 14 she says that **his body is like polished ivory decorated with sapphires**. The word for "body" (מֵעֶה, mē'eh) usually refers to internal organs (cf. 5:4), but in this context it refers to the external "private part" of the man's lower body.[51]

The description concludes with praise for his **mouth** (חֵךְ, ḥēk, palate). Is this simply an expression of admiration for the physical features of the mouth (7:9)? Or is this expressing delight for his mouth as an organ of speech (cf. Prov 5:3; 8:7; Job 31:30; 33:2)? The **lips** have been mentioned earlier (v. 13). It is quite possible that the reference is to the man's speech (cf. RSV and NRSV; "his speech is most sweet"). If so, the woman climaxes the description of her lover by praising the **sweetness** of the speech that flows from his mouth. The two lovers

---

[50]Longman, *Song*, p. 172.

[51]BDB says "the external belly," p. 589. Weems says it most likely refers to the man's genitalia ("Song," p. 415). Longman agrees (*Song*, p. 173). The term stands parallel to "arms" (יָד, yād, lit., "hand"), which may also refer to the penis (see 5:4).

engage in dialogue all the way through the course of the book. Speech is the element that establishes and sustains their relationship.

This male is the essence of physical manhood; he is royalty. He is tall (**his appearance is like Lebanon**, like the cedars), dark (ruddy, probably due to being out in the sun; cf. 1:6), attractive (radiant), and strong (his legs are pillars of marble). In addition, he smells wonderful.

The woman uses exotic royal language to represent her lover and then to declare this lover hers. No one else is like him. He is outstanding among ten thousand. She claims him as her sole possession: **This is my lover, this my friend,**[52] **O daughters of Jerusalem**. The term "friend" used primarily by the man for the woman is an expression of equality and the mutuality of respect.

**⁶:¹Where has your lover gone,
    most beautiful of women?
Which way did your lover turn,
    that we may look for him with you?**

**²My lover has gone down to his garden,
    to the beds of spices,
to browse in the gardens
    and to gather lilies.**
**³I am my lover's and my lover is mine;
    he browses among the lilies.**

**⁴You are beautiful, my darling, as Tirzah,
    lovely as Jerusalem,
    majestic as troops with banners.**
**⁵Turn your eyes from me;
    they overwhelm me.
Your hair is like a flock of goats
    descending from Gilead.**
**⁶Your teeth are like a flock of sheep
    coming up from the washing.
Each has its twin,
    not one of them is alone.**

---

[52]Whereas the man frequently refers to the woman as "my friend" (NIV, darling), this is the only time the woman refers to the man as my friend (רֵעִי, rēʿî).

⁷**Your temples behind your veil**
    are like the halves of a pomegranate.
⁸**Sixty queens there may be,**
    and eighty concubines,
    and virgins beyond number;
⁹**but my dove, my perfect one, is unique,**
    the only daughter of her mother,
    the favorite of the one who bore her.
The maidens saw her and called her blessed;
    the queens and concubines praised her.
¹⁰**Who is this that appears like the dawn,**
    fair as the moon, bright as the sun,
    majestic as the stars in procession?

6:1-3 Verses 1-3 continue the dialogue and the search motif between the daughters of Jerusalem and the woman. Now that they understand the royal status of this man (5:10-16), the daughters are quite willing to enter into the search for him on behalf of the woman: **Which way did your lover turn, that we may look for him with you?** (v. 1b) The woman replies: **My lover has gone down to his garden, to the beds of spices, to browse in the gardens and to gather lilies** (v. 2). The playful teasing between the two and with the daughters continues. The woman does not need to search for her lover after all. She knows exactly where he is. He is in his garden. In other words, he is present with her. His garden is really her garden, her self.

Now she affirms the mutual love they hold for each other. The browsing and the gathering (v. 2b) in the woman's garden that was once locked is a declaration of the reciprocal relationship. Their interdependence is highlighted by the refrain that the woman proclaims: **I am my lover's and my lover is mine** (v. 3; cf. 2:16; 7:10). This commitment to one another is the basis from which their attraction toward one another grows. And it is with this declaration that the man launches into a description (*wasf*) of his darling or "friend."

6:4-7 Verses 4-7 contain the second physical description the man offers of his **darling** (see earlier 4:1-7). This *wasf* is not as detailed as the first, omitting any mention of the lips, neck, and breasts. The man compares her beauty to the fortified cities of **Tirzah** and **Jerusalem** (v. 4). Tirzah was the capital of North Israel during the time of Jeroboam I (1 Kgs 14:17; 15:33). The woman's beauty is

majestic and noble, like those of the great cities in Israel's past and present history.

The phrase **majestic as troops with banners,** (אֲיֻמָּה כַּנִּדְגָּלוֹת, *'ǎyummāh kaggidgālôth*; the same phrase is used in v. 10b) is unclear because of the uncertainty of the word for "banner" (דָּגַל, *dāgal*). Various forms of the word are used several times in the book (2:4; 5:10; 6:10b). The term seems to have military overtones. In this verse, with the two fortified cities in the background, the phrase might be rendered, "as awe-inspiring as military forces drawn up for battle before fortified cities." Her beauty is able to conquer the strongest defense of any man. It may also be possible that the root meaning of the term "banner" (*dāgal*) means "to look" or "to see."[53] If so, then a paraphrase of the verse might be, "as awe-inspiring as these sights [i.e., Tirzah and Jerusalem]." Either way, the beauty this woman possesses inspires, even intimidates the man. He reinforces this feeling by appealing to her in the next line to **turn your eyes from me; they overwhelm me** (v. 5). He is afraid to even look into her eyes.

Following the description of the overwhelming splendor of the woman, the man now focuses on a few detailed features of the woman's head: her **hair, teeth,** and **temples**. The images of these three features are almost identical to the descriptions given of them in 4:1-7.

6:8-10 Verses 8-10 contain a comparative motif whose purpose is to express admiration for the woman who is one of a kind. The woman is compared to the many beautiful women found in the king's harem. The king's harem consists of three levels: **queens, concubines,** and **virgins** (v. 8). The gradation in number from sixty to eighty may be similar to the numerical sequence used elsewhere in the Old Testament (Amos 1-2; Ps 62:11; Job 40:5). That is, it is poetic parallelism and refers to an unlimited number of beautiful queens and concubines. The number of women in the king's court was a matter of boasting and pride.

In contrast to all the beautiful women of the king's court, this woman is the one and **only** woman for him (v. 9). The man would rather have her and only her than all the women in the king's harem. The phrase **my dove, my perfect one** is identical to the phrase used in 5:2. It is an expression of exclusivity. True love does not deal in numbers or in statistics.

---

[53]BDB, p. 186.

To emphasize her uniqueness, he adds that she was **the favorite of the one who bore her**. The clause, **the only daughter of her mother**, is not a statement claiming she was an only child. It simply is another way of proclaiming her uniqueness in her mother's eyes (for a treatment of the role of mother in the Song see 3:4). There is one and only one like her. This text evokes images of the parable Nathan told David about the rich man who had many flocks and the peasant who had only one ewe lamb (2 Sam 12:1-5).

In contrast to the women in the king's harem who possess no identity of their own and who remain anonymous (v. 8), this woman has a distinct identity. She has a place where she belongs and where she is known: in her mother's house and with her lover. As a result of her unique identity she is praised by the **maidens, queens** and **concubines** (v. 9b). These are the very ones with whom she is compared and contrasted. They appear to long for such an identity and relationship. Provan says the contrast in these verses is between exclusive love on the one hand and love that manifests no commitment on the other.[54]

In verse 10, the man expresses his admiration for his bride through the mouth of others: **Who is this that appears like the dawn, fair as the moon, bright as the sun, majestic as the stars in procession?** "Who is this" recalls the same rhetorical question in 3:6 and later in 8:5. The verse concludes with the exact phrase with which verse 4b concludes, except the NIV translates it differently in each place. Here the NIV translates the phrase *'ăyummāh kaggidgālôth* as "majestic as the stars in procession." The NRSV translates the phrase identically in both verses: "terrible as an army with banners." In verse 10, the moon and sun may be understood as a part of the heavenly armies. In comparing the woman to them, she may be seen as awesome as these "armies" or heavenly hosts (Yahweh is described as "LORD of hosts;" Isa 47:4; 51:15; Jer 10:16; 31:35; Amos 5:27). Or if the root meaning of the word "majestic" (*dāgal*) means "to see," then the phrase could be paraphrased as follows: "as awe-inspiring as these sights" [i.e., the dawn, the moon, the sun] (see v. 4 above).

[11]I went down to the grove of nut trees
to look at the new growth in the valley,

---

[54]Provan, *Song,* pp. 339-340.

to see if the vines had budded
  or the pomegranates were in bloom.
¹²Before I realized it,
  my desire set me among the royal chariots of my people.ᵃ

ᵃ*12* Or *among the chariots of Amminadab*; or *among the chariots of the people of the prince*

6:11-12 One of the problems in verses 11-12 is the difficulty in knowing who speaks. Is it the man or the woman? One cannot know for certain. It appears to be the woman. The woman in 7:12 utters similar language. If so, she is responding to his invitation to rendezvous in **the grove of nut trees**, literally the "nut garden" (גִּנַּת, *ginnath*), where they will enjoy the sexual pleasures of one another (cf. 2:10-15).

Verse 12 is the most difficult verse to translate and to interpret in the Song. It is so because of the obscure language of the Hebrew text. The Hebrew text reads, "I did not know, my soul [or "desire"] set me chariots, my noble people [or "Amminadib"]."[55]

LaCocque observes that allusions to the ark of the covenant are strong in verse 12. The phrase at the end of the verse literally is translated "my noble people." The phrase can also be understood as a proper name, Amminadib (cf. KJV) which is quite similar to Abinadab. In 1 Samuel 6 the ark of the covenant is placed on a chariot and sent away by the Philistines, finally coming to rest in the house of Abinadab (1 Sam 7:1). Later in 2 Samuel 6, the ark is brought on a chariot from Abinadab's house to Jerusalem.[56]

In addition, verse 12 may recall images of the prophet Elijah being lifted up into heaven on a chariot of fire (2 Kgs 2:11-12; 13:14). LaCocque concludes that the woman is being compared with the chariot that carried the ark and that transported the prophet into the heavens: "The shepherd's love transforms the Shulammite into the (sacred) chariot that transported the ark of the covenant to and from the house of Abinadab."[57] Her beau has made her "the

---

[55]For a summary of the various translations of this verse see Pope, *Song*, pp. 184-192.

[56]Longman offers two worthwhile observations regarding translating the phrase as a proper noun: 1) "It is something of a last resort to appeal to a proper name in a difficult text." 2) "The Amminadab of the Bible has no special connection with love. . ." (*Song*, p. 187).

[57]LaCocque, *Romance*, p. 141.

most prestigious chariot in Israel's history."[58] Though LaCocque's interpretation is intriguing, he may be relying too much on other images outside the Song.

The image of **chariots** (מֶרְכָּבוֹת, *mirkābôth*) recalls the reference to Pharaoh's "chariots" in 1:9 and especially to the description of the litter of Solomon in 3:10 where the same word is used (there the NIV translates the word "seat"). In 3:6-11 the occupant of the litter was Solomon. Here the occupant appears to be the woman. Perhaps this verse envisions the woman being transported to the man's chariot, a seat of honor reserved exclusively for her.[59] In the end, one can merely speculate on its meaning.[60] The only certainty about the verse is that it "expresses strong passion."[61]

VII. THE FINAL DESCRIPTION OF THE WOMAN (6:13–7:9a)[62]

[13]**Come back, come back, O Shulammite;**
    come back, come back, that we may gaze on you!

Why would you gaze on the Shulammite
    as on the dance of Mahanaim?

6:13 Verse 13a contains the words spoken by a group to the woman. Is the group male or female? In light of their request to **gaze on** the **Shulammite**, some would argue that the group is male. They are enamored with her beauty and wish to enjoy her presence. If so, the man responds in 13b by expressing displeasure at their gazing.

If the group were male, however, this would be the only appearance of a male chorus in the Song. It is more natural to assume that this is another exchange of dialogue between the daughters of Jerusalem and the woman. If so, then the exchange expresses the admiration the women have for the young woman's beauty and her response of embarrassment over their gazing at her.

---

[58]Ibid., p. 147.

[59]Longman, *Song*, p. 187.

[60]Walsh interprets the verse as an expression of the man's desire for the woman. She translates it as follows: "I am trembling, you have made me as eager for love as a chariot driver is for battle" (*Desire*, p. 90).

[61]Longman, *Song*, p. 187.

[62]The Hebrew versification of this unit is 7:1-10.

Several explanations have been offered for the meaning of **the dance of Mahanaim**. The term "Mahanaim" (מַחֲנָיִם, *maḥănāyim*) means "two camps."[63] The term may refer to the way the dance was performed. Participants gathering in two lines or camps, respond to one another. Or it may refer to the woman moving between two lines of dancers (see New English Bible). Related to this is the possibility that "the dance of Mahanaim" may refer to some kind of exotic choreographed dance performance.[64] Longman speculates that the phrase refers to the dance of two war camps and suggests paraphrasing it in the following way: "Watching her is as mesmerizing as watching two armies battling with one another."[65] Another speculation is that the term refers to the *origin* of the dance. Mahanaim was the place where Jacob met the angels (Gen 32:1-2; 2 Sam 17:24). It is also the home of Ishbaal, the son of Saul (2 Sam 2:8-9). If the reference is to origin, then Mahanaim is the place where the dance was performed to honor some special historical event that took place there. One can only conjecture on the meaning.

In verse 13, the woman is called a **Shulammite**. This is the only place in the Song where she is referred to in this way. Three basic interpretations have been offered as an explanation.[66] First, it has been equated with the town of Shunem (Josh 19:18; 1 Sam 28:4). As such, the woman is sometimes associated with the beautiful Abishag, the Shunammite (1 Kgs 1:3,15; 2:17-22).[67] Second, it is the name of the goddess Ishtar, who was the goddess of love and war in Mesopotamian culture. And third, it is a feminine form of the name Solomon ("Solomoness"), whose root means "peace." Of these three, the third seems the most plausible because of other references to Solomon in the book. Just as the man is a Solomon-type in the eyes of the women, so the woman may be a Solomoness-type in the eyes of the man.[68]

---

[63]BDB, p. 334.

[64]Jacob referred to the place where he met the angels as "the camp of God" (Gen 32:1-2).

[65]Longman, *Song*, p. 193.

[66]See Pope for a more detailed analysis of these three interpretations, *Song*, pp. 596-600.

[67]There is no evidence that the two names refer to the same place. Their similarity is more of a coincidence.

[68]Adding some weight to this interpretation is the fact that the definite article is attached to the word. So she is "the Solomoness."

Chapter 7:1-9 is the fourth and final praise song (*waṣf*) found in the book (cf. 4:1-7; 5:10-16; 6:4-10). Unlike the others that moved from the head down, this one moves from the feet up. This description is also the most complete *waṣf* of the three devoted to the woman. The other two praise songs of the woman's body focus exclusively on the head (6:4-10) and the upper body (4:1-7). This *waṣf* scans the whole body of the woman from feet to head (7:1-5). The *waṣf* describing the man scans his body from head to legs (5:10-16).

¹How beautiful your sandaled feet,
　　　O prince's daughter!
　Your graceful legs are like jewels,
　　　the work of a craftsman's hands.
²Your navel is a rounded goblet
　　　that never lacks blended wine.
　Your waist is a mound of wheat
　　　encircled by lilies.
³Your breasts are like two fawns,
　　　twins of a gazelle.
⁴Your neck is like an ivory tower.
　Your eyes are the pools of Heshbon
　　　by the gate of Bath Rabbim.
　Your nose is like the tower of Lebanon
　　　looking toward Damascus.
⁵Your head crowns you like Mount Carmel.
　　　Your hair is like royal tapestry;
　　　the king is held captive by its tresses.
⁶How beautiful you are and how pleasing,
　　　O love, with your delights!
⁷Your stature is like that of the palm,
　　　and your breasts like clusters of fruit.
⁸I said, "I will climb the palm tree;
　　　I will take hold of its fruit."
May your breasts be like the clusters of the vine,
　　　the fragrance of your breath like apples,
⁹　　　and your mouth like the best wine.

7:1-2 Because the woman's **feet** are mentioned first (7:1), along with the imagery that follows, some scholars propose that verses 1-6 describe the wedding dance of the bride. However, the dance of

Mahanaim in 6:13 is not a dance that the woman performs. Instead, gazing at her is *like* (note the particle **as**, כְּ, *kᵉ*) gazing at some kind of dance performance.

The man begins by praising the woman's **sandaled feet**. There may have been something sensual about the top of a woman's feet being exposed in a pair of sandals.[69] The woman is referred to as a **prince's daughter**. All through the book, the couple use regal terms to describe each other (cf. v. 5; also 1:4,12). The description of the woman's **legs** (lit., thigh, יָרֵךְ, *yārēk*), **navel** (שֹׁר, *šōr*), and **waist** (belly, בֶּטֶן, *beṭen*) are some of the most physically intimate descriptions found in the book. It is one way by which the man can express his deep love and commitment to her.

To what does "navel" (*šōr*) refer? It could be, by extension, a reference to the umbilical cord, which is how the word is used in Ezekiel 16:4. However, its positioning lies between the **legs** (thighs) and the **waist** (belly) implying in all likelihood that this is a reference to the vagina.[70] The vagina is more likely to be moist with the liquid of **blended wine** than is the **navel** (v. 2). The woman's **waist** is described as **a mound of wheat encircled by lilies**. A round rather than flat stomach was viewed as a most desirable trait. It also indicates that she was well fed (cf. 4:3).

7:3-5 Your breasts are like two fawns, twins of a gazelle (v. 3). The imagery is similar to 4:5, except for the omission of the phrase "browse among the lilies." Moving on up the body, her neck is compared to **an ivory tower** (v. 4; cf. 4:4).

As the man describes the features of his lover's face, her **eyes**, **nose**, **head**, and **hair**, he compares them to special geographical locations that in that day were know for some unique feature. So he mentions **Heshbon**, **Bath Rabbim**, **Lebanon**, and **Mount Carmel**.

---

[69]The courageous woman, Judith, delivered the Israelites from their enemies by seducing the general with her beauty. She is described in the following way: ". . . she fastened her hair with a tiara and put on a linen gown to beguile him. *Her sandal ravished his eyes,* her beauty captivated his mind and the sword severed his neck!" (Judith 16:8-9; emphasis mine).

[70]BDB says, the word is "now oft. interpreted as = vulva," (p. 1057). Provan argues that the context in the Song favors the vaginal area, "It is with this area, after all, that water and fertility have been closely associated already in 4:1-15 . . ." (*Song*, p. 353). His mention of water and fertility refers to the next phrase in the verse, "blended wine." Pope also favors this translation (*Song*, p. 417).

The one part of the woman's body he does not praise in earlier *wasfs* is her nose. Here he describes it as being **like the tower of Lebanon looking toward Damascus** (v. 4). Contemporary readers might think that this is hyperbole gone awry! But a long nose was a sign of strength and beauty. The tower of Lebanon may either be a reference to a military tower located in Lebanon or to a towering mountain in the Lebanon range.[71] Whatever the analogy, the emphasis is on the prominence, straightness, and splendor of the woman's nose.

Her hair is compared to **royal tapestry**. The Hebrew text reads, "the hair of your head is like purple." The ideal of feminine beauty may have included dyed hair. The NIV offers an appropriate translation. "Purple" signifies royalty. Thus **the king is held captive by its tresses**. Once again the lover is compared to a king and as king the loveliness of her hair enraptures him. In verses 1-5, the reader captures a glimpse of a different standard of feminine beauty where long noses and necks, round bellies, and small breasts are the desired features.

7:6-9a The description concludes in verses 7-9 with a poem of yearning; the man expresses a desire for physical union. He compares her **breasts** to **clusters of fruit**. He desires to scale up the **palm tree** (the proper name "Tamar" is derived from this Hebrew word) and **take hold of its fruits** (vv. 7-8). He uses a litany of senses to express his physical desire for the one that he loves: smell, taste, touch, and sight.

In the context of a covenant relationship, expression of sexual desire is a part of creation (Gen 1:28-30). The enjoyment of the physical body is reciprocal between the two. She offers her "vineyard" to him and he responds.

VIII. CARING FOR THE VINEYARD (7:9b–8:4)

May the wine go straight to my lover,
 flowing gently over lips and teeth.[a]
[10]I belong to my lover,
 and his desire is for me.
[11]Come, my lover, let us go to the countryside,
 let us spend the night in the villages.[b]

---

[71]Pope, *Song,* p. 627.

¹²**Let us go early to the vineyards**
        to see if the vines have budded,
    if their blossoms have opened,
        and if the pomegranates are in bloom—
        there I will give you my love.
¹³**The mandrakes send out their fragrance,**
        and at our door is every delicacy,
    both new and old,
        that I have stored up for you, my lover.

ᵃ**9 Septuagint, Aquila, Vulgate and Syriac; Hebrew** *lips of sleepers*   ᵇ*11* **Or**
henna bushes

7:9b-13⁷² At this point in the dialogue, the woman interrupts. **My
lover** (דּוֹדִי, *dôdî*) is used in the Song only by the woman to refer to
the man. So the words of the man appear to end abruptly at this
point and the woman begins to speak in verse 9b.⁷³

She expresses her longing for her lover in a statement of mutual possession: **I belong to my lover, and his desire is for me** (v. 10;
cf. 2:16; 6:3). Here the poet reverses the order of the statement from
its earlier use. The mutual desire that they possess for one another
is a sexual desire (תְּשׁוּקָה, *t°šûqāh*). The woman makes a bold solici-
tation to the man: **Come, my lover, let us go to the countryside, let
us spend the night in the villages.** This is the most direct invitation
she makes to the man in the book (contrast 2:10-13). She openly and
unashamedly speaks of her desire for him.

The woman extends the invitation to the man to meet her for a
secret tryst. She invites him to the **vineyards to see if the vines have
budded** (v. 12; cf. 6:11). Sometimes "vineyards" refers to the woman's
body (1:6). Other times, as here, it refers to a place of lovemaking.
She makes her intentions for taking him there quite explicit: **there I
will give you my love.** Verses 12-13 describe a spring-type motif similar to the song of springtime found in 2:11-13.⁷⁴ Love is associated
with the coming of spring in the Song of Songs. **Mandrakes** were
thought to possess an aphrodisiac quality and to induce human

---

⁷²The Hebrew versification is 7:10b-14.

⁷³The RSV and NRSV omit the term "my lover" (*dôdî*) and assume the
man continues to speak until the next verse.

⁷⁴The blooming of the pomegranate was a symbol of the coming of spring
(cf. 6:11).

fertility (Gen 30:14-16). It is oftentimes referred to as the "love apple."[75] The roots of the mandrakes also have the appearance of genitalia.

In other parts of the Old Testament, farming is used as a metaphor to describe sexual activity (e.g., Samson claims that the Philistines "plowed with my heifer"; Judg 14:18). "Semen" is the English word that usually translates the Hebrew word "seed" (זֶרַע, zera'; e.g., Gen 38:9). Childless women are frequently described as "barren" (Gen 11:30; 25:21; 29:31). So when the male seed does not germinate, it is because the "ground" of the woman is not fertile; her "soil" is barren.

Walsh maintains that what is striking about the Song is that the farming metaphor is not used. Instead the woman is described as a "garden" and a "fruit" and a "vineyard." Walsh notes that a vineyard takes more tender loving care than does a field. When a farmer plows a field, the focus is more on the end *product*, reproduction. With a vineyard, it is more on the *process*.[76] After harvest a field can lie fallow for awhile and not be harmed. On the other hand, a vineyard is "high maintenance" and demands constant attention.[77] As such, a vintner working in a vineyard conjures up more relational terms (Isa 5:1-7).

[8:1]If only you were to me like a brother,
    who was nursed at my mother's breasts!
Then, if I found you outside,
    I would kiss you,
    and no one would despise me.
[2]I would lead you
    and bring you to my mother's house—
    she who has taught me.
I would give you spiced wine to drink,
    the nectar of my pomegranates.
[3]His left arm is under my head
    and his right arm embraces me.

---

[75]J.C. Trever, "Mandrake," *IDB*, 3:256.

[76]Walsh, *Desire*, pp. 87-94.

[77]Ibid., p. 90. It is difficult to know if the Song sets up an *intentional* contrast between farming and caring for vineyards.

⁴Daughters of Jerusalem, I charge you:
   Do not arouse or awaken love
   until it so desires.

8:1 The woman continues to express her song of yearning to the young man. She longs to display her affection to her lover publicly, as though he were her **brother** (v. 1). This is the first reference to her lover as a brother. Earlier he referred to her as a "sister" (4:9,10,12; 5:2). The word does not convey blood relations but is an expression of romantic affection.⁷⁸

For some unknown reason, the lovers are not able to express publicly their love and affection for one another. Currently if they did, others **would despise** them (v. 1). Is it because of the censure on public display of affection that was a part of the culture, even for married couples? Or is it because in the eyes of most, they are not considered a married couple? The problem with the former is that public display of affection between wedded couples was acceptable (see Gen 26:8; 29:11). Could it be that if she kissed him she could be mistaken for a prostitute (Prov 7:13)? It appears that in these verses the couple is not married. Their relationship remains a secret. Those interpreters who view the Song as a plot that unfolds a developing relationship, run into difficulties at this point.

8:2 Reference to the **mother's house** has been made back in 3:4. In the Old Testament the usual reference is to the "father's house." Israelite society was patriarchal. So the custom was for the woman to leave her "father's house" and reside in the house of her husband's father. But in the Song of Songs, the mother's house becomes central. It may be central because it is a place that symbolically represents the secret desires of the woman.⁷⁹

8:3 Verse 3 describes one of the few times in the Song that actual physical contact is made between the two (see 2:6). Numerous allusions are made to contact and expressions of desire for physical union, but few times does it actually occur.

8:4 The poem concludes in verse 4 with the repetition of the refrain

---

⁷⁸Weems suggests that the reason the woman longs for her lover to be blood relations is that then, as nearest kin, he could marry her and their relationship would be publicly validated ("Song," p. 428).

⁷⁹Various lovemaking spots are identified in the book: the vineyard (2:14-15); the garden (4:16); the mother's house.

that admonishes the **daughters of Jerusalem: Do not arouse or awak-
en love until it so desires** (cf. earlier 2:7; 3:5). The woman admonishes
the daughters not to rush into love, not to open one's "vineyard" to
another without making a mutually exclusive commitment. Casual love
is perverse and destructive. Only in the context of a covenant promise
is love able to express itself in its most fulfilling way.

IX. CONCLUDING ANTHOLOGY OF POEMS (8:5-14)

The remainder of the poems in chapter 8:5-14 are loosely connected to one another. No dialogue takes place between the poems. They
should not, however, be considered later additions because the language used in them echoes earlier phrases and images. Verse 5a seems
to stand on its own as some kind of refrain. Verses 6-7 are a single unit
that expresses the climactic message of the book. Verses 8-10,11-12,
and 13-14 all appear as relatively independent units of material.

⁵**Who is this coming up from the desert**
> **leaning on her lover?**

Under the apple tree I roused you;
> **there your mother conceived you,**
> **there she who was in labor gave you birth.**

⁶**Place me like a seal over your heart,**
> **like a seal on your arm;**
> **for love is as strong as death,**
> **its jealousy**[a] **unyielding as the grave.**[b]
> **It burns like blazing fire,**
> **like a mighty flame.**[c]

⁷**Many waters cannot quench love;**
> **rivers cannot wash it away.**
> **If one were to give**
> **all the wealth of his house for love,**
> **it**[d] **would be utterly scorned.**

[a]6 Or *ardor* [b]6 Hebrew *Sheol* [c]6 Or / *like the very flame of the* LORD
[d]7 Or *he*

8:5 It seems most likely that the daughters of Jerusalem ask the
following question, **Who is this coming up from the desert . . .**
(v. 5a)? The question, "Who is this," appeared earlier in 3:6 and

6:10. In 3:6 the reference is made to Solomon's litter coming from the desert. The referent of "who is this" in that context is Solomon. Here, however, the referent is the young woman who is said to be **leaning on her lover**. The woman is depicted as being content and secure in the arms of her lover. The times of danger and anxiety are over. The question, "who is this . . . ," follows the admonition given to the daughters in verse 4 as it also did in 3:5. But what it means for her to be coming up from the desert escapes us.

It is probably best to assume that the woman speaks in verse 5b, even though it is possible that the man is speaking. She speaks of rousing her lover. The word for **roused** (עוּר, *'ûr*) could either speak of arousing from sleep or of exciting love.[80] It is from the same root word used twice in the refrain, "Do not arouse or awaken love until it so desires" (2:16; 3:5; 8:4).

She arouses her lover **under the apple tree**. Earlier she had compared her lover to "an apple tree" standing out from among all the other "trees of the forest" (2:3). It was from apples that the woman sought refreshment (2:5). Later the man compared the woman's breath to the fragrance of apples (7:8). For love to blossom under trees is not only an ancient motif but a contemporary one as well. It is under the apple tree that the woman claims **your mother conceived you**. This phrase may be analogous with "my mother's house" mentioned earlier in verse 2. It is a place where the lovers can fulfill their sexual desires. The woman and her lover are now engaging in the same act that brought him into the world.

8:6-7 Verses 6 and 7 serve as the climactic verses of the Song of Songs. The verses contain wisdomlike reflections that are more contemplative than the erotic tone woven in the rest of the book. The words appear to be spoken by the woman (6a uses masculine suffixes) and expand the theme expressed in the two refrains repeated through the book. The one refrain expresses the theme of mutual commitment: "My lover is mine and I am his" (2:16; 6:3; 7:10). The other refrain is an admonition not to share love "until its time" (NRSV). The NIV translates the refrain, "Do not arouse or awaken love until it so desires" (2:7; 3:5; 8:4). These refrains come to full expression in the affirmation in verses 6-7.

---

[80]BDB, p. 735.

Four metaphors or images describe the resilience and abiding nature of **love**: it is **like a seal**, it is **as strong as death**, it **burns like blazing fire**, and it is like **many waters**. The woman requests the man to **place me like a seal over your heart** (v. 6a). Seals were often placed on letters or jars or tombs to indicate possession. The seal was impressed on the person or object by a stamp or a cylinder. In this case, the seal identified her as belonging to him, or more than likely, she requests that she be allowed to own him. The seal is placed on *him* not on the woman.

For love is as strong as death (v. 6). Death is the most powerful adversary in Scripture. Only God is stronger than death (Hos 13:14). Death and the **grave** are never satisfied; they have an unquenchable thirst for more and more (Prov 27:20). It is death that the writer of Ecclesiastes considers his biggest foe in the battle to understand the meaning of life. But in this passage, love is not doing battle with death. Rather, love is compared to the fortitude and robustness that death possesses. Death is personified as an active power that doggedly pursues every human being. Death is relentless; it will not release anyone from its clutches. In the same way, love will not let another loose whom it has brought into its grip. It is persistent. As Paul declared in 1 Corinthians 13:8, "love never fails."[81] Love is deadly serious.

Love's **jealousy** is **unyielding as the grave**. In this context, the Hebrew word the NIV translates "jealousy" (קִנְאָה, *qin'āh*) is not a negative term as we normally understand it. No object of jealousy is identified. A more positive word to use is "passion." However, it is more than passion, if one associates passion primarily with sex. The Hebrew word conveys the idea of intense single-minded devotion (Zech 1:14-17; 8:2). So it is best to translate the word "zeal" or "fervent love."[82]

Another metaphor used to describe love in verse 6 is the image of fire. The intensity of love is such that it **burns like blazing fire**. The last word in verse 6, **mighty flame** (שַׁלְהֶבֶתְיָה, *šalhebethyāh*), can be translated one of two ways depending upon how one understands

---

[81]"Love" (אַהֲבָה, *'ahăbāh*) is used eleven times in the Song: 2:4,5,7; 3:5,10; 5:8; 7:7; 8:4,6,7(2×).

[82]BDB suggests "ardent love" (p. 888). Elijah uses the word to describe his devotion to the LORD, "I have been very zealous [lit., "with zeal I have been zealous"] for the LORD God Almighty" (1 Kgs 19:10).

the last two Hebrew letters in the word, *yāh* (יָה). The letters could be understood as a superlative, which is how most translations render it. So the RSV translates it "a most vehement flame." The NRSV renders it "raging flame." And of course the NIV chooses "mighty flame." A second way of translating the ending is as an abbreviated form of Yahweh (Yah). In that case, the word would be translated "flames of Yahweh."[83] The zealous abandonment of human love is then compared to divine love. However, since the name of God is avoided all through the book, which appears to be intentional, it seems preferable to translate the suffix as a superlative.[84]

The final image used to depict love is as mighty **waters**. The image of water contrasts nicely with the image of fire. In the Old Testament **many waters** (מַיִם רַבִּים, *mayim rabbîm*) denotes the raging powers of chaos which, like death, only God can subdue (Gen 1:1-31; Ps 69:1-2; Isa 51:9-10). The love between these two lovers is like the raging powers of the primordial waters of the earth. The next line in verse 7, **rivers cannot wash it away**, is simply a parallel image emphasizing love's awesome force.

If one were to give all the wealth of his house for love, it would be utterly scorned (v. 7b). This is the final sapiential observation made in the poem. While in 8:1 the woman is scorned (בּוּז, *bûz*) by the society around her, now she scorns (*bûz*) those who buy love. The phrase, "all the wealth of his house," is identical to that used in Proverbs 6:31 for a man who must pay for an adulterous affair. "All the wealth of his house" may refer to the bride price or dowry that was a part of the negotiation done when a daughter was given away in marriage to the groom's family. As such, it may be the background to what the brothers are doing in the following verses (vv. 8-10). It may further anticipate what takes place in verses 11-12 when Solomon engages in financial transaction regarding his "vineyards" (women?). On this occasion, the woman declares that love is not a commodity to buy or sell. It is only for those who give themselves freely to one another.

---

[83]This would be the one time then in which the name of Yahweh is used in the book. Numerous other examples exist in the Old Testament that use the abbreviated form "yah," which is rendered as "iah" in English: Jeremiah, Josiah, Isaiah, Zedekiah.

[84]To translate the suffix as a divine name also involves an emendation; one must redivide the consonantal text.

⁸We have a young sister,
>   and her breasts are not yet grown.
What shall we do for our sister
>   for the day she is spoken for?
⁹If she is a wall,
>   we will build towers of silver on her.
If she is a door,
>   we will enclose her with panels of cedar.
¹⁰I am a wall,
>   and my breasts are like towers.
Thus I have become in his eyes
>   like one bringing contentment.

8:8-9 Either the woman's brothers are speaking in this passage or the woman quotes the words of her brothers. They allege that their sister is not yet ready for marriage because **her breasts are not yet grown** (v. 8). They ask the question, **What shall we do for our sister for the day she is spoken for?** The phrase "when spoken for" (שֶׁיְּדֻבַּר־בָּה, *šey°dubbar-bāh*) in this context means when someone proposes marriage to her. The same phrase is used when David "spoke for" Abigail to come and be his wife (1 Sam 25:39).

When it came to the courtship and marriage of a sister, brothers seemed to have played an important role in the process. Laban negotiated with the servant of Abraham regarding the marriage of his sister Rebekah to Isaac (Gen 24:29-60; cf. Judg 21:22). Something similar appears to be happening in this text. The brothers refuse to see that their little sister has grown up. Though eventually they want to give her away in marriage for the sake of the dowry, for the time being they conclude that she is not yet ready to take that step. So they must do what they can to protect her virginity.

In verse 9, the brothers compare their sister to **a wall** and **a door**. What is the relationship between a wall and a door? Are the two terms synonymous or antithetic? A wall is designed to protect or to ward off. The **sister** who is like a wall is resistant and inaccessible. A door can serve a dual purpose. It can either open a wall or keep it closed. It can be either for entering or for shutting out. It is the brothers' and family's primary obligation to protect the virginity of their women. When Shechem violated Dinah, the daughter of Jacob, her brothers sought vengeance on him and his family (Gen 34:1-31).

Women needed protection from predatory men (recall Absalom's response to the rape of Tamar; 2 Sam 13:20-22). This appears to be the case in 2:15 with the metaphor of the little foxes ruining the vineyard of a woman that was in bloom. Until the day she is married, the brothers sought to make her a wall and a *closed* door. Both images are images of defense. The brothers build embellished defenses to protect the woman. The **towers of silver** and the **panels of cedar** serve as "a kind of chastity belt."[85] Elizabeth Huwiler suggests that in building the "decorative defenses" the brothers

> increase the woman's value in two ways: first by adorning her with silver and cedar, and second by ensuring her inviolability. The brothers here, like Solomon (and the tenants?) in the next subsection, are set up to be "utterly scorned" in the terms of verse 7. All of these men suggest thinking in terms of the wealth of the household/kingdom, rather than in terms of love.[86]

8:10 The woman (sister) replies with impudence in verse 10, affirming her chastity by claiming that she **is a wall** (recall her self-description as an enclosed garden in 4:12). But contrary to her brothers' assessment, she argues that she is ready for marriage: **my breasts are like towers** (a poetic extension of the wall imagery). In 7:8 the lover described the woman's breasts as "clusters of the vine." By standing up to her meddlesome brothers, she shows that she is not only physically mature but mentally and emotionally mature as well. This stands in stark contrast to the picture conveyed in 1:6 where she complies with her brothers when they send her to the vineyard as punishment. Now she is no longer under her brothers' care. She is not just family property.

She concludes by declaring that she brings **contentment** (peace; שָׁלוֹם, *šālôm*) to her lover. Earlier she is described as "leaning" or resting content in her lover's arms (8:5). The feeling of contentment is mutual.

[11]Solomon had a vineyard in Baal Hamon;
**   he let out his vineyard to tenants.**
Each was to bring for its fruit
**   a thousand shekels[a] of silver.**

---

[85]Pope, *Song,* p. 681.
[86]Huwiler, *Proverbs, Ecclesiastes, Song of Songs,* pp. 288-289.

¹²**But my own vineyard is mine to give;**
    the thousand shekels are for you, O Solomon,
    and two hundredᵇ **are for those who tend its fruit.**

ᵃ*11* That is, about 25 pounds (about 11.5 kilograms); also in verse 12
ᵇ*12* That is, about 5 pounds (about 2.3 kilograms)

8:11 The speaker of these verses is not clear. Some say the male lover is speaking. If so, then these verses stand parallel to 6:8-9 where the man expresses his commitment for his one and only love over the harem of the king. It seems likely, however, that it is the woman who speaks in light of the declaration that "my own vineyard is mine to give." "Vineyard" is a metaphor used in the Song to describe the woman (cf. 1:6).

The mention of Solomon's vineyard in **Baal Hamon** is a reference to an actual vineyard. However, given the use of "vineyard" in the next verse it is more likely the vineyard refers to Solomon's harem. Thus a contrast is made in verses 11 and 12 between Solomon's vineyard and the vineyard of the woman.

Baal Hamon was a luxurious private vineyard owned by **Solomon**, though the place is not mentioned in Scripture. The name literally means "possessor of abundance" and carries a double entendre here in speaking of the wealth of Solomon. Snaith facetiously concludes that Solomon's nickname is "own-a-lot."[87] For Solomon his vineyard was simply a source of revenue. He has no personal relationship with it. The **tenants** actually care for his vineyards. Solomon remains distant. The **thousand shekels** that Solomon received from his vineyard may be an enigmatic reference to his harem, which consisted of seven hundred wives and three hundred concubines (1 Kgs 11:3-10). Whether it is or not, Solomon's harem is set against the next verse where the woman chooses to give herself to only one man.

8:12 But my own vineyard is mine to give.[88] Earlier she was not able to keep her own vineyard (1:6). But now in her maturity she is able to experience liberation from being the property of someone else. Neither her brothers nor **Solomon** can own her. She gives her-

---

[87]Snaith, *Song,* p. 127.
[88]Literally, "my vineyard, which is for me, is before me" (לְפָנָי, *l°phānāy*). *L°phānāy* is usually translated something like "at my disposal" (Gen 13:9; 20:15; 24:51; 34:10).

self freely to the one she loves. Solomon, in contrast, has no such relationship of mutual reciprocity. His relationships are business ventures; they are only displays of power. **Two hundred** shekels was the amount paid to **those who tend** the **fruit** of Solomon's vineyard. These verses set up a stark contrast between the casual, detached love of Solomon and the mature, intimate love of the woman for the man. The woman's desire for love also imitates the spiritual quest humans have for God.

> [13]**You who dwell in the gardens**
> > **with friends in attendance,**
> > **let me hear your voice!**
> [14]**Come away, my lover,**
> > **and be like a gazelle**
> **or like a young stag**
> > **on the spice-laden mountains.**

8:13-14 The Song concludes in a way that characterizes the whole book. That is, it concludes with a dialogue between the two lovers. The man speaks in verse 13 expressing his desire to hear her **voice**. Earlier he had expressed a similar longing to hear his lover's voice (2:14). The woman replies with an echo of words she had spoken in 2:17. Her invitation is for him to come to **the spice-laden mountains**, that is, to herself. In offering the invitation, she lets her lover hear her voice. The love that they offer one another is never static. It is always moving forward. Love is a journey into the unknown future, in which two people are willing to risk sharing their lives unconditionally with one another.